T0301327

Private Equity Operational Due Diligence

Founded in 1807, John Wiley & Sons is the oldest independent publishing company in the United States. With offices in North America, Europe, Australia and Asia, Wiley is globally committed to developing and marketing print and electronic products and services for our customers' professional and personal knowledge and understanding.

The Wiley Finance series contains books written specifically for finance and investment professionals as well as sophisticated individual investors and their financial advisors. Book topics range from portfolio management to e-commerce, risk management, financial engineering, valuation and financial instrument analysis, as well as much more.

For a list of available titles, visit our Web site at www.WileyFinance.com.

Private Equity Operational Due Diligence

Tools to Evaluate Liquidity,
Valuation, and Documentation

JASON A. SCHARFMAN

John Wiley & Sons, Inc.

Published by John Wiley & Sons, Inc., Hoboken, New Jersey.
Published simultaneously in Canada.

For general information on our other products and services or for technical support, please contact our Customer Care Department within the United States at (800) 762-2974, outside the United States at (317) 572-3993 or fax (317) 572-4002.

Wiley also publishes its books in a variety of electronic formats. Some content that appears in print may not be available in electronic books. For more information about Wiley products, visit our web site at www.wiley.com.

Library of Congress Cataloging-in-Publication Data:

Scharfman, Jason A., 1978–
   Private equity operational due diligence : tools to evaluate liquidity, valuation, and documentation / Jason A. Scharfman.
      pages cm. – (The Wiley finance series ; 731)
   Includes bibliographical references and index.
   ISBN 978-1-118-11390-5; ISBN 978-1-118-22416-8 (ebk);
   ISBN 978-1-118-23747-2 (ebk); ISBN 978-1-118-26243-6 (ebk)
  1. Private equity.   2. Real estate investment.   3. Reasonable care (Law)   I. Title.
   HG4751.S33 2012
   332.63'2–dc23

                                                                      2011048538

Printed in the United States of America

10 9 8 7 6 5 4 3 2 1

I dedicate this book to my wife, Rachel, for her endless support, to my brother, Barry, to my parents, Gloria and Michael, and to my entire family for their never-ending encouragement.

Contents

Preface   xiii

CHAPTER 1
Introduction to Private Equity Operational Risk   1
  Introduction to Operational Risk   1
  Operational Risk Compared to Operational Due Diligence   3
  What Is Operational Due Diligence?   4
  Operational Due Diligence in the Field of Private Equity   8
  Operational Due Diligence as Distinguished from Operational
    Management of Portfolio Companies   9
  Timing of Operational Due Diligence in the Investing Process   10
  Operational Due Diligence Process   13
  Historical Perspectives of Private Equity Operational Risk   16
  Items Typically Covered during the Operational Due Diligence
    Process   23
  Core versus Expanded Operational Due Diligence Reviews   25
  Shared Commonalities between Private Equity and Real Estate
    Operations Risk   30
  Differences in Operational Risk Factors between Private Equity
    and Real Estate   32
  Country- and Industry-Specific Risk Considerations   33
  Investment and Operational Due Diligence: Nexus or
    Blurred Lines?   39
  Differences and Similarities with Hedge Fund Operational
    Due Diligence   40
  Notes   49

CHAPTER 2
Importance of Operational Due Diligence for Private Equity Funds   51
  Understanding the Goals of the Operational Due
    Diligence Process   52
  Common Arguments against Operational Reviews of Private
    Equity Funds   55

Common Arguments in Favor of Performing Operational
    Reviews of Private Equity Funds   75
Conclusion   82
Notes   82

CHAPTER 3
Beginning the Operational Due Diligence Review: Core Issues   85
Goal Self-Assessment   85
Designing an Operational Due Diligence Program for
    Private Equity   87
When Does the Operational Due Diligence Process Begin?   101
Signaling Effects of Operational Flags   104
Requesting and Collecting Documentation   104
Nondisclosure and Confidentiality Agreements   106
Document Collection: What Documents Should
    Investors Request?   113
Document Collection Negotiation Techniques: Avoiding a
    Pass-the-Buck Environment   117
Document Collection: Hard Copy or Electronic?   119
Fund Manager On-Site Due Diligence Considerations   125
Key Risk Consideration Areas to Cover   128
Conclusion   133
Notes   133

CHAPTER 4
Additional Operational Due Diligence Considerations:
An Expanded Analysis   135
Core Issues versus Expanded Analysis   135
Compensation Structures   138
Introduction to Private Equity Fund Fees   139
Manager Investment in Funds   140
Evaluating Service Providers   141
Additional On-Site Visit Considerations: Negative Operational
    Due Diligence   148
Additional On-Site Visit Considerations: Interview Techniques
    and Question Design   150
Asset Raising and the Use of Placement Agents and
    Third-Party Marketers   159
Cash Management and Controls   162
Business Continuity and Disaster Recovery   165
Understanding the Trade Life Cycle Process   168
Legal, Compliance, and Regulatory Risks   171

Insurance 173
Technology and Systems 174
Tax Practices 175
Diagnosing and Mitigating Reputational Risk 177
Conclusion 179
Notes 179

CHAPTER 5
Valuation Techniques, Methodologies, and Standards **181**
Limited Partner Distinction between Fund Level and Portfolio
  Company Valuation Approaches 181
Valuation Considerations for Newly Formed Funds 182
Introduction to Valuation 182
GIPS Statement on Private Equity 183
IPEV Guidelines 185
FAS 157 189
Use of Third-Party Valuation Consultants 191
Valuation Output Process Documentation 194
Valuation Committee Review Scope 196
Additional Limited Partner Valuation Considerations 197
Conclusion 197
Notes 198

CHAPTER 6
Legal Due Diligence **199**
Operational Due Diligence Specialists versus Generalists 199
Common Private Equity Fund Structures 201
Understanding the Private Placement Memorandum 201
Common Document Risk Assignment Terms 206
Exculpation and Indemnity 206
Trends in Indemnification and Exculpation Clauses 217
Other Legal Documents Considerations 227
Conclusion 228
Notes 228

CHAPTER 7
Financial Statement Due Diligence **233**
Audit Standards 233
Accounting Standards 235
Other Financial Statement Formats 237
Considerations That Are Unique to Private Equity and Real
  Estate Financial Statements 241

Understanding Financial Statement Sections   244
Other Financial Statement Sections   245
Understanding FAS 157   251
Conclusion   254
Notes   254

CHAPTER 8
Distinguishing the Assets Class: Real Estate–Specific Concerns   **257**
Real Estate Trade Flow Process   257
Sample Real Estate Process   258
Real Estate Valuation   262
Monitoring Conflicts of Interest   266
Fraud Considerations: Mortgage Fraud and
    Straw-Man Borrowers   269
Understanding Real Estate Fund Fees   270
Property Holdings Legal Considerations   271
Conclusion   272
Note   273

CHAPTER 9
Putting It All Together: Asset Allocation and Ongoing Monitoring   **275**
Incorporating the Results of Operational Due Diligence into
    Asset Allocation   276
Evolution of Minimum Operational Risk Regime (MORR)   283
Operational Risk Correlations to Portfolio Transaction
    Frequency   285
Operational Lift-to-Drag Ratio   286
Negotiating Private Equity Side Letters   290
Ongoing Monitoring: Operational Due Diligence Monitoring
    for Private Equity Funds   292
Conclusion   296
Appendix: Mathematical Conepts   297
    The Derivative   297
    The Chain Rule   298
    The Second Partial Derivative Test   299
    Notes   300

CHAPTER 10
Boards, Committees, and Activism   **301**
Private Equity Fund Advisory Boards   301
Different Types of Advisory Boards: Limited Partners versus
    Pure Advisors   302

Ongoing Operational Due Diligence Monitoring Advisory
  Benefits   303
Balancing the Role of Inner Circle versus Broadly
  Representative Advisory Boards   305
Advisory Board Criticisms: Crowding Out, Power
  Aggregation, and Redundant Board Layers   306
Information Flow Considerations from Underlying Portfolio
  General Partner to Limited Partners   307
Limited Partner Due Diligence Considerations for a Private
  Equity Fund of Funds   308
Additional Private Equity Advisory Board Considerations   311
Conclusion   313
Notes   313

CHAPTER 11
Case Studies and Scenarios   **315**
Case Studies   315
Hypothetical Scenarios   326
Notes   335

CHAPTER 12
Trends and Future Developments   **341**
Use of Third-Party Administrators   341
Increased Focus on Material Nonpublic Information
  in the United States   345
Increased Reliance on Audit-Type Certifications   348
Increased Use of Operational Due Diligence Consultants   350
Pooling Operational Due Diligence Resources among
  Multiple LPs   352
Operational Benchmarking   353
ILPA Guidelines   354
From Self-Regulation to Mandatory Registration   355
Impact of Dodd-Frank on Operational Due Diligence   356
Conclusion   357
Notes   358

About the Author   **359**

About the Website   **361**

Index   **363**

Preface

People tend to not take operational due diligence in the field of private equity very seriously. The risk category that operational due diligence is supposed to evaluate—operational risk—is not as narrowly defined as other related types of risks, such as credit risk, counterparty risk, currency risk, and so forth. Depending on the context, the implications of the term *operational risk* can change. In part, the broadness of the field and subsequent confusion about exactly what is meant when discussing operational risk and operational due diligence are likely contributing factors to the lack of attention paid to this risk category.

When an investor first decides to take the plunge into private equity investing, it is often an anticlimactic choice. In some cases, hundreds of millions of dollars are committed by institutional Limited Partners (LPs) to private equity funds, but the money may not generate returns for years. Yet, with such a long-term commitment of capital into a traditionally illiquid and complex asset class, it would seem only logical that LPs would seek to perform at least as rigorous a due diligence analysis on a private equity fund as they perform on other asset classes, such as hedge funds. In investing arenas outside of private equity, operational due diligence has slowly gained acceptance over the years. Within the alternative investment arena in general and hedge funds in particular, a key driver of increased focus is the losses that have been caused by fraudulent activity, which in turn was facilitated by weak operations. In recent memory, investors have seen a number of headlines and articles about the hundreds of millions in losses associated with names such as Bernard Madoff, R. Allen Stanford, Jerome Kerviel, Tom Petters, and Samuel Israel III, which help to explain the meteoric rise in interest in operational due diligence in the alternative space. Even as this book is being written, alleged UBS rogue trader Kewku Adoboli has been charged with fraud that resulted in a loss of over $2 billion. Because of a series of similar private equity frauds, LPs and, however begrudgingly, General Partners (GPs) have begun to respect the need for private equity operational due diligence.

But operational due diligence involves a great deal more than fraud detection. Sometimes honest GPs and LPs simply do not have the requisite skills, resources, or foresight to avoid underperformance or losses due primarily to operational concerns. Proper operational risk management within a fund is not simply a matter of throwing experience or money at the problem. Rather, operational risk evolves within a fund organization over time. To effectively manage its own internal operational risk exposure, a fund's management must be actively involved in all aspects of operations oversight. At different times and during different types of market events, private equity funds may react differently and the ensuing consequences may not be uniform for their internal fund operations.

Operational due diligence is an ongoing diagnostic process. Much like private equity investing itself, however, operational due diligence on private equity investments requires a measured dose of patience. Due diligence can be more art than science, and a thorough analysis will allow investors to detect funds that will have an increased likelihood for underperformance or for failure in the event of unexpected stresses.

This book seeks to accomplish several goals, but in particular the author wishes to convince LPs of the benefits of designing, performing, and maintaining a robust operational due diligence program for private equity funds. To support this cause, I have outlined a brief history of operational risk coupled with an introduction to the unique aspects of operational due diligence on private equity funds.

The second aim of this book is to provide LPs with the tools necessary to execute detailed comprehensive operational due diligence reviews of private equity funds. To accomplish this, I have outlined the elements of core and expanded operational due diligence reviews. I have provided comprehensive chapters dedicated to analyzing approaches to valuation, legal, and financial statement risks. In Chapters 3 and 4 you will see a red flag icon (like the one set next to this paragraph) that indicates key operational risk areas in which deficiencies have historically tended to signal larger problems.

I also offer a summary of historical private equity frauds and hypothetical case studies to familiarize LPs with the scenarios they may encounter when performing operational due diligence. This discussion also includes a review of the key considerations LPs should take into account when reviewing real estate funds.

Additionally, this book seeks to broaden the discussion surrounding operational risk assessment in private equity funds beyond the notions of "pass" or "fail." To accomplish this, I have provided an introduction to incorporating the results of operational due diligence reviews into the asset allocation process. This book also includes discussions regarding ongoing operational monitoring techniques and the role of advisory boards in due diligence.

Finally, one of the other goals of this book is to foster an increased understanding among investors in the private equity community about the rights of LPs to perform comprehensive operational due diligence reviews and the ways in which GPs approach operational risk management. It is likely that there will be readers who disagree with some of the opinions and conclusions presented in this book. Debates are welcomed, and I encourage all those interested in private equity to throw their hats into the arena, to join in and discuss the issues and enhance the larger community's understanding and focus in the field of operational risk.

A detailed, comprehensive operational due diligence program for private equity funds requires time, resources, and skill to develop and refine over time. The benefits of implementing such a program with discipline, uniformity, and caution are that it will allow Limited Partners to weed out managers with weaker operations, make investment decisions with stronger convictions, facilitate ongoing monitoring, and avoid losses associated with operational risks. It is my hope that the techniques and advice in this book are taken up by LPs and more risk-conscious GPs. Perhaps Ben Franklin's saying best sums up the importance of operational due diligence in the illiquid, complex, and often opaque field of private equity investing: "An ounce of prevention is worth a pound of cure."

JASON SCHARFMAN
March 2012

Private Equity Operational Due Diligence

CHAPTER 1

Introduction to Private Equity Operational Risk

Private equity investing is a unique asset class that can offer a number of attractive benefits to investors. Compared to more traditional investments, some of the benefits associated with private equity investing can include the ability to focus on long-term capital growth with higher uncorrelated returns. Despite these benefits, as is the case with any asset class, private equity investing is also fraught with a number of unique risk sets and challenges that investors must consider. These risks can include traditional investment-related risks such as style drift, excessive risk taking, and overall poor performance. When investing in private equity, investors are also exposed to a series of what may be thought of as risks that are not purely related to investments. These risks have become commonly grouped together under the moniker of operational risks. But what exactly is this mysterious risk category known as operational risk?

INTRODUCTION TO OPERATIONAL RISK

Noninvestment-related risks can be often grouped into different categories due to certain shared similarities. These noninvestment risks also go by many names depending on with whom you are speaking. Some may refer to these noninvestment related risks as fat-tail risks. The term *fat-tail risks* is used due to the severe effects that these risk may have, coupled with the perceived infrequency with which they actually cause damage. Others may use the terms *business risk* or *organizational risk*. The term that most individuals who focus on analyzing and monitoring these risks have settled on in recent years is *operational risk*.

The concept of operational risk is not unique to the world of private equity. Indeed, it is not even unique to asset management or the financial industry in general. Concerns related to risk management falling under the heading of operational risk are present across a number of industries that have nothing whatsoever to do with the business of investing or managing money. The FAA System Safety Handbook for pilots has a section dedicated to Operational Risk Management (ORM) and defines the goals of ORM as "protecting people, equipment, and other resources, while making the most effective use of them."[1] In the medical field, surgeons have procedures in place to mitigate literal operational risk, to prevent mistakes such as wrong-side surgery when conducting actual operations on patients.[2]

With such a well-developed field spanning multiple disciplines, why in recent years has there been a flurry of interest in a subject that is supposedly so well fleshed out? After all, with a large body of research on operational risk in other fields not related to asset management or private equity, could a discussion of operational risk and due diligence in a private equity context actually yield anything new? While the field of private equity investing has continued to increase in complexity and specialization, the issues of operational risk and due diligence areas applicable to private equity as they are in other fields. This ambivalent situation can perhaps be best summed up by a comment that Pablo Picasso is rumored to have made following a viewing at Lascaux Cave of some of the earliest prehistoric cave paintings ever discovered: "We have invented nothing."

Regardless of the field or context in which operational risk is being discussed, often times it seems both practitioners and academics alike have a difficult time pinning down an appropriate definition of this broad topic. Part of this problem perhaps stems from the typically broad number of topics and disciplines that operational risk generally encompasses. Within the financial and specifically asset management world, defining operational risk is often a contentious exercise at best. Indeed, as Chapter 2 discusses in more depth, many in the asset management world and private equity communities in particular, may not even see a real need to devote material resources toward analyzing operational risk in private equity funds.

Indeed, why bother attempting to develop a definition of something if there is a commonly held belief that the very thing attempting to be defined is not itself of any consequence? Stated plainly, as the reader may be able to gather from the title of this book, operational risk not only matters but should be of paramount importance to any investor even considering investing in private equity. As an aside, for those in the private equity community who may disagree with this statement, I invite them to read this book, fully consider the benefits of developing a private equity operational risk assessment program and ultimately think about whether or not they would find making a more informed decision (e.g., a decision based on an understanding of not only the investment risks of a particular private equity investment, but the operational risks as well) to be the most prudent course

EXHIBIT 1.1   Common Private Equity Operational Risk Categories

Risk Category
Cash controls
Trade life cycle processing
Valuation
Transparency and fund reporting
Liquidity management
Technology and systems
Legal and compliance
Counterparty oversight
Quality and roles of service providers
Business continuity and disaster recovery

by which to proceed. Ultimately, more informed investors tend to make better investment decisions and realize fewer losses due to operational risks.

Within the private equity world, there are any number of factors that can fall into the category of operational risks. Common operational risks are outlined in Exhibit 1.1.

The list of common private equity operational risks in Exhibit 1.1 are the general risks that come to most individuals' minds when they first hear the term *operational risk*. As this chapter discusses in more detail, the operational risk category lacks a true universal definition. Within the private equity world, there is no operational risk rule book. Furthermore, no private equity legislation, regulatory guidance, or other laws describe what falls under the term *operational risk* and it is therefore usually defined by what is covered by the operational due diligence process. As such, in a private equity context, *operational risk* is very much a term whose definition is driven by the market. Investors, fund managers, and private equity service providers alike are effectively left to their own devices in some regards to come to terms with this concept. That being said there are certain risk factors, as discussed throughout this book, which most in the private equity community would group into the category of operational risk. It is upon this foundation that we will begin to place the building blocks of the discussion of the operational due diligence process.

OPERATIONAL RISK COMPARED TO OPERATIONAL DUE DILIGENCE

Now that we have introduced a basic understanding of what is commonly meant by operational risk we can next focus on operational due diligence. The two terms are occasionally used synonymously in practice; however, there is a distinction between the two. The term *operational due diligence* is correctly utilized when employed to refer to the processes of gathering data about a particular private equity fund. The type of data collected during the operational due diligence process is operational risk data. After this data has been collected during the operational due diligence process, an investor then can perform an analysis of this data to come to a determination as to the amount of operational risk present at a particular private equity fund. This analysis stage, as compared to the data collection stage, is also typically considered to be a part of the operational due diligence process.

Operational due diligence can be thought of as the process of performing due diligence on these operational risks. But this definition does not really tell us much. So, what exactly do those in the private equity community mean when they refer to operational risk and operational due diligence?

WHAT IS OPERATIONAL DUE DILIGENCE?

With the basic understanding now in place we can now begin to think about what exactly operational due diligence actually entails within a private equity context. Operational due diligence is a peculiar subject. Indeed the acronym that is commonly used in the industry is "ODD," although this book will use "ops dd." Many investors and fund managers may have a general idea about what operational due diligence encompasses. Some investors may even think operational due diligence to be limited to the seemingly easy-to-diagnose areas such as post-trade analysis and other back-office processes. Any such risks would certainly be obvious to detect for anyone who devoted the time to take a look—they are hiding in plain sight. While these statements are certainly overgeneralizations, they definitely contribute to the understanding of what encompasses operational due diligence.

What is less obvious perhaps is that while each individual's exact notions of what is meant by operational due diligence may vary, the range of variations can be quite wide. This is one of the reasons why operational due diligence is a multifaceted and fairly deep field of due diligence and lacks one universal definition that would sum up all of these aspects into one unique package. The lack of a universal definition is brought even more into focus in the complex work of alternative investments.

Under the broad umbrella category of alternative investments, it is even more difficult for investors and fund managers to explain how operational due diligence processes may vary among different types of investments such as hedge funds and private equity investing. It is the latter category, private equity, upon which this book will focus. By introducing the various related concepts, due diligence techniques and approaches, as well as trends in this field, this book attempts to provide guidance toward fostering a more complete understanding for the parties involved in private equity investing, including investors, fund managers, and private equity service providers of what the field of a robust operational due diligence program entails. Perhaps this will foster a more universal definition of the term among members of the private equity community.

But perhaps we are getting ahead of ourselves. As intimated earlier, the world of private equity is a category of alternative investing unique unto itself, replete with its own series of challenges and opportunities. This uniqueness and the general ways in which investors and fund managers may have approached the concept in the past have developed into a situation in which, among most individuals in the private equity community, operational due diligence in the private equity world tends to be an amorphous concept.

Focus on Fraud Detection

When many private equity investors first hear the term operational due diligence, they may immediately begin to focus on fraud detection. Indeed, when first beginning to think about the subject of items that may influence the ultimate investment decision other than purely investment-related concerns, there is a strong temptation for investors to focus on concerns related to fraud in the management of a private equity fund. Certainly, this is understandable for several reasons.

Due to the fat-tailed risks associated with fraud it is certainly reasonable, and from a pragmatic standpoint logically prudent, that due diligence surrounding potential issues of fraud should be of penultimate concern during every stage of the entire due diligence process. Private equity investors logically want to avoid all losses, but losses due to fraud can leave a particular sting and any potential recovery from such losses is often a sticky business. When an asset management fraud occurs it can generally lead to total losses with little hope for recovery. Indeed if recovery by defrauded investors does occur it is often only after a long extended process steeped in legal costs. Moreover, any recovery process typically only results in partial recovery because the capital "pie" to be divided does not meet the needs of all investors. Of course, there are rare exceptions in which investors recoup the entire amount of their initial investment.

Additionally, in the wake of a series of frauds, Ponzi schemes, and the like, in the alternative investment arena concerns related to fraud are still at the relative forefront of the general investment collective consciousness. Furthermore, regardless of whether a private equity fund manager has a long track record of stellar performance, coupled with experienced well credentialed professionals and a highly compelling investment thesis for a fund—if the entire thing is a fraud—none of the other due diligence that may have been performed regarding the merits of the investment strategy (i.e., investment due diligence) and the quality of the managers' reputation (i.e., reputational due diligence) matters very much.

In the context of fraud detection, the distinction matters little whether an investor is performing investment due diligence, operational due diligence, or any other subcategory of the two. Stated plainly, if the due diligence process fails to detect fraud, it has failed.

Now of course there are different levels of fraud. There is the complete and total fraud often employed under the model of the Ponzi scheme (e.g., Madoff) and then there are other types of fraud that may not be so apparent or so completely ruinous to an organization (e.g., a private equity manager claiming that they have 80 percent of the portfolio independently valued when in actuality it is more like 70 percent). In the latter example, the fraud may not result in any losses at all, however, the private equity fund manager is still committing a fraud in the broadest sense of the word by misrepresenting the truth of the facts and circumstances relevant to their particular organization. So if a due diligence process fails to detect these "white lie" lesser frauds, has it failed?

It would be easy perhaps to give into the temptation to state, quite directly, yes. However, this seeks to impose black-letter bright-line pedagogy on a mutable subject matter. In fact, one approach toward reaching an answer to this question relates to issues of the weights with which a particular areas of the underlying items queried by the due diligence process both matter to an investor and directly relate to the potential severity with which overlooking such an item could create losses or future liabilities (i.e., clawback) for investors via fraud.

So, for example, there may be little potential for investor losses due to fraud solely related to the fact that a private equity firm may claim to use the more well respected, and expensive, Fund Accounting System A while in fact they utilize the cheaper and less robust Fund Accounting System B. Certainly this is an important misrepresentation that would raise red flags, lead investors to consider what else a fund manager may be lying about, and ultimately affect an investor's determination whether or not to invest with a particular private equity manager. However, if the private equity manager utilizes the accounting system in only a limited capacity and accomplishes all the necessary accounting tasks with Fund Accounting System B, then the potential for direct investor losses due to fraud (i.e., perhaps that the fund's accounts were not properly maintained) is minimal as related to the fund manager's misrepresentation of accounting systems utilized.

Therefore, in the overall scheme of things certain instances of fraud may be more or less deadly to a particular investor in terms of their ultimate consequences to generate losses. However, the opportunity for fraud is still prevalent throughout multiple areas of a private equity organization at both the management company and fund level. As such, investors' sometimes seemingly zealous focus on fraud detection and prevention is certainly reasonable. Fraud concerns however, should not overshadow other goals of the operational due diligence process. After all, an organization can be run with the best of intentions in a nonfraudulent manner but still be a complete operational disaster. In such cases, whether a private equity fund fails due to fraud or a weak operational infrastructure, regardless of the potential recovery options when a fraud occurs, both situations have the same initial destructive effects.

Universal Definition of Operational Due Diligence

Depending on who you talk to and what their general role is (e.g., investor, fund manager, fund operations personnel, service provider, etc.), you will likely receive a multitude of answers to questions regarding the meaning of operational due diligence. From the investor's perspective, the author has heard the head of an alternative investment allocation platform describing the work of their operational due diligence team along the following lines, *"Sure we do comprehensive work. These operational due diligence guys go in and make sure that the fund manager doesn't have two different driver's licenses or has never spent time in jail."*

If you talk to someone with an accounting background they may interpret the term literally to mean due diligence on the operational aspects of a firm, such as the back-office accounting work. They would be correct. Others, as our example illustrates, may consider operational due diligence to consist of fraud detection and background investigations (e.g., making sure that their private equity manager is not the next Bernard Madoff). They, too, would be correct.

Others with a focus on controls might describe operational due diligence as focusing on the flow of cash throughout an organization.

Still others might describe operational due diligence as making sure that the fund manager is properly valuing securities and not stealing from the firm. Still others may consider operational due diligence to be all of the leftovers from the rest of investment due diligence process (e.g., things that don't quite fit neatly into the parts of due diligence that are used to determine the merits of a particular private equity fund and whether it will be profitable or not). These opinions are also correct. We could go on with this list but by now the reader should have the idea that operational due diligence is viewed by some to be a catch-all hodgepodge of different disciplines and subjects cobbled together into a developing field with its own unique moniker.

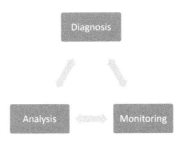

EXHIBIT 1.2 Functions of a
Core Operational Due Diligence
Process

Core Operational Due Diligence Process Functionality

Within this potpourri of concepts and terminology, as with all areas of due diligence, be they operational investment or otherwise, are a series of basic processes, techniques, and risk factors that can be found. It is these areas that are the core of operational due diligence, and should be the bedrock upon which a larger due operational diligence process is founded. As outlined in Exhibit 1.2, by diagnosing, analyzing, and monitoring operational risk in private equity investments, investors can foster a deeper understanding of any operational risk exposures, mitigate those exposures, and avoid taking unnecessary operational risks when investing in private equity.

OPERATIONAL DUE DILIGENCE IN THE FIELD OF PRIVATE EQUITY

Many investors will not be directly managing their own private equity funds but instead entrusting capital to a third party to manage on their behalf in a commingled investment vehicle also known as a private equity fund. There are several categories of private equity fund strategies including:

- Venture capital (VC) funds
- Leveraged buyout (LBO) funds
- Mezzanine financing funds
- Distressed debt investing funds
- Crossover funds
- PIPE transactions
- Interval funds
- Real estate funds

In addition to these strategies there also exist private equity fund of funds, which are private equity funds that invest with other private equity funds. This book will provide an overview of the general universal elements of operational due diligence for private equity funds in general and will also pay particular attention to certain of the specific risks associated with different classes of funds just referenced including real estate funds. With an understanding of the basic landscape of private equity fund strategies, we can begin to discuss in greater detail the investor's role in the private equity process.

To begin with, despite all of the benefits that an investment in private equity funds may offer, the asset class does have its detractors. It is an asset class that has been referred to as having "lottery-like characteristics."[3] Private equity groups have been called "amoral asset strippers" and "casino capitalists."[4] Franz Müntefering, former vice-chancellor of Germany, referred to private equity firms as "Heuschrecke," or locusts, and went so far as to publish a so-called locust list that included such firms as Carlyle, Goldman Sachs, KKR, and Deutsche Bank.[5] Others have referred to private equity investors as vultures or buzzards.[6] Groups such as the Service Employees International Union have criticized the tax advantages enjoyed by many private equity firms as compared to the employees of the portfolio companies that they manage.[7]

Putting the rhetoric aside, private equity can indeed be classified as one of the alternative investment asset classes in which manager selection plays the most crucial role in all asset classes.[8] Therefore, one of the key considerations in assessing the potential benefits and risks that will be factored into an investor's decision making process to invest in private equity will not only be related to the scope of the underlying investments and/or portfolio companies that will be held in the private equity fund, but also to the competency, skill, and quality of the operational infrastructure of the private equity fund manager themselves.

OPERATIONAL DUE DILIGENCE AS DISTINGUISHED FROM OPERATIONAL MANAGEMENT OF PORTFOLIO COMPANIES

As is the case in many disciplines and particularly in finance, the terms and concepts associated with operational risk and operational due diligence can have more than one interpretation, particularly in a private equity context. As such it is important to clarify the specific context within private equity in which the term is being used here. For the purposes of this book, operational due diligence refers to the due diligence on operational risks that investors will perform on *private equity funds*.

This is to be distinguished from any operational planning or management assessment that a private equity fund manager would perform on underlying portfolio investment companies. While many of the core operational concepts and techniques that will be discussed in this book are certainly relevant, those types of operational reviews fall more into the context of investment management than they would operational due diligence and are therefore best left for other texts focused more exclusively on such subject.

Before we proceed, so that all readers are on the same page it is worth pausing for a moment to define some basic terminology that will be used throughout this book:

- **Private equity firm.** For the purposes of this text, a *private equity firm* will refer to the management company of a private equity organization. A private equity firm will typically manage several private equity funds.
- **Private equity fund.** The term *private equity* fund refers to a private equity investment vehicle that adheres to a particular strategy. A particular private equity fund may be offered in a variety of different investment vehicle formats so that investors from different jurisdictions can invest in a particular investment strategy. Motivations for such different investment vehicles can include jurisdictional and tax concerns.
- **General Partner or GP.** The *general partner*, commonly referred to as a GP, is the managing partner of a private equity company. To clarify the General Partner is not typically a single individual but rather a legal entity that is organized by the private equity firm's principals to oversee the management of a private equity fund. These entities are commonly organized as a limited liability companies.
- **Manager or Investment Adviser.** In many cases, a private equity fund will have an intermediary level entity known as the *Manager* or *Investment* Advisor between the general partner and investors, which technically may serve as the manager of a particular private equity fund.
- **Limited Partners or LPs.** Investors in a private equity fund are commonly referred to as *Limited Partners* or *LPs*. This term comes from the fact that many private equity funds are organized as limited partnerships and, therefore, the investors that subscribe (i.e., invest) in those funds are limited partners.

TIMING OF OPERATIONAL DUE DILIGENCE IN THE INVESTING PROCESS

During the initial private equity fund assessment process investors are faced by a series of due diligence challenges. These challenges often broach the due

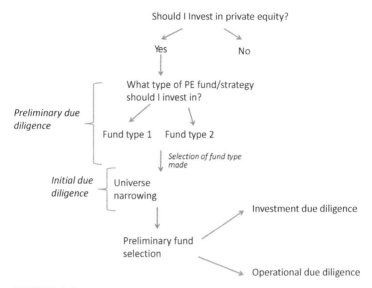

EXHIBIT 1.3 Typical Private Equity Decision-Making Process

diligence process first with investment considerations, which are then subsequently followed by various stages of both investment and operational due diligence. Exhibit 1.3 provides an outline of a typical decision-tree process that may be followed by investors as they progress from first considering an investment in private equity down through to the actual due diligence processes that such an investment may entail.

The process shown in Exhibit 1.3 is by no means set in stone. An investor may begin the operational due diligence process in parallel with the investment process. In certain cases, in much the same way that an investor may have certain minimum criteria regarding the investment merits of a particular private equity manager or fund, so too may similar operational requirements be in place. In these cases, in order to prevent an investor from unnecessarily expending the necessary time and resources required to perform a full operational due diligence process on a particular manager, an investor may attempt to perform an initial operational screening, or smell test, as it may sometimes be called, in order to evaluate whether the private equity fund or manager should be discarded out of hand, based on a preliminary failure to adhere to an investor's minimum operational requirements.

An example of such a requirement might be that an investor may, as either a function of their own internal policies or perhaps on a case-by-case basis as determined by the sector of the particular market a private equity fund is anticipated to be active in, determine that as a minimum operational requirement the investor will not allocate capital to a private equity fund that is not associated with a firm that has managed capital before. For nonprivate equity firms, such a minimum operational requirement could be perhaps equated to the presence of a minimum track record that is maintained for a number of years. A requirement that would be typical for a hedge fund, for example, is a three-year track record. Returning to private equity, another operational requirement could be previous experience in managing funds in a particular sector. To illustrate, an investor may come across a private equity fund that has traditionally invested in health-care (pharmaceutical) funds and then launches a fund focused on infrastructure or technology-based sectors.

While the technology-based sector may indeed be related to health care, such as a private equity fund that invests in medical device companies fueled by technological innovations, the original fund in our example invested primarily in pharmaceuticals and an investor may consider these two funds to be different enough that the technology-based sector fund would not pass the minimum screening requirements. As such, if these initial screens or filters are not successfully met by the funds then, regardless of the results of the subsequent operational due diligence process and any operational risks or strengths detected, the fund has effectively been doomed to fail before the process even started because it has been determined by the investor that such a fund will not be suitable. Exhibit 1.4 outlines a typical process

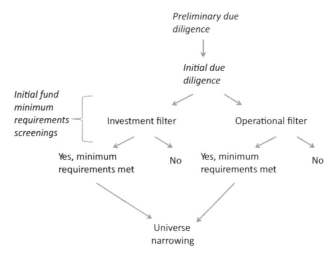

EXHIBIT 1.4 Investment and Operational Filtering Stages in Private Equity Decision-Making Process

employing these initial investment and operational screens, which must be passed before proceeding through the remaining due diligence process flow.

OPERATIONAL DUE DILIGENCE PROCESS

Once an investor has moved through the initial fund screening and selection processes, it is time to begin the operational due diligence process. This process, to which the bulk of this text is devoted, will focus on performing operational due diligence on a particular private equity fund and its affiliated entities, such as a management company. This is in contrast to the more general operational due diligence screening outlined above, which facilitates the universe defining stage of the process. To mark our progress along the path of an investor's fund-focused operational due diligence review, it is at this stage that a number of funds have successfully passed the operational minimum criteria. We will limit our focus at this stage to operational universe definition criteria as opposed to either solely investment universe definitions or both investment and operational minimum universe criteria.

With the universe now defined by those funds that an investor has both a sufficient amount of investment interest in, as well as those that possess the required minimum operational qualities to merit further due diligence, an investor can now proceed. At this point, an investor will typically approach a new series of sequential stages focused less on minimum criteria requirements and more on assessing minimum operational practices and weaknesses within each particular fund and firm. In making these determinations, these operational due diligence processes often are marked by a number of broad stages through which an investor progresses before coming to a final operational determination regarding the private equity fund. A common four-stage process is outlined in Exhibit 1.5.

EXHIBIT 1.5 Stages of Analysis in Investor Private Equity Due Diligence Process

As the firm stage in the process suggests, the operational due diligence process typically begins with an investor being approached by, or approaching, a private equity firm. The first stage of the operational due diligence process will therefore generally begin with an investor developing a dialogue with the private equity firm. During this stage a basic understanding of the firm's key players, the funds managed, and its organization will come to light.

The next stage of the operational due diligence process typically involves investors focusing their efforts more on an investment strategy managed by the firm. During the course of this stage, investors will likely begin to focus their due diligence process on items specifically related to a certain fund. Generally, this process will entail investors familiarizing themselves with investment personnel, such as portfolio managers who may devote the majority of their time to a particular fund. Additionally, this stage is often where the real meat of the operational due diligence process occurs and many fund specific operational policies, procedures, and controls are discussed.

The final stage in the broad four-stage process involves investors reaching through the private equity fund itself and looking through to the investments, actual or proposed, in which the fund under consideration currently invests or intends to invest. In many of the private equity situations investors will face, the private equity fund under consideration will be allocating capital to an underlying company or series of companies.

In such cases, the operational due diligence process may involve not so much an assessment of the investment merits of such investments (e.g., why is the private equity fund planning on investing in this particular sector, or why is company A more deserving of funding from the private equity fund than fund B?) but rather may pose questions regarding appropriate policies, procedures, controls, and transparency at the private equity firm, and oversight and reporting of these investments such that the operational risks associated with funding these underlying companies is appropriately monitored and mitigated. Of course, contingent on the scope and amount of other due diligence being performed, an investor may gauge the depth at which he looks through to such underlying companies. The point of referencing this stage in the operational due diligence context is that just because an investor has put on their operational due diligence hat and has undertaken a review focused primarily on operational type risks, it is often not advisable for investors to shut themselves off completely from a particular area of review because it may border, however tangentially, on investment-related matters.

Based on this description, one may imply that the broad stages in the operational due diligence process are sequential in nature (i.e., first operational due diligence is performed on the fund, then the firm, and then, if applicable, portfolio companies). This is not necessarily the case, and many investors may opt to advance through each of these stages out of order, or simultaneously, or in an overlapping fashion.

The suggested sequence seems to be the most logical and practical route for most investors to follow. Many investors prefer this approach because it allows them to start with a big picture view and then drill down into more focused areas. The reason for conducting the process in an incongruous fashion may be due to considerations of the operational due diligence process aligning with any investment due diligence. Additionally, as is often the case in private equity, an investor may need to fire on all cylinders in order to meet a particular funding date upon which a fund will realize a close and stop accepting new capital.

In the case where an investor is performing operational due diligence on a private equity fund of funds, a fifth stage can be added to the process. This five-stage process is summarized in Exhibit 1.6.

Under this five-stage category operational due diligence process, the "Private Equity Fund" category is effectively transformed into "PE Fund of Funds." This switch is made in reference to the fact that there is now an additional player in the mix, the fund of funds, as not just an investor making a direct investment into a private equity fund. The previous, "Private Equity Fund" category, which was used to reference the stage of the process at which an investor approaches performing operational due diligence on a direct private equity manager now is slotted beneath the "Private Equity Fund of Funds" stage. If you think about it for a moment, this addition

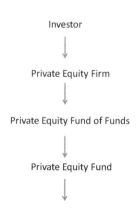

Investor

↓

Private Equity Firm

↓

Private Equity Fund of Funds

↓

Private Equity Fund

↓

Private Equity Fund Portfolio Companies

EXHIBIT 1.6 Stages of Analysis in Investor Private Equity Due Diligence Process

of the Private Equity Fund of Funds category and subsequent reordering of the process adheres to the same logical process utilized in the four-stage process. An investor will typically start with a big-picture view of the private equity firm, a category that is the starting point for both four- and five-stage processes, and then progresses into subsequent levels of more refined detail.

HISTORICAL PERSPECTIVES OF PRIVATE EQUITY OPERATIONAL RISK

Now that we have established a basic understanding of what is generally implied by the term *operational due diligence*, we can next proceed to a discussion of the roles of operational risk and operational due diligence in a private equity context. To facilitate this discussion, it is perhaps useful to first consider the current state of the private equity operational due diligence world. In recent years investors have begun to focus more on operational risk across all investment classes ranging from traditional long-only investments to alternative investments. As with the evolution of most areas of risk management and due diligence, in the early stages of this acceptance reviews of operational risks were typically couched into primarily investment-related processes.

Before going any further, it is important to highlight that the purpose of this discussion is to provide the reader with a general sense of the development of operational due diligence in a private equity context. Due to the general nature of this discussion, the goal is not to imply that there were organizations several years ago, for example, that did not have distinct dedicated operational due diligence functions. Rather, such organizations were generally more the exception rather than the norm. As there was an increased acceptance of the importance of operational risk management in an asset management context, the carving out of distinct operational due diligence functions then became more common. In recent memory, perhaps the most obvious and notable point of demarcation fueling the development of operational due diligence was the uncovering of Madoff's Ponzi scheme.

Madoff's Ponzi Scheme and Operational Due Diligence

Some may say, perhaps rightly so, that the Madoff scandal was the exception rather than the norm. Others may say that Madoff was not a private equity manager and, therefore, any increased awareness or lessons learned from the Madoff scandal are simply not applicable. Many practitioners in the hedge fund profession had immediate gut reactions that Madoff's scheme was not a hedge fund and, therefore, it should not be held up as an example to which the entire hedge fund or even broader alternative investment industry should be compared.

While well-intentioned, such notions are patently incorrect. This head-in-the-sand attitude borders on asset-class xenophobia and certainly does not foster an open-minded approach toward learning from mistakes. By conducting such operational case studies of fraudulent activities both investors and fund managers, regardless of what asset classes they primarily participate in, can certainly learn a great deal about not only what steps they may take to prevent fraudulent activity, but also what concerns might be at the forefront of their current or prospective investors' minds.

Corgentum Consulting, an operational risk consultancy (and also your author's employer) that works with investors to perform operational due diligence reviews on asset managers places an emphasis on studying historical operational due diligence case studies. Corgentum has found that case studies can not only inform an investor's operational due diligence processes in order to avoid fraud, but can often provide a framework by which an investor can expand the existing scope of their operational due diligence reviews to focus on areas previously not vetted, in which the opportunity for fraud may be more apparent than previously through. In general, while the merits of modeling fraud to predict future fraudulent activity with any certainty is limited by the nature of the next unanticipated fraud, such research and analysis of prior frauds certainly yields a much more comprehensive operational due diligence process and results in more informed investors, as compared to not analyzing such frauds.

Returning to our discussion of the development of operational due diligence, the pre-Madoff and post-Madoff worlds of operational due diligence is perhaps best thought of as the 23rd equatorial parallel above and below which lie investors who either have embraced operational due diligence or those who have not. The Madoff fraud was also important because it had a resounding effect on the way in which many investors approached the concept of operational due diligence. A Corgentum Consulting study found a so-called *Madoff Effect* by which investors tend to tailor their operational due diligence around recent frauds while minimizing certain other operational risks.[9]

The Madoff scheme has become one of the most-cited illustrations of fraudulent activities and Ponzi schemes. It is used in this context because of the preeminent initial and subsequent attention and media coverage from investors and the press. Many other frauds in recent years, which occurred both before and after Madoff's Ponzi scheme were revealed, have fueled an increased awareness of the dangers of ignoring operational risk and not performing operational due diligence. Examples of these fraudsters include

R. Allen Stanford (Stanford Financial Group), Tom Petters (Petters Group Worldwide), Arthur Nadel (Scoop Management), Nicholas Cosmo (Agape World), and Helmut Kiener (K1 Group). Even service providers got in on the act with the revelation of fraudulent activity by prominent attorney Marc Dreier that stole millions from asset managers with the fraudulent sale of nonexistent securities.

Such was the spate of Ponzi schemes, as opposed to other fraudulent schemes, in the media, that the term "Ponzimonium" came into the public consciousness. This increased awareness on the part of investors and fund managers of the importance of understanding operational risk and performing operational due diligence had a lasting effect among investors across all asset classes, including private equity. It is in this post-Madoff world that the techniques described in this book are focused.

However, before discussing operational due diligence techniques and approaches, it is first helpful to obtain an understanding of how we arrived at the current environment as it relates to the world of private equity investing. To that point, before analyzing the current framework for operational risk analysis in private equity funds, it is useful to gain an initial understanding of the basic history of private equity investing. This historical perspective will allow investors to better understand how we arrived at the present state of private equity operational due diligence.

A Brief History of Private Equity

The earliest private equity investments were not really via modern pooled fund structures as we know them today. Instead, the concept of individuals pooling together capital to fund private, and often risky, ventures has in its earliest beginnings extending back hundreds, if not thousands, of years. For example, merchants in the ancient world would pool their assets together to finance trade expeditions with other countries.

The first private equity deals of the modern era consisted of groups of financiers and companies putting together private pools of capital to extend loans or fund various infrastructure projects. The focus was on one project or deal at a time. Examples of such early private deals include the financing of the Transcontinental Railroad in the United States via the conglomeration of Credit Mobilier and Civil War financier Jay Cooke in the mid-1800s.[10] These types of transactions were eventually followed by more sophisticated deals, such as the buyout of the Carnegie Steel Company by J.P. Morgan from Andrew Carnegie in 1901.[11] Even the roots of large companies such as International Business Machines (IBM) grew because of the combined efforts of groups of wealthy individuals combining pools of capital with combinations of other less-successful businesses to produce better managed, more efficient, and profitable firms.

For the next 40 years or so, the sophistication of private equity deals continued to gradually increase; however, deal originations predominately remained limited to a select group of wealthy individuals. The mid-1940s saw the rise of the first modern private equity firms and fund structures, with a particular focus on venture capital. During this period the appeal of private equity firms was broadened and firms began to solicit capital from a number of sources and did not limit capital inflows solely to wealthy families. This was especially true with the growth of venture capital firms during this time, such as the American Research and Development Corporation (ARDC).

ARDC was founded by General Georges Doriot and Carl Compton to invest in developing firms that had technologies rooted in military applications from World War II. ARDC invested primarily in companies with ties to the academic juggernauts of MIT and Harvard and the firm's investments included the High Voltage Engineering Corporation and the Digital Equipment Company.[12] The focusing on continued investment in innovation in science and technology continued to fuel the growth of venture capital into the 1950s with the growth of Silicon Valley firms such as Draper Gaither and Andersen.[13]

In the more modern era, private equity has gone through a number of so-called boom and bust cycles. These include the increased focus on junk-bond-financed leverage buyouts throughout the early 1980s through the early 1990s. The firm of Drexel Burnham Lambert was a leader in this area until the firm was effectively shut down as a result of an insider trading scandal involving Dennis Levine and Ivan Boesky. Perhaps the most famous leveraged buyout (LBO) deal during this time was the record-setting $25 billion takeover of RJR Nabisco. This deal was immortalized in a book and a movie, both called *Barbarians at the Gate*.[14]

It was during this period that the modern focus on regulation first began to have a noted impact on private equity investment activities. Fueled in part by a political backlash against jumbo deals such as the RJR Nabisco buyout, firms that underwrote junk bonds came under increased scrutiny, particularly in relation to their beneficial tax treatment. After the failure of Drexel Burnham Lambert, coupled with significant increases in defaults among junk-bond-issuing companies, the U.S. Congress took action. In August 1989, they implemented the Financial Institutions Reform, Recovery and Enforcement Act of 1989. This Act, driven by the savings and loans (S&Ls) crises of the 1980s, prevented S&Ls from investing in junk bonds.

For the next few years, post–RJR Nabisco, private equity continued to grow and shirk with the ebb and flow of investors' demand. Notable deals during this time period include the sale of Snapple Beverages to Quaker Oats, and buyouts by private equity groups of Continental Airlines, Domino's Pizza, and Petco.

The next stage of private equity was realized by the growth of the venture capital investment in technology and Internet companies. Notable firms that received venture capital funding during this dot-com period included Netscape, Yahoo!, and Amazon.com. The dot-com bubble eventually burst, turning into what many have called a "dot-bomb".

It was around this time that additional legislation had a material impact on the activities of private equity. After the failure of such firms due to a number of accounting and management scandals that brought down companies such as Enron, Tyco International, and WorldCom, the Sarbanes-Oxley Act of 2002, commonly referred to as SOX, was enacted. SOX imposed a number of increased reporting and transparency requirements for publicly listed companies. After the passage of SOX, many venture capital firms could no longer afford the increased cost of compliance for initial public offering exit strategies, which further stagnated the growth of such private equity investments.

After this period of decline, and the eventual resurgence of private equity during the 2000s, several private equity firms took a page from their own playbook and considered pursuing their own offerings via a combination of private and public offering strategies. One of the most notable offerings during this time period was the initial public offering of the Blackstone Group in 2007. The credit crisis of 2008 saw many private equity firms transition to focus on purchasing debt in existing LBOs or private investments in public equity, commonly known as PIPEs.

Now that we have developed a basic summary understanding of the modern roots of private equity investing, it is worth noting a few items. First of all, private equity, as its name implies, has largely succeeded in remaining just that, private. While some of the large mega-deals and tax benefits granted to asset managers such as private equity firms have garnered attention, in general from a regulatory perspective private equity firms—as compared to banks, insurance companies, and even hedge funds,—have for the most part undergone less scrutiny.

These historical developments have served to drive a wedge between both the efforts investors allocate toward performing operational due diligence on private equity firms as well as a growing desire among investors in other asset classes for operational transparency. As such, if one looks at the development of operational risk standards in general, private equity investors have been seemingly less focused on leveraging developments in the field of operational risk management and due diligence to push for increased operational transparency and best practices.

EXHIBIT 1.7 Milestones in Recent History of Operational Risk Development

Year / Time Period	Notable Development in Operational Risk
Mid-1980s	U.S. House of Representatives' Committee on Energy and Commerce inquiries into accounting profession
1985	(i) National Commission on Fraudulent Financial Reporting / Treadway Commission; (ii) formation of Committee of Sponsoring Organizations ("COSO")
1988	(i) Creation of the Basel Capital Accord by the Basel Committee on Banking Supervision; (ii) Publication of the Hampel report
1990s	Series of rogue trader events
1991	Formation of the Cadbury Commission
1992	Publication of the Cadbury Code and the COSO report, "Internal Control-Integrated Framework"
1995	Report of the Greenbury Committee
1996	Formation of the Hampel Committee
2001	Myners report published
2002	Enactment of Public Company Accounting Reform and Investor Protection Act of 2002 (SOX)
2004	Basel II implemented
2007	(i) Markets in Financial Instruments Directive ("MiFID") enacted; (ii) Publication of Guidelines for Disclosure and Transparency in Private Equity (the "Walker Guidelines");
2010	(i) Enactment of Dodd-Frank Wall Street Reform and Consumer Protection Act; (ii) Passage of Alternative Investment Fund Managers Directive ("AIFMD")

The development of operational risk in a modern context can be traced back to the work of groups such as the Treadway Commission and the development of the Committee of Sponsoring Organizations through to the Basel Accords and the enactment of SOX.[15] Exhibit 1.7 provides an overview of the major highlights in the development of operational risk.

As a result of the impact of these regulatory developments, throughout the course of the development of operational risk, investors in other classes seemed to gain leverage from these developments and began to integrate them, with varying degrees of success, into their own due diligence processes. Perhaps facilitating their focus was the ease by which the targets of regulatory developments could be equated to funds in which they invested. Another contributing factor toward integration was likely the market events driving the implementation of subsequent regulations that promoted increased operational transparency and quality.

For example, it is easy to imagine how an investor reading about rogue-trader-type events in the early 1990s carried out by individuals such as Nick Lesson at Barings Bank, could begin to integrate questions regarding any controls or processes a firm may have in place to prevent rogue traders from operating. As more and more types of these questions were integrated into an investor's operational due diligence process over time, coupled with increased regulatory action, so too does the scope of an investor's operational due diligence focus begin to grow.

Private equity funds however, do not have many of the high-profile characteristics associated with such frauds and subsequent losses. Continuing our trading example, private equity firms generally do not trade nearly as frequently as more traditional funds or even some low-volume hedge fund strategies. As such, an investor performing due diligence on private equity funds during the same time period may not have brought any such concerns to the forefront of their due diligence process because of the seemingly different nature of the risks. Furthermore, even if they had, such an investor would likely have been the exception rather than the norm. To borrow from Keynesian economics, the invisible hand of the market will dictate the appropriate course of action.

If enough investors or regulators do not place enough pressure on a particular manager, industry, or asset class, then a manager may believe, however foolishly, that they have nothing to gain from either establishing high degrees of operational quality or being able to demonstrate operational transparency in a digestible, easy-to-follow format that highlights their operational strengths. This has in effect created what economists refer to as a multiplier effect. However, it seems in relation to operational risk concerns related to private equity (as compared to other asset classes) that the effect has been virtually stagnant on an absolute basis and effectively negative as compared to both other asset classes and the increasing complexity of private equity operational infrastructure.

So is it fair to say that operational due diligence is merely a poor victim of circumstance, cast by the wayside as a field of lesser import, subservient to other more legitimate areas of due diligence? Not necessarily, as recent developments have suggested an increased interest in this area. Consequently, when examining the history of the development of operational due diligence in a private equity context from an investor's perspective it seems as if it is only in very recent times that the majority of investors have opened the door to entertaining discussions of private equity in the operational due diligence process. Without this increased investor attention and pressure brought to bear an environment is continually created that not only accepts poor operational quality but fosters it.

This trend of increased attention and resource allocation makes sense for a number of reasons that Chapter 2 discusses in more detail. For now, one of the most notable reasons that readers should keep in the back of their minds is the fact that, all else generally being equally, there is a positive correlation between an operational quality and positive investment performance.

ITEMS TYPICALLY COVERED DURING THE OPERATIONAL DUE DILIGENCE PROCESS

Earlier in this chapter, we refer to something known as a "basic" or "core" operational due diligence process." The term *core process* is utilized here to refer to the basic building blocks of operational due diligence. A core process encompasses a review of, at a minimum, those operational risk factors that are necessary to allow an investor to reach an informed opinion, and ultimately come to an operational determination, regarding a particular private equity fund. In an absolute bare-minimum core process, if one of these operational risk factors is not examined it is highly unlikely, if not impossible, to question if an investor has truly taken the operational due diligence process seriously. The bare-bones minimum items in a private equity operational due diligence core review process are included in Exhibit 1.8.

After reviewing this list, an investor may comment, "I think that business continuity is a very important risk factor, particularly because the private equity fund I am considering is located in Caribbean country X, which is prone to hurricanes and power outages. So I would consider it very important to look at these areas during the operational due diligence process as well."

EXHIBIT 1.8 Sample Core Operational Risk Factors

Trade flow analysis	Legal documentation review
Cash oversight, management and transfer controls	Valuation policies and processes
Compliance infrastructure	Quality and appropriateness of fund service providers
Fund reporting	Financial statement review
Human capital	Custody procedures and third-parties

Such a question certainly raises valid concerns and often arises during early discussions concerning core operational due diligence process factors. It affords us with an opportunity to reiterate exactly what the goal of a core process often is. It is, as the name implies, to get to the heart of what key operational risks are typically associated with private equity. In developing a core process, an investor may consider the operational risk factors included in the core list to be thought of as containing the low-hanging fruit of the operational risk spectrum.

Cash oversight, management, and transfer controls, for example, is one of the operational areas that is fertile ground for the breakdown of operational processes resulting in either outright fraud and theft or operational risks with less nefarious motivations such as improper transfers of cash due to a lack of appropriate transfer controls. The opportunity for noticeable operational weaknesses and subsequent actual losses due to the breakdown of operational processes is prevalent in this area. As such, most investors would include a review of the cash management and transfer process in one form or another, in their core operational due diligence process.

This can be contrasted with a category such as business continuity and disaster recovery. As our hypothetical investor questioned, depending on the circumstance, business continuity can be an important factor to review as well, is it not? The answer, of course, is yes. But as the rewording of the investor's query may have suggested, the answer to such a question is very circumstance dependent. Such is the case with most rules or maxims in life— there are exceptions.

As a general rule however, in the field of operational due diligence exceptions to such rules tend to lean more toward conservatism in approach. Such conservatism ultimately results in the inclusion of more operational risk factors, which necessarily broadens the scope of the operational due diligence review. Therefore, to clarify, two different private equity funds under review could each have different core operational due diligence processes that would vary by the number of operational risk factors included in each review. What then is the point, you may ask, of having a core process? The answer is that a core process gives investors a starting point from which to work. Additional factors can be added to the process on a case-by-case basis for each fund as prudence and common sense dictates. So, returning to our hypothetical investor's original example, it would be considered certainly advisable to add to the core process the business continuity and disaster recovery category for a private equity manager located in an area that experiences a great deal of weather-related events such as hurricanes.

This list of factors, as with any of the core lists included throughout this book, are by no means all-inclusive. Rather, the purpose of discussing a core process is to provide investors with a general idea of the baseline amount of

EXHIBIT 1.9 Core Process and Informed Operational Opinion Formation

operational risk factors they should consider analyzing before deciding to pursue an operational due diligence program. If an investor is not prepared to devote the necessary resources, time, and energy into vetting each of the types of factors included in a core process, then they may want to reassess their goals in performing operational due diligence to begin with.

Corgentum Consulting advises clients that as a firm we cannot give an informed opinion regarding a private equity manager unless, at a minimum, the firm has the opportunity to review certain core operational risk factors. Think of it this way: How can an investor form any sort of opinion regarding the operational strength of the private equity firm or fund if they do not understand the basics of the operations? In order to get these basics down there are certain key fund documents and processes that must be reviewed. The goal of the core process is to draw a line in the sand, below which a risk opinion cannot be formed. This concept is summarized in Exhibit 1.9.

CORE VERSUS EXPANDED OPERATIONAL DUE DILIGENCE REVIEWS

Once a core process has been developed and then amended or enhanced, it is no longer a core process. Rather, depending on your perspective, these additions have effectively altered the DNA of a core process such that it has become a different species of operational due diligence review entirely. Perhaps we could refer to this process as a core plus level of review. At some point, depending on the number of additional operational risk factors added to the core process, an investor may be more comfortable with dropping the core association all together. We can refer to a more broadly scoped process

EXHIBIT 1.10 Sample Core Operational Risk Factors

Operational Risk Factor	Operational Risk Factor Type
Trade flow analysis	Core
Cash oversight, management and transfer controls	Core
Compliance infrastructure	Core
Human capital	Core
Legal documentation review	Core
Valuation policies and processes	Core
Quality and appropriateness of fund service providers	Core
Custody procedures and third parties	Core
Technology and systems	Expanded
Review of regulatory interaction	Expanded
Business continuity and disaster recovery	Expanded
Information security	Expanded
Insurance coverage	Expanded
ISDA reviews	Expanded
Board of directors	Expanded
Tax practices	Expanded

as an expanded level of review. Exhibit 1.10 outlines an example of the operational risk factors included in a core as compared to an expanded operational due diligence review process.

Due to the number of additional operational factors included in the expanded operational due diligence reviews, these require more resources to complete. The same can be said when comparing a below-core level of review to a core level of review, which necessarily contains more operational risk factors. Exhibit 1.11 provides a theoretical outline of the resource allocation percentages dispersed among the components of the due diligence equation (e.g., investment due diligence and operational due diligence) for each of the three levels of review previously discussed.

A few comments should be kept in mind when considering the theoretical resource allocation guidelines outlined in Exhibit 1.11. First, a critical assumption in reviewing the resource guidelines is that the sum of each of the respective processes totals 100 percent. It is further worth clarifying that this 100 percent sum of all due diligence efforts is to be applied on a case-by-case basis. This is in contrast with an investor's total due diligence resources. It is worth noting this distinction because an investor may have access to more total due diligence resources than they are deploying to a particular fund review. These other nondeployed due diligence resources could simply be sitting on the sidelines or employed in other projects. This situation does

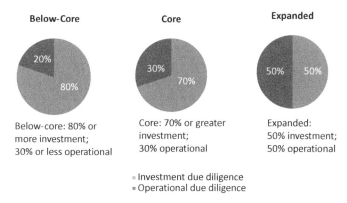

Below-core: 80% or
more investment;
30% or less operational

Core: 70% or greater
investment;
30% operational

Expanded:
50% investment;
50% operational

■ Investment due diligence
■ Operational due diligence

EXHIBIT 1.11   Resource Allocation among Below-Core, Core, and Expanded Operational Due Diligence Review Processes

not necessarily represent an investor being spread too thin by performing too many due diligence projects in any single time period.

Furthermore, an investor may deploy these due diligence resources toward funds on which they may be performing only preliminary due diligence. This initial screening could then feed the more comprehensive due diligence reviews further down the line. As such, one series of due diligence resources are being utilized to keep others busy. Regardless of the situation, this 100 percent assumes that for each particular project an investor is allocating 100 percent of designated due diligence resources toward a particular review. An example of a scenario that would not apply to the theoretical allocation guidelines outlined earlier would be when an investor decides to reduce the percentage of resources dedicated to investment due diligence but does not reallocate these resources to operational due diligence. This of course assumes that such investment and operational due diligence resources are swappable and available, which in the real world might not be the case, but in order to facilitate our discussion of resource allocation such theoretical guidelines and assumptions are employed.

Secondly, it is worth reiterating that the percentages in Exhibit 1.11 are intended to represent resources allocated toward the respective areas of due diligence and not the time allocated to such processes. While there is generally a positive correlation between the extent of resources dedicated toward a particular due diligence function and the time it takes to complete such a review, there are a number of variables involved that can skew such notions that a direct correlation is present. For example, one must first consider what is meant by the term *time* in this context. Is it the number of cumulative hours required to complete an initial due diligence review or perhaps the absolute time period necessary for completion of an initial due diligence review?

The difference in these two slightly different interpretations in the use of the time principal is perhaps best illustrated by the following example. Consider two different investment organizations making an investment in the same private equity fund. The first such investment organization, Firm 1, employs a total of five due diligence analysts. Four of these analysts focus on investment due diligence and one on operational due diligence. Next let us consider the second investment organization, Firm 2. This company employs three due diligence analysts. Firm 2's due diligence analysts are primarily dedicated to investment due diligence but donate a portion of their time as necessary toward operational due diligence. Putting aside the requisite competencies and skill sets of each analyst, as well as the likely benefits in quality and efficiency to be realized by Firm 1 in having a dedicated operational due diligence analyst, we can now examine a scenario by which the time to completion of each review is evaluated. Let us further assume that both Firm 1 and Firm 2 begin their due diligence reviews of our private equity fund on Monday, January 1, in the year 20XX. Further, let us assume that Firm 1 dedicates its one operational due diligence analyst to the review but only dedicates two out of its four investment due diligence analysts to the review of the fund (the other analysts are busy reviewing different funds).

Contrast this with Firm 2, which dedicates all three of its due diligence analysts to the job. As the due diligence work proceeds, Firm 2, having an overall smaller due diligence team as compared to Firm 1, decides to burn the midnight oil and dedicate all of their waking hours solely on this review. Firm 2, however, has the disadvantage of not having a dedicated operational due diligence analyst. As such, the review process takes longer for Firm 2 than it would have if it had regarded the analysts as being two individuals, with one dedicated to investment due diligence and the other toward operational due diligence. (Chapter 4 discusses strategic operational due diligence allocation in more detail). As a result of their stalwart dedication to the process, the due diligence process for Firm 2 subsequently takes two-and-a-half weeks (approximately 300 hours). Firm 1's due diligence process for the private equity firm in regard to total time is completed over a span of four weeks but in total takes only approximately 250 hours. The question now becomes which process took longer, Firm 1's or Firm 2's? The answer of course depends on the particular definition of process time to completion. Most investors would likely view the four-week time period taken by Firm 1 to be the longer time period. Viewed from the perspective of an investor performing an initial due diligence review of a private equity fund with an eye toward meeting a particular funding deadline, such an absolute view of time would likely be more practical.

Below-Core

100%

- Investment due diligence
- Operational due diligence

Below-core extreme example:
100% investment due diligence and no operational due diligence

EXHIBIT 1.12 Extreme Example of Below-Core Process
Allocation to Investment Due Diligence

It is also worth noting that the percentages in Exhibit 1.11 are merely
guidelines. Certainly, as compared to the chart, an investor performing operational due diligence at a below-core standard could certainly increase the
amount of resources dedicated to investment due diligence and dial down the
percentage increased toward operational due diligence. While such a change
is certainly not advisable, some operational due diligence is better than none
at all. An extreme example of such a change in allocation percentages with
100 percent of an investor's due diligence resources being allocated toward
investment due diligence and no resources allocated toward operational due
diligence is shown in Exhibit 1.12.

Furthermore, returning to our original theoretical resource allocation
paradigms, the allocation separation points themselves are once again merely
guidelines and not to be viewed as hard checklist points of demarcation
among the different levels of review that are set in stone. So, for example, an
investor may allocate only 65 percent of their total due diligence resources
toward investment due diligence. Does this mean that they cannot claim to
have a core process? No; rather, this indicates two points to be considered.

First, because they are dedicating less time (e.g., 65 percent as opposed
to 70 percent) of their total due diligence resources toward investment due
diligence, it is assumed that this 5 percent is being reallocated toward operational due diligence to account for the entire 100 percent of allocated
resources. As such, a trade-off from investment due diligence resources that
increases the operational due diligence resource allocation certainly can be
viewed as pumping up a process that might not, according to the theoretical
guidelines, be considered a core process because of the increased allocation
toward operational as opposed to investment due diligence. Second, the
terms *below-core, core*, and *expanded* utilize operational due diligence as
a frame of reference as opposed to investment due diligence. Therefore, as

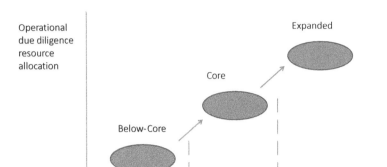

EXHIBIT 1.13   Operational Due Diligence Resource Allocation as a Driver among Transitions from Below-Core, to Core, to Expanded Review Levels

described earlier, by increasing the amount of resources dedicated to operational due diligence, an investor would tend to progress along the spectrum from below-core to expanded as summarized in Exhibit 1.13.

SHARED COMMONALITIES BETWEEN PRIVATE EQUITY AND REAL ESTATE OPERATIONS RISK

For the purposes of this text, we will consider real estate funds to be a subset of the larger category of private equity funds. That being said, due to the unique challenges of the real estate asset class, and associated real estate funds, this book will outline several of the differences and similarities between private equity and real estate funds.

In general, regardless of the asset class there are certain universal categories of due diligence considerations that are applicable. This maxim applies to both investment due diligence and operational due diligence. From an investment perspective, these similarities could include performing due diligence on a manager's research function, the ability of a fund manager to generate alpha, and a manager's approach toward and execution of a risk management program. Regardless of whether an investor is considering an investment in a mutual fund, separate account platform, hedge fund, private equity, or real estate fund, general universal categories of investment considerations would likely be present in the due diligence programs of prudent investors. This is not meant to imply that cookie-cutter, one-size-fits-all due diligence approaches are employed across all asset classes. On the contrary, once these general categories are established, the difference in the due diligence process among the asset classes in terms of the diagnostic approach, as well as the types of risks being vetted, should be necessarily customized to each specific asset class, subclass, and fund type. For example, an investor would likely utilize a different approach to analyze the risk management function of a mutual fund than it would an event-driven hedge fund.

Similarly, there are certain universal categories that generally arise from an operational perspective as well. Some examples of the types of operational risk areas that prudent investors would incorporate into their operational due diligence function regardless of the asset class or fund type under consideration could include such axiomatic categories as valuation, business continuity and disaster recovery, and cash transfer controls. Similar to the manifest investment considerations, each of these operational risk areas would likely be incorporated by investors into their operational due diligence process, regardless of the asset class or fund type.

This larger, universal group of factors, both investment and operational, can be further narrowed down when performing due diligence on similar asset classes. Turning specifically to private equity and real estate, there is a subgroup of universal factors that are certainly more applicable among these two asset types than among two dissimilar types of investments. In other words, when performing operational due diligence on a private equity fund and real estate fund, many more similarities in approach will be employed than when performing operational due diligence reviews of a mutual fund and a real estate fund.

One prevalent issue in an operational due diligence analysis of a private equity and real estate fund is valuation. Both types of funds typically involve investments in hard-to-value and illiquid companies and pieces of property. Long gone are the days when a statement from a private equity or real estate firm claiming that everything is held at cost was sufficient. An investor performing operational due diligence on both real estate and private equity funds should devote substantial efforts to not only understanding the particular type of illiquid assets being held but also the valuation processes and approaches employed in determining such valuations. See Chapter 5 for further discussion of valuation.

As this example illustrates, there are a number of similarities between the two operational due diligence processes for both private equity and real estate funds due to some of the shared similarities between the two types of funds. Investors can utilize these similarities to enhance the efficiency of their operational due diligence reviews. That being said, a number of operational differences also exist between the two types of funds, as discussed in more detail in the following section.

DIFFERENCES IN OPERATIONAL RISK FACTORS
BETWEEN PRIVATE EQUITY AND REAL ESTATE

In addition to a number of similarities, private equity and real estate funds also have differences that become apparent during the operational due diligence process. As previously suggested, real estate funds present a number of unique considerations for investors. These considerations may be asset or industry specific, but for ease of reference and for the purposes of this discussion we can consider real estate to be the odd-man-out and private equity the norm. Under this approach, an investor more familiar with common private equity operational risks, when approaching an operational due diligence review of a real estate fund may be unfamiliar with some of the differences to be on the lookout for. For example, a private equity fund that invests in underlying companies may not have to deal with considerations related to a fund that owns property or manages and rents structures on that property.

So continuing our example, consider the difference in assets that may be held by a private equity fund and a real estate fund. Let us say a private equity fund, PE Fund 1, owns equity in a company that makes applications for smart phones. Next consider a real estate fund, RE Fund 1, which owns a shopping mall located on Main Street. Now let us consider both of these funds with regards to the universal operational risk category of cash controls referenced above. An investor performing operational due diligence on PE Fund 1 would likely focus on a number of different cash-related considerations, including the ways in which cash moves into and out of the fund, the cash transfer and approval process, and the processing of any subscription and redemption. We can now contrast this to an investor performing operational due diligence with regard to cash controls on RE Fund 1.

Remember, this is a real estate fund that owns and manages a shopping mall. A shopping mall has tenants. Tenants pay rent. Rent payments need to be collected and processed. This means that in addition to the cash considerations outlined with regards to PE Fund 1, an investor performing operational due diligence on our real estate fund, RE Fund 1, also needs to consider these additional levels of tenants cash flows. The additional areas an investor would likely need to delve into during the operational due diligence process include how rents are actually collected, to which bank accounts rents are deposited, and how interest on any overdue rents is accrued and collected. These are all additional operational risk considerations that would not otherwise be relevant for the investors' operational due diligence review of PE Fund 1, and are therefore specific to real estate funds.

As this example illustrates, there are a number of additional and unique considerations specific to real estate and private equity. While there are certain similarities among private equity and real estate funds, there are also a number of differences between these two types of funds. Investors cannot simply lump the two groups together into a generic operational due diligence process. A more detailed discussion of operational due diligence approaches and the unique operational risk consideration related to real estate is presented in Chapter 8.

COUNTRY- AND INDUSTRY-SPECIFIC RISK CONSIDERATIONS

Before proceeding any further, it is perhaps advisable to pause for a moment to discuss country- and industry-specific concerns that arise in the context of an operational due diligence review. While these concerns are applicable to both private equity and real estate funds, in certain cases each type of fund may have their own unique considerations, as well.

Country-Specific Considerations

First, we turn to country-specific considerations. Different countries have their own laws, regulatory structures, tax codes, and approaches toward fund establishment and operations. When performing operational due diligence on different funds located in different countries, it is advisable for investors to familiarize themselves with any country-specific matters. Regional considerations often come into play in the context of operational due diligence reviews. These regional considerations may be particularly prevalent in the context of operational reviews of real estate funds when the manager is often located in the region or country around which property holdings of a particular fund may be centered. To illustrate, a U.K.-based fund may be focused on pan-European properties. By contrast, a German-based fund might invest in German properties. Each of these countries may present a regulatory backdrop that can be rife with unique operational challenges.

These types of country-specific items can include unique laws, regulatory requirements, and investor reporting or financial statement preparation formats. Oftentimes, investors performing operational due diligence outside of their nature country may be unfamiliar with the landscape, legal or otherwise, outside their own primary jurisdiction. In these cases, many times an investor runs the risk of relying too heavily on the local (i.e., outside the investor's primary jurisdiction) private equity manager to provide guidance on certain issues. Now of course, any sort of guidance contained in a private equity fund manager's documentation will usually be surrounded by so many legal disclaimers that an investor would virtually lack any recourse if they were given bad advice, but nonetheless investors need a starting point by which to familiarize themselves with the lay of the land.

However, an investor should not solely take the private equity manager's word for it. Oftentimes laws and regulations, regardless of which country they were created in, are open to interpretation. After all, arguments in favor or against certain interpretations of laws are what keep lawyers, judges, and politicians employed in the first place. Consequently, an investor may need to seek the advice of local legal counsel, tax advisors, or others to get a sense of not only the local general practice (e.g., in Country X most private equity funds are organized as a limited liability company), but also an investor's options within a particular jurisdiction (e.g., under the rules of Country X the private equity manager could have decided to create a legal structure that minimized taxes, but opted for a different legal structure because it would benefit the firm itself more directly).

Depending on the jurisdiction of the private equity fund structure, as opposed to the respective jurisdiction of any investors, a private equity fund may have a number of advantages regarding tax regimes. Indeed, the selection of a particular jurisdiction for the creation of a fund may be highly influenced by not only legal concerns, but tax considerations as well. In the hedge fund world preferential tax treatments are the primary motivating factors for the growth of fund registrations in offshore jurisdictions throughout the Caribbean and Europe such as the Cayman Islands, Luxembourg, Liechtenstein, the Isle of Man, and the Channel Islands–based Gemini tax treaty twins, Jersey and Guernsey. The same is true in the private equity world, with many traditional hedge fund offshore jurisdictions being utilized for fund structures. Additionally, depending on where the investing activity of the private equity fund is centered, either the private equity firm and/or the manager or investment adviser for the fund may be registered in a location that has beneficial tax status, as compared to the nature of underlying investments.

This is true even in the situation of a private equity fund-of-funds where the underlying investments are themselves investments in other private equity funds. An example of one such structure would be a private equity fund of funds with a focus on Indian private equity funds. Many such funds, via the previously mentioned affiliations with a parent firm and investment advisers, are legally centered around an unexpected location—Malta.

Malta, one of the world's smallest and most densely populated countries, is separated from India by the Arabian Sea and a distance of approximately 4,000 miles. Yet Malta, like many other small offshore jurisdictions, had the foresight to make enough political changes to effect a favorable tax environment and encourage many companies, investors, and asset managers to engage in business relations with a country they would not have otherwise considered. The tiny island country of Malta has over 50 tax treaties in place with countries such as India, Switzerland, France, Germany, Sweden, and the United Kingdom. The United States and Malta have also recently ratified a new income tax treaty that became effective on January 1, 2011.

Through Malta's numerous double taxation tax treaties, foreign (i.e., non-Maltan) investors receive relief in the form of tax credits that significantly lower the tax bill for foreigners who utilize Malta as a registration hub. However, the point of this discussion is not to inform investors about the intricacies of structuring Maltese tax efficient private equity structures. Rather, the point is this: Investors seeking to invest in an India-focused private equity fund of funds may, because of the favorable tax regimes outlined, find themselves forced to at least obtain a basic familiarity with the sometimes technical laws of a completely different country. In order to perform an informed operational due diligence review of a fund, investors need first to understand what they are analyzing.

So if an investor is simply told that a particular fund is based in Malta because of tax treaties, and then has no understanding or experience with common practices in a particular country, they are left with two options. Option number 1 involves effectively taking the private equity manager's word for it. Option number 2 is for an investor to attempt to make an independent assessment of the manager's statements and opinions in this regard. Chapter 2 provides a more detailed analysis of performing operational due diligence on private equity investments, which will necessarily involve investors developing an independent understanding of any information provided by a private equity manager. Suffice it to say that the second option is clearly superior. Indeed, most prudent investors would certainly prefer to put the time and effort into not simply taking a private equity manager's word for it, but independently determining the facts and coming to their own individual assessment of the situation. At a minimum, such a process allows investors to make more informed allocation decisions, which should after all be one of the primary goals of due diligence to begin with.

Industry-Specific Considerations

Among the larger subset of private equity funds there are a number of fund-specific factors that can arise during the course of the operational due diligence process. As outlined above, these items can relate either to the unique structuring of the fund, jurisdictional issues, or these operational risks can also be the result of risks inherent in the underlying portfolio companies or assets in which the private equity fund itself invests. For the purposes of this text, we will refer to such risks as *industry-specific risks*, in contrast with the previously mentioned country-or regional-specific risks.

It is worth noting that investors should not run the risks of placing these industry- and country-specific risks into independent silos. In much the same way that investment risk and operational risk interact, so too must investors consider in parallel the interactions between country-specific and industry-specific operational risks. But what exactly are these industry-specific risks? After all, from an operational perspective, aren't the nuts and bolts of most private equity and real estate funds the same?

For example, an investor may consider private equity funds that primarily invest in timber or timberland. At first glance, due diligence, apparently falling into the category of investment due diligence, would focus on the benefits of timber investing and any correlation timber may have to other assets. When narrowing down the universe to a specific private equity fund timber fund, investment due diligence may then focus on questions such as:

- What competitive edge does this manager bring to the table?
- Is the methodology utilized for biological tree growth in line with industry standards?
- How does this manager sustain their investment edge?
- What factors are considered in coming to a determination regarding the appropriate timing of tree harvesting?
- What, if any, risk management oversight does the manager have in place for this fund?
- Is this manager making accurate projections about the future market for hardwoods and softwoods?

When the operational due diligence process begins, often in conjunction with the timing of the investment due diligence process, other asset-specific considerations may come to the forefront (some of which may be related to investment due diligence). For example, investing in a timber fund, which is sometimes referred to as a *timber investment management organization* (TIMO) is a unique exercise as compared to other types of private equity investments. Timber investing involves knowledge about a number of distinct fields including forestry, botany, and cutting, milling, and processing trees. The skill sets that are involved in investing in private equity funds that invest in other real assets besides timber are completely different. Other types of real asset funds could include those that make investments, either directly or indirectly, in oil and gas, gold and other precious metals, energy, infrastructure, and agriculture. These funds each have different areas of focus.

The considerations of investing in agriculture are completely different from those invested in funds whose development of real assets such as oil and gas involves drilling or mining operations. Depending on the type of operation and the source material (e.g., oil, gas, coal, etc.) being sought, drilling and mining operations similarly involve unique skill sets such as knowledge of geology, the storage of waste products from drilling and mining operations, and safety concerns and appropriate insurance amounts required for dangerous activities. Compared to timber, these knowledge bases are completely different. Specifically, when investing in TIMO funds, some areas that should be understood by an investor performing operational due diligence include:

- If new timberland is acquired, does the manager take steps to ensure experienced lumberjacks and foresters continue to work with the same land as it changes hands from owner to owner?
- What systems are in place to model disease rates in the trees produced to grow timber?
- What precautions are taken to ensure disease does not infest trees?
- How does a manager account for increases in land value on which trees are located?

As potential investors in private equity funds are reading this discussion, they may comment, "Wait a minute. I understand these concerns and the unique considerations of different assets classes even among similar subsets of asset classes such private equity funds that invest in real assets. But I thought that these were more investment-related concerns; why would I need to consider such issues in an operational due diligence process?"

The answers can lie in several areas. Every investment due diligence process is different. Certain investment due diligence processes may pursue a broader scope of review than others. As unfair as it may seem, operational due diligence is sometimes the dumping ground for the leftovers that were not covered, either intentionally or inadvertently, during the investment due diligence process. As suggested, this may not be as the result of any sinister plan or design to punish or overwhelm the operational due diligence process.

On the contrary, due to a number of factors unique to each individual investor or investment organization, considerations, including time and resource constraints, may be in place that influences this decision. For example, an investment organization that allocates to private equity could make a strategic choice to have investment personnel focused on sticking to their knitting and focusing more on the purely traditional investment-related merits in the due diligence process whereas, the operational due diligence function could be asked to fill in the holes in these areas. Therefore, the operational due diligence role becomes increasingly expanded in such due diligence frameworks.

Returning to our original investor query, operational due diligence is one of the most important functions of the entire due diligence process. Yet operational risk cannot be viewed in a vacuum. The investment and operational processes can often play off each other in a symbiotic relationship to produce due diligence synergies that yield risk insights greater than the sum of their respective investment and operational parts.

A law student in the United States, and most likely in other countries around the world as well, is taught that a good lawyer is able to defend both sides of an argument. After all, when the student graduates and eventually goes into practice, there is no guarantee, regardless of which area of law they may specialize in, that they will become either solely a plaintiff's or a defendant's lawyer. As such, there is a joke about a lawyer who is engaged by a client to represent him or her in a particular matter. The details of the court appearance are arranged by the client's assistant and the lawyer shows up at the courthouse on the appointed day. Before the hearing begins, the lawyer turns to the other side's legal counsel and asks, "Which side am I representing?" and then begins to argue accordingly. Clearly, no reasonable lawyer would undertake a court appearance without adequate preparation; however, this story is in some cases a bit like operational due diligence in certain organizations, particularly in those with dedicated operational due diligence functions.

An operational due diligence process typically starts after that of investment due diligence. When the handoff to the operational due diligence department occurs, an investor is typically fairly far along in the process and progressing rapidly toward making an investment decision. Typically, the investment side of the due diligence process has already developed a number of opinions and convictions regarding the strengths and weaknesses of the private equity fund and organization. This process can serve as a guide on which the operational due diligence function can hang its hat, and can utilize to begin to navigate through the operational due diligence process.

These types of risks might not have been the type that the operational due diligence process may have traditionally focused on. Oftentimes, such issues will be driven, or certainly rooted in, investment-related considerations. As such, during the operational due diligence process an investor may likely read the investment related file and have to argue a particular side one way or another with a manager in order to utilize as leverage to either obtain additional information or ultimately negotiate better terms prior to investing. As Chapter 2 discusses in more detail, knowing where to pick your battles in the operational due diligence process can be an important strategic skill set that investors must master in order to maximize the benefits of the operational due diligence process.

INVESTMENT AND OPERATIONAL DUE DILIGENCE: NEXUS OR BLURRED LINES?

The beneficial nexus between investment and operational due diligence processes should not be confused with the establishment of a homogenous due diligence process that perhaps compromises efficiency and shared understanding with a lack of independence and functional due diligence competencies. The entire due diligence equation is displayed as follows:

$$\text{Investment Due Diligence} + \text{Operational Due Diligence}$$
$$= \text{Total Due Diligence}$$

From this equation we can see that an investor's entire due diligence process consists of a combination of both investment due diligence as well as operational due diligence. With due diligence performed exclusively in one area, such as investment due diligence, the equation is unbalanced and incomplete. Both components of this equation, investment and operational due diligence, should not operate in isolation. This is particularly true of the field of operational due diligence. In order to make a fully informed operational risk assessment of a private equity fund, an investor must be cognizant of several investment-related facts specific to a private equity fund's basic investment strategy and tenants. Such understandings are useful for a number of reasons. Examples of this can be found in such operational risk areas as valuations.

An investor performing operational due diligence cannot determine the effectiveness of valuation policies and procedures if they do not have an understanding what the private equity fund is investing in. Without such discussions, the operational due diligence process runs a risk of being separated from the investment process. Furthermore, such collaborative dialogues between investment due diligence and operational due diligence functions can also yield both sides of the total due diligence equation, developing a deeper understanding of the total risks involved in investing in a particular private equity manager.

If such collaborations between the investment and operational due diligence processes become too involved, then, of course, the lines between such processes may become blurred and investors run the risk of dissolving these two distinct processes into a homogenous process. Such a homogenous process is detrimental to the benefits provided by an investor maintaining an independent operational due diligence process. When such independence exists, the ultimate operational determination is much less likely to be tainted by investment considerations. In summary, the benefits of collaboration between the investment and operational due diligence processes must be tempered with the measured concern of the loss of independence of each distinct process.

DIFFERENCES AND SIMILARITIES WITH HEDGE FUND OPERATIONAL DUE DILIGENCE

Similarities with Hedge Fund Operational Due Diligence

Due diligence processes across all asset classes, whether within the realm of alternative investments or more traditional investment strategies, share certain characteristics and goals. These similarities certainly apply to both traditional notions of investment and operational due diligence. As outlined earlier, there are a number of differences and similarities even among similar asset class types such as private equity and real estate. Similarly, narrowing our focus to alternative investment operational due diligence, there are both a number of similarities and differences between hedge fund and private equity operational due diligence. The similarities between such funds may have been first driven by the investment side, with activist hedge funds being considered as alternatives to private equity funds.[16]

It should be noted that the previously mentioned similarities are fundamentally found in the core operations of fund management and certain shared commonalities of operational risk. Also contributing to similarities among the operational due diligence processes and actual operations management of hedge funds and private equity is the increasingly shrinking operational divide between traditional notions of both types of funds via a growing wave of hybrid funds. The term *hedge fund* is an umbrella term that encompasses a wide variety of trading strategies. Increasingly, these trading strategies may have an increasing number of private equity-like features. This has resulted in the growth in recent years of so-called hybrid or crossover funds.[17] Further blurring the line between hedge funds and private equity are rumors and concerns of collusion between hedge funds and private equity funds.[18]

In order to highlight some of the similarities between the operational due diligence processes employed for both private equity funds and hedge funds, it is perhaps best to frame this discussion first in the context of the goals of the due diligence process. The shared goals of investors performing operational due diligence on both private equity funds and hedge funds include risk diagnosis, mitigation, and monitoring. While the specific ways in which such processes are carried out differs, as discussed in more detail in the "differences" section further on, there are common goals to both approaches. Indeed, these goals may be shared among investors performing operational due diligence not only on hedge funds and private equity funds but on other types of funds as well.

In terms of the actual operational risk factors analyzed during the operational due diligence process, many investors may incorporate the same basic operational risk factors into their own core review process. These factor similarities, as with the other similarities outlined in this section, should not imply that hedge fund operational due diligence and private equity operational due diligence are interchangeable processes, as will be highlighted in the section on differences. Returning to the core factor similarities, these sometimes overlapping operational risk factors are not necessarily exact copies of each other in every respect.

On the contrary, the similarities are more likely to be among generic umbrella operational risk categories. Differences are often apparent as investors begin to dig into the meat of these categories. This should make sense, as certain core operational processes of hedge funds and private equity funds are similar in basic function; however, such similarities only extend up to a certain point. In pure private equity and hedge fund plays, each of these different asset classes involves a fund possessing markedly different portfolio of assets. These differences are of course blurred by the previously mentioned evolution in recent years of private equity and hedge fund hybrids that may hold increasingly similar asset types, particularly in terms of an illiquid asset profile. That being said, despite any asset type differences, similarities in large umbrella core operational risk factor categories still exist.

Another way we can view the similarities in the investor operational due diligence reviews between hedge funds and private equity is to evaluate the due diligence exercises in terms of the actual due diligence processes employed. On a high level from a process perspective, the basic waypoints along the operational due diligence process for hedge funds and private equity funds have many similarities. Such a process is outlined in Exhibit 1.14.

Chapter 3 outlines the intricacies of each of the different steps regarding this process in more detail. However, for the purposes of our current discussion, a number of similarities exist in terms of the core steps necessary to perform operational due diligence reviews of both hedge funds and private equity funds.

With the previously mentioned similarities in the high-level operational due diligence processes related to hedge funds and private equity, it is also

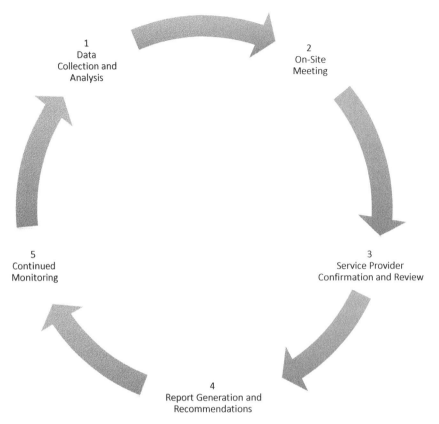

EXHIBIT 1.14   General Operational Due Diligence Process for Private Equity and Hedge Fund Operational Due Diligence

worth considering the similarities between the operators of the processes. In certain cases, this will be a single investor performing both investment and operational due diligence on their own behalf. In other cases, an investor may represent an institutional entity such as an endowment, foundation or corporate pension or a professional larger investment allocator such as a fund of funds.

Regardless of the organizational affiliation of a particular investor, the role of an investor may fall into a number of different roles depending on a number of factors including the size of their particular organizations as well as their organization's approach toward operational due diligence. That is to say, an investor may be solely dedicated toward investment due diligence related matters, or solely dedicated toward operational due diligence, or, as is more likely the case in the current state of the private equity community, dedicated to a blended due diligence analysis consisting of a combination of investment and operational rules. In the latter case, these blended roles typically slant more heavily toward the investment due diligence side as opposed to the operational side. However, a growing number of investment organizations are allocating dedicated resources toward monitoring operational risk in private equity investments.

Regardless of the specific designated role of the individual, there are certain skill sets that are recommended to perform operational due diligence. On a core level, many hedge fund and private equity operational due diligence reviews will have some degree of overlap among operational risk factors covered on a high level. Logically, it then follows that there will be other similarities in the skills and basic competencies required to perform these reviews. But exactly what skills are required to perform operational due diligence in this regard?

While other texts provide a more complete overview in this regard, for the purposes of our discussion, we can begin developing our understanding in this regard by first acknowledging that operational due diligence is a multidisciplinary subject.[19] Due to the multifaceted nature of this subject, an individual performing operational due diligence will at a minimum need to have some degree of experience with many different disciplines. Some of the common requisite basic skills can include knowledge of accounting, back-office operations, information technology, the law, compliance, and vendor evaluation. Many times a single individual will not, even on a generic level, possess a sufficient degree of familiarity with all of these different areas to be an effective operational due diligence analyst. In these situations, often an investor may work in a team environment consisting of operational due diligence analysts from different backgrounds that as a group possess such requisite skills.

Alternatively, an investor may opt for the sometimes more efficient solution of engaging the services of a third-party operational due diligence consultant who specializes in this field. For reference, a more detailed description of operational due diligence consulting arrangements is offered in Chapter 3. For now, the point of this discussion is to highlight that, due to some degree of shared similarities in the underlying core operational risk factors typically analyzed by investors during the operational due diligence process on both hedge funds and private equity funds, similarities also exist in the skills sets required to properly execute operational due diligence on these funds. Similarities between Private Equity Fund of Funds and Hedge Fund of Funds

It should also be noted that many of the similarities outlined above are also applicable to funds that invest in private equity funds and hedge funds. When investors are seeking to invest in fund of private equity funds and fund of hedge funds, it is advisable that they perform operational due diligence on these types of investment vehicles as well. While performing operational due diligence on such funds is a bit of a different exercise than performing operational due diligence on a direct private equity fund or hedge fund, there are a number of similarities between such vehicles (e.g., fund of private equity funds and fund of hedge funds) that are comparable to goal and process similarities of direct funds outlined above.

Differences with Hedge Fund Operational Due Diligence

Based in part upon the different traditional investment approaches and operational infrastructures supporting these approaches of both hedge funds and private equity funds a number of differences are apparent with regards to operational due diligence on both hedge funds and private equity funds.

Less Trading Frequency   One notable difference between private equity and hedge funds relates to the analysis of a factor that is generally a shared factor in the umbrella core operational risk category discussed in the similarities section. As suggested above, cracks begin to emerge once investors start the process of digging into the details of the different umbrella categories between private equity and hedge funds. One of the most obvious factors in this regard is trade life cycle analysis and posttrade operations. Hedge funds as a whole tend to engage in much more frequent trading activity as compared to private equity funds.

Such generalizations are of course contingent upon the investment strategy around which a particular hedge fund or private equity firm is based. However, to utilize an extreme example, let us consider a venture capital fund as representative of our private equity fund and a high-frequency *commodity trading advisory* (CTA) to be representative of our hedge-fund strategy. CTA hedge funds may execute tens of thousands of trades, or more, on a daily basis. A venture capital fund, putting aside any consideration of trading around positions or currency hedging, may execute a trade once a month if it is lucky. These are two very different operational animals. As such, an investor performing operational due diligence on these types of funds will still inquire into the subject of trade operations, but this is effectively where the similarities end.

A high-frequency trading operation must have the ability to execute trades in real time. On a postexecution basis the staff, systems, policies, and procedures must be in place to confirm, allocate, and settle large volumes of trades in an efficient, if not automated, manner. With such high-frequency trading operations, even with direct-exchange *Financial Information Exchange* (FIX) connectivity, trade breaks between the hedge fund and the trading counterparties can occur. In such cases, the posttrade operations team's middle and back offices must be capable of investigating and resolving any such breaks in an effective manner. Without such operational systems and knowledgeable staff, the hedge fund will, at best, not be able to function efficiently, and at worst just grind to halt.

Contrast this with a venture capital firm. When the decision is made to allocate new or additional capital to a particular portfolio company after a capital call, this is generally a fairly straightforward repeatable process that occurs infrequently and with a generally low trade volume (certainly low, compared to most CTA funds). However, because such trading activities are chunkier and less frequent in nature does not mean that there are not just as many operational risks that could result in significant losses as there are in a high-frequency trading operation. On the contrary, the deadly magnitude of such risks may be even greater in a private equity fund precisely because of the chunky nature of these trades, which are often at much larger individual amounts, compared to thousands of very small high-frequency trades. The operational risks are still there, they just may be in different places.

More Concentrated Portfolios Similar to the notions of different trading frequencies outlined previously, private equity funds, as compared to hedge funds, often have more concentrated portfolios consisting of fewer total aggregate positions. Such general trends can have ramifications across a number of different operational risk areas, as analyzed during the operational due diligence process for both hedge funds and private equity. An example of such an area is valuation. To explain this in more detail, it is worth introducing the context in which valuations are commonly evaluated in the scope of an operational due diligence review. While Chapter 5 offers a more detailed discussion of valuation, we can begin here with an introduction to valuation.

Before discussing valuation, we must consider a few points regarding the operational due diligence process itself. An operational due diligence review is not the same as a traditional audit. First, an auditor is typically engaged by an investment vehicle (e.g., a hedge fund or private equity fund) to perform an audit. In this case, an investor is typically performing operational due diligence on their own behalf and not at the behest of another individual. Second, an operational due diligence analyst will most likely not have the level of transparency that an auditor will have.

This is likely due in part to the point mentioned earlier. Many hedge funds and private equity funds may approach the entire due diligence process in general, beyond the pleasantries of the initial marketing efforts, as an exercise in information control. Furthermore, a skilled hedge fund or private equity firm can often conduct a sleight-of-hand, employing the age-old magician's aid of distraction, regarding the levels of transparency and types of information they provide to certain investors. Furthermore, based on their already prepared materials, such as a stock off-the-shelf due diligence questionnaire or marketing presentation, they may be able to lead an investor down a primrose path of operational distractions, which can cause an investor to focus their operational due diligence efforts on certain risk areas, while certain operational weaknesses are shielded from inquiry. Despite the cat-and-mouse elements of these processes, a skilled operational due diligence analyst can navigate this process effectively and can generally collect all the necessary information to perform a detailed operational assessment of a fund.

With these points in mind we can now return to the subject of valuation. An operational due diligence analyst will likely never have sufficient information to conduct an independent valuation of an asset held in a portfolio of a private equity fund. Furthermore, for a newly forming private equity fund, when operational due diligence is typically performed there is no fund yet likely in existence, or if it has been formed it is likely just a legal shell with no capital funding as yet, and, therefore, there is nothing in the portfolio to value.

Rather an investor performing operational due diligence at this stage must evaluate what is available to them. That is the policies and procedures regarding the valuation process. It is from these pieces of operational information that a due diligence analyst can make a determination as to how conservative and consistent a fund will be with their valuation process. Examples of the areas an investor can look at include the frequency at which such valuations will occur; the processes, methodologies, and valuation inputs that are utilized; and whether any independent parties such as third-party valuation consultants, will be utilized in determining valuation. Valuations are typically a paramount concern among many investors performing operational due diligence on private equity funds because of the highly concentrated nature of private equity portfolios.

This can be contrasted with the issue of valuation in the hedge funds. Depending of course on the hedge fund strategy, the number of positions in a hedge fund, as compared to a private equity fund, is likely to be much more diversified and less concentrated. In more liquid hedge-fund strategies, such as equity long-short, the bulk of the portfolio is publicly listed, highly liquid, and can be priced virtually in real time from a variety of third-party independent pricing sources such as Bloomberg and Reuters. Such positions from a valuation perspective are the complete antithesis of concentrated, illiquid private equity fund holdings. Consequently, an investor approaching the issue of valuation during the course of an operational due diligence review of a hedge fund must take a different approach to understanding valuation. Yes, there are similarities with regard to the evaluation of valuation policies and procedures, as there was when an operational due diligence review of private equity was performed. However, different considerations that were absent in a private equity context, such as which valuation sources are utilized by the manager and the way in which a larger number of valuation inputs are accounted for, must also be considered.

No Actively Traded Portfolio for New Funds Another key difference between the operational due diligence processes for hedge funds and private equity relates to the nature of new private equity vehicles that are undergoing initial capital raises. Many investors seeking to invest in a private equity fund may do so during the initial capital raising period of a private equity fund. It is at this stage of the funding process, depending on the structure of the fund, that investors may be asked to put up a certain amount of capital to get the ball rolling. Beyond this initial investment, investors are also expected to make capital commitments, which are called upon by the private equity fund. When the call comes, investors commit their funds, subject to their previous agreements.

This is to be contrasted with most hedge fund strategies. Oftentimes, even for a newly formed hedge fund, the fund is actively trading in some form. This trading could be with the hedge fund principle's own proprietary capital, sometimes referred to simply as prop capital, or via a combination of prop capital and external funds. Additionally, due to the ongoing rolling nature of hedge fund subscriptions and redemptions, putting any considerations of lockup periods and gates aside, money is actively flowing into and sometimes out of the fund, on an ongoing basis. The point is that an investor approaching a fund is trading and therefore, has to be able to handle the related pretrade and posttrade operational processes. Therefore, when an investor is performing operational due diligence, they then have an opportunity to analyze an active functioning organization that is likely operating, at least from an operational perspective, in much the same way it will be after an investor allocates capital. This results in an investor being likely to have a much better opportunity for operational data collection and analysis in a hedge fund, as compared to a private equity fund.

Document Collection Differences Due to the fact that a newly formed private equity fund has not yet been in operation for a substantial period of time, a number of differences can be seen in the operational due diligence document collection process, as compared to hedge funds. A hedge fund that has been in operation for a period of one year has likely produced audited financial statements. An investor can then collect and review such statements during the operational due diligence process. A newly formed private equity fund does not have such documentation available. Investors can utilize a number of techniques to broach this issue, including examining statements of any previous vintage funds managed by the private equity firm. Despite such techniques, an investor familiar with performing operational due diligence on hedge funds who is now performing operational due diligence on private equity funds should approach the document collection process with these differences in mind.

More Asset-Specific Knowledge Required Another difference between private equity fund and hedge funds from an operational perspective is related to the more concentrated nature of private equity portfolios. Hedge funds, depending on the strategy, may generally trade in instruments and securities for which exchanges or markets may exist. These markets may not necessarily the highly liquid markets that are present from equities but in general there is some sort of exchange by which assets may be traded, however thinly. This is not to imply that hedge funds solely hold liquid positions. In particular, since 2008 many hedge funds realized that positions that they believed to be quite liquid were in fact not, and many such positions were placed and still remain in side-pockets. As we move along the spectrum of liquidity from highly liquid to less liquid we tend to be more in the arena of private equity. With this drought of liquidity comes a number of both asset type and individual asset-specific concerns that investors must consider during the operational due diligence process.

In a general sense, asset-type concerns for private equity funds can include items such as the general category of investments made into underlying portfolio companies. Certainly additional granularity can be added by inquiring into what a particular private equity fund may be exchanging capital for. Is a fund receiving direct equity in an underlying portfolio company, a combination of equity and stock options, or perhaps equity in a particular deal alone? Regardless of the type of security held, there is likely less of a secondary market for such assets as opposed to more highly liquid positions, which are commonly held to some degree by hedge funds.

Asset-type concerns can be further contrasted with individual asset-specific concerns. Typically such concerns arise in relation to one-off unique assets commonly seen in real estate. While it is true that certain similarities do exist among certain property types (i.e., there are common characteristics that are applicable among two different shopping mall properties), each property also has unique considerations. Oftentimes during the operational due diligence process for such funds, an investor will need to gain an understanding of these asset-specific considerations such that they can effectively analyze operational risk areas including valuation, as referenced previously. Such asset-type and individual-asset specific concerns are often not as prevalent in hedge fund operational due review processes.

NOTES

1. FAA System Safety Handbook, Chapter 15: "Operational Risk Management," December 30, 2000.
2. See Dennis I. Dickstein and Robert H. Flast, *No Excuses: A Business Approach to Managing Operational Risk* (Hoboken, NJ: John Wiley & Sons, 2009).
3. Larry E. Swedrow and Jared Kizer, *The Only Guide to Alternative Investments You'll Ever Need* (Bloomberg Press, November 12, 2008), 132.
4. See Christine Buckley, "TUC Calls for Action on 'Casino Capitalists,'" *The Times*, February 21, 2007 (summarizing the comments of Brendan Barber from the United Kingdom's Trades Union Congress).
5. See Ralph Atkins and Patrick Jenkins, "German Business Welcomes the Private Equity 'Locusts'," *Financial Times*, May 5, 2005.
6. See Richard A. Booth, "The Buzzard Was Their Friend—Hedge Funds and the Problem of Overvalued Equity," *U. Pa. Journal of Business and Employment Law* 10:3, Summer 2008.
7. See Thomas Heath, "Ambushing Private Equity," *Washington Post*, April 18, 2008.
8. See Cyril Demaria, *Introduction to Private Equity* (Hoboken, NJ: John Wiley & Sons, 2010).
9. See Corgentum Consulting, "The Madoff Effect—An Analysis of Operational Due Diligence Trends," June 2010, www.Corgentum.com.
10. See M. John Lubetkin, *Jay Cooke's Gamble: The Northern Pacific Railroad, the Sioux and the Panic of 1873* (University of Oklahoma Press, 2006).
11. Les Standiford, *Meet You in Hell: Andrew Carnegie, Henry Clay and the Bitter Partnership That Transformed America* (Crown, 2005).
12. Hans Landström, *Handbook of Research on Venture Capital* (Edward Elgar Publishing Limited, UK, 2007), 11.
13. See William H. Draper III, *The Startup Game* (Palgrave MacMillion—a division of St. Martin's Press LLC, 2011).
14. See Bryan Burrough and John Helyar, *Barbarians at the Gate: The Fall of RJR Nabisco* (HarperCollins, 2009).
15. See Jason Scharfman, *Hedge Fund Operational Due Diligence: Understanding the Risks* (Hoboken, NJ: John Wiley & Sons, 2008), Chapter 1.
16. See Douglas Cumming, *Private Equity: Fund Types, Risks and Returns and Regulation* (Hoboken, NJ: John Wiley & Sons, 2010), 159.
17. See Pierre-Yves Mathonet and Thomas Meyer, *J-Curve Exposure: Managing a Portfolio of Venture Capital and Private Equity* (West Sussex, England: John Wiley & Sons, 2007), 34 (discussing the convergence of private equity and hedge funds).

18. See James Mackintosh and Martin Arnold, "French Probe Buyout 'Collusion,'" *Financial Times*, June 6, 2007 (outlining the inquiry by the French financial regulatory authority, Autorité des Marchés Financiers, into allegations that activist hedge funds may have pressured a company's management to put companies up for sale without disclosing agreements in place to sell the hedge fund's stakes in those companies to private equity firms).
19. See Jason Scharfman, *Hedge Fund Operational Due Diligence: Understanding the Risks* (Hoboken, NJ: John Wiley & Sons, 2008), 69.

Importance of Operational Due Diligence for Private Equity Funds

In most disciplines related to the concept of investing, there is little argument as to both the scope of the fields covered by the particular discipline and whether any particular field can be justified in the first place. Analyzed in a straightforward manner, the discipline of investment due diligence in private equity would generally be agreed to be broadly related to selecting, analyzing, and funding private equity funds. Furthermore, in order to invest in private equity it would certainly seem justified that there be a discipline dedicated to this exercise. Another less obvious example would be the discipline of risk management. Even outside the world of private equity, risk management is a well-established field in asset management that covers areas relating to diagnosing and mitigating risk or even facilitating calculated risk taking. Furthermore, it is likely that almost everyone both within and outside of the private equity community would plainly acknowledge that risk management is essential. Operational due diligence, however, is not as well understood and appears to be odd man out.

Many investors seem unsure about whether or not they should be performing operational due diligence reviews on private equity funds. Even operational due diligence analysts who primarily focus on other asset classes such as hedge funds often seemed confused, if not downright resistant, about performing operational due diligence on private equity funds. There are a number of reasons for this confusion and resistance, many of which are primarily routed in the nature of private equity funds as a whole. Before discussing such objections in detail, it is advisable to first make a brief detour and revisit our discussion in Chapter 1 regarding the reasons an investor should consider performing operational due diligence to begin with. A good place to start this discussion is with the goals of the operational due diligence process.

UNDERSTANDING THE GOALS OF THE OPERATIONAL DUE DILIGENCE PROCESS

Before undertaking a discussion of the merits, or lack thereof, in performing operational due diligence on private equity funds it is beneficial to take a step back and consider the purposes or goals of the operational due diligence process to begin with. After all, without an understanding of the motivations behind the actions of performing due diligence, it is not really a fair evaluation. So what is the goal of operational due diligence? As previously intimated, the primary goals of many investors are driven not by lofty aspirations but are rather rooted in concerns related to operational risk. Specifically, one such major concern is the possibility of fraud. Therefore, the corresponding goal is to avoid exposure to fraudulent activity. As we previously acknowledged, this is certainly a reasonable and important goal. Exhibit 2.1 presents a summary of many other common concerns and corresponding goals.

Other Goals: Operational Process Learning

In addition to diagnosing, analyzing, and mitigating operational risk, investors may also have a number of affiliated ancillary goals that are associated with the operational due diligence process. One such goal could be to not only come to some sort of conclusion regarding the operational

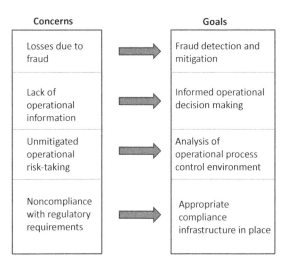

EXHIBIT 2.1   Common Operational Due Diligence Concerns and Goals

infrastructure of a particular private equity fund, but also to actually learn something during the process. A common approach would be for an investor to perform operational due diligence on a private equity fund with the goal of being able to understand the internal operational processes of a particular private equity fund and also be able to explain them to another investor.

Typically many investors will either read a series of documents collected from a manager, or sit in a meeting with a private equity manager's operations staff. During the process, many investors, particularly when faced with the volume of information coming their way, feel overwhelmed. When this happens, many investors, and rightfully so, default to a head nodding approach toward due diligence. For example, during an on-site meeting, a private equity firm's chief operations officer (COO) will sit with an investor and walk them through the back-office processes. Within a few minutes, an investor who is not actually trying to understand a process with the goal of having to explain it to someone else will end up simply trying to assess it. This typically results in investors nodding in agreement with the COO's explanations. While this head-nodding may indicate that the COO can continue explaining subsequent operational steps, the investor may at best be logging this information into his or her short-term memory.

If, on the other hand, an investor was approaching this discussion with the goal of explaining the operational infrastructure of the private equity fund to a third person, a different dialogue would likely take place. At this point, it is perhaps worthwhile to discuss another ancillary goal of the operational due diligence process: How it is documented?

Other Goals: Operational Due Diligence Process Documentation

Some investors perform operational due diligence with the goal of simply coming to an assessment of the operational risks present in a particular private equity fund. In these cases, investors may give less consideration to how they document the data collected and the analysis process that led to this ultimate conclusion. It is common practice for many investors to seek to document, in some way, shape, or form, the operational due diligence process.

Some investors may only produce documentation that contains conclusions of the operational due diligence process. Others, such as Corgentum Consulting, produce extensive, detailed operational due diligence reports that outline not only the operational strengths and weaknesses of a particular private equity fund, but also the details of each operational process. There are a number of benefits in producing such a detailed document, perhaps the most important of which is that it facilitates an information-based approach toward reaching a conclusion regarding the operational attributes of a particular fund. Compare this to other approaches that may offer only summary conclusions and effectively ask readers of the report to trust the report writer without questioning the details.

Another benefit of documenting the operational due diligence process, and the subsequent operational infrastructures of a particular private equity fund, is that it requires an investor to put things into writing. Many times investors may believe that they understand a particular operational concept in detail. Such an understanding is facilitated when someone who is very knowledgeable about particular operational practices, such as the COO of a particular private equity fund, explains them. Oftentimes investor preconceived notions of detailed understanding are deflated when they sit down to either explain the same operational processes to a third person in the same amount of detail or are required to convey the information in writing.

This is not meant to imply that investors are not capable of paying attention during the private equity operational due diligence process or are otherwise incapable of following through with detailed descriptions of operational processes. What this discussion is attempting to highlight is that investors who do not set the goal and prepare to re-explain certain processes, either orally or via a documented operational due diligence memorandum, often run the risk of letting details fall by the wayside.

Other Goals: Benchmarking and Ongoing Monitoring

Another goal that many investors may, or should, have when performing operational due diligence is to facilitate the development of operational benchmarks. These benchmarks can be utilized to facilitate ongoing monitoring of a particular fund under review. Furthermore, the development of such operational benchmarks can broaden an investor's operational knowledge base and enhance the quality of future initial fund reviews.

These goals relate directly to the previously referenced goals of operational process learning and process documentation. By developing a measured understanding of operational processes and documenting this understanding, investors can then begin to construct a database of operational risk information. Corgentum Consulting has developed such a proprietary database to facilitate operational benchmarking. This benchmark analysis allows investors and consultants to compare a particular private equity fund's operational competencies and processes to the practices of other funds.

This benchmark analysis not only facilitates such a comparison to other market practices but allows for effective exception reporting as well. An example of this exception reporting would be the use of third-party valuation consultants. For example, let's say that an investor has developed operational information regarding a database of 100 different private equity funds. Then, consider that a particular private equity fund utilizes one third-party valuation consultant, called ABC valuation consultants. If the other 99 funds in the database use other valuation consultants, then an exception has been produced from the database. While this might not be representative of a larger trend because of the limited sample size of the investor's own database, from the investor's perspective they are not likely to have any familiarity with or have performed any prior due diligence on ABC valuation consultants. Therefore, in our example, ABC valuation consultants represent an anomaly that should be researched. This is not meant to disparage the work of ABC's valuation consultants. Indeed, this firm may be quite well known in the private equity community, yet the firm is not known to our investor. The investor may only be able to keep track of such information via the previously mentioned operational due diligence documentation procedures that facilitate such benchmarking.

Investors performing operational due diligence on private equity funds may also be performing this exercise with the goal of facilitating ongoing monitoring. Ongoing monitoring refers to any operational due diligence processes that occur after an initial operational evaluation is complete. This process is typically performed after an investor has made an allocation to a fund. Regardless of the arguments in favor of and against performing such ongoing monitoring (which will be discussed in more detail in the next section), investors may wish to collect operational data with the goal of facilitating this ongoing monitoring. Similar to the benefits of operational benchmarking processes, investors can learn from their own internal operational due diligence process documentation. Oftentimes many items will be in processes or under developmental operational changes at the time of the initial operational review. By documenting such processes, investors then have a road map that can guide future monitoring of a private equity fund's progress. This is of course more easily facilitated by having a documented operational risk evaluation, compared to when such an operational due diligence memorandum or report is not produced.

COMMON ARGUMENTS AGAINST OPERATIONAL REVIEWS OF PRIVATE EQUITY FUNDS

Now that we have provided an introduction to some of the common goals investors may have when approaching the operational due diligence processes, we can next begin to consider some of the arguments for and against performing operational due diligence reviews of private equity funds.

As suggested above, as absurd as it may seem to some, others are still either not sure or totally unconvinced about the merits of performing operational due diligence on private equity funds. These objections are often raised despite a series of convincing arguments to the contrary, which strongly favor performing operational due diligence on private equity funds. However, before delving deeper into such arguments, let us first focus on the questions raised and objections in this regard.

Doesn't Increased Government Regulation Sufficiently Insulate Investors from Operational Risk?

In the context of the recent fervor with which financial regulatory regimes throughout the world have sought to place restrictions on risk-taking and enhance transparency, fund disclosures, and the frequency of such oversights, many investors may raise the question, "Why bother performing operational due diligence on private equity funds?" After all, isn't the increased pressure by the government going to cause any potentially serious operational risks hidden in a private equity fund to come to the surface and receive appropriate corrective action?

Indeed, support for this line of thinking/questioning may be found in the revival of interest in both new private equity fund establishment and fundraising from jurisdictions with purportedly robust regulatory, anti-money-laundering, and tax information exchange regimes.[1] The answer to such questions is a succinct no, but rather than bluntly dismiss such considerations, it is perhaps worth considering the recent push toward government regulation in the form of regulatory registration in the United States with the Securities and Exchange Commission (SEC).

In the United States, such registration requirements as they relate to private equity funds are perhaps most easily discussed by examining the rise and fall of the so-called Hedge Fund Registration Rule. In 2006, one investor, Philip Goldstein, challenged this registration requirement on a number of policy and legal grounds. Specifically, Mr. Goldstein's objections included the fact that the SEC, by requiring registration of hedge funds as investment advisers under the Investment Advisers Act of 1940, was in effect exceeding its authority and incorrectly conflating the terms *client* and *investor*.[2]

The courts agreed with Mr. Goldstein and the rule was subsequently overturned. Despite what could be arguably deemed a victory for the alternative investment community, in the wake of the 2008 financial industry bailout, the political tide eventually turned toward an environment of increased regulatory oversight. At the forefront of this regulatory charge were U.S. Senators Grassley and Levin via the introduction of the *Hedge Fund*

Transparency Act. After this initial proposal a host of government personalities joined the bandwagon in jockeying for the regulatory reigns. The most vocal were Treasury's Timothy F. Geithner and SEC Chairman Mary L. Shapiro. A number of industry groups both in the hedge fund and private equity community also indicated that they supported regulation in one form or another.

The SEC was eventually able to regain their standing in the regulatory hierarchy under this retraction from an industry environment that once fought tooth and nail against regulation, to an almost resigned understanding that increased regulation was inevitable. Under Title IV of the relatively recently enacted Dodd-Frank Wall Street Reform and Consumer Protection Act, most private funds that include hedge funds and private equity funds will be required to register with the SEC. While there are certain exemptions in place, such as for funds that oversee less than $150 million in assets under management and for certain venture capital funds, in general this new registration requirement represents a major change to the regulatory environment for private equity funds in the United States.

Many investors will likely view these new registrations requirements as a good thing. Regardless of whether an investor is for or against regulation, many investors also hold the belief that such regulation enhances the level of scrutiny to which a private equity fund will be subjected. Some investors extend this argument even further in order to provide themselves with an additional level of comfort with regard to fund operational oversight. Certainly, their logic goes, with this increased regulation the government will catch any material operational weaknesses as a result of an enhanced regulatory process. Such increased scrutiny, these investors may reason, obviates the need for operational due diligence on private equity funds. Ultimately, increased regulation is likely an overall positive development for the private equity industry. However, taken in the context of due diligence, these proposed regulations will do little to promote a higher standard of operational due diligence. For example, the *Hedge Fund Transparency Act* requires hedge funds to disclose the name of a fund's accountant and broker. If a hedge fund will not disclose this information, any responsible investor would never allocate to the fund, regardless of whether such a disclosure is a regulatory requirement or not.

In Europe, motivation toward increasing regulatory oversight of asset managers was perhaps most notably realized in recent history in the early stages via the enactment of the Markets in Financial Instruments Directive (MiFID) in November 2007 that replaced the previous Investment Services Directive. MiFID was passed so expediently in part because of the four-level Lamfalussy procedure promulgated by the Committee of Wise Men (yes, that is its real name). This procedure was set up by the European Counsel in 2000 to make the European Union (EU) securities regulation process more transparent.[3]

Several years later, following up on the MiFID initiative, the Alternative Investment Fund Managers Directive (AIFMD) was adopted by the European Parliament in November 2010. AIFMD has implications for hedge funds and private equity managers both inside and outside the European Union. In an attempt to balance regulatory oversight with market concerns, AIFMD pioneered the concept of a so-called EU passport that allows for non-EU alternative investment managers and alternative investment funds to eventually utilize the same European passport as their European Union counterparts.

Regarding private equity, AIFMD contains requirements that directly impact private equity operations. Some of the most notable changes include the requirement that a private equity fund appoint an external valuation firm as well as an independent custodian. Another somewhat contentious requirement relates to the fact that private equity funds under AIFMD are required to disclose business plans for the portfolio company to the company, its other shareholders, and its employees. Those who have argued against such enhanced disclosure requirements argue that it will place European Union private equity funds at an informational disadvantage. Furthermore, they argue that such regulations may go too far.

To support this argument, they may cite that enhanced disclosure-reporting requirements overextend the private equity industry's already acknowledged need for transparency. They may refer to regulations such as the United Kingdom's 2007 Guidelines for Disclosure and Transparency in Private Equity, which are referred to as the Walker Guidelines. These guidelines were published in November 2007 and adopted by the British Venture Capital Association (BVCA). Apparently EU regulatory bodies have sought to go beyond even the well-intentioned self-regulatory approaches (the BVCA and a group of major private equity firms commissioned Sir David Walker to write the rules that they subsequently adopted) and to insist on further transparency and disclosures.[4]

Regardless of the actual nuts and bolts of the enhanced regulatory oversight to be carried out, coupled with any additional enhanced reporting requirements, perhaps the biggest misconception concerning the enhanced regulatory environment is the associated cache that often accompanies notions of private equity fund registration. Such enhanced regulatory oversight and even reregistration requirements run a very high risk of creating a false sense of confidence among many private equity investors. This is the very same misplaced confidence in regulators that led to the ongoing perpetration of many outright frauds such as Madoff's Ponzi scheme. Specifically, the proposed regulations are a missed opportunity to raise the standards of operational due diligence on two primary fronts, and serve as a rebuttal to the misplaced belief that the need for operational due diligence is supplanted by increased regulatory oversight.

Disclosure Requirements Will Not Provide Sufficient Operational Transparency

The private equity registration regulations, while making some changes designed to enhanced disclosure transparency such as modifications in Form ADV or the fairly recent requirements of Form PF, essentially turn back the clock on private equity operational information disclosure requirements to the pre-Goldstein era, when private equity funds were required to be registered with the SEC. As noted previously, few new disclosure bells and whistles are added; however, the operational disclosure requirements that the SEC finally settled on have set the operational information disclosure bar very low.

A Higher Standard of Diligence Will Not Be Required for Fund of Funds of Hedge Funds and Consultants

Many hedge fund investors who lost money with fraudsters like Madoff were introduced to these funds via "professional" money managers such as fund of hedge funds or feeder funds. These entities were supposed to be performing a certain level of operational due diligence. The new proposed regulations will not place increased responsibility or liability on these professionals to perform a minimum level of operational risk reviews.

In summary, private equity regulation is not a replacement for investor operational due diligence. U.S.-based private equity funds will be required to produce a uniform minimum amount regulatory documentation. This base level is far below the minimum amount of operational risk information that any responsible investor should require as part of the operational due diligence process. Investors should not expect to rely on the regulators to properly vet the operational risks associated with private equity investing. As it has in the past, private equity regulation will only create an artificial operational informational floor that some private equity funds may continue to attempt to hide beneath.

Isn't Operational Due Diligence Simply Opening a Pandora's Box?

This argument against operational due diligence is typically rooted in the multifaceted nature of this discipline. Oftentimes operational due diligence can be equated to the concept of performing construction in an old house. Let us say that in order to perform construction, say install a new bathroom, you need to cut a hole in a wall to run plumbing pipe through. However, when you cut open this hole you find a multitude of other problems you did not know existed. In effect, you have opened a Pandora's box of troubles. Stated less dramatically, you must now devote time, energy, and resources toward fixing these previously undiscovered issues.

Operational due diligence can be the same. Issues within a particular organization may not be apparent at first glance. Only after an investor starts to learn more about a particular private equity fund's operational infrastructure may problems begin to become visible. Oftentimes operational risk issues are interrelated, even across multiple functions in a firm. For example, a weakness in the trading systems utilized may have ramifications for valuation and fund accounting. Once an investor starts to dig into these initial issues, a series of more troubling issues may be skulking underneath. Some investors who argue against performing operational due diligence on private equity funds may say, why bother with the whole process if you will potentially uncover a seemingly endless series of problems?

Furthermore, some investors may raise related objections to operational due diligence being performed on private equity, with regard to the knowledge required to diagnose certain linked Pandora's-box-type risks. An example could be exogenous risks, which are those risks that come from outside the private equity fund itself. Perhaps a nice way to illustrate some of the arguments against performing operational due diligence that are related to both these Pandora risks as well as to anti-exogenous concerns is by returning to an example that Chapter 1 discusses.

Investors must include country-specific considerations when performing operational due diligence. As an example of such considerations, Chapter 1 discusses tax regimes in different countries. The tax program of a particular jurisdiction is an example of an exogenous type risk. The tax code for a particular region is promulgated by the government and taxing authorities of that particular region and not the private equity fund itself. Any risks associated with future tax code changes, for example, as opposed to tax implications based on how a fund chooses to structure itself, primarily come from outside the fund. In Chapter 1 we also utilize the example of an investor who is performing operational due diligence on an Indian private equity fund of funds. Many such funds are domiciled in Malta due to the double-taxation treaty between India and Malta.

Based on the logic of the argument presented earlier, an investor may not want to open the so-called Pandora's box of operational due diligence issues, and similarly they may not want to become involved in understanding the specific benefits and intricacies of the Malta tax code as related to their proposed investment in an Indian private equity fund of funds.

When faced with such questions, an investor effectively has two options. Option number one involves an investor effectively acknowledging that they are interested in investing in India and yet don't know anything about Malta's tax treaties. Moreover, they do not care to expend the time, resources, and effort in researching such matters and, as long as it is not illegal or detrimental to the fund or their investments, they are content to take the private equity manager's word on the details. Investors selecting this option do not have the knowledge because they have not performed any independent reviews of common industry practices to determine if what the private equity manager says is actually so.

How does such an investor know whether the private equity manager had made a strategic choice to select a particular jurisdiction, offshore or otherwise? Has the private equity manager taken measures that comport with common practices? Or has the fund made a shrewder choice that has other ancillary benefits (such as increased insulation from liabilities) that may be less obvious to uninformed investors? The answer, plainly, is that an investor pursuing the first option does not know, and this is where this argument falters. By not looking into such issues and performing operational due diligence, an investor is not making an informed independent assessment of the operational risks present in a particular fund.

The second, and better, option, is for an investor to incorporate an understanding of such matters into their larger operational due diligence process. But wait a minute, you may saying to yourself, this seems unfair! The questioning may continue as follows, "Why should I, as an investor, be forced to expend time, energy, resources, and my own capital to understand this? Is it not reasonable for an investor to rely on the experience of both the private equity fund manager and their lawyers and accountants to structure the fund in an appropriate and legal manner?"

These are valid questions and they do raise genuine legitimate concerns regarding who should bear the onus of both responsibility and cost regarding operational due diligence. Such questions are worth asking if not solely for the didactic nature of discussions they foster. After all, perhaps such lines of inquiry regarding the second option of incorporating such seemingly nonprimary jurisdictional concerns (e.g., by not focusing on understanding Malta's tax regimes and instead focusing solely on India) are legitimate. Furthermore, investing, particularly in a private equity context, is a time-sensitive process. When considering an investment in a newly formed private equity fund, investors allocation decisions, and subsequently their due diligence timelines are driven primarily not by the scope of their own due diligence processes but rather by working toward meeting a particular fund closing deadline. Therefore, as suggested in the questions posited, perhaps a more heuristic approach coupled with reliance on the private equity manager and their advisers is not so crazy after all.

Such an approach to investing, and certainly to operational due diligence, is the antithesis of the informed decision making goal of operational due diligence. While private equity fund managers and even some investors are comfortable, "taking someone else's word for it" and blindly relying on others' statements, most prudent investors would view such an approach as fostering ignorance bordering on a miasma of barbarism. Since it is not very productive to outline all of the criticisms that may be associated with the first option, let us instead focus on the benefits of option number two. By incorporating a broader scope into the nature of such multijurisdictional considerations, investors can realize a number of benefits. First, regardless of the conclusion reached, investors will be making an informed allocation decision. Second, by performing an independent review of even a small handful of key operational factors, they could be avoiding organizations with weak operational infrastructures.

What about Other Pressure from Investors?

Assuming that the reader no longer relies solely upon government regulations, then a second objection often raised to performing operational due diligence reviews on private equity funds has its grounding in economics. (Specifically, the "invisible hand of the market" theory of John Maynard Keynes.) With a grounding in the invisible hand orthodoxy, an investor may question the merits of performing private equity operational due diligence by asking something to the effect of, "Won't other investors demand operational best practices?" This question then perhaps logically advances down the objection path to the following line of reasoning, ". . . and won't the removal of whatever the market determines to be 'unnecessary' or 'excessive' operational risk result in the survival of only the operationally strong funds?" This effectively is arguing that a Darwinian survival of the fittest occurs with regard to private equity operational risk so that only the strongest operational players remain standing. Survival, for the purposes of this discussion, can generally mean sufficient capital to stay in business.

When we take a moment to break down this argument we can see that it rests on four basic premises. The first such premise is that information freely flows among private equity investors. Private equity, just like hedge fund investing, as well as many other fields of asset management is a marketplace in which information is exchanged. Investors who have particular operational concerns regarding a particular private equity fund do not necessarily call up other investors to let them know about their concerns. Would not the free exchange of ideas foster a more transparent and ultimately safer investing environment for all? At first there may appear to be benefits in sharing information, but in the long run there a number of reasons why the encouragement of this practice is not an easy sell. First, among professional investment organizations such as private equity fund–of-funds who are paid by investors to create a portfolio of underlying private equity funds, there are few incentives to encourage groups to share information. From an economic perspective, if one private equity fund of funds has significant operational concerns regarding a particular private equity fund that it has performed due diligence on, another private equity fund of funds will not be likely pay for such information.

Furthermore, another fund of funds may look suspiciously on information supplied by a direct competitor. Additionally, from the point of view of market competition it may actually profit the private equity fund of funds that has the information not to pass it along. If another private equity fund of funds, invests in the questionable manager's fund, then it may realize substantial losses or even go out of business altogether. By not sharing its original operational concerns with its competitors, the first private equity fund of hedge funds allows for a natural thinning of the competitive herd, which may ultimately benefit its own organization.

A second reason why private equity investors may not broadcast information concerning any operational concerns they may have with a particular manager relates to liability issues. When an investor begins the operational due diligence process, some private equity firms may ask an investor to sign a confidentiality agreement. Even if such a confidentiality agreement is not requested, many of the documents an investor collects and reviews will likely include legal disclosures and statements that indicate that the material the investor is analyzing is confidential. Regardless of the express or implied nature of the investor confidentiality relationship, investors who, based on a due diligence process, then turn around and broadcast concerns they may have to other investors may be breaching this confidentiality. Putting confidentiality concerns aside, assume that an investor does share operational concerns they have based on the due diligence with other investors. Let us further assume that such operational concerns have not been manufactured by the investor for whatever reason, but that they are actually true.

So now we have a scenario in which an investor has performed operational due diligence on a private equity fund, come to a decision not to invest based on genuine operational concerns that are grounded in fact, and shares his operational concerns with another investor considering the same fund. We live in a litigious society. This is particularly true in the United States. If a private equity fund learns that an investor is bad-mouthing its offerings and potentially scaring off other investors, the private equity fund may well sue. The suit may be based on a breach of confidentiality or perhaps claims of defamation, libel, or slander. People and organizations sue for all kinds of reasons. You don't need to be right to file a lawsuit; you need only have a gripe. If you were wrong, you will eventually lose. The problem is that litigation can be quite costly from both an economic and reputation standpoint. Additionally, litigation is not a quick solution and can take years, if not decades. Most investors would rather avoid the possibility of a lawsuit and instead keep their concerns to themselves. What this boils down to is that most investors effectively say, "I did my own due diligence and protected my own organization. It's the next guy's problem to find out what I found out." Not exactly a neighborly sentiment, but no one said investing in private equity was a civil exercise.

The second premise of the argument against performing operational due diligence reviews of private equity funds is that investors are universally informed about and hold the same general standards regarding operational best practices. Nothing could be further from the truth. Some investors do not even believe that it is necessary to perform operational due diligence on private equity funds. With such an absolute dictum on avoiding the subject, certainly these investors are neither informed about operational risk in private equity funds nor have they formed any sort of meaningful opinions regarding operational best practices in private equity funds. Putting these extreme cases of investors aside, even if different investors are performing operational due diligence on private equity funds, there is certainly not a universal consensus among all investors as to what constitutes a level of operational risk below which it is not worth investing. Each investment organization is unique and each investor has their own internal benchmarks for the minimum core processes (which we discuss in Chapter 1). Of course, 99 percent of the private equity community could believe that a certain operational practice is not investible and that it would be ludicrous to even consider it, such as having no cash controls whatsoever in place. However, there is no way to say with any certainty that all private equity investors feel the same way. There is just not enough transparency among private equity investors to come to a final determination.

Third, the line of reasoning previously described assumes that all investors apply the same level of standard toward operational due diligence to private equity reviews. This reasoning is not practical because some investors may, foolishly, not be performing any sort of operational due diligence on private equity funds. Setting aside these considerations, other investors who perform operational due diligence may allocate different amounts of resources to this area. Some investors may adhere only to what could be called a core process, while other investors may pursue an expanded process or a process that falls somewhere in between. Furthermore, some investors may employ experienced operational due diligence teams while other investors may have operational due diligence analysts who are primarily experienced in investment due diligence. With this diversity among resources and investor skill sets, it is difficult to support an argument that assumes that investors universally apply the same standards of operational due diligence to private equity.

Finally, the argument above implies that private equity funds with poor operational infrastructures either fail or stay in business. Viewing private equity in such black-and-white terms does not fit with practical observations of private equity funds. In much the same way that a private equity fund is not self-limited to categorizations of being either an strong investment or going out of business, so too do similar notions apply toward a private equity fund's operational risk management. A private equity fund can be operationally mediocre but still remain in business. It, of course, will not be operating as efficiently as it could, but it may not grind to a halt anytime soon. Furthermore, such an operationally mediocre private equity fund may also be unnecessarily exposed to high amounts of operational risk that could substantially increase the potential for failure related to its weak operational infrastructure. However, until such failures occur the fund may not falter to an absolute standstill.

Illiquidity (the Lockup) Argument

Putting exogenous factors aside, that is, those elements that come from outside the private equity fund itself, there may be other stalwart objections raised against the operational due diligence process itself, due to factors that are inherent in private equity funds themselves.

The first of such arguments may come directly from the general characteristics of private equity investing. Generally, for a new private equity fund, an initial capital raise occurs. During this time is when most due diligence (including investment due diligence) is performed. After the fundraising period, investors are effectively "locked in" to the investment for the term of the fund.

The only necessary or required ongoing interaction between the private equity fund and investors is the mailing of financial statements, which typically will not even come from the private equity fund but from the fund's administrator, and calls for capital that are also referred to as drawdown requests.[5] Therefore, because investors are "locked in," the basic question becomes why bother performing operational due diligence? The investors won't be able to act upon the advice by, for example, submitting a redemption request or even adding more capital depending on the particular circumstances and results of any operational due diligence.

It is at this point that it is worth distinguishing between the two broad stages in the investing process at which operational due diligence can be performed. The first period, before an investment is made, is termed *initial operational due diligence*. The second such period refers to operational due diligence after an investment has been made and is termed *ongoing operational due diligence*.

Many of the previously referenced arguments against performing operational due diligence on private equity funds relate to the initial operational due diligence stage. The present argument relates more to an argument against ongoing operational due diligence than it does to initial ongoing operational due diligence. At face value the "actionability" of the results of the operational due diligence process is more prevalent during the initial operational due diligence stage (e.g., an investor can decide whether or not to invest after factoring in the results of the operational due diligence process). Once an investment has been made, the supposed "actionability" of the operational due diligence data gathered is effectively useless—an investor cannot redeem or add more to his or her capital.

Before delving into the concept of actionability, it is ridiculous to hold the opinion that it is better for investors not to provide themselves with the option to learn about particular operational risks simply because they feel they may not have the ability to do anything with the information. This is equivalent to observing the situation of an individual, whom we can refer to as Mr. Ig Norant, whose house is on fire, and not caring that there is a fire hydrant outside his house because he doesn't have a hose to connect to it. Perhaps if Mr. Norant knew about the fire hydrant he could improvise a hose or seek help from a neighbor with a hose. Maybe Ig does not even need a hose at all. Perhaps Mr. Norant, whose house has since burned to the ground, could have used a bucket to collect water from the hydrant to put out the fire. Sadly, Ig is now warming himself by the smoldering pile that used to be his house. Mr. Norant firmly believes that ignorance is bliss and out of sight is out of mind.

Even if an investor believes that he or she cannot do anything with certain pieces of information it is often much more advisable to obtain this information and make a more informed decision about any action or inaction rather than preferring to keep their head in the sand. In fact, operational risk information obtained during the ongoing operational due diligence process is indeed actionable from a number of different perspectives.

Consider, for example, that an investor may have a seat on a private equity fund, with a seat on the fund's board or on an advisory board. In these cases, an investor may learn certain pieces of information but may also perform further operational due diligence. This ongoing operational due diligence process may be driven by a desire to monitor operational concerns that were originally noted during the initial operational due diligence process or this may be part of a regular ongoing program that does not focus on any specific operational concern. However, regardless of the motivation for performing such ongoing operational due diligence, if an investor confirms additional operational concerns or uncovers new operational concerns they may be able to take actions on such concerns based on their role on the board of the fund or the advisory board.

An investor may not be fortunate enough, however, to sit on the board of a fund or an advisory board. If based on an ongoing operational due diligence review an investor develops or reconfirms operational due diligence concerns, then an investor has several options. First, they can communicate such concerns to the fund manager. The private equity firm may not necessarily want to take action based on such concerns, yet they at least will be made aware of them. It is difficult sometimes for a private equity firm to be conscious of a third party's opinion of their own internal operations. In some cases, a firm may not know that a certain practice either deviates from current market practice or is of concern to investors. In these cases, the firm may be willing to make a change once an investor's concerns are communicated to them. If an investor had not performed any sort of ongoing operational due diligence, they would have not necessarily have any such concerns to communicate to the fund manager and no change would be effected.

Furthermore, by performing ongoing operational due diligence on a private equity fund, regardless of whether a fund is amenable to making any particular changes, an investor is still accomplishing something very important. They are sending a message to a manager that someone, even if it's one investor, is not only conscious of such issues but that they are watching. Investing is often a long-term relationship. Private equity firms are in the business of raising money for managing private equity funds. If an investor, particularly a large one, raises operational concerns as the result of ongoing operational due diligence and such issues are completely ignored or minimized, this will leave a proverbial bad taste in the investor's mouth. Investors tend to be a bit like elephants in this regard: They do not forget. So when the time inevitably rolls around for Private Equity Fund 1, in which the investor raised their initial operational concerns, to close and for a new fund, Private Equity Fund 2, to raise capital, this investor is not interested. And why should they be? So they can continue to be ignored. No thank you, there are plenty of fish in the sea and an investor may choose to do business elsewhere. Many private equity funds are beginning to realize the folly of this penny-wise, pound-foolish approach and are slowly minimizing their previous resistance to ongoing operational due diligence reviews from investors.

Even If I Perform Operational Due Diligence, My Private Equity Fund Could Still Fail for Operational Reasons

In raising objections to the operational due diligence process being performed on private equity, some investors may raise the following questions: "Why perform operational due diligence on private equity funds if my fund could still fail for operational reasons? And what about fraud? After all, if my private equity manager is a fraud and they want to steal, they will figure out a way to do it regardless of any operational due diligence review I perform." While this line of reasoning may seem a bit drastic at first, it does raise a number of valid arguments that should be addressed.

In approaching these objections we must first highlight a key point about operational due diligence. Posit the following objection to performing operational due diligence reviews of private equity funds. Operational due diligence is not an insurance policy. It is not a guarantee in any way, shape, or form. Anyone who tells you otherwise is lying. Anyone who attempts to sell operational due diligence as an insurance policy, guarantee, seal of approval, or anything else might also be trying to sell you a certain bridge in Brooklyn. Operational due diligence is a process via which an investor can diagnose, analyze, and monitor operational risk. Operational due diligence can be thought of as a hedge against operational risk. By performing a competent operational risk review of a particular factor, an investor is effectively taking the bulk of the risks associated with that particular factor off the table.

To facilitate this discussion, we can think of a private equity fund as having a certain fixed amount of operational risk. Whatever this amount of operational risk is or how we interpret it, operational risk, regardless of the granularity with which we delve into a certain area will approach some definite limit as we approach infinity. If we assume this premise, then within that finite operational landscape or plane, we can demonstrate that by utilizing a particular process an investor can effectively shrink the portion of the operational risk plane that they have not performed operational due diligence on. This necessarily will reduce their exposure to operational risk factors that are left not reviewed on the finite operational risk plane. This concept is summarized in Exhibit 2.2.

We can further consider the finite operational plane in the context of the core and expanded levels of operational due diligence review that we discuss in Chapter 1. Each of these theoretical levels of review relates to the scope of the operational risk factors encompassed by each process. As the name implies, the term *core* refers to a process that encompasses a review of, at a minimum, those operational risk factors that are necessary to allow an investor to reach an informed opinion, and ultimately come to an

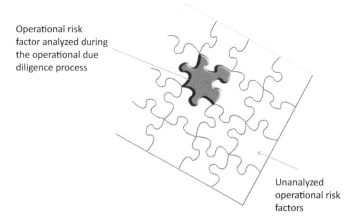

Operational risk factor analyzed during the operational due diligence process

Unanalyzed operational risk factors

EXHIBIT 2.2 Representation of Fixed Operational Plane with Individual Operational Risk Factor Selection

operational determination, regarding a particular private equity fund. An example of the core operational due diligence process plotted on the finite operational plane is shown in Exhibit 2.3.

Moving down the spectrum from a core to expanded process increases the number of operational risk factors included in the operational due diligence process. This relationship is summarized in Exhibit 2.4.

While the addition of each incremental factor does not necessarily imply transitions among the theoretical levels of below-core, core, and expanded

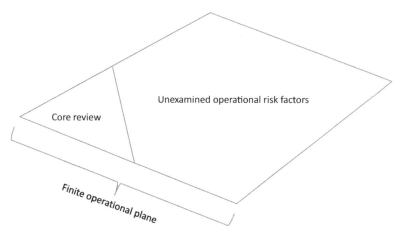

Unexamined operational risk factors

Core review

Finite operational plane

EXHIBIT 2.3 Entire Finite Operational Risk Plane with Core and Expanded Risk Segments

Number of operational risk factors included
in the operational due diligence process

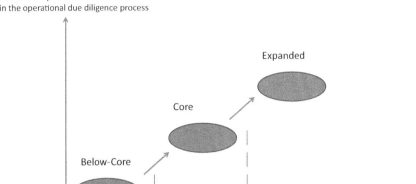

EXHIBIT 2.4 Comparison of Operational Risk Factor Inclusion to Operational
Due Diligence Process Scope

there is an increase in process scope with each additional operational risk
factor included in the due diligence process.

Returning to our discussion in terms of the finite operational plane,
an expanded process broadens the scope of the core process to include
additional operational risk factors that generally result in an investor making
a more informed operational determination. In this case, the broader the
scope of an investor's operational due diligence review from core to an
expanded process, the greater the number of operational risk factors that
are included. Considered in the context of the finite operational plane, we can
see how an expanded level of review shrinks the size of the total unexamined
area of operational plane. This concept is outlined in Exhibit 2.5.

Now that we have developed an understanding of the concept of the
operational plane coupled with the notions of expanding processes scope
based on risk factor inclusion that subsequently reduced the unexamined
factors, we can return to our analysis of the argument against performing
operational due diligence based on the potential for losses or fraud due to
unexamined operational risk factors.

If investors had infinite resources, time, and an unending army of qualified superb operational due diligence analysts, they could still not completely
eliminate the possibility for losses due to operational reasons. Fraud, for example, cannot be modeled but only analyzed and studied on a historical

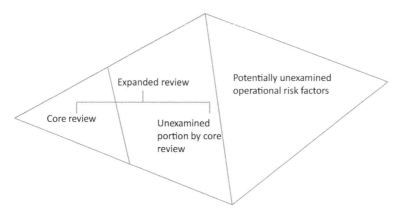

EXHIBIT 2.5 Entire Finite Operational Risk Plane with Core and Expanded Risk Segments

basis. The next fraud could be carried out in a completely different manner from a previous fraud. Therefore, any such backward-looking model utilizing historical inputs could not accurately determine a future fraudulent occurrence. This is not meant to imply that it is not fruitful for investors performing operational due diligence to brainstorm and develop models to try to predict such fraud. Indeed, their predictions may very well be correct. Rather, what this discussion of the fraud modeling is meant to illustrate is that any model of fraud in an operational risk context cannot be said to predict the occurrence of the magnitude and type of fraud with certainty.

Furthermore, returning to our original discussion, investors do not have limitless resources. Additionally, private equity funds should not be subjected to limitless scrutiny. As Chapter 3 discusses in more detail, an investor has a small window of opportunity during which operational due diligence may be conducted in regard to the attention and time a private equity manager is willing to commit. During this window of opportunity an investor may have only so many bites at the apple, so to speak, during which they can gauge particular operational risk factors. Beyond a certain point, a private equity manager will likely not entertain an investor's operational due diligence inquiries and will ask them to either accept the fund or leave it. An example of the delicate balance of the relationship between private equity investors and fund managers is shown in Exhibit 2.6.

With such an eventually limited window of opportunity, it is unreasonable to look toward the operational due diligence process to serve as a magic panacea for all non-purely-investment-related losses.

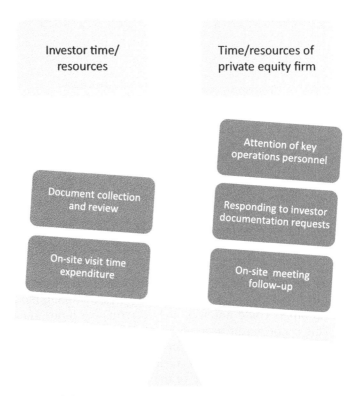

EXHIBIT 2.6 Model Representation of Balancing of Time and Resources Allocated to the Operational Due Diligence Process by Investors and a Private Equity Firm under Review

The "Information Barrier" Argument

Another common argument that is often raised in the context of arguing against performing operational due diligence reviews of private equity funds relates to the nature of information that is available to investors when approaching a private equity fund. As previously mentioned, when an investor performs initial operational due diligence on a private equity fund that has not yet funded, there is a paucity of data points in certain operational risk areas, which may impair an investor's ability to fully vet these areas. This dearth of information, to some investor's minds, may be a reason for not performing operational due diligence.

This illustrates a concept known as *the information barrier*. Certain investors who support not performing operational due diligence on a private equity fund may feel that if there is not what they consider to be "enough" operational risk information, then why bother? From this perspective, operational due diligence requires a critical mass of operational risk factors to be meaningful. After all, isn't this a corollary to the concept of the core operational due diligence processes previously described?

The answer is both yes and no. From the affirmative perspective, yes as our description of the core process is still valid. The theoretical construct of the core process is that it is meant to describe the minimum amount of operational risk factors covered during an operational due diligence process upon which a meaningful operational determination may be based. Transitioning to our below-core level of operational due diligence review, it is here where we approach the concept of the information barrier utilized to attack the merits of performing operational due diligence on private equity funds. In this regard, these arguments falter in an analysis of the below-core level of review as compared to performing no operational due diligence at all.

Put another way, if an investor is left with the option of performing zero operational due diligence as compared to performing a below-core level of review, which is preferable? A comparison of information barriers as compared to these hypothetical operational due diligence level thresholds is outlined in Exhibit 2.7, which may provide some guidance in this regard.

Those in favor of utilizing the information barrier concept to support a defeatist concept (i.e., nothing is better than something) opt in favor of performing zero operational due diligence. A more prudent investor believes the contrary: some operational due diligence is better than nothing. Of course, the operational due diligence does not need to remain at this below-core level. Even with a newly forming operational due diligence fund there is certainly enough operational risk data available to support satisfying a core level process.

The information barrier concept is also sometimes further extended by those who object to performing operational due diligence, into ongoing

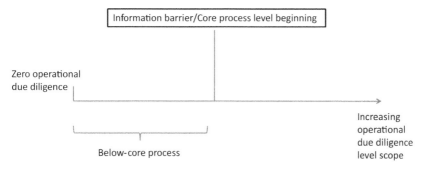

EXHIBIT 2.7   Comparison of Information Barriers Incorporated into Hypothetical Operational Due Diligence Level Thresholds

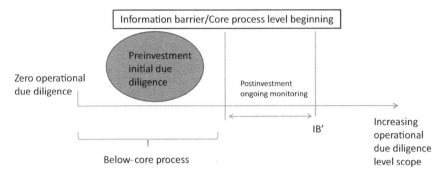

EXHIBIT 2.8 Comparison of Preinvestment and Postinvestment Information Barriers Incorporated into Hypothetical Operational Due Diligence Level Thresholds

operational due diligence. That is objecting to performing operational due diligence not only when considering an initial private equity investment, but also once an investment has already been made. Examples of the lines of reasoning used to support such arguments with regard to the information barrier outline that a subsequent information barrier is effectively erected after the initial funding is made. This second information barrier, which we can refer to as IB′, represents the level to which this information barrier reaches. The relationship between the initial information barrier and IB′ with regard to the hypothetical operational due diligence thresholds is shown in Exhibit 2.8.

As we progress through the initial operational due diligence process into the postinvestment process, then the second information barrier comes to light. In this regard, the information barrier that those raising an objection to performing operational due diligence refers to relates to the general nature of private equity investing. As noted above, private equity funds often do not trade as frequently as compared to other alternative investment vehicles such as hedge funds. Continuing this trading frequency notion, hedge funds often frequently report more frequently to investors. With this increased trading activity also comes more frequent changes in valuations. Additionally hedge funds have more frequent changes in items such capital flowing into and out of the fund on a more continual basis.

Private equity funds by contrast have limited open periods during which capital is raised before closings are implemented. Similarly, capital calls are typically more regularly scheduled as compared to monthly capital inflows and outflows that may be present in a fund such as a hedge fund. The purpose of our comparison with hedge funds here is that there is often more contact, activity, and subsequently more operational data points in regard to certain areas that effectively destroy or severely limit any such concerns related to the postinvestment ongoing monitoring information barrier. Investors allocating to private equity, it may be argued, slam into this information wall with almost the same severity that they do in the initial preinvestment operational due diligence process. In rebuttal to such arguments, and in support of performing ongoing operational due diligence monitoring, we can rely on many of the arguments we previously outlined with regard to overcoming the first information barrier.

COMMON ARGUMENTS IN FAVOR OF PERFORMING OPERATIONAL REVIEWS OF PRIVATE EQUITY FUNDS

Smaller Windows of Opportunity

One argument that lends support to the reasons as to why an investor should perform operational due diligence relates directly to the nature of most private equity investing in new funds. When a new private equity fund begins, it typically raises a pool of capital up-front and then closes. This initial capital close may be the only capital close that the fund undergoes. In other cases, a private equity fund may undergo multiple closes dependent upon a number of factors, including the capital raising environment as well as the nature of the private equity fund investments. When an investor begins a relationship with a private equity firm it is common that he or she will deposit a certain amount up-front with the fund and be committed to the rest. The private equity then calls down this capital from investors at regular intervals and/or as needed. The term of private equity funds generally extend for a number of years. Therefore, investor's capital is effectively locked up during this time period. While we have outlined some of the concerns this raises with regards to performing ongoing operational due diligence in the postinvestment stage, we can focus on the initial preinvestment operational due diligence stage of the process for the moment.

Investors who are considering an investment in private equity are left with the prospect of having their capital locked into a particular investment private equity fund for quite a while. This is particularly true when compared to hedge funds, which in recent years have tended to eschew longer lockups and embrace more frequent liquidity. Investors considering private equity should consider this future illiquidity, when coming to a determination as to whether or not they should perform operational due diligence at all. Due to the fact that their capital will be effectively locked up for a number of years, it certainly suggests that performing due diligence would be prudent. This is particularly true if an investor has made his or her mind up, however mistakenly, that they do not need to perform ongoing operational due diligence once an investment had been made. After an investor subscribes capital to a private equity fund, there is virtually no going back. The private placement memoranda and subscription agreements of most funds will contain legal language to this effect as well.

An investor who is considering whether to perform initial operational due diligence on a private equity fund should consider what his or her respective goals are. One common goal, which we have previously discussed in this book, relates to the notion of making more informed decisions. This is certainly a prudent and reasonable goal. In this case, an investor choosing not to perform operational due diligence on a private equity fund prior to investing is effectively stating that they do not want to make the most informed investment allocation decision possible.

We can make this statement because, even if an investor performs operational due diligence on a particular private equity fund and feels that he or she have learned nothing that was not already covered during the investment process, they have in fact learned something. The most important take-away an investor can have from such a process would be to learn that there was nothing else that he felt he did not know. No stone left unturned, so to speak.

Of course, this example is offered to demonstrate a point. In practice, an investor can learn a great deal of new information and gain additional insights during the operational due diligence process. It is these pieces of operational risk data that allow investors to then make more informed decisions. An informed decision is not always the correct (i.e., profitable) one; however, the more information an investor has, the higher the probability that she will make better decisions. Furthermore, the more information they collect the more informed such a decision will be.

However, let's assume that despite the benefits of making more informed decisions, an investor may still be unconvinced regarding performing initial operational due diligence on a private equity funds. It is at this point that we can revisit a concept outlined earlier. Investors in private equity typically only get a limited window during which initial operational due diligence can be performed. This time period generally runs up until a specific capital close date. After this date, because of the longer lockup period discussed earlier, an investor's capital is effectively stuck in the fund. With this limited window and long capital lockup period, an investor is asked to make a fairly quick decision that can have long-lasting consequences. Under such a scenario it is advisable for investors to seize the opportunity to learn as much as possible about a private equity firm and fund during this period.

This "as much as possible" notion relates to a second piece of the operational due diligence. Once an investor has made the determination to perform initial operational due diligence, they must next consider the scope to which such a review is performed. Such illiquidity and lockup considerations should also factor into considerations of what degree of operational due diligence should be performed. Compared to other asset classes, such as hedge funds, the longer lockups and smaller operational due diligence window suggest that an investor must maximize the opportunity for initial operational due diligence up-front and under a tight time frame. Due to these reasons, it is advisable that investors conduct the most detailed and broadly scoped operational due diligence reviews of private equity that their own internal organizational resources allow.

In order to conduct such expansive reviews, this means that investors will likely be required to dedicate an inordinate amount of due diligence resources in the direction of private equity when considering a new investment in a private equity fund. Such large, focused resource allocations however, should not necessarily be a surprise to investors. Performing due diligence in general is a bit of a chunky exercise. From a workflow perspective, operational due diligence itself can be quite lumpy. By this we mean to say that the workflow is very up-front intensive. When considering making a potential investment in a fund, be it a mutual fund, hedge fund, or private equity fund, for example, an investor will likely perform a certain degree of due diligence before investing. This due diligence process typically begins with an investor performing initial investment due diligence. This can be performed in a multitude of ways including attending industry conferences, searching performance databases, speaking to industry contacts, and working with investment consultants.

After the decision as to whether invest or not with a particular fund has been made, an investor will then move on to the next project. If no new investments are being considered, outside of considerations of ongoing monitoring, then the due diligence function may be relatively stagnant. When the next investment is considered the due diligence machine starts up in full gear again. The chunky nature of this work as it is driven by each individual investment is summarized in Exhibit 2.9.

Once an investor has identified a prospective fund the operational due diligence process typically begins. Of course, there is no formal point at which the operational due diligence does, or should, start. Rather, it can be incorporated into the initial due diligence processes outlined earlier in a number of ways. The most common method of such incorporation, as is likely similar with many investment criteria utilized to weed out potential funds from a large list, is as a filter. So, for example, a potential investor, in

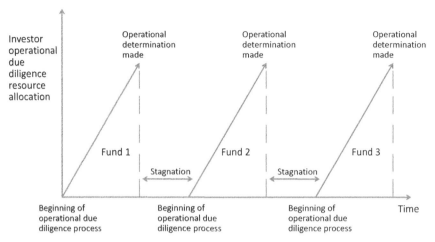

EXHIBIT 2.9 Chunky Nature of Initial Operational Due Diligence Resource Allocation

addition to setting certain minimum primarily investment-related requirements for a potential private equity fund, may also impose certain operational requirements including assets under management size, number of personnel, presence of clean regulatory history, and so on.

After this initial screening process is complete and a fund has been identified upon which a potential investor wants to conduct more extensive due diligence, typically this is where the heavy lifting in the operational due diligence process comes into play. The bulk of operational due diligence work typically occurs at this initial (i.e., preinvestment) stage for investors because they are dealing with an unknown entity.

One of the purposes of operational due diligence is so that the investor can educate themselves about a private equity firm and fund operations in order to make a more informed investment decision. As such, the slope of the initial learning (and resource allocation) curves is generally steepest in the beginning. This relationship is summarized in Exhibit 2.10.

In reviewing Exhibit 2.10, the reader should realize that the relationship between the number of operational due diligence reviews performed, as indicated by resource expenditure in the chart, and a particular investor's level of operational competency is not necessarily linear. On the contrary during the early days of an operational due diligence program an investor may make large incremental gains in the amount they know about operational risk. Such large gaps in knowledge advances tend to plateau over time; however, the relationship may not always be as smooth as the graph implies.

EXHIBIT 2.10 Comparison of the Level of Investor Competency to Operational Due Diligence Resource Expenditure

With an understanding of the nature of operational due diligence resource allocation coupled with the common smaller windows during which operational due diligence may be performed on private equity funds, we can see the logical reasons that support performing operational due diligence on such funds. Furthermore, due to illiquidity considerations outlined in more detail further on, investors will likely broaden the scope of such operational due diligence reviews as compared to other asset classes.

Longer Capital Lockups

As outlined earlier, due to the structure of private equity investing, after a potential investor decides to allocate to a private equity fund they have, for all intents and purposes, locked their capital up for the term of the fund. While the time over which a fund runs its course may vary among firms and private equity investment strategy types, the average length is often much longer than compared to other alternative investments such as hedge funds. For example, hedge funds may impose lock-ups of capital for perhaps one to two years whereas the average length of an LBO fund is approximately six years.[6]

When there is the potential that an investor's money will be locked up for a longer period of time, the investor must necessarily have a higher level of conviction in making such an allocation decision. In order to obtain comfort with this less liquid investment, many investors will require more due diligence to, at a minimum, feel more comfortable with parting with their money for several years. This longer-term structure effectively reduces the opportunities for ongoing monitoring. This means that investors have fewer bites of the apple to perform operational due diligence as referenced in the smaller window of opportunity discussion section.

Therefore, it only makes sense that an investor should not only perform initial operational due diligence on a private equity fund, but that the scope of such due diligence should at least meet, if not exceed, that of more liquid asset classes such as hedge funds. Furthermore, in comparison to other alternative asset classes, this longer-term lockup structure suggests that investors have more to lose by not dedicating increased amounts of resources to private equity operational due diligence during the preinvestment stage.

Performing Operational Due Diligence Facilitates Process Documentation and Creates a Paper Trail for Litigation Support

There are numerous topics that private equity firms would generally prefer not to have in-depth discussions with investors about during the operational due diligence process. These topics may understandably include fees (and subsequent negotiations surrounding fees, including fee reductions), personnel turnover, poor performance of past private equity funds run by the firm, and so on.

Another overarching topic relates to the loss of money. This topic is particularly of note when individuals or groups who advise on or manage money on behalf of other investors (e.g., financial advisors, brokers, private equity fund of funds) lose money for their clients via investments in private equity funds. Investors, or their advisors, ultimately allocate to a particular private equity fund because they want to generate profits. Private equity firms want to generate profits in their funds. If a private equity fund makes money it is a win-win situation for both investors and the private equity firm. On the other hand, when investors lose money it is another story entirely, and certainly not one that private equity firms would likely wish to discuss with investors during the operational due diligence process.

If a private equity fund makes bad investments and enough people lose enough money, then investors may sue to seek recovery. Note the use of the word *enough*. In this case, it refers to losses sufficient to economically justify a lawsuit. Investors may allege numerous types of awful conduct by a fund manager when losses ensue, such as that the fund manager was reckless in investments or perpetrated fraud. Regardless, of whether the merits of such investor's suits have a rational basis, when such a suit ensues several things happen.

First, this generates negative reputational consequences for the firm. Second, from a practical standpoint, if a lawsuit follows the normal progression, eventually it will come to a stage in the process known as *discovery*. During discovery a series of documents and pieces of information are requested and collected by the parties suing each other. During the discovery process the types of due diligence documentation that may be required to be produced include those from the private equity fund manager itself as well as from those who advise on or manage money on behalf of other investors. Let us unpack these two types of due diligence documents in more detail. The private equity fund manager may be required to produce documentation related to any due diligence, operational or otherwise, that they may have performed on underlying portfolio companies, for example.

We can next turn to our second group, those who advise on or manage money on behalf of other investors. It is in this case, and the one that is most relevant to our present discussion, in which an advisor or manager of other people's money, such as a broker or private equity fund of funds, will be required to produce what could effectively be referred to as a *due diligence file*. It should be noted that the term *due diligence file* is not a legally defined one; however, for our purposes we can define it simply enough as all documents related to the due diligence process.

These documents in such a file can include:

- Copies of any communication (e.g., emails, document requests lists, log of phone calls, etc.) between the PE fund of funds and the underlying PE funds
- Details of any internal discussions regarding the decision to invest (or not invest) with a particular PE fund (e.g., meeting minutes, records of the votes of any internal committees)
- Copies of any documents collected from the underlying private equity fund
- Documentation of any analysis performed on these documents (e.g., reviews of financial statements and legal documents, etc.)
- Conclusions drawn based on reviewing documents (e.g., internal memorandum)
- Details and agendas of any on-site visits
- Details of any service provider reviews and any documentation reviews from service providers

So if litigation proceeds and during the course of the discovery process if a financial advisor or a private equity fund of funds cannot produce a detailed due diligence file, they are likely to be off to a very bad start. As noted above, this due diligence file should include not only copies of documents collected from the underlying private equity fund in which capital was placed, but also an outline, in written form, of the steps taken to perform operational due diligence. While the stages of the due diligence process themselves are useful, a due diligence file should also demonstrate implementation of the operational due diligence program. If a financial advisor or private equity fund of funds can produce such a detailed file, then from a litigation perspective they may have a leg to stand on.

By performing operational due diligence and developing a detailed due diligence file, an investor will not only create a more uniform due diligence process, but will also be forced to document their operational conclusions. As discussed previously, this documentation process often forces investors to clarify their thinking with regard to the operational risks present in a particular private equity fund, and ultimately make more decisive operational determinations. Furthermore, as outlined earlier, performing operational due diligence on private equity funds lends itself toward documenting such a process. When such a due diligence file is created as a result, then in the event of a worst-case scenario, where, for example, a private equity fund of funds ends up losing investor funds in bad private equity investments and litigation ensues, they will be in a much better position to defend themselves, and perhaps save themselves hundreds of thousands of dollars in lawyer's fees and millions of dollars in investor compensation to boot.

CONCLUSION

In conclusion, performing operational due diligence on private equity is a good idea. It provides investors with the opportunity to diagnose, analyze, avoid, and potentially mitigate unnecessary exposures to operational risk. Operational due diligence is also a process that lends itself to being documented. This documentation process allows investors who manage money on behalf of others to potentially insulate themselves from liability in the event they are sued due to losses related to due diligence, make potentially more informed decisions, and have more conviction in these decisions.

NOTES

1. See Philip Millward and Julian Ashworth, "Opinion: Cautious Optimism in Cayman for Primary Private Equity Fundraising," *Private Equity Wire*, April 4, 2011.
2. See François-Serge Lhabitant, *Handbook of Hedge Funds* (Hoboken, NJ: John Wiley & Sons, 2006), 39.

3. See Walburga Hemetsberger, *European Banking and Financial Services Law: Third Edition* (Brussels: Groupe De Boeck S.A.), 2008, 270.
4. See Simon Walker, "BVCA Response to EU Commissioner's Comments on Walker Guidelines," www.bvca.co.uk/assets/features/show/BVCAresponseto EUCommissionerscommentsonWalkerguide.
5. The timing of capital calls and associated cash flows management can be quite volatile. For a discussion of this, see Andre Frei and Michael Studer, "Quantitative Private Equity Risk Management" in *The New Generation of Risk Management for Hedge Funds and Private Equity*, ed. Lars Jaeger (Institutional Investor Books, 2004).
6. See Kamal Ghosh Ray, "Merger and Acquisitions," PHY Learning Private Limited, New Delhi, 2010, 495.

CHAPTER **3**

Beginning the Operational Due Diligence Review: Core Issues

C hapters 1 and 2 provide an introduction to the field of both operational risk in general, as well as positioned operational due diligence considerations in a private equity context. With this background now in place, we can proceed to a discussion of how an investor can actually begin the process of performing an operational due diligence review on a private equity fund.

GOAL SELF-ASSESSMENT

As we discuss in Chapter 2, before diving headfirst into the operational due diligence process, it is often critical for investors to determine what they are looking to get out of the process. There is not always a universal answer in this regard. Some investors may have several goals when approaching the operational due diligence process. Others may be more single-minded and seek to achieve one primary goal. Certain common goals that are often associated with operational due diligence include fraud detection and mitigation, more informed operational decision making, operational process learning, and process documentation. Regardless of the actual goals an investor may have, it is a highly productive exercise for an investor to go through this self-assessment process to determine not only what goals they may have in mind but what outputs, if any, are to result from this process. In this way, investors can be sure that when they design a process there is an alignment of expectations and the procedures that are necessary to reach these goals.

When performing fund manager due diligence, there is a general consensus that checklists used in evaluations may be flawed, at best. A checklist is a self-limiting approach that can foster a due diligence process in which certain key risks are completely avoided. But without a checklist, are

85

investors resorting to an amorphous, free-form approach to due diligence, and is each new fund review a unique case? Of course not—there are certain key processes and components of the operational due diligence process that can serve as a good starting point for virtually all reviews. In performing this goal self-assessment, one question for investors to consider is whether their review approach is goal-driven or process-driven.

To facilitate investors completing their own goal self-assessment process, we can first examine what goals are in place for their other operational due diligence procedures. Additionally, investors may want to consider viewing the process from a fresh perspective. The types of questions they may want to ask themselves include:

- Are there are process similarities we can leverage from other operational due diligence reviews?
- Are there any key risk areas to which my organization is particularly sensitive?
- How will this process differ from any existing operational due diligence reviews we perform on nonprivate equity managers?
- What operational risk areas are of most concern to our organization with regard to private equity?
- What output is required from my private equity operational due diligence process?

An investor's goal self-assessment process is also important because it allows investors to consider the unique aspects of private equity operational due diligence. Many investors who are considering implementing a private equity operational due diligence program may already be performing other types of operational due diligence reviews to varying degrees for other asset classes and nonprivate equity managers with which they invest. If this is the case, there is a high degree of likelihood that an investor may stick to their knitting, so to speak, and apply many elements of the same operational due diligence processes. After all, there is no reason to recreate the wheel if there is a fairly robust operational due diligence process already in place. This assumption is only partially correct, however. Certainly, as Chapter 1 discusses, there are a number of similarities between operational due diligence processes across both all asset classes and more specifically between fund managers such as hedge funds and private equity. In this regard, the processes do indeed share attributes that may be leveraged. However, by applying the same cookie-cutter process to different types of managers, say hedge funds and private equity, investors run the risk of not incorporating the unique operational aspects of private equity into their review process.

DESIGNING AN OPERATIONAL DUE DILIGENCE PROGRAM FOR PRIVATE EQUITY

Once an investor has gone through the goal self-assessment process, they can next approach the design of an operational due diligence program. During the goal self-assessment process an investor has likely made a number of choices that have implications for the scope and scale of the operational due diligence process. It is in this way that operational due diligence program design is closely related to process development design. Such choices will necessarily have an impact on process design.

Operational Due Diligence Scope Considerations

One example of the interaction between the results of the goal self-assessment process and operational due diligence process design, relates to resource expenditure. If an investor has very high expectations of the operational due diligence process and wants a broad net to be cast in an attempt to uncover any and all operational risks, then this same investor must also be prepared to allocate the appropriate resources in this regard. Operational due diligence resource allocation can be a bit of a tricky business. As any analyst will likely tell you, operational due diligence is one of those areas where the more work an investor does, the more there seems to be to do. Such notions can refer to the fact that when an investor reviews a particular document, such as a manager's own due diligence questionnaire (DDQ), there may be an additional series of questions that come out of that process.

Similarly, the more an investor expands the scope of the operational due diligence process, the more operational risk factors are necessarily reviewed. This relationship is summarized in Exhibit 3.1, utilizing the previously introduced below-core, core, and expanded review level concepts.

Returning to the phenomenon of increasing process scope toward factor review, in this context it is useful to introduce a concept known as *operational fringes*. When an operational due diligence process of a certain finite scope is employed, this in turn implies that other operational due diligence factors are left not reviewed, or at least not reviewed completely, even if they may be touched upon tangentially. In this case, a finite due diligence process often borders on the edges, or fringes, of certain issues. An example of this is illustrated in Exhibit 3.2, showing the operational fringe phenomenon in a comparison of core and expanded process reviews.

To better clarify the concept of operational fringes, consider an investor employing a core operational due diligence process that has as one of its goals, developing an understanding of the trade life cycle process. As part

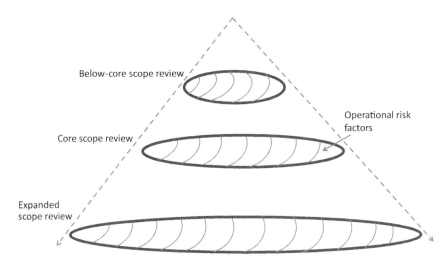

EXHIBIT 3.1 Positive Correlation between Increasing Operational Scope Review and Operational Risk Factors Included in Review Process

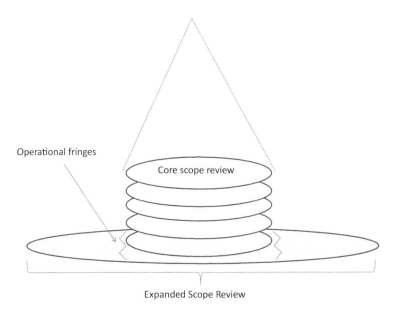

EXHIBIT 3.2 Operational Fringes Presence in Comparison between Core and Expanded Scope Reviews

of this process, an investor will typically examine the trading process from the time a decision is made to trade through to execution and settlement. As part of this process, an investor will likely encounter a variety of trading systems and accounting systems that may be used within and between different firms. Therefore, in order to effectively evaluate the trading process an investor now needs to be able to gauge the appropriateness and efficiency of these trading systems. Perhaps in this investor's core process a review of the information technology framework of the private equity firm is not included. It is at this point that a decision must be reached. He or she can decide to either stop or proceed with a basic understanding of the trading and accounting systems. He can expand his process to an expanded approach and include technology and systems. He also has the option of learning "just enough," however he defines it, about the technology and systems functions of the firm to be able to assess the trading and accounting systems. The difference between the "just enough" approach and the full-blown expanded approaches is that the investor utilizing the "just enough" approach isn't necessarily interested in evaluating the entire information technology infrastructure of the private equity firm. On the contrary, this investor has decided that they will need to know just enough about the firm's technology and systems to facilitate the primary operational risk review goal included in their core review process of understanding the trade process.

A reader might be tempted to call this investor lazy. After all, if he is going to look at the information technology function to begin with, why not go all the way? However, this investor may not be lazy but rather have a number of different considerations that may not allow him to expand the process. For example, an investor could be resource-constrained and not have enough time, money, or manpower to perform an expanded operational due diligence review. Furthermore, such an investor may not feel that he has the internal operational competencies to review a private equity firm's information technology infrastructure. Does this mean that this investor would be completely correct to ignore this subject entirely? Of course not. An investor faced with such a situation has a number of options, including hiring qualified personnel with technology backgrounds to assist in such reviews or working with a third-party operational due diligence consultant.

Another reason why an investor might not expand beyond their core review process is because they are working under time constraints. Certainly, cutting back in the due diligence department is not advisable, but some investors may find themselves in this situation. We will discuss in more detail further on the different approaches that investors can take toward developing operational due diligence time lines, to avoid being in a crunch situation when managing multiple reviews.

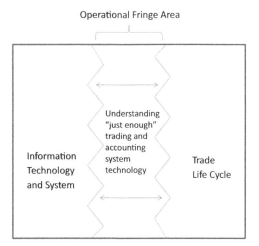

EXHIBIT 3.3   Example of an Operational
Fringe Area between Trade Life Cycle and
Information Technology and Systems
Operational Risk Factors

Returning to our investor who has a choice to make, let's assume that
he decides to pursue this "just enough" approach. The investor includes
a review of the trade life cycle in his core process, but does not expand
the process fully to include information technology, and therefore is now
conducting a review along a so-called *operational fringe*. Stated in another
way, this investor is broadening the scope of the core review process but
only just enough to review the necessary information in a noncore scope,
without fully broadening the review scope into that factor. An example
of the operational fringe area utilizing the trade life cycle and information
technology and systems operational risk factors is shown in Exhibit 3.3.

Operational Due Diligence Resource Allocation

After an investment has gone through a self-assessment of goals and has
utilized that self-assessment to further their understanding of the review
level and scope considerations, an investor can next consider the resources
that will be allocated toward operational due diligence. One primary question an investor must first consider relates to what, if any, resources an
investor is allocating toward operational due diligence in the rest of their
organization. Some investors may be new to the concept of operational due
diligence. These investors may not have any internal dedicated operational

due diligence resources at all. Other investors may have individuals performing operational due diligence, which are focused on other areas such as investment analysis. Before determining the appropriate amount of resources to allocate toward private equity operational due diligence reviews, it is perhaps useful to provide an introduction of common operational due diligence frameworks that are typically employed.

Understanding Operational Due Diligence Frameworks　In order to provide some guidance in this area we can introduce the research findings of Corgentum Consulting in this regard. Corgentum conducted a series of studies related to trends in operational due diligence frameworks utilized by different investment organizations. In order to facilitate this study, a series of proprietary data sets were constructed. Data were culled from a variety of different sources including interviews and surveys with employees working at investment organizations that perform operational due diligence. Other data were collected from publically available databases and regulatory archives, including those maintained by the U.S. Securities and Exchange Commission, the United Kingdom–based Financial Services Authority, the Hong Kong Securities and Futures Commission, and the Cayman Islands Monetary Authority.

For the purposes of these studies, Corgentum classified operational due diligence frameworks into four style buckets: *dedicated, shared, modular,* and *hybrid*. Each of these operational due diligence style buckets refer to the framework implemented at an investment organization to perform operational due diligence reviews. These style buckets do not address which individuals or groups at an investment organization hold the authority to make the ultimate operational conclusion regarding a particular manager.

Furthermore, these style buckets do not address which individuals or groups, such as an investment committee, has the final authority to make the final allocation decision to a manager. A definition of each of the style categories follows:

1. **Dedicated.** An operational due diligence framework where a fund of hedge funds has at least one employee whose full-time responsibility is vetting the operational risks at hedge fund managers.
2. **Shared.** An operational due diligence framework where the responsibility for reviewing the operational risk exposures at hedge funds is shared by the same individuals who have responsibility for investment due diligence. No full-time dedicated operational due diligence staff are employed.
3. **Modular.** An operational due diligence framework whereby the operational due diligence process is classified into functional components and

parsed out among different specialists with relevant domain specific knowledge.

4. **Hybrid.** A hybrid operational due diligence framework refers to an approach that encompasses some combination of the three previously described approaches (dedicated, shared, and modular).

In regard to the modular framework, it is important to note that in a modular operational due diligence framework, these domain experts typically have other responsibilities within the larger fund of hedge funds organization outside of their operational due diligence responsibilities. Examples of the titles that these functional domain experts typically hold within the fund of hedge funds organization would be General Counsel, Chief Technology Officer, Chief Compliance Officer, and Chief Financial Officer.

Under a modular approach, the work of these domain experts is often pieced together by an individual or group of individuals that we will refer to as operational generalists. The operational generalist can be thought of as an information aggregator who pieces together the disparate functional reviews completed by the domain experts to facilitate the fund-of-hedge-funds organization progressing toward an operational risk conclusion. The operational due diligence duties of the operational generalist can be very similar to those of operational due diligence analysts under a dedicated framework and can include such things as on-site manager visits and operational risk report generation.

Under a modular framework the operational generalist or group of individuals performing the operational generalist function can be either a dedicated operational due diligence professional (i.e., fitting into the definition of the dedicated approach) or the operational generalist(s) themselves can serve other functions within the organization and may even be domain expert(s) in their own right. An example of this would be an individual whose title is Chief Operating Officer and who has other responsibilities within the fund of hedge funds organization, yet who also serves as the operational generalist piecing together the operational due diligence work of the functional domain experts. Exhibit 3.4 summarizes the role of the operational generalist in a typical modular framework.

Returning to the hybrid framework, an example of a hybrid framework would be a fund-of-hedge-funds organization that employs a full-time operational due diligence analyst (i.e., dedicated framework) while including in-house domain experts as needed. Continuing this example, these domain experts would not be a part of the standard operational due diligence review process followed by the fund-of-hedge-funds (e.g., such as a modular approach) but utilized on an ad-hoc basis. Another example of an operational due diligence framework that would fall under the hybrid classification

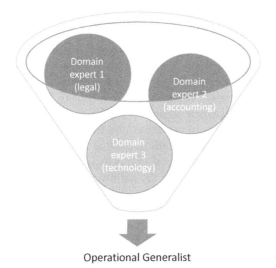

Operational Generalist

EXHIBIT 3.4 Example of Modular Operational
Due Diligence Framework

would be a fund-of-hedge-funds that outsources the operational due diligence function, either in part or entirely, to a third-party operational risk consultant. Therefore, within those managers that fell into the hybrid classification it is important to note that a significant diversity of subapproaches existed.

General Framework Trends The summary results of these Corgentum studies are summarized in Exhibit 3.5.

It should be noted that names such as "hedge funds (and not private equity)" are not meant to imply that an investment organization invests only in hedge funds. On the contrary, this category title refers to an investment

EXHIBIT 3.5 Operational Due Diligence Frameworks at Fund-of-Hedge-Funds Globally

Operational Due Diligence Framework	Hedge Funds Only	Private Equity Only	Hedge Funds and Private Equity
Dedicated	27%	18%	29%
Shared	31%	32%	28%
Modular	14%	28%	22%
Hybrid	28%	22%	21%

organization that may allocate to several different types of managers varying across asset classes, such as long-only managers. To be clear, "hedge funds (and not private equity)" indicates an investment organization that invests in hedge fund managers, and may also invest in other asset classes, but that does not invest in private equity funds. Similarly, the "private equity (and not hedge funds)" category is not meant to imply an investment organization that invests solely in private equity funds, but rather identifies an organization that invests in private equity funds and not hedge funds.

Additionally, in this regard, dedicated does not refer to a firm that has an operational due diligence function that is focused solely on private equity reviews. Instead dedicated falls into the definition of a dedicated framework outlined earlier (i.e., individuals whose sole role is to perform operational due diligence reviews, as opposed to other reviews).

The figures outlined in Exhibit 3.5 outline some interesting trends in relation to investors' historical views toward performing operational due diligence in hedge funds and private equity. As compared to hedge funds, historically investors have seemed to allocate fewer dedicated resources toward operational due diligence. This trend seems to reverse when an investor performs operational due diligence on both hedge funds and private equity funds. Specifically, the study data suggests that investors who allocate to private equity, and not to hedge funds, allocate fewer dedicated resources toward operational due diligence. This can be compared to the marked difference, almost 9 percent greater, of investment organizations that allocate dedicated resources toward hedge fund operational due diligence.

The argument could now be raised that perhaps in general more investment organizations allocate more capital toward hedge funds than private equity; however, as with most studies the data are not meant to conclusively prove any certain investor behavior but rather to imply what prevailing trends might be in practice. Such a marked difference between the two suggests that historically more investors have allocated resources toward conducting hedge funds operational due diligence reviews as opposed to private equity.

Turning to the shared framework, the data suggests that only minimal differences exist between the operational due diligence frameworks of investors who allocate to hedge funds and private equity respectively. These differences are somewhat magnified when we examine the operational due diligence frameworks employed by investors who invest in both hedge funds and private equity. A slight decline can be noticed in this regard, of only 3 or 4 percent for hedge funds only and private equity only respectively.

Proceeding to the modular framework, we can notice a stark disparity between the hedge fund and private equity groups of investors. While only 14 percent of those investment organizations that allocate resources to hedge funds and not private equity employed modular frameworks, double that amount utilized modular frameworks among private equity and not hedge funds investors. This large disparity is diminished slightly to 22 percent for hedge funds and private equity investors. Finally, turning to the hybrid framework, we can see a slight bias toward the hybrid framework among hedge fund investors as compared to private equity only as well as investors that allocated to both hedge funds and private equity.

So what can we take away from this study? Taken in the context of other study data, it seems as if private equity investors have historically shied away from utilizing dedicated operational due diligence resources to perform operational risk reviews of private equity firms. Instead, the data suggests that these investors, when performing such reviews at all, have tended to benefit from the shared due diligence resources of their organization or a modular framework of internal specialists competencies. The data also seems to indicate a convergence of more evenly distributed operational due diligence framework utilization across the four categories listed earlier among investors who perform operational due diligence on both private equity and hedge funds. Among these investment organizations, there tends to be a slight bias in favor of dedicated frameworks with shared frameworks following as a close second.

Process Construction Concerns: Resource Dilution and Process Homogeneity

In processing the study conclusions in the context of an investor determining which framework and how many resources to allocate toward operational due diligence on private equity funds, it is also worth considering the case alluded to earlier, of an investment organization that already maintains an established operational due diligence department. This dedicated department can be employed to review, for example, hedge fund investments, or even multiple types of investments such as hedge funds, fund-of-hedge-funds, and long-only funds, then this investor has already effectively made a commitment toward operational due diligence. In this regard, many such investment organizations would view adding reviews of operational due diligence of private equity funds as iterative to the existing process. That is, it could easily be integrated into the existing operational due diligence function already in place. Such organizations may however run the risk of having both *resource dilution* as well as *process homogeneity*. We can address each of these concepts individually.

An existing operational due diligence function with a fixed number of employees represents a finite pool of due diligence resources from which an investment organization must execute its review, analysis, and monitoring of operational risks of all managers and generally across all asset classes. The word *generally* is used because of differences among firms; for example, one investment organization may have a policy of not performing operational due diligence on any affiliated managers or on any long-only managers. When a new asset class such as private equity is added to the pool of funds that remain under the purview of the operational due diligence function, this group now has a series of additional issues to address. Putting aside considerations of any unique or particular skills required to perform operational due diligence reviews on private equity funds that may not already be present, it is worth evaluating the workflow aspect of these changes. Assuming that all other investment activity remains effectively stable throughout the firm (e.g., an investment organization is not investing solely in private equity) then the finite resources of the pool now have to be used for more operational due diligence reviews than previously. Particularly when considered in the context of balancing potential operational due diligence review scope expansion, such additional review requirements can dilute this pool of finite resources and result in the *resource dilution* phenomenon.

A second consideration, *process homogeneity*, also relates to scope expansion. If an organization already maintains a finite operational due diligence function that then begins an expansion into private equity reviews, it is worth considering, as outlined earlier, how this process is approached. Many times, if the existing investment organization has what they determine to be well-defined operational due diligence processes, a certain amount of institutional entrenchment tends to be present.

When comparing operational due diligence methodologies across different private equity allocators, consistency of approach is often a key concern. These concerns, however, must be counterbalanced with the notion that all private equity funds are not created equal. In order to successfully vet the entirety of operational risks present at a fund, an investor must sometimes be prepared to add an element of flexibility to their approach. Such flexibility can often lead to covering areas not traditionally addressed in detail during the course of standard methodology reviews. Such flexibility often sheds more light on the operational risks already uncovered during standard methodology reviews. Similarly, flexible approaches tend to allow investors to uncover a series of operational risk factors that were previously not reviewed under standard methodologies. Inflexible operational due diligence approaches, which can result from the previously referenced institutional creep of existing operational due diligence methodologies into subsequently added asset classes, can suffer from a *check-the-box mentality* that can be detrimental to investors. Furthermore, inflexible operational due diligence approaches are more susceptible to fraud as they are easier to manipulate from the perspective of the private equity fraudster. Investors should seek to have an element of flexibility in their operational due diligence process to design the most appropriate review specifically tailored to meet the needs of each unique fund manager, while at the same time not sacrificing the benefits afforded by having minimum uniform standards in place.

One example of the ways in which flexible and inflexible operational due diligence standards can differ relates to the notion that different private equity investors may have different sensitivities and priorities in regard to the operational riskiness of a hedge fund. For example, one investor may place only minimal importance on a fund manager's business continuity and disaster recovery plan, while this may be of high importance to another investor. An overly rigid operational due diligence methodology overlooks these different investor sensitivities. Additionally, operational risk concerns may also vary among different managers. Continuing our example, business continuity and disaster recovery may be of increased importance to a manager that trades more frequently than a fund that executes only a few trades a month. Inflexible operational due diligence methodologies often ignore the nuances of different investor operational risk thresholds and the potential increased weight of certain operational risk factors for different managers.

Another problem with inflexible operational due diligence methodologies is that entrenched processes can often yield operational due diligence reports that contain reams of irrelevant information as a result of their boilerplate check-the-box approaches to due diligence. Overloading investors with volumes of such information can result in important details and risk considerations becoming lost. This leaves investors with the problem of searching for an operational risk needle in a haystack of immaterial information. A flexible approach to operational due diligence can assist in mitigating this information overload.

With these considerations in mind, investors with established operational due diligence processes already in place that simply add on private equity as the next new thing can run the risk of applying an inflexible generic operational risk process that can dampen sensitivities and produce operational risk reviews that do not consider the unique operational sensitivities present in private equity funds.

Developing an Operational Due Diligence Timeline

An investor who performs operational due diligence does not undertake the process in a vacuum. Investors operate on timelines. When faced with the decision as to whether to invest in a particular private equity firm, there is often a finite hard deadline after which the fund will not accept additional capital. Certainly a private equity fund might have multiple periods during the capital-raising period when it accepts capital, a phenomenon often referred to as instituting a soft close and then reopening. However, after any such periods there is a definite point after which an investor will no longer be able to invest, commonly referred to as a hard close. Therefore, an investor does not have an unlimited time period in which to consider whether they will allocate to a private equity fund. Therefore, investors must strategize how best to plan their operational due diligence process with this time line in mind. Returning to our discussion of the goals of operational due diligence, most investors would likely agree with the benefits of making the most informed private equity allocation decision possible. Therefore, investors must plan their private equity operational due diligence time line for a particular fund with the goal of accumulating and analyzing all of the relevant data to facilitate this informed decision making.

The question now becomes how much lead time is enough to allow an investor to appropriately review and come to a decision regarding the amount of operational risk present in a particular private equity fund. The answer to this question is firmly rooted in notions of both the investor's own resources and the scope of the review being performed. All other things being equal, if two different investors approach the challenge of having to perform an operational due diligence review of a particular fund, then the time it takes to perform such reviews will vary contingent upon a number of different factors.

First, the most obvious way in which such processes may differ relates to process scope. Assuming that two equally skilled operational due diligence functions of equal size are deployed to perform a review of a particular manager, the investor seeking to cover more operational ground (i.e., review more operational risk factors) will necessarily take longer to complete the review compared to an investor reviewing fewer operational risk factors. Of course, a single-skilled operational due diligence analyst may be able to conduct reviews more efficiently than two or more unskilled or inexperienced analysts, which can serve to make up time differences in review processes.

Another consideration, in addition to process scope, relates to how much other due diligence work has already been performed. If an investor has performed only minimal investment due diligence and is looking toward the operational due diligence function to perform much of the heavy lifting in the due diligence area, then the operational due diligence process will likely take longer as well. This can be particularly true with regard to process documentation concerns. If, for example, the investment due diligence process produced a one-page summary memorandum regarding a manager's particular investment merits, but the operational due diligence function is expected to produce a 50-plus page tome on a manager's weaknesses, then obviously just from a documentation perspective, it is a much more time-intensive exercise. Contrast this with an investment due diligence process that produces a great deal of detailed internal documentation that already touches on a number of different issues, either tangentially or directly, that operational due diligence may touch on as well. This will likely both speed up the process from an operational due diligence perspective as well as lessen the process documentation burden on the operational due diligence function. Such reviews will likely be completed on a more expeditious time line.

Operational Smell Tests Are a Bad Idea

While developing an operational due diligence time line, it is also worth noting that investors may uncover items during the operational due diligence process that merit further review. Operational due diligence is one of those areas where it is often difficult to perform a "smell-test" for a fund. The notion of a "smell-test" will often come about when an investment analyst approaches an operational due diligence analyst within the same organization. The investment analyst will ask the operational due diligence analyst to take "a quick look" at the manager and let the investment analyst know if there are any issues. The investment analyst's motivation can be directly influenced by when the operational due diligence process begins within an organization.

Some investment organizations may not begin the operational due diligence process until after a certain level of investment conviction for a particular private equity manager is reached. Other investors may begin the operational due diligence in parallel with the investment due diligence process. In the former type of organization, returning to our previous example, an investment analyst may not want to waste the time and effort required to reach a particular level of institutional conviction with regard to a private equity manager, if soon afterwards the operational due diligence function will come along and either veto the manager entirely or note a series of operational issues.

Not to inflate the head of the operational due diligence analyst, however, in such cases, it is often advisable for the operational due diligence analysts to take a position similar to that of the Supreme Court of the United States. In the history of the United States there have been several occasions when the President has asked to the Supreme Court for an advisory opinion on matters. That is there was not an actual case or controversy before the Supreme Court to decide, but rather, the President was seeking legal advice in one regard or another. A notable example of this was when President George Washington asked the Supreme Court for advice relating to his Neutrality Proclamation regarding the French Revolution.[1] In this case, as with subsequent other examples, the Supreme Court declined to render such an opinion because they are not the attorneys to the President. Rather their approach is, either let us consider the issue in its entirety or not at all. Operational due diligence is a bit the same way.

From an initial evaluation perspective, an investment organization may have certain minimum criteria that are required in order for a particular private equity manager to be considered eligible for investment. These criteria can include minimum factors such as a previous track record of a certain length (e.g., three years or more) or certain firm-wide assets under management size (e.g., $1 billion or more). Generally, any individual does not need to be a fully fledged operational due diligence analyst in order to make such determinations and it is often fairly obvious whether a private equity manager complies with these guidelines.

Outside of such considerations, however, operational risks may be much more difficult to ascertain unless a complete operational due diligence process is conducted for a particular manager. A good example of this relates to the way in which different pieces of information from different documents collected from a private equity manager interact. Often an investment analyst may have collected certain pieces of documentation during their preliminary investment due diligence process. The investment analyst will typically forward these documents to the operational due diligence analyst for review when asking them to perform the so-called smell test. As will be outlined in more detail further on, there is a particular art to document collection that this investment analyst may not have been aware of. As such, all of the documentation that an operational due diligence analyst may require to perform a review may not present. Additionally, by being asked to conduct a cursory review of documents, an operational due diligence analyst may not catch certain latent pieces of information that may be inconsistent with other documents. Continuing our example, an operational due diligence analyst in smell-test mode may not catch the names of certain entities referenced in the fund's offering memorandum that are not addressed elsewhere in other documents. It could potentially turn out that this entity could be related to significant operational issues (e.g., an affiliated custodian) that could either prevent an investor from moving forward with a particular investment due to operational concerns, or alternatively slow down the process significantly.

Therefore, investors are faced with the problem of not knowing what they will find until they actually undertake the work of performing a review. So what is an investor to do? One solution is to build in an appropriate time buffer or cushion into the operational due diligence process to allow for the uncovering of unexpected operational risk factors that require further review along the way.

WHEN DOES THE OPERATIONAL DUE DILIGENCE PROCESS BEGIN?

Now that an investor has gone through self-assessment of goals and come to a general determination as to the scope and framework to be employed in the operational due diligence process for private equity funds, an investor can next turn their attention toward beginning the process of reviewing a particular private equity fund. Before delving into the specifics, however, it is worth considering some of the major waypoints in the operational due diligence process. This broad five-stage process is outlined in Exhibit 3.6.

The first stage in the broad five-stage process is "Data collection and analysis." This stage involves two distinct primary parts. The first such section relates to data collection, which includes document collection. The

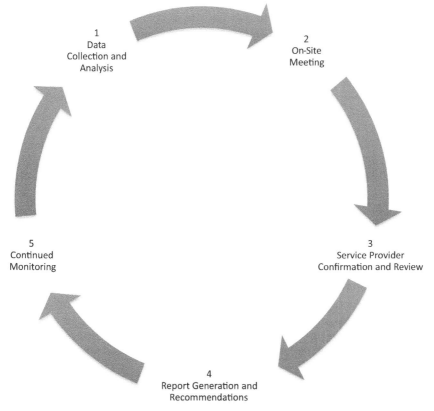

EXHIBIT 3.6 The Operational Due Diligence Process

document collection process is discussed in more detail further on. The data analysis portion involves actually reviewing and analyzing the data collected during this stage, including the operational risk data that has been culled from document review. The type of documents collected can include legal documents and financial statements. (Chapters 6 and 7 discuss techniques for analyzing these documents in more detail.)

The next stage in the operational due review process requires an on-site meeting. The on-site meeting stage refers to the process by which an investor actually travels to visit the private equity manager at his or her own offices. The on-site process has a number of benefits that investors can realize. The greatest benefit is that face-to-face communication between investors and a private equity firm's personnel often yields enhanced quality and depth of information, as opposed to teleconferences, webinars or even video conferences. In cases where an investor feels such a visit is prohibitively expensive, they may want to pursue these non-face-to-face options. However, such a practice is not advisable.

Moving on from the on-site visit, we can next approach the third stage in the five-stage process. This stage involves service provider confirmation and review. It is important to note the positioning of this stage in the process. While an investor may wish to conduct individual stages outside of the prescribed order, or even simultaneously, there is a method to the relative order. Considering, for example, the positioning of the service provider review stage of the process, an investor may prefer instead to confirm service provider relationships before the on-site visit and then perform a more detailed review of service providers after the on-site visit. There is nothing wrong with such a re-jiggering of the order. Investors each may have different considerations motivating the order in which they carry out such a process. However, a key element is that each of the steps referenced in the process be completed.

Returning to the service provider confirmation and review stage, during the operational due diligence process it is advisable that an investor reach out to a private equity fund's service providers to confirm, at a minimum, that the relationship actually exists. An investor should then take further steps to review the nature of the relationship that a service provider may have with a private equity fund or firm respectively. Additionally, an investor should review the quality and appropriateness of the service provider in relation to the types of services being offered to the private equity firm or fund as mentioned earlier. (Chapter 4 offers a more detailed discussion of service providers.)

Now that we have an understanding of the various components of the operational due diligence process, we can next begin to focus on when the process actually starts. Before starting this discussion, however, it is perhaps useful to pause for a moment to consider the following often repeated story:

> *An individual who is having a great deal of emotional problems walks into a psychologist's office. The patient sits down and before the session begins she begins talking about her problems and crying. The psychologist politely picks up some papers and starts to read them. He then interrupts the young woman and says, "Excuse me, we haven't begun yet." Upon hearing his instructions the woman calms down, stops crying, dries her eyes, and sits there patiently waiting for him to finish shuffling some papers. The psychologist then points out to her that he has just been able to stop her from crying simply by disrupting her behavior pattern.*

Operational due diligence is similar in its effects. Many investors, and private equity funds, may be under the perception that the operational due diligence review process only begins when interviews start to take place (e.g., via on-site visit or telephonically).

This should not be the case at all. Operational due diligence in a private equity context is not a formalistic engagement. Unlike, for example, the practice of law there is no Geneva Convention, nor are there Civil Practice Law Rules, Federal Rules of Evidence, or any other formal rules that govern how to perform operational due diligence or, for the purposes of this discussion, when the process begins. This is not to say there are not standards, both legal and otherwise, that do and should apply toward operational due diligence approaches and practices. However, in general terms, there is no one formal legal rule or document that outlines what an investor, or firm, must do when performing operational due diligence. The legal standards for operational due diligence, if there are any, are typically interpretations of the amount of due diligence required to comply with certain standards (e.g., "reasonableness" or "appropriate measures to reduce risk").

Now that we have established that the operational due diligence process does not have a formal beginning, we now come to the general first step in the operational due diligence process for investors. Generally, an investor's first point of contact with regard to operational due diligence (after initial introductions have been made) is to request materials (e.g., documents) related to both the private equity firm and any funds under consideration.

We discuss the actual document request list in more detail further on; however, one point of consideration (and an item that can raise a red flag) would relate to the private equity firm's response to the actual document request process.

SIGNALING EFFECTS OF OPERATIONAL FLAGS

At this point it is beneficial to introduce a concept that we will utilize throughout this book. In finance, signaling theory relates to the concepts of symmetric and asymmetric information, by which the actions of certain groups, such as companies, may send signals to the market by either acquiring or selling their own stock.[2] In the context of operational due diligence, a signaling effect can also said to be present when certain key operational risks are present. An example of this would historically be a fund that held self-custody of assets. Without the oversight of a third-party custodian, there are more opportunities for this fund to either perpetrate fraud; since they are holding custody of assets there is effectively no one stopping them from taking the assets and running away, or, more plausibly, there is increased potential for operational issues resulting from this situation, where there is a lack of appropriate controls.

In this case, a signaling effect often results from these key operational risk areas, such as a lack of checks and balances or a lack of process independence. Throughout the book, when such issues are discussed, a red flag symbol will be placed at the beginnings of these sections to highlight the signaling effect of these particular operational risk factors associated with each respective flagged section. Readers should be conscious that the term *red flag* is employed here in a broad context. The term red flag may have different meanings to different people. Some investors may view the presence of any red flag items at a private equity fund as being not investible. Others may opt to evaluate each red flag issue on a case-by-case basis. Still others may eschew a binary system—that is, no flag or red flag—entirely and prefer a multitiered flag color system consisting of mid-level operational risk areas that would be marked with yellow flags.

Regardless of the gradations or the color scheme employed, certain key operational weaknesses or practices can be signals of much bigger operational problems or risk area. As such, when performing operational due diligence it is advisable for investors to vet these operational risk areas more deeply and be on the lookout for these red flag items.

REQUESTING AND COLLECTING DOCUMENTATION

As previously noted, the process of beginning an operational due diligence review on a private equity fund often begins with a documentation request. Document collection and review is the lifeblood of the operational due diligence process. By not collecting and reviewing documentation, an investor is effectively going into the rest of the due diligence process blind—and at a major disadvantage. Even the document requests and collection process itself can offer insight into how the result of the operational due diligence process will proceed and may alert investors to any red flags that may be on the horizon.

When the operational due diligence process begins, after introductions are out of the way, an investor generally has two options: submit a document request themselves or ask the fund to provide them with due diligence documents. The distinction between these two options is in who drives the process—the investor or the fund.

Each option has its pros and cons and, as with many things in the field of operational due diligence, there is no one right answer as how to best proceed. Each investor may have a different preference and the selection of how to begin the document collection process may indeed be driven by the way in which operational due diligence interacts with other parts of the larger due diligence process.

For example, for an investment organization that begins the operational due diligence process only after substantial investment due diligence has been conducted, many of the needed documents may already have been collected. If this is the case, an investor may find it more efficient to request only the additional documents that fill in any holes that remain from the initial document collection process.

On the other hand, an investor who performs operational due diligence in parallel with the larger due diligence process, either as a distinct operational due diligence process or as part of the complete due diligence process, may seek to have the fund provide them with documents to kick things off, and then go back to the fund with more specific document requests if necessary.

Regardless of which approach is taken, when an investor first makes the document request to the private equity firm, not all firms will automatically comply. In many cases, the fund manager may immediately comply with certain document requests. In other cases, a manager may eventually comply with other document requests after a delay, perhaps because the manager does not have these documents readily available. A manager may also state such platitudes that the firm does not distribute such documentation but the investor is welcome to review such documents during an on-site visit to the manager's offices. In still other cases, a manager may state flat-out that a firm does not share such documents. In situations where the manager does not immediately comply, the document collection process can turn into an exercise in negotiation. Before discussing the negotiation aspect of this process, it is worth considering an often overlooked consideration that is present in not only the document collection process, but also in the due diligence process as a whole—confidentiality.

NONDISCLOSURE AND CONFIDENTIALITY AGREEMENTS

When an investor first begins the document request process, an investor can learn a thing or two about the private equity firm themselves based on their response. This is a type of metacommunication, or details embedded in the response to the document request itself. Certain private equity firms may respond to these data requests differently. When faced with a document request, a private equity firm may ask an investor to sign a nondisclosure agreement (often referred to as an "NDA") or a confidentiality agreement (often referred to as a "confi").

NDAs could be referred to as a subset of confidentiality agreements. In general, some confidentiality agreements can be broader and cover a larger scope than a traditional nondisclosure agreement. From a more practical perspective, it could also be argued that it does not effectively matter what the agreement is technically labeled (e.g., either NDA or confi). The names are used for the same agreement and relate to the same subject matter—protecting confidential information. Agreements of such types become important in business operations when one party or both are providing certain information of a confidential nature to the other and wish to protect their rights in so far as it relates to the information being disclosed and what happens in the event of a nonpermitted disclosure. In general, when presented with such documents, investors are generally more concerned with the contents of the documents than with the subtle differences perhaps implied by the names "NDA" or "confidentiality agreement."

However, before diving headfirst into reviewing the NDA, or having an attorney do so, it is worth pausing for a moment to consider the implications of the request from the private equity firm itself on the operational due diligence process. In this perspective, for the purposes of this stage in the operational due diligence process, the focus is not necessarily on the content of the document, but rather on the question of whether a private equity firm asks an investor to sign a confi or an NDA.. When a private equity firm is presented with an initial due diligence inquiry from an investor, they may not likely ask such an investor to complete a confidentiality agreement. This is understandable from an investor's perspective because the minute legal documents are introduced into the initial getting-to-know-you stage, it can bring the conversation to a grinding halt.

Once the due diligence processes progresses a little further, for example, to the document request stage, the private equity firm may certainly very reasonably ask an investor to enter into a confidentiality agreement with the firm. Before discussing why it is generally a positive sign when a private equity firm under consideration asks an investor to sign such a form, we should consider some of the arguments for, and against, such agreements.

To start with, some on the private equity side may be against bringing up the issue of confidentiality at all at this stage in the due diligence process. For example, they may feel, and perhaps rightly so, that requesting that an investor enter into such an agreement will forestall the process before it gets underway. Most investors are not likely to simply sign such agreements, but they are likely to consult with legal counsel and attempt to negotiate the terms of this document.

Another objection that may typically be raised by private equity personnel is that such NDAs or confis are not required. These individuals believe that there is an implied confidentiality in place. After all, most of the materials that an investor will receive as part of both their initial due diligence process as well as in reply to any specific document requests at this stage may even have language indicating that such documentation is to be maintained in confidence. That is, there is a sort of gentleman's agreement among all private equity participants that such information would not be shared outside of the confidences of the private equity firm and an investor. In reply to such objections, your author humbly quotes Sir Harry Vaisey, who was a senior judge in the Chancery Division of the High Court of Justice in England and Wales and who defined a gentleman's agreement as "an agreement that is not an agreement, made between two persons neither of whom is a gentleman, whereby each expects the other to be strictly bound without himself being bound at all."[3]

As abhorrent as it may be to those with a legal background, some private equity personnel overseeing an investor's operational due diligence inquiries, such as representatives of investor relations or even senior operations personnel themselves, may seek to reinforce these notions of gentlemanly civility in the private equity community. This involves situations where a private equity fund will seek to manufacture its own sort of ad hoc confidentiality acknowledgment. One such example, which your author has seen on more than one occasion, states, *"In regards to your due diligence request, please be aware that we regard the materials we will be sending you as confidential. We request that you treat them as such and that you please do not share with anyone outside your organization. Please indicate that you agree to this provision in a reply e-mail."*

Before discussing such generally well-intentioned attempts to replace the formalities of a legal document with a quick e-mail, it is worth reminding investors of the types of firms they are investing in. Private equity firms are multimillion-dollar complex investment organizations. In certain cases, as unbelievable as it may seem, these well-funded private equity organizations with existing and ongoing relationships with likely a multitude of law firms, may not have a standard confidentiality agreement on hand. Furthermore, as we have discussed, some private equity firms may not even ask an investor to sign such confidentiality agreements altogether.

Now let us return to our good-hearted private equity employee asking an investor to confirm by e-mail that they will behave and not share any of the materials that they are sent. First, assuming that an operational due diligence analysts replies yes, from a legal perspective it may be debatable whether he has the authority to bind his entire firm to confidentiality. Second, such a reply of confidentiality may be altered or changed entirely by the barrage of other small print disclaimers in the footer of most e-mails these days. Third, if an investor, or an operational due diligence analyst at an investment organization, indeed agrees to maintain the "materials" sent in confidence, then such confidentiality concerns do not necessarily automatically apply to all other communications, electronic or otherwise, between the private equity firm and the investor. So for example, just because an investor has supposedly consented via e-mail to confidentiality of materials sent to an investor, the same confidentiality does not necessarily apply to materials handed, and not sent, to an investor during an on-site due diligence meeting. Furthermore, such confidentiality does not likely apply in perpetuity to other materials that may be sent past a certain time interval.

Yet another argument that private equity personnel may raise in objection to introducing a confidentiality agreement at this stage of the game relates to investors' motivation. What benefit, they may ask, will it serve investors to share information they obtain during the due diligence process with others? This line of thinking frankly misses the point. Investors are not generally collecting such information with a goal of bartering it for profit among others. On the contrary, most investors are collecting such data to facilitate their own decision making as to whether to allocate to a particular private equity fund.

During the course of this decision-making process, for example, it is not outside the realm of possibility that, in the hypothetical collegial gentleman's community of the private equity world, one gentleperson could inquire upon another as to their opinion of a particular firm. This inquiry could be made of an individual who has already made the determination as to whether to invest in a particular private equity fund, and such information would perhaps be common knowledge among the private equity elite, either because he spread the word or others did. For the purposes of our example, we will refer to the investor who initially performed due diligence and ultimately did not invest with the private equity fund under consideration due to operational concerns, to be the first investor. The second investor in our example will be the investor who is currently performing due diligence on the private equity fund and is seeking counsel from the first investor.

In this case, the lack of a confidentiality agreement in place with the first investor has now caused difficulties for the private equity firm when dealing with the second investor. This is particularly true if the first investor found things that they believed to be unfavorable and advised others not to invest. Without such a confidentiality agreement in place initially, the private equity fund may have little basis for seeking recourse against the first investor. This can be particularly frustrating for a private equity firm if the first investor was perhaps mistaken regarding certain operational conclusions they have made. Perhaps the first investor was not very adept at operational due diligence and not successful in piecing the often disparate operational facts together at the particular private equity firm to make a completely informed operational decision. Furthermore, what if this investor, who ultimately made the decision not to allocate to the private equity fund, performed his due diligence some time ago and is now, when asked, recommending that others do not invest as well. Under such a scenario, an investor may not only be advising others with incomplete information, but also based on stale operational data. Perhaps based on decisions of individuals such as our first investor not to invest, the private equity firm has since made marked operational improvements that would now result in a different investing outcome.

From the perspective of the private equity firm, the argument may concede that each of these may be well-founded issues that a firm must contend with during the due diligence process. However, from a practical perspective they may, playing devil's advocate, raise the question of "So what?" After all, a private equity firm is not likely to be privy to the private discussions of such investors. Furthermore, if a particular investor, the second investor in our example, decides not to invest with a particular manager or puts the breaks on the due diligence process as a result of the advice of his investing compatriot, then he is not very likely to point the blame at the bearer of this advice. As such, even if a confidentiality agreement was in place, what recourse if any does a private equity firm have? The answer plainly is still little, if any. However, let us say that the investor who decided not to invest tells not just one individual of the intricacies of a particular firm, but broadcasts such opinions to several individuals. Furthermore, let us say that this individual shares their opinion in a public forum such as on the Internet or during a TV interview. Does the answer change? Many private equity funds do not stay in business by suing their prospective investors. However, without such a confidentiality agreement in place, the investor would likely have a much stronger shield in place than any sort of litigation-type sword a private equity firm may try to brandish in their defense.

Returning to the second investor, this individual may not be, as discussed previously, seeking to sell the information obtained during the operational due diligence process to other investors. On the contrary this individual may simply be seeking perspective. As such, in approaching the first investor, or any investor for that matter, he may inquire as to how common certain practices employed by the private equity fund under consideration are in practice. In doing so this second investor may directly, or inadvertently, reveal certain pieces of information. Once again the investor's intentions may be well and good, but he is revealing information obtained from the private equity firm during the due diligence process—information that, if construed negatively, the private equity firm would rather likely not have disclosed, particularly when it cannot respond to such potential concerns. Now, of course, it may be naive at best to believe that people who enter into confidentiality agreements always uphold them. However, from the perspective of the private equity firm, if an investor is going to share the information obtained during the due diligence process one way or another, then having the options afforded to them by a confidentiality agreement certainly are preferable. Reverting back to our practicality objection, if an investor has such a confidentiality agreement in place, they may be less likely to share such information with others. The fact that they are bound by confidentiality will, hopefully, be in the back of their minds before they begin to spread the word one way or another.

Reviewing the issue of confidentiality from an investor's perspective, many investors may welcome with open arms the prospect of not having to sign a confidentiality agreement. This prospect may seem attractive on multiple fronts. After all, an investor is not binding himself or herself to any sort of obligation to protect information or keep their mouths shut. Furthermore, when an investor is not asked to sign any sort of nondisclosure agreement, this means there is no such document for them to review. An investor does not have to expend the time and resources necessary to have such a document reviewed, and most likely negotiated among their own lawyers and the private equity fund's lawyer. Not having to sign such an agreement seems like a good deal for investors.

Yet, what such a viewpoint might overlook is the reciprocal nature of such agreements. In nondisclosure agreements, not only is a private equity firm typically seeking to protect their information from being spread about by investors, but it is also offering protection of any investor information communicated to the private equity firm as well. So, for example, let us assume that during the due diligence process a private equity firm learns certain facts or preferences that a particular investor may have. An example of this could be mundane investor restrictions such as the need to maintain full portfolio transparency. Or, perhaps, during the course of the due diligence process, an investor happens to mention that he or she have had a great deal of personnel turnover at their investment organizations, or that recent asset flows into the investment organization from third parties may not have been particularly strong lately. Similar to the examples outlined earlier, the presence of a confidentiality agreement will not necessarily prevent a private equity fund from discussing such information with others, but having one in place certainly couldn't hurt an investor's chances of keeping such information confidential.

Other situations in which an investor may want to have their information protected relate to the maintenance of confidentiality in the postinvestment period. Occasionally in private equity, as in most industries, mistakes eventually happen, particularly when the potential for human error is more prevalent. An example of this relates to when a private equity firm responds to certain investor documentation requests. In this example, we will consider two different investors. Investor A is a current investor in a private equity fund that has gone through its first soft close. Investor B is an investor who started the due diligence process on the private equity fund after Investor A and missed the first soft close. Investor B is now in the final stages of the operational due diligence process and is in document collection and review stages with a goal of coming to an operational determination, and subsequent allocation decision, before the private equity fund's hard-close date. For our example, we will assume that the private equity fund does not require investors to sign confidentiality agreements during the due diligence process. One commonly requested document may be an offering memorandum for a private equity fund under consideration. Let us assume that Investor B has included the offering memorandum in his document request list. The private equity firm's investor relations manager, Molly Dowell, is happy to comply with Investor B's request. Relying on the knowledge that an investor is, from the perspective of the private equity firm in this case, implicitly purported to possess regarding implied confidentiality, Ms. Dowell expeditiously sends along the offering memorandum to Investor B. Unfortunately, Molly has made an error. Instead of sending along the sample offering memorandum that the firm had scrubbed to be in generic format, she sent an actual offering memorandum that had been issued to a previous client: Investor A, to be exact. Investor B has not only received an offering memorandum, but he also knows the identity of Investor A and that this same investor has at a minimum performed due diligence on the private equity fund. As sloppy as such a practice may seem, these kinds of mistakes unfortunately happen all the time, particularly during the often frenzied capital raising period of a private equity fund approaching a close. But we digress, returning to our example, what about poor Investor A? Not only does he not likely know that his personal details have been transmitted to Investor B, even if he did he likely has little recourse. Remember there was no confidentiality agreement in place to protect both the confidential information of the private equity firm *and* the investor.

Now the reader may be saying to themselves, "Wait a minute! Why are we talking about *recourse*? What damage has been done to Investor A?" Well, we don't know exactly. As with most things, however, you don't generally seek recourse until after the damage is done. Perhaps unbeknownst to Ms. Dowell or her employer, the private equity firm Investors A and B had separate business dealings that are now negatively impacted by the knowledge mistakenly imparted to Investor B. There are any number of scenarios in which such sensitive information getting into the wrong hands can cause problems. The point of this entire discussion regarding confidentiality agreements, and as applicable to our current example, is that most private equity firms when speaking to investors during the due diligence process, operational or otherwise, keep their eyes on the prize—raising money. As a result, subtle issues such as the benefits of confidentiality agreements may be intentionally, or even consciously, ignored by such firms at their own peril. Furthermore, investors, for the reasons discussed earlier, may consider it a plus in terms of expediting the process. Not to have such agreements perhaps removes a roadblock on the path toward reaching an allocation decision. However, for all of the reasons just noted, confidentiality agreements can be a good thing for both private equity firms and investors.

Furthermore, when a private equity firm does not ask an investor to sign a confidentiality agreement, it has a strong signaling effect. The private equity firm is in essence indicated that they have made a decision, either proactively or by silence, regarding the ways in which they approach issues of information confidentiality. Some may argue that such silence on the matter is not necessarily an affirmation of a disregard for the importance of maintaining information confidentiality but instead a lack of desire to press the issue. Or perhaps, even worse, relying on the weak argument that arguably this is not an issue they have actively considered. After all, the obstreperous may continue, if the private equity firm's counsel did not advise them that such confidentiality agreements were required, then what harm, legal or otherwise, is the firm doing by not implementing a required procedure of requiring investors to sign such agreements? Regardless of whether such silence on the issue with investors is rooted in misplaced blame on legal counsel or well-intentioned, albeit absentminded, oversight, the appearance of a private equity firm's lack of desire to consider the issue of information confidentiality in a measured way during the document collection stage is reminiscent of the famous Latin maxim *qui tacet consentire videtur*, which is loosely translated as, "He who is silent appears to consent."[4]

DOCUMENT COLLECTION: WHAT DOCUMENTS SHOULD INVESTORS REQUEST?

With a firm understanding of the goals of the operational due diligence process, and resource framework allocation considerations, as well as the meta-signaling effects embedded in the reply to the initial document request submission, we can proceed to the meat of the document collection process—what documents should an investor request? Unfortunately, there is no secret list of documents investors should request.

Indeed, the document request process should not be driven by specific document names at all. Rather, the document request list should be topic-driven. So for example, an investor will likely have better results in designing a document request list that seeks to cover certain topics such as legal and compliance, and then utilizing these general topics to drive the specific documents to be requested, such as a private equity fund's offering memorandum or a private equity firm's compliance manual. This is an area in the document collection process where a combination of the art and science of operational due diligence come together.

As noted earlier, depending at which stage of the overall due diligence process operational due diligence begins, the types of documents collected that relate to operational due diligence may be collected in part during a predecessor investment due diligence stage of the process or operational due diligence may be brought in to start fresh. In order to facilitate our discussion of the types of documents, an investor should collect during the operational due diligence process, we will assume the latter option, that an investor is approaching the operational due diligence process of a particular private equity fund from a fresh perspective. This is not to suggest that an investor should eschew any knowledge or insights garnered from any previous investment-related due diligence. Such an assumption will allow us instead to establish a model paradigm from which investors can either subtract or add as applicable to their respective due diligence processes.

Furthermore, as discuss earlier in this chapter, the operational due diligence process can be driven by either the investor or the private equity fund. In the former case, an investor submits the document request list to the fund. In the latter case, an investor performing operational due diligence will request that the fund provide them with due diligence documents. For the purposes of the following discussion, we will also assume that an investor is proceeding with the document requests process. Depending on the type of review being performed, as well as balanced against the previously discussed differing approaches toward the positioning of the operational due diligence process in the larger due diligence scheme, such a fund-driven process may be appropriate at different stages. However, in order to facilitate our discussion, we will assume that the investor is directing the process.

The document request list itself is not meant to be all-inclusive. Furthermore, if a particular private equity firm or fund, as applicable, does not possess any of these documents, it does not mean that the operational due diligence processes should grind to a halt and the fund should be cast aside. Rather, this list is meant to outline a series of generally agreed-upon documents, each of which focus on the primary operational competencies of a private equity management company and fund, respectively. In reviewing the list, a cautionary word is necessary. First, the names or titles given to a particular document in this list are not necessarily the exact same name that every private equity firm in the world will utilize. Further complicating the issue is that two different private equity managers may call certain documents that are similar in substance, by two different names. Another wrinkle that may appear is that a private equity firm may decide to group analogous procedures and policies into a single document, while another firm may split each of these policies into several different documents. In this way, the initial document request and collection can be a bit like playing one side of Battleship, the famous board game in which players attempt to sink each other's navy by guessing at the positions of ships represented by different squares on a grid, as summarized in Exhibit 3.7.

In much the same way, investors may guess at the appropriate name of a particular document, as used in the context of each private equity organization, in order to unlock access to the document itself.

Now with the appropriate background in place, the following is an outline of a suggested baseline document request list.

For the Private Equity Management Company

I. Core Compliance / Regulatory Documentation:
   1. Compliance Manual
   2. If not included in compliance manual:
      a. Employee personal trading procedures
      b. Electronic communication policy
      c. Antimoney laundering policies and procedures
   3. Form ADV (if U.S. SEC registered)

II. Other management company core documentation:
   4. Organizational charts
   5. Business continuity and disaster recovery plan
   6. Valuation policy and procedures
   7. Certificate of incorporation
   8. Certificate of good standing (if applicable)

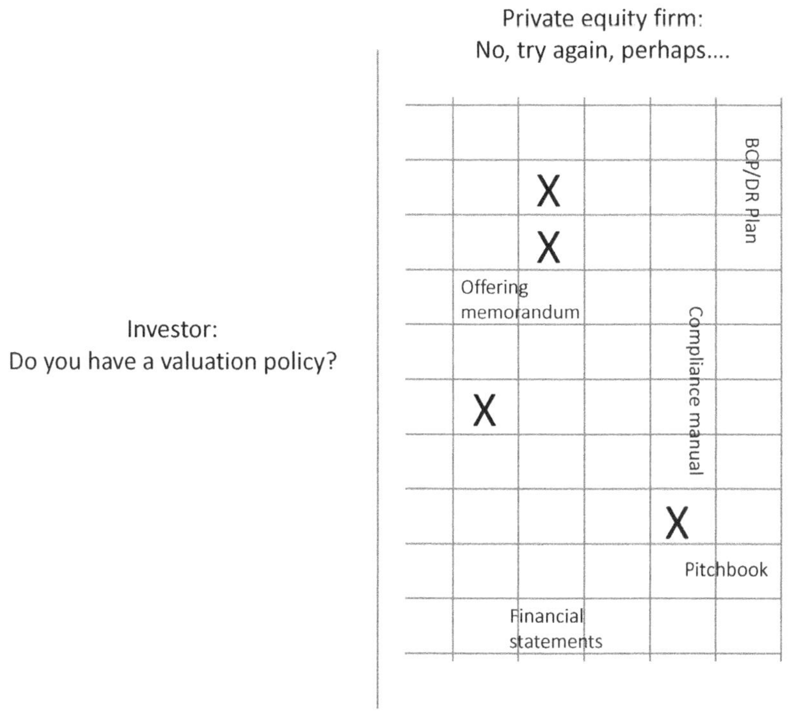

Private equity firm:
No, try again, perhaps....

Investor:
Do you have a valuation policy?

EXHIBIT 3.7 Locating the Appropriate Document May Sometimes Become a Guessing Game for Investors

For the Private Equity Fund(s) under Consideration
III. Core fund legal documentation:
   9. Offering memoranda
   10. Subscription documents
   11. Articles of association (if applicable)
   12. Limited partnership agreement (if applicable)
IV. Other core fund documentation:
   13. Previous similar fund's audited financials (if available)
   14. Letters to investors (e.g., monthly or quarterly) for previous funds (if available)
   15. Performance track record for similar fund's (if applicable)
   16. Samples of recent marketing materials (pitchbook, etc.)
   17. Private equity fund manager provided DDQ
   18. Certificate of formation
   19. Details of insurance coverage (including copies of insurance certificates)

As indicated previously, the document request list outlined is merely meant to be a baseline from which investors can begin the operational document review process. When reviewing this list, investors should be careful not to shoot themselves in the foot before the process starts. One way many investors may become tripped up by such a baseline document list is that they get trapped into a self-limiting request mode. An example of the way in which such a scenario plays itself out, is when a single private equity strategy is being offered via multiple types of investment vehicles. Typically, each of these vehicles is typically created to cater to certain types of investors based on tax status and/or jurisdiction. Generally, each of these investment vehicles is generally managed in substantially the same manner, which is sometimes referred to as a *pari passu* format. While private equity funds, unlike hedge funds, are less likely to be offered in common master-feeder structures, these different private equity investment vehicles may contain different terms. While we delve into a more detailed discussion of legal document analysis in Chapter 6, for now suffice it to say that an investor, at this stage of the game, would do well to collect the legal documents of these pari passu investment vehicles. An investor may raise the following question in this regard, "Why should I be interested in other vehicles in which I am not invested?" There are a number of responses to this, including to make sure that the funds do not have the ability to engage in affiliated transactions and to inquire as to whether one fund may contain significantly different terms. Additionally, the offering memorandum of the pari passu vehicle could contain reference to other entities or affiliated parties that may not be referenced in the offering memorandum of the primary investment vehicle that is being considered for investment. However, as with most items in the world of operational due diligence, you simply do not know if there is anything worth considering in these other documents if you do not collect and review them. Therefore, investors must be cautious not to self-limit themselves by being overly stuck in the mud with regard to baseline document request lists.

In reviewing the previous list, it is also worth noting a unique aspect of private equity investing that directly influences the documents to be collected. The private equity fund under consideration may have already been formed as a legal entity and as such there are generally legal documents for the fund available. However, the fund may not have commenced operations. Without actually having been funded yet by investors or having participated in any deals, the private equity fund on which an investor is performing operational due diligence is effectively not much more than a legal shell. As a legal shell, the fund therefore has not yet been active for the length of a fiscal year and cannot produce audited financial statements, as well as a host of other documents. This is unique challenge for investors seeking to perform operational due diligence on a newly formed private equity fund, but one that is surmountable and not an absolute roadblock. While Chapters 6 and 7 offer discussions of the particular aspects of reviewing legal and financial documents, one common technique that investors can employ when faced with the unique challenge of performing operational due diligence on an as-yet uncreated private equity fund relates to collecting documentation of any previously managed funds. While such an analysis is not a perfect replacement for performing a review of documentation that had been generated specifically for the new fund under consideration, it is often an acceptable, and perhaps the only, substitute. At a minimum, such a review gives an investor a flavor for the documentation format that the new fund under consideration may utilize. Furthermore, a review of such documentation of a previously managed fund will also provide an opportunity for an investor to gauge any specific choices a private equity firm may have made with respect to certain items such as accounting conventions or legal documentation choices.

DOCUMENT COLLECTION NEGOTIATION TECHNIQUES: AVOIDING A PASS-THE-BUCK ENVIRONMENT

In much the same way that there is no secret list of documents investors should request from a private firm, there are no magic words of enfeoffment investors may recite in order to convince a private equity firm to provide such documents. Typically an investor will submit the document request list electronically via e-mail, although such details may very well be communicated via telephone or even in person.

In certain cases, a private equity firm may respond only partially to an investor's request list. Why? you may ask. Are they trying to pull something over on the investor? Giving the private equity firm the benefit of the doubt, there are a multitude of reasons. Providing certain documents while completely ignoring other documents is a negotiation technique that we refer to as *tsunami tactics*.

For those who may be unfamiliar with the term, a tsunami is a very large wave. When an investor first requests documentation from a fund, and the private equity firm begins to reply with such documentation, investors can find themselves virtually drowning in a sea of very voluminous and often complex documentation. In these cases, the burden has now been shifted toward investors to weed through such documentation and figure out exactly what is missing. This investor onus is often multiplied when a private equity firm may be inclined to state that certain of the requested documents are effectively covered in another document. In many cases, the referenced document may only contain scant if any details on the subject that the originally requested document was meant to contain. In these cases, the investor must then review the document and be equipped with enough ammunition to go back to the firm and continue the document negotiation process.

The success of these tsunami tactics is further fueled by an investor-driven phenomenon known as the *piñata problem*. This refers to an investor's perspective when presented with a flood of manager documentation. For the investor, beginning an operational review is a bit like busting open a *piñata* in that an investor does not exactly know what is falling out, but it all looks enticing. This excitement can cause investor's eyes to glaze over and items can get lost in the details, particularly when an investor performing operational due diligence is operating under a tight deadline.

In other cases, in order to limit the burden on a private equity firm, the firm may indicate to investors that they must obtain certain documentation directly from third-party service providers of the firm or previous funds. An example of this might relate to audited financial statements from previously managed funds, which an investor might find useful to collect and review. Some private equity firms may want such audits or other statements related to the previously managed funds to come directly from the administrator or auditor as opposed to directly from the private equity firm. Perhaps they are motivated by mistaken notions of potential liability if such documents were to come directly from the private equity firm as opposed to from the service providers.

Regardless, to equate what the private equity firm is saying to a non-private equity context, this is the equivalent of a customer going into a restaurant, asking the waiter for a glass of water, and the waiter hands the customer a bucket and a map to the nearest well. Not very user-friendly, to say the least. In certain instances, investors may want to collect certain items of documentation directly from a third-party service provider of a private equity firm. However, a key distinction here is that the choice should be the investor's. The private equity firm should not be allowed to skate by with such diversionary tactics. As with most things in the due diligence process, when an investor is faced with such a response they should look skyward for a big bright signal flare. The private equity firm is being just plain lazy at best. At worst, they are betting that an investor will not follow through and follow up on actually contacting the firm, potentially signing off on a service provider provided confidentiality agreement, likely waiting for the private equity firm to sign off on the service provider sharing the documentation with the investor, and then the investor actually receiving the documentation. What if the investor should dare to have a question regarding such documentation that they would like to inquire about with the service provider? Well, the process could be extended even longer. The likely signal, in this case, is that the firm is seeking to make the operational due diligence process difficult. Some private equity firms may even flat-out tell investors who utilize third-party consultants to perform operational due diligence that they do not like the process. Investors should consider this to be a signal to ramp up the due diligence process.

There is an old adage, "You can catch more flies with honey than you can with vinegar." Your author has found that in terms of document collection, this adage is correct. There is no need to begin the process as if it were an adversarial one. However, when a fund starts to put up roadblocks such as those discussed and becomes involved in gamesmanship of the process, then perhaps the adage "Nice guys finish last" is more appropriate. In certain cases, investors should not be afraid to put their foot down and call private equity funds on the carpet. Often a few correctly chosen words or demonstrations that an investor will not put up with shenanigans is enough to show a private equity firm that you are serious about the operational due diligence process and that they should take the process seriously as well.

DOCUMENT COLLECTION: HARD COPY OR ELECTRONIC?

Another point worth noting in regard to the document collection and request process relates to the actual format in which documentation is transmitted from the private equity firm under review. In general, the document request list is transmitted to the fund electronically via e-mail. This is common with most modern communication, as opposed to a long-form, hard-copy letter.

Of course, this same request could be submitted in person or over the phone; however, electronic document request submissions are generally preferred for several reasons. First, as an investor you have a written detailed written record of exactly what documents you may have requested. Second, as suggested earlier, it is more difficult for the fund to fake their way through this list by submitting a partially complete response. However, putting the document request format aside, we can return to the format in which the private equity fund responds, that is, the format or manner in which the requested documents are delivered.

Putting the previously discussed considerations of confidentiality and nondisclosure agreements aside, when faced with a document request list a private equity firm typically has four primary responses for each document requested. The firm can:

1. Provide the document in the same form requested (e.g., if an e-mail was sent requesting the document, the fund can provide the document electronically).
2. Advise the investor that the firm adheres to a policy of not distributing that particular document but the investor may review the document in the firm's offices during an on-site meeting.
3. Refuse to provide the document.
4. Provide the document in one of the more difficult-to-manage formats (e.g., hard copy).

The reader's eyes are not deceiving them with regard to the last option. As unbelievable as it might seem in the twenty-first century, certain private equity firms still believe it is appropriate to distribute documentation in hard copy format. Likely a chief motivation for submitting hard-copy document, as opposed to an electronic one, is confidentiality. Perhaps private equity funds are also concerned that if information is submitted to an investor electronically an investor may be inclined, with a few clicks of the mouse, to forward the document to other parties.

While the intention behind both of these concerns is certainly grounded in laudable notions from an operational risk perspective (e.g., protecting confidential information), unfortunately, technology has evolved past the point of making hard copy transmission of materials any sort of hurdle toward sharing such documentation and protecting confidentiality. The best way to perhaps illustrate this point is by example. In the early days of the modern private equity era, investors may have been forced to review all documents in hard copy. Then along came an invention called the mimeograph machine. This allowed copies of documents to be made. Therefore, an investor did not need to review an original document from the fund but could rather review a replica.

Similarly, an investor could make their own mimeograph (e.g., photocopy) and send it along to a friend unbeknownst to the private equity firm. Of course, modern photocopy technology still allows for copies to be made—strike one against the so-called security of hard copies. The reader may ask, "What about watermarked documents?" We will get to this in a moment. But assume for the sake of argument that documents are not encoded with any watermarks or other security technology that would, for instance, prevent photocopying.

Fast forward to modern times and consider a private equity firm that, despite an investor's best efforts to convince a private equity fund otherwise, adheres to a policy of providing certain documents solely in hard copy. The investor then patiently waits by the mailbox, and one day finally receives the requested document in hard copy. Then, perhaps for the ease of electronic storage, potentially enhanced searchability once the document is in electronic form, and a host of other benefits, an investor then runs the document through a scanner. Yes, the modern scanner is a widely available and cost-effective tool that has just circumvented the fund's half-hearted attempt at protecting information. There are a number of better methods the fund could have used to protect this information without the inconvenience and delays of the hard-copy document distribution process.

In order to put in place increased document security, while at the same time streamlining the process for investors and not involving third parties, a private equity fund could easily send documents electronically with a host of identifying and security measures. Common document security measures can include watermarking the electronic document with the investor's contact information, defining a time after which the document is no longer accessible, and password-protecting the document. There are also a number of other benefits that a private equity firm can realize by implementing these types of document security controls, including increased tracking of where investors' documents are sent, which is often an added benefit, and in some jurisdictions a requirement, for compliance purposes.

However, the implementation of such procedures requires the fund to be up to speed with modern technology, which some private equity firms are not. Additionally, such electronic document security measures also require a little bit of effort to actually implement, beyond simply buying the technology, to install these security measures, which some private equity funds do not want to exert.

The next time a private equity firm insists on providing certain documentation only in hard copy to an investor, the investor may do well to have a reasoned discussion with the firm. If the firm cannot provide a thorough explanation, then perhaps this is a signal of a lack of adaptability in other operational areas as well.

Due Diligence Questionnaires: Uses and Considerations

In reviewing the previously referenced document request list, the reader may notice the inclusion of "Private equity fund manager provided due diligence questionnaire." Indeed, if the private equity firm does not automatically volunteer such a document. One of the most initially useful documents investors will likely receive when performing due diligence on a private equity fund is the due diligence questionnaire, which is also known as a

DDQ. The DDQ we are discussing in this case is one that has the private equity manager has prepared on their own accord and not at the request of any specific investor. Such due diligence questionnaires are created with the intention of making a generic questionnaire that can be distributed to every investor. Often, such DDQs may attempt to address many of the most common topics covered during both the investment and operational due diligence processes. DDQs are essentially the highlights of the firm's most frequently asked questions—or, that is to say, the ones the private equity fund wants to answer. Many investors may fail to realize that DDQs, just like pitchbooks, are marketing documents. A competent private equity manager will most likely attempt to present the information in the DDQ in the most positive light possible.

This DDQ provided by a private equity fund manager should be contrasted with a DDQ that an investor will provide to a private equity fund and ask them to complete. When considering these options, many investors often raise the question of whether they should require a private equity fund to complete their own DDQ, sometimes called a request for proposal (RFP), or whether it is sufficient to rely on the manager-provided DDQ. In regard to the operational aspect of due diligence, there has been a growing trend in recent years not to require a private equity manager to complete a custom operational DDQ. Despite some shortcomings, these manager-provided DDQs are often good starting points for the process. Before asking a hedge fund manager to complete a DDQ or RFP, investors should bear in mind the following issues:

- What is the goal in having the manager complete your particular DDQ or RFP?
- How will you follow up with a manager who responds vaguely or to a different question than the one presented in the DDQ? Will you require new responses in writing?
- Will you accept a previously prepared DDQ in lieu of your specific format? How will you determine when a manager-provided DDQ meets this standard?
- How will you incorporate the information from the DDQ into your larger due diligence process?
- How often do you anticipate having the manager update the DDQ?

In addition to these questions, there are a number of other considerations that investors should take into account, with regard to the question of whether to ask a fund to complete a bespoke DDQ:

- An off-the-shelf investor questionnaire often results in similarly generic responses.

- When investors require custom DDQ completion, the element of surprise during the due diligence process is often lost, as investors are effectively showing their hand by revealing questions in advance.
- Many investors have a tendency to use the DDQ as a crutch and in place of extensive operational due diligence.
- The opportunity for the give-and-take of an in-depth operational due diligence process is often lost when due diligence is conducted primarily via DDQs or RFPs.

A final word regarding DDQs: Often when an investor asks a fund manager to complete a customized DDQ on their behalf, investors run the very real risk of falling into a so-called *copy and paste mentality*. This occurs when a private equity fund manager, perhaps by copying and pasting information from their own DDQ into an investor's DDQ, completes a customized DDQ on behalf of a particular investor. The investor reviewing this questionnaire may then be very tempted to either take this information at face value with no further inquiry, or simply cut and paste the relevant pieces of this information into their own documentation of the due diligence process. This is an example of a garbage in, garbage out process that simply results in the investor's due diligence processes being reduced to an exercise in language manipulation as opposed to due diligence. Investors who are aware of such pitfalls can navigate the process accordingly to devote the bulk of their efforts toward developing an understanding of and inquiring about operational procedures, as opposed to simply regurgitating a private equity fund manager's own descriptions about their own processes.

Beginning the Document Review Process: Document Errors

Some readers may have experienced, from their university or parochial days, instructors who took a relatively hard line toward grading papers. These professors adhered to a strict policy of reading a student's paper up until the point where they encountered a basic error in grammar or spelling. One of the underlying premises is that if a student could not take the basic precautionary measures and check their paper for basic spelling and grammar, then the professor should not extend the student the courtesy of continuing to read the paper. The professor may either fail the student entirely or award credit for the student's paper up only until the point where the error was detected.

Now, what does any of this have to do with operational due diligence? If such a standard were applied to operational due diligence it is likely that many investor due diligence reviews of a private equity fund's materials would be stalled before they started.

Private equity firms and funds, just like investors, are not infallible. While both groups are indeed error-prone, in the context of the document review portion of the operational due diligence process, the focus is on any documentation errors made by the private equity firm in preparing those documents. From the private equity firm's perspective, such errors may be understandable. After all, it is often difficult for one to check their own work, and a private equity firm may be too close to its own documentation to realize certain errors that are apparent from an outsider's, such as an investor's, perspective. While understandable, it certainly does not mean that all such errors are excusable.

Documentation errors can be grouped into two basic classifications. The first such type of documentation error is the previously mentioned rudimentary grammar and spelling errors. There is not much to say about such errors, other than the fact that the presence of too many mistakes suggests a lack of oversight in document preparation and a generally sloppy attitude. If a private equity firm cannot even prepare an error-free document, how can an investor be sure they will not make mistakes in basic operational processes?

The second type of error relates to factually incorrect or stale information. Instances of these errors occur when a document provided by the private equity firm is an inaccurate description of actual practices in place. An example of this would be a manager-provided DDQ that describes a firm that requires two signatory approvals for all cash transfers but which, during the operational due diligence process, is revealed to require only one signatory. The statement in the DDQ is factually incorrect. Another type of related error as referenced earlier is stale information. Stale information can come about in a number of different ways. The most common is when a private equity firm does not update certain materials frequently enough to reflect changes within an organization. One example could be when a firm no longer utilizes a certain service provider and has switched to a new one—such as external legal counsel—but has not reflected this information in documents such as their fund-offering memorandum or manager-provided DDQ. Another common type of document error that typically results from stale information arises when employees have departed a firm but they are still referenced in certain documentation. This error may frequently arise in documents that a private equity manager updates with less frequency, such as a business continuity and disaster recovery plan. Such plans typically contain chains of command or call-tree lists that reference individuals by name. Upon the departure of an individual from the firm, a private equity firm's personnel may have taken care to remove this individual's name from documents that may be deemed to be more investor-facing such as DDQs, but may be less likely to revise documents such as a business continuity and disaster recovery plan.

It is worth noting that the purpose of this discussion is not to suggest that the vast majority of private equity firms do not put thought into preparing their documents or take reasonable precautions in ensuring these documents are free of errors. However, the point of this discussion is to provide investors with insight into the fact that they must be vigilant in reviewing documents for such errors. After all, isn't that part of the point of the entire operational due diligence process? If investors could be assured that all documents were error-free, then part of the function of the necessity of due diligence process would be obviated.

So what is an investor supposed to do when they come across some errors? Well, a good first step is not to simply ignore them. An investor should make an ongoing list of such documentation errors. A process that investors frequently follow in coming to an operational determination as to the overall levels of operational risk present at a private equity manager, the sum total of these errors should be evaluated cumulatively. In isolation any one of these errors may not be damming but viewed together, perhaps the sheer numbers of such errors or the type of such errors may be enough to shift an investor's conviction one way or another.

FUND MANAGER ON-SITE DUE DILIGENCE CONSIDERATIONS

In the broad five-stage operational process, after document collection and analysis comes the on-site meeting. On-site visits are of paramount importance in the operational due diligence process. Investors seeking to cut corners, due to cost or resource constraints would be ill-advised to cut back in the area of the on-site visit. First, even in this world of free Internet-based satellite maps, the most obvious reason is to confirm that the fund manager actually maintains an office. An on-site visit also provides an investor with the opportunity to confirm the size and scale of the fund manager's internal office space—an area that satellite photos may be of little help in viewing. Insights that can be gained in this area can facilitate answering a number of questions including:

- Is the fund manager's space shared or subleased to any entities that were conveniently not referenced in any of the fund's documentation?
- Does the firm claim to have 50 employees but show only 20 desks?

- Is everyone conveniently out to lunch or on vacation during the day of the on-site visit?
- Is secure access maintained to the firm's offices?
- Is secure access maintained to certain areas such as server rooms?

Another benefit of the on-site visit is the additional information that can be garnered via face-to-face communication. Operational due diligence is one of the areas that can suffer greatly from an attempt to replace on-site visits with web conferences, video conferencing, or teleconferencing. In certain instances such conferencing options may support on-site meeting follow-up. However, investors should not try to use technology to replace the benefits of face-to-face communication. During an on-site visit investors can gauge people's reactions—facial and body language and other signals—to certain questions.

Additionally, on a conference call, these types of conversations often take place among several individuals at once. In such large groups, the candor and frankness of a private equity firm's operational employee may be tempered as to not express any negative or controversial opinions that he might otherwise express in a one-on-one, in-person setting. Additionally, in the real world there is no pause or mute button available. A more genuine reaction is obtained via in-person communications. Furthermore, an investor's presence in an office affords the opportunity for any operational systems to be observed by the investor or their operational due diligence representative. While it is possible to demonstrate systems and technology that may be employed in a private equity firm's operations during web conferencing, such demonstrations can be rehearsed and manufactured. The prepackaged nature of such web presentations is a poor substitute for an actual on-site observation.

Now that we provided an overview of the benefits of investor's performing on-site visits to a private equity manager during the course of the operational due diligence process, we can next discuss certain considerations that investors should have in mind when approaching scheduling of the on-site visit. Similar to the document collection process, discussions between investors and private equity managers can often provide signaling insights into a manager's attitude toward the operational due diligence process.

When scheduling an on-site visit dedicated to operational due diligence in particular, a private equity firm, depending on their approach, may hear the word operational and immediately assume that an investor need only meet with people with some version of the word "operational" in their title. Such a response is, of course, ridiculous, but one that your author has observed, in one shape or another, on multiple occasions. Another common response is those who may be more comfortable discussing the merits of a private equity fund's portfolio and less comfortable about traditional operational areas and may scatter as soon as an investor approaches to perform operational due diligence. This may sometimes be seen among investor relations personnel. Perhaps motivated by fear that they are beyond their primary domain of expertise, they may think it best to defer to more traditional operations personnel, such as a chief operating officer or chief financial officer. While they may be well-intentioned, as investor relations personnel most certainly are, they often miss the point that they can be helpful during the operational due diligence process. The value of investor relations and client service personnel can come both in the form of the information they possess as well as the ability they may have to assist investors in navigating the on-site meeting process in general.

When scheduling the on-site meeting, another common inquiry that investor relations may ask is "How long is this going to take?" Once again, such a question may seem harmless and well-intentioned. This is particularly in light of some investors' belief that the amount of time spent on-site during an operational due diligence visit directly correlates to the quality of the review. Such investor beliefs are misplaced, and this commonly held misconception is illustrated in Exhibit 3.8.

Rather, there is a point beyond which such on-site meetings can result in diminishing returns or even in damaging the ongoing relationship between the investor and the private equity firm, which is required to complete the

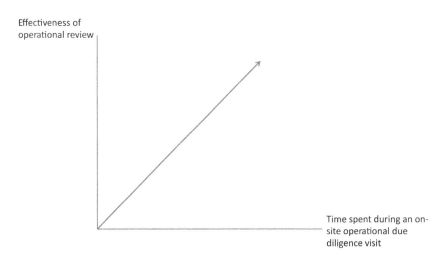

EXHIBIT 3.8 Misconception That There Is a Positive Correlation between Increased On-Site Meeting Length and the Effectiveness of an On-Site Operational Due Diligence Review

post-on-site operational due diligence review process. There is no magic number of hours for how long an on-site operational due diligence visit should or must take. The length of time required is often contingent in part on several factors, including the transparency of the private equity firm in sharing documentation prior to the on-site meeting, and the amount of time the investor spent preparing for the on-site meeting. An unprepared investor will likely spend more time covering basic operational issues, as compared to one who has devoted a significant amount of time to preparing for the meeting who can instead focus more on why strategic operational decisions were made as opposed to the operational basics that may be covered relatively quickly by an informed investor. Similarly, an investor could be willing to put the time in to prepare prior to the on-site meeting; however, if the private equity firm has minimal documentation or if they attempt to stonewall the investor by sharing virtually nothing in advance, then the on-site meeting will necessarily take longer because the investor had little to work with prior to the on-site meeting.

Returning to our "How long is this going to take?" question, depending on the context in which it is asked as well as the tone, such a response can once again have a direct signaling effect. The signal that can be sent is that a private equity firm is not really interested in seizing a particular opportunity to demonstrate their operational strengths to a particular investor and instill the strong sense of confidence that a fund may have in its operations, but rather just going through the motions with the hopes that they "pass the test" and secure an allocation.

KEY RISK CONSIDERATION AREAS TO COVER

The baseline document request list was designed around the common areas that investors are likely to cover. This process is intended to be more goal-driven as opposed to focusing on any particular document or operational concern. To facilitate our understanding of how each of these key operational risk areas may be covered during an on-site private equity fund manager visit, it is to discuss the types of questions that may be asked.

The following list of questions is by no means all-inclusive. Rather, questions have been included that should provide an introductory overview of each key risk area. Generic questions such as "What are your firm's advantages as compared to peers?" have been omitted from the list. Such open-ended questions definitely can add value during the operational due diligence process, but for ease of analysis they have been omitted.

Firmwide Issues

- Have any partners or founders of the firm since departed the firm?
- Provide a detail of any affiliated entities.
- Are any members of the firm related? Does the firm maintain a policy on relatives working together? If so, how does it prevent potential conflicts of interest?
- What is the alignment of interests between the firm and its investors? Amount of principal and employee capital invested? Deferred compensation structure, and so forth?
- Side letters: Do other investors have them? What are their terms?
- Is the private equity firm locked into any long-term contracts, such as office space leases, technology service contracts, and so on?

Assets Under Management

- What are the current assets under management for the firm? For each fund?
- What were the assets under management a year ago for the firm? For each fund?
- What has been the peak of assets under management? When was it reached?
- What is the breakout of investors by investor type in the firm? In each fund?
- What is the geographical breakout of the firm's investor base?
- What is the anticipated investor pipeline for the current private equity fund under review?
- When is the first anticipated closing date for the fund? Is it a hard close or a soft close?
- What percentage of assets under management do the following represent (as a percentage of both firm and fund assets under management):
  - Largest investor
  - Three largest investors

Personnel and Employee Turnover

- Provide details of historical employee turnover (additions and departures).
- Does the firm have any additional planned hires?
- If the firm indicates that someone has left on good terms, can you contact this former employee as a reference?
- What does the firm do to ensure retention of key employees? Are non-compete agreements utilized?

Legal and Compliance

- What is the structure of the firm's compliance organization?
- Are employees dedicated solely to compliance or do they have shared responsibilities?
- Does the firm work with any third-party compliance consultants?
- If registered with any regulatory entities, does the firm work with any third-party compliance consultants?
- Is any compliance training performed? If yes, what topics are covered by compliance training?
- Do you perform any electronic communication monitoring?
- What are the general policies regarding employee personal account dealing?
  - Is a restricted list maintained?
  - Are minimum holding periods in place?
  - Is pretrade approval required?
  - What sort of posttrade reviews are conducted?
- Has there been any previous litigation against the firm, fund, or any employees?
- Is there any pending litigation against the firm, fund, or any employee(s)?
- Are third-party research networks utilized? If so, what measures has the firm taken with regards to material nonpublic information?
  - Is a restricted list maintained?

Insurance Coverage

- What types of insurance coverage does the firm maintain?
- What are the terms of this coverage?
- Which carriers provide this coverage?
- What are the amounts of such coverage? How did the firm determine these amounts?
- Does the private equity fund self-insure for anything (as opposed to obtaining third-party coverage)?
- Has the firm ever issued a claim on any of its insurance policies?

Firm and Employee Reputation

- What is the employment history of the firm's senior management? Did they leave their previous firms on good terms? Can they provide references?
- Is there anything in senior managements' past that is noteworthy from a reputational risk perspective (e.g., criminal convictions, sanctions by regulators, etc.)?

- Is senior management involved in any current litigation or disputes that may be distracting (e.g., a messy divorce, dissolution of former business partnerships, etc.)?
- Does senior management have any outside business interests? If yes, what is the nature of these interests? How much of senior management's time do they take?

Counterparty Oversight

- Does the firm have any existing relationships with trading counterparties?
- What counterparty relationships are anticipated for the new private equity fund under consideration?
- What is the review and approval process for new counterparties to be added to the firm?
- Where are new counterparties sourced from?
- Does the firm have an existing counterparty review process? If yes, how frequently are existing counterparties reviewed? Who at the firm is responsible for conducting existing counterparty reviews?

Transparency and Fund Reporting

- What types of reporting does the firm anticipate distributing to investors in the new private equity fund?
- What is the timing with which such reports will be distributed?
- What is the method of delivery of such statements (e.g., via e-mail or via a centralized investor relations website)?
- Does the firm adhere to a practice of distributing performance estimates for funds?
- When have audited financial statements historically been available?
- Have there been any historical fund performance restatements? If yes, what happened?

Technology and Systems

- What third-party and proprietary systems are currently in place?
- What types of hardware are utilized (e.g., desktop PCs and servers) systems are utilized?
- Have any systems been customized or upgraded by the firm? Are there any plans to do so?
- What are examples of the types of problems that arise with the firm's current systems?

Information Security

- What are the firm's information security defenses?
- What kinds of firewalls are in place?
- Does the firm, either itself or via a third-party provider, perform penetration testing?
- Does the firm, either itself or via a third-party provider, perform social network type penetration testing?
- Does the firm log employee network activity?
- Has the firm taken any steps to monitor employee usage profiles to monitor for unusual computer usage or director access?
- Is the use of remote storage devices such as zip drives permitted?
- How often are employees required to change their network passwords?

Personnel and Employee Turnover

- Provide details of historical employee turnover (additions and departures).
- Does the firm have any additional planned hires?
- If the firm indicates that someone has left on good terms, can you contact this former employee as a reference?
- What does the firm do to ensure retention of key employees? Are non-compete agreements utilized?

Business Continuity Planning and Disaster Recovery (BCP/DR)

- Does the firm maintain written BCP/DR procedures?
- Is the plan tested? If so, how often? When was the most recent test?
- Are BCP/DR plans tested from a technology perspective solely or are personnel tests employed as well?
- Who is in charge of updating the plans?
- What are the firm's data backup capabilities?
- Does the firm have backup power-generation facilities?
- Does the private equity firm have a disruption gathering location?
- Has the private equity firm ever had to activate its BCP/DR plan? If yes, what happened?
- If the private equity firm has multiple offices, how are these offices supposed to coordinate with each other in the event of a business disruption in either location?

Quality Roles of Service Providers

- What service providers do you anticipate utilizing for the current private equity fund for which you are raising capital?
- How long have you worked with your current service providers?

- What services do you receive from each of your service providers?
- How long have you worked with your current service providers?
- Are you happy with your service providers or are you thinking of switching?
- What are the terms and length of contract with your service providers?
- Have you experienced any turnover of personnel at the service provider that has impacted the level of service the fund receives?

CONCLUSION

This chapter provides an introduction to some of the primary issues an investor should consider when beginning the operational due diligence review process for private equity funds. The process should begin with goal self-assessment so that investors ensure that they design an operational due diligence process that comports with their notion of the process. With these goals in mind, investors should next consider the anticipated process scope and then proceed to consider operational due diligence resource allocation. As part of this framework selection design process, investors should consider framework design and selection considerations. With a firm grounding in goals and process, an investor can next begin the document-collection process. As part of this process, this chapter covered common document request items as well as the ways in which signaling effects can provide insights as to potential operational issues. Additionally, this chapter outlines some of the document collection considerations surrounding confidentiality agreements, as well as the role of negotiation in the document collection process. Finally, this chapter provides an overview of on-site visit considerations, as well as an introduction to the baseline types of issues that investors should cover during the operational due diligence process. With such a measured approach, investors will be able to build a strong foundation for a thorough operational due diligence process for private equity funds.

NOTES

1. See David Sloss, *The U.S. Supreme Court and International Law: Continuity or Change* (Cambridge University Press, 2011), 26.
2. See Scott Besley, *Essentials of Managerial Finance* (Thomson South-Western, 2008), 516.
3. See Bryan A. Garner, *A Dictionary of Modern Legal Usage 2nd Edition* (Oxford University Press, 2001), 384.
4. See George Frederick Wharton, *Legal Maxims, with Observations and Cases* (Baker, Voorhis & Co., 1878), 279.

4

Additional Operational Due Diligence Considerations: An Expanded Analysis

This goal of this chapter is to introduce some additional operational due diligence techniques that are available when investors are seeking to increase the scope and depth of their operational due diligence reviews. In Chapter 3, we provide an overview of some of the basic considerations that may be in place with regard to beginning the operational due diligence process. As part of this introduction we covered some basic documents an investor might seek to collect during the operational due diligence process. We also introduced several basic topic-focused questions investors may seek to cover during the initial stages of the operational due diligence review. Building upon this foundation, we can now move toward discussing the process expansion into a more comprehensive framework.

CORE ISSUES VERSUS EXPANDED ANALYSIS

Earlier in this book, we consider the notions of a *below-core*, *core*, and *expanded* operational risk theoretical resource allocation paradigms. With a firm introduction to the core process already established, we can next proceed to an outline of the expanded review. The expanded review process seeks to build upon an investor's core process, such as by broadening the scope of the operational due diligence in a number of ways. An example of expanded risk analysis is compared to a core process in Exhibit 4.1.

It is worth noting a few points regarding Exhibit 4.1. An investor may object to the classification of certain operational risk categories. That is to say, investors may consider certain operational risk categories to be more appropriately placed in the expanded column than in the core column or

EXHIBIT 4.1   Comparison of Core and Expanded Processes

Risk Category	Core	Expanded
General firm overview	√	√
Assets under management review	√	√
Trade flow analysis	√	√
Cash oversight, management and transfer controls	√	√
Compliance infrastructure	√	√
Valuation policies and processes	√	√
Legal/Compliance	√	√
Regulatory	√	√
Quality and appropriateness of fund service providers	√	√
Reporting	√	√
Technology and systems	×	√
Information security	×	√
Human capital	×	√
Business continuity and disaster recovery	×	√
Operations connectivity	×	√
Tax practices	×	√
Insurance	×	√
Counterparty management	×	√
Human capital	×	√
Administration/administration agreement	×	√
Fund reporting	×	√

vice versa. Consider for example the operational risk category for technology and systems. Some investors may feel that a private equity firm's information technology function is so crucially important that this category should be placed in the core process review camp as opposed to the expanded review. This investor may be perfectly correct. The point of comparing the core and expanded categories is not to say that one should be focused on one at the expense of the other. Rather, this is intended to suggest a starting point from which an investor may develop his or her own operational due diligence process. In certain instances, an investor may be justified in adding technology and systems to the core category.

Another way in which an investor may transition from a core review to an expanded process is to increase the depth of the review across existing core operational risk categories. Of course, the ability to conduct such increasing depth core expanded reviews may be limited in scope by the particulars of the fund itself. For example, an investor may want to fully vet certain operational risk areas, such as custody, but may be limited by the operational practices of the fund itself. An investor during a core review process may have inquired about whether the fund held self-custody of any assets. If the investor was pursuing a more expanded review process, they may want to dig deeper by inquiring about the details of the custodial relationship, such as attempting to confirm a private equity firm's balances with a custodian, gain an understanding of fees charged, have a discussion or on-site visit with the custodian to understand their processes and procedures, discuss the ways in which assets are overseen, and even collect and review a copy of the service level agreement (SLA) between the private equity fund and the custodian. Anything beyond this level of review is really a function of the operational particulars of each unique private equity firm. As such, there is only so far an investor can dig into a particular operational issue from a generic perspective, beyond which the operational risk factor must be viewed in the context of the fund under review itself. An example of such a transition from a core process to a more expanded process in a particular operational risk category, the custody category in this case, is outlined in Exhibit 4.2.

Additionally, an investor may still also want to transition to blend by casting a larger net as compared to a core process (e.g., increasing scope) but limit the increase in scope to such a degree that increased depth across each of the new total set of examined operational risk factors is now covered, as

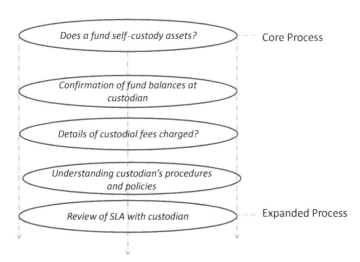

EXHIBIT 4.2   Example of Core to Expanded Process Transition through Increasing Depth in the Particular Operational Risk Category of Custody

compared to the previously more shallow coverage across each operational risk factor in the core review.

COMPENSATION STRUCTURES

A key area that is typically included in most investor's operational due diligence reviews of a private equity firm relates to employee compensation. The question of compensation, from the investor's perspective, effectively boils down to three primary questions. The first question relates to the ways in which the existing fund employees are compensated. This is of particular importance for an investor approaching a private equity firm during the due diligence process for a newly forming private equity fund.

The question of compensation is focused on the alignment of interest between a private equity employee and the fund in which they will be involved. Such an alignment of interest is often paramount for investors. Investors generally believe that a private equity employee whose compensation is directly tied to the performance of a particular fund will work harder on that fund than they would a fund whose performance may only tangentially affect their compensation. Furthermore, many investors generally hold the belief that private equity employees will be more incentivized to act in the best interests of the fund, as opposed to their own best interests, if their compensation is directly linked to fund performance.

The second of the three primary questions related to compensation is, "Does the firm offer compensation packages that are competitive enough to attract top talent?" If the answer to this question is no, then an investor must question how the private equity firm is going to continue to grow to attract either seasoned analysts from other firms who may be a useful addition to the current firm, and perhaps more effectively participate in portfolio oversight and help to generate increased fund returns.

The third and final compensation question is whether an employee's compensation will vest over a specified period of time. Vesting is a technique whereby compensation does not become immediately available to an employee unless certain goals are met. This is a type of deferred compensation scheme that seeks to reward employees throughout the life of a particular private equity fund. By deferring compensation over a long period of time, and more closely aligning long-term compensation with fund performance, vesting can also seek to promote employees' focus on sustained profitability throughout the lifetime of a fund.

There are a number of different approaches to vesting private equity firms, such as time vesting and performance vesting.[1] *Time vesting* refers to a concept whereby compensation will continue to vest as long as an employee remains with the firm. If the employee departs, the vesting period ceases. In certain cases, depending on the termination devices employed, the employee may receive only their prorated portion of the full amount to the degree with which vesting occurred. Another option may be *cliff vesting*, whereby an employee who is not fully vested (i.e., departs before the full vesting period is complete) receives nothing. *Performance vesting* refers to a concept whereby vesting will occur based on the achievement of certain performance-related targets. Common performance vesting targets can include yearly performance targets for the private equity fund itself. Another type of performance target for the private equity fund itself is so-called *catch-up performance vesting* whereby performance targets are aggregated over the entire vesting period to allow for a fund to potentially catch up for early poor performance. In addition to performance vesting targets related to the performance of a private equity fund itself, so too may performance metrics be linked to the underlying performance of portfolio companies of a particular private equity fund itself. Examples of such a performance metric may be tied to notional enterprise value or variations of EBITDA.

Employee compensation is a rich and sometimes complex subject that investors should take care to analyze during the operational due diligence process. In addition to the three questions outlined, there are a host of other related compensation issues and ways in which a private equity firm may add additional bells and whistles to the compensation process. As suggested earlier, one of the core issues that investors should focus on in evaluating these compensation issues should be to evaluate whether there is a true alignment of interests between employees and the private equity funds that they may be working on.

INTRODUCTION TO PRIVATE EQUITY FUND FEES

Another area that investors should focus on in the operational due diligence process relates to fees. Depending on the structure of the private equity fund that an investor is analyzing, a number of different fees may be assessed to investors. There are some common issues related to most fees that investors should consider. The first of these relates to the actual number of fees charged. For example, an investor may be willing to tolerate a higher management fee if it is only one of the fees charged. Some funds may try to nickel-and-dime investors via a host of smaller fees that, in or of themselves, may seem smaller, at least smaller than the management fee (continuing our example), but in aggregate are larger in magnitude. Examples of these other fees that can sometimes rear their heads in real estate funds in particular can include asset management fees, income performance fees, forward commitment performance fees, and property management fees.

Another general consideration regarding fees is the timing of fee collection. The two basic options are whether the fees are collected in advance or in arrears. Collection in advance means that the funds are collected at the *beginning of a period*. Collection in arrears refers to a concept where fees are collected at the *end of the period*. If fees are collected in advance, it is generally considered less beneficial for investors primarily because of the time value of money. Investors are required to part with the money allocated to the fee sooner than they would have had to if the fees were collected in arrears.

Another consideration relates to the potential for the linking of any fees to benchmarks or subject to high-water marks or hurdle rates. The latter two considerations are particularly applicable to carried interest fee calculations.

MANAGER INVESTMENT IN FUNDS

Earlier in this chapter, we provide a basic overview of compensation structures related to private equity funds. In particular, one area of focus that is often highlighted during the operational due diligence process relates to the alignment of interest between private equity employees and the performance of a particular private equity fund. A related issue, which is often paramount in investor's minds, is how much capital the private equity employees themselves have invested in the firm's funds. Such concerns in this area are generally focused around the senior management of the private equity firm including the fund managers themselves. The point of this inquiry, from a due diligence perspective, is to once again gauge the alignment of interests between the private equity firm employee and the fund's interests.

While the private equity manager may indeed have a duty—fiduciary, legal, or otherwise—to act in the best interest of investors, many consider such an alignment of interests to be crucial. The theory behind this is such that an employee whose compensation is tied to the fund has so-called *skin in the game*, which can motivate them not only to perhaps act in the best interests of the fund but to generate stellar performance as well. It is worth noting that in regard to private equity funds, as a particular fund may be in the process of being funded, an investor may also commonly look at how much capital a private equity firm's employees and principals are anticipated to allocate to a particular fund.

Assuming that this premise is valid, we should next consider the question of how much is enough. Certain investment organizations may have hard rules in place regarding these capital requirements. These rules may come in the form of actual dollar requirements. Other investors may approach such requirements with a percentage-based analysis. For example, a private equity firm's principals and employees must consist of at least 5 percent of the newly formed fund's assets under management during the time of the first funding close; otherwise an investor may not invest. There is no single magic answer to the question of, "How much skin in the game is enough?" Different investors may develop their appropriate internal guidelines to such questions. A good opportunity to establish such guidelines is during the creation of an investor's operational due diligence program. It is at this stage when investors are less likely to be led into gray areas that may blur their original operational due diligence program guidelines.

Returning to the subject of due diligence upon the amount of principal and employee capital invested in the firm's funds, whether dollar or percentage guidelines are imposed, it is worth considering the ways in which a private equity fund may respond to inquiries on this issue. As Chapter 3 outlines, operational due diligence is a process that can involve give-and-take between investors and private equity firms. In certain cases, the private equity firm may attempt to erect informational roadblocks that can impede the effectiveness of an investor's operational due diligence work. A common roadblock is raised by private equity funds when posed with the question of how much capital a particular fund manager may have invested and/or is anticipated to invest in the newly formed private equity fund. Often an investor may be faced with a response such as "Our portfolio managers have invested a significant portion of their liquid net worth in the firm's funds."

While perhaps well-intentioned, such a response is effectively useless to investors seeking to evaluate in any real way the alignment of interests among the portfolio managers and the firm's funds. When presented with such an informational roadblock, investors can perhaps better gauge the financial commitment of the portfolio managers by looking for more of a quantitative metric in response to the question "What percentage of fund capital is represented by principals and employees?" The combination of the interplay of such two questions is an example of technique that we will refer to as *backdooring* and which we discuss in more detail in the question design section of this chapter.

EVALUATING SERVICE PROVIDERS

In order to evaluate the quality of service providers, investors must first understand exactly what service providers they are going to analyze. The term *service provider* may have different meaning and scope depending on an investor's perspective. Most investors would likely include a third-party firm such as a private equity fund's auditor. To broaden the scope a bit, an investor could also include legal counsel among the list of a private equity fund's service providers that she analyzes as part of the due diligence process. However, what about a third-party administrator? Does this fall within a core review process? Many investors would likely say yes. When we broaden the scope even further, it tends to get into a grayer area. Consider, for example, a third-party service provider such as an information-technology consultant utilized by a private equity manager. Would this fall into the scope of a core review? Some investors may not think so. Instead, others would say it is important to review such a service provider.

To play devil's advocate, some investors may go so far as to ask, who cares? After all, if a private equity fund utilizes a subpar information technology consultant there isn't any sort of potential for fund losses. Is there? We can table this question for now (the answer is yes, by the way), but, for the purposes of our discussion, we will instead focus on which service providers would potentially be included in an investor's operational due diligence review. Broadening the scope even further, we can look at service providers such as insurance carriers. Now an investor may be asking, "Wait a minute, an insurance carrier—that's not a real service provider." Certainly insurance carriers are real service providers, but more important for the purposes of this discussion some investors could likely broaden the scope, perhaps in an expanded review, to a private equity firm and fund's insurance carriers. The question comes down to how broadly an investor will define such service providers. An example of such a broadening process is outlined in Exhibit 4.3.

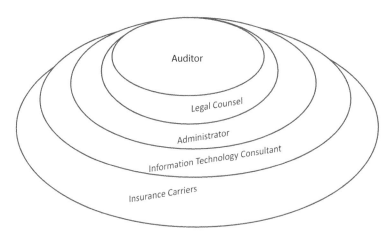

EXHIBIT 4.3 Example of Broadening Scope of Service Provider Definitions

Regardless of the scope of the review employed, before analyzing any service providers, it is useful for investors to ensure that they have an understanding of the basic functions of service providers. Before progressing with a discussion of service providers, however, it is also important to consider any specific relationships a private equity fund under consideration by a potential investor may have. This is a point worth highlighting—a private equity firm may have certain service provider relationships that are not directly applicable to the private equity fund under consideration and vice versa. Now, this is not to say that it is not appropriate (and not advisable) to evaluate these relationships, but that the nature of the relationship (as to between the fund and firm) should be distinguishable. An administrator is a good example of this. An administrator has a relationship with a fund, not a firm. Investors will not ordinarily invest in a private equity firm; they will invest in a fund. This is not to imply that an investor should not inquire into service providers on both the fund and firm levels. However, it is important for investors to understand these firm and fund distinctions, particularly when delving into the scope of service provider relationships.

With this caveat out of the way, we can now begin our discussion of private equity fund service providers. Common service providers utilized by private equity firms and funds include the auditor, administrator, legal counsel, custodian, information technology providers, compliance consultants, and cash-management firms. We discuss the respective roles of each of these service providers in the sections that follow.

Auditor

From a traditional perspective, private equity fund auditors have been primarily responsible for overseeing the maintenance of a private equity fund's official books and records. Auditors are also responsible for the preparation of a fund's audited financial statements. Over time the role of auditors has evolved to offer a greater degree of services including assistance with fund regulatory matters, assistance with management of the internal accounting function, such as providing software for this function, tax planning, and compliance with tax reporting requirements. Chapter 7 provides a more detailed discussion of the role of the auditor.

Administrator

At their most basic level, fund private equity fund administrators typically offer two primary types of services: fund accounting, which includes independent pricing of the portfolio, and shareholder servicing.

Within the fund accounting function, the types of services traditionally provided include:

- Trade capture
- Valuations
- Calculation of profit and loss on a daily, weekly, and monthly basis
- Calculation of fees and accruals
- Calculation of net asset value and preparation of financial statements
- Investment accounting
- Fee calculations
- Partnership accounting
- Financial accounting/general ledger maintenance
- Daily profit and loss and net asset value reporting
- Performance measurement
- Tax preparation
- Reporting for investment managers and their investors
- Preparation of weekly/monthly financial statements

The primary services provided by the shareholder services function generally include:

- Overseeing the subscription and redemption processing, that includes receiving and processing all the relevant documentation and complying with hedge fund-specific criteria such as required redemption notice periods, lockups, and potential redemption penalties
- Ensuring compliance with the anti-money-laundering and know-your client requirements in each jurisdiction
- Tax reporting for investors

Similar to the audit industry, administrators have been eager to meet the growing demands of their hedge fund clients in recent years by both enlarging the suite of services offered and increasing the integration of their traditional administration services with other hedge fund service providers.

Other types of services offered by administrators in recent years include:

Corporate Services

- Maintaining minute books and the statutory records
- Convening meetings, providing company secretaries, and preparing all necessary filings
- Managing regulatory requirements and liaising with company registrars
- Calculating net asset value and preparing financial statements

Other Types of Services

- Assistance with fund creation and setup
- Maintenance of financial records
- Corporate secretarial services
- Coordination of the audit process and stock exchange reporting
- Prime broker reconciliation
- Structuring of alternative investment instruments and products

With the growth of the private equity administration industry, many third-party administrators have developed into either large standalone firms that have been in the administration business or are companies affiliated with large investment banks that typically have large prime-brokerage operations as well. Administrators often have offices across multiple time zones, in order to provide 24-hour rolling coverage, and in certain offshore hedge fund havens around the world such as the Cayman Islands and Bermuda.

There has also been a tendency in recent years for certain private equity managers who do not have the expertise or resources to manage an internal accounting function to outsource this function to the fund's administrator. As a result, several hedge fund administrators have developed technology platforms in recent years that provide straight-through processing and connectivity between a hedge fund and a third-party administrator's front, middle, and back-office functions.

As Chapter 12 discusses, while the use of third-party administrators has gained traction in recent years, some large private equity and real estate funds still self-administer. Fund self-administration can present a number of conflicts of interest in regard to process independence and is generally considered to be an operational strike against a firm.

Legal Counsel

A private equity firm's external legal counsel provides advice and services on law-related matters. Depending on the jurisdictional location of both the investment manager and the underlying hedge fund vehicles, many hedge funds have both domestic (also referred to as *onshore*) and international (commonly called *offshore*) legal counsel. The typical types of basic services offered by law firms to hedge funds include:

- Initial fund creation documentation
- Ongoing legal advice
- Assistance with maintenance of continual legal filing requirements
- Changes in fund documentation

Certain law firms also provide higher levels of service, including:

- Compliance consulting
- Mock regulatory audits
- Employee training on both investment- and non-investment-related issues

Custodian

At the most basic level, a private equity firm utilizes a custodian to physically hold a fund's assets. A custodian acts for a fund in much the same way that an individual's personal bank acts as a custodian of checking and/or savings accounts. Of course, this basic concept becomes blurred by book-entry securities settlement, contract- or agreement-based securities, and even further complicated when considering that physical custody is only one way in which a private equity firm may have custody of a client's assets. The idea of "constructive custody" or the ability of a private equity firm adviser or its affiliate to access or move assets or cash out of an account further complicates the custodial landscape for investors and advisers alike. Potentially further complicating custody issues are uncertificated, sometimes called noncertificated, securities.

Recently the rules regarding custody requirements were significantly changed. Prompting such changes were a series of enforcement actions brought by the Securities and Exchange Commission (SEC) that alleged misuse, misappropriation, and theft of client monies. While the Madoff and Stanford scandals made big headlines, a number of smaller Ponzi schemes and asset misuse enforcement actions and private litigation brought against advisory firms and their principals, and even technology personnel, emphasized gaps in the previous custodial regulatory environment. To close these loopholes the United States Securities and Exchange Commission adopted amendments to the Rule 206(4)-2 that was known as the *Custody Rule*. These amendments to the Custody Rule have placed a number of increased requirements on both U.S. SEC registered investment advisers as well as custodians, such as:

- Investment advisers must have a reasonable basis for their belief that account statements distributed by qualified custodians, which much be sent at least quarterly.
- Investment advisers that hold self-custody may be required to receive a so-called written internal control report at least annually.

- Subject to certain exceptions for private fund advisors, investment advisers will be required to undergo an annual surprise examination of client assets for which the adviser has custody.

Another key point of inquiry for any hedge fund investor when evaluating a private equity firm's relationships with a custodian is whether assets held at the custodian are in the name of the custodian or the hedge fund. Assets that are not held in the name of the hedge fund could potentially expose those assets to other capital commitments of the custodian. If, for example, the custodian were to become insolvent, this could put a hedge fund's investors at greater risk of losing their capital then they would be if the assets were held in the name of the private equity firm.

Investors should also be on the look-out for situations in which a private equity firm does not utilize a third-party custodian. In certain instances, a private equity firm may create an affiliated entity to serve as a custodian, perhaps to give the appearance that an independent custodial relationship is in place. The potential conflicts of interest surrounding affiliated custodial relationships are largely considered by many investors to be too great. In summary, many investors performing operational due diligence reviews on private equity funds with regard to affiliated custodial relationships frankly agree with the adage, "The juice is not worth the squeeze." In other words, any benefits associated with self-custody of assets are not worth the operational risks associated with the potential conflicts of interest that are likely to be present.

Information Technology Providers

Private equity firms often address their information technology needs via a combination of internal and external efforts. Information technology firms can provide support across a number of different areas at a private equity firm, including basic initial firm systems installation and ongoing support. Increasingly, information technology consultants oversee the installation and maintenance of trading systems and platforms, Internet systems, enterprise systems, customer relationship management (CRM) systems, and software development. IT firms also oversee the development of integrated network, computer, voice, and security solutions, including communications room design, electronic communication solutions, and secure remote connectivity. Information technology firms can also assist in planning for technology-related business continuity and disaster-recovery concerns. During the operational due diligence process, investors should be conscious of the scope and scale of service being provided by third-party information technology consultants.

ADDITIONAL ON-SITE VISIT CONSIDERATIONS: NEGATIVE OPERATIONAL DUE DILIGENCE

While the focus of most investor's on-site operational due diligence processes may be squarely centered on the operational policies, procedures, and processes in place at the private equity fund, there is another aspect of due diligence that many investors may overlook. This relates to a concept which for the purposes of this book will we refer to a *negative due diligence*.

This concept relates to the understanding that the investor due diligence process is a reciprocal one. If private equity firms and investors are honest about the operational due diligence process, it is one in which each party has certain wants and needs. An investor wants, at a minimum, to avoid exposure to fraud and weak operations and, at best, select private equity firms with strong operational infrastructures. To accomplish this, an investor needs the cooperation of the private equity firm to collect certain pieces of information and to conduct certain steps, such as an on-site visit, to complete this process. Turning to the private equity firm, it too has wants and needs in this process. It wants to ultimately obtain investment allocations from investors to be placed in the funds that it manages. In order to accomplish this from an operational perspective, the private equity firm needs to demonstrate, or at least convince, investors that it is not a fraud and that strong operations are in place. Because of sometimes conflicting wants and needs, the private equity operational due diligence process can have an adversarial aspect. When going up against an adversary, even one that you are not looking to defeat but rather enter into a business relationship with, it is useful to learn as much about your adversary as possible. This book is primarily about methodology, tools, and techniques that investors can use to diagnose, monitor, and analyze their adversary in this process—the private equity firm.

On the other side of the table we have the private equity firm. This is where the concept of *negative due diligence* comes into play. Negative due diligence, or reverse due diligence, refers to the process that the target of a due diligence analysis itself performs upon the investor that is investigating it. This is not to imply that the private equity firm has any right to begin submitting document requests lists to investors or seeking an on-site visit with them. Private equity firms should not be performing the same type of due diligence on investors that the investors are performing on them. This is not the type of due diligence we are referring to in this case; instead, we are referring to a different type of due diligence. It could almost be thought of as due diligence light. The relationship between traditional due diligence and negative due diligence is summarized in Exhibit 4.4.

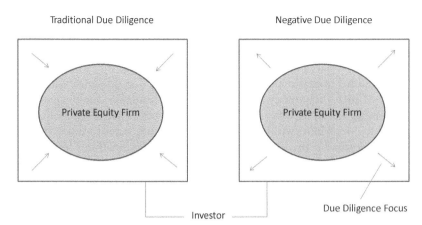

EXHIBIT 4.4   Comparison of Traditional and Negative Due Diligence Processes

Putting aside any anti-money-laundering safeguards, under the negative due diligence concept a private equity firm should take basic steps to gather initial background information about the investor. Generally, a private equity firm will have a basic understanding of an investor's investment organization, but they may not have taken the time to maintain an understanding of who is actually performing operational due diligence. This can be particularly true when an investor may engage a third-party consultant to assist in the operational due diligence process. In these cases, from the perspective of the private equity firm, this lack of due diligence can put them at a significant disadvantage during the operational due diligence process. What types of information are we talking about?

As indicated earlier, operational due diligence does not need to be adversarial in nature, but it can certainly evolve into an adversarial process. If such an adversarial development is the case, it is certainly reasonable for a fund to know their adversary. For example, has the investor published any articles that could provide insights into particular operational views that the investor holds? Does the investor have a certain background, either professionally or from his or her educational discipline, that could provide guidance as to any areas they might focus on in the operational due diligence process?

Consider if the individual performing operational due diligence has a background working at a former financial regulator. For the purposes of our example, we can refer to him as Joe Regulator. While your author is not a gambling man, we could likely wage dollars-to-doughnuts that during the course of his operational due diligence review process Joe is likely to focus more heavily, or at least have the ability to dig deeper, on certain regulatory- and compliance-related matters, compared to an average investor. Contrast this with another investor performing operational due diligence who used to work as Chief Technology Officer at a hedge fund. For the purposes of our continuing example, we can refer to this investor as Mr. Micro Chip. As compared to Joe, Micro would likely, at a minimum, want to poke around the server room of a private equity firm. If he sees something he doesn't like, Micro is likely more equipped than Joe to dive deep into information technology-related issues. The point of this example is to demonstrate that if a private equity firm is armed with such knowledge, they can prepare accordingly. Unfortunately for many private equity firms, and perhaps fortunately for many investors, remember that, after all, in the context of our present discussion operational due diligence is a somewhat adversarial exercise; many private equity firms do not devote the necessary time or resources to take a few moments to learn about investors' or operational due diligence analysts' backgrounds.

Such a lack of effort in the negative due diligence process certainly could have a signaling effect to investors. An investor may well posit that, if a fund has not taken the time to learn some basic details about the investor performing operational due diligence beyond when they are planning to invest and how much, this may be a red flag representative of larger operational problems, such as a lack of thoroughness. For example, is the fund equally lax when examining any trading counterparties or similar firms with which it might have balance sheet exposure?

ADDITIONAL ON-SITE VISIT CONSIDERATIONS: INTERVIEW TECHNIQUES AND QUESTION DESIGN

Another key area that can be considered in relation to the on-site visit process relates to the nature of the interview process itself. While one of the primary functions of the operational due diligence process may be to focus on operational information collection and evaluating that information, there is also a great deal of information that can be gathered from the on-site process itself. This type of meta information can provide investors with due diligence insights that can be just as informative as the actual operational due diligence process. As with most aspects of the operational due diligence process, such pieces of information may only be accessible to investors if they utilize appropriate techniques to collect such information.

Interview Techniques

These techniques relate to the concept of interview techniques. One such technique may be in the way in which an investor approaches the entire operational due diligence process. For example, consider the old adage previously alluded to in this book, "You can catch more flies with honey then you can with vinegar." If investors take a more aggressive or adversarial approach toward the operational due diligence process, they will most likely receive a much different reaction from a private equity fund than if they approach the process in a more friendly way. There is actually a whole field of research dedicated to interview techniques that draws on elements from multiple disciplines including sociology and psychology. Being nice or friendly, perhaps via the engagement of small talk, is a technique known as rapport building. Research has shown that rapport building can produce more open and productive interviews.[2] Other techniques can include utilizing active listening, detachment, body language, and vocal tone, and how to respond to anger. Expanding such techniques may also include interview techniques that focus on lie detection, as well.

Question Design

Another often overlooked area of operational due diligence during the on-site visit relates to the concept of question design. A related field to the discipline of interview techniques examines the ways in which investors ask certain questions. While the goal of an investor is ultimately to obtain certain pieces of operational information to facilitate an analysis of this information, investors can and should utilize the on-site visit to collect additional meta data by putting thought into the way certain questions are asked. The science of question design techniques broadly includes the concepts of closed and open questions. Closed questions, which are sometimes referred to as closed-ended questions, attempt to solicit a curt "yes" or "no" answer. Open questions, also sometimes referred to as open-ended questions, are instead focused on letting the interview subject, in this case the private equity firm, answer a question at length. Within the subset of open questions a variety of different question types can be employed by investors performing operational due diligence including reflective questions, directive questions, pointed questions, indirect questions, self-appraisal questions, diversion questions, and leading questions.[3]

The role of such interview techniques and question design in the operational due diligence process is perhaps best illustrated by way of example. Consider an investor who is performing operational due diligence on a private equity fund. For the purposes of this example, we can refer to this investor as Invest A. Gator. As part of the operational due diligence process Mr. Gator seeks to meet with the Chief Compliance Officer of the firm, Mr. Stick Ler, as well as several other operational professionals. When Mr. Gator arrives at the firm he is met by the private equity firm's head of investor relations, Tom Fundmoney. Mr. Fundmoney shares a few pleasantries with Mr. Gator and then leaves him in a conference room by himself. As the day progresses, Mr. Gator meets with a series of operations personnel, each of whom provide him with an overview of various issues regarding the private equity firm's operations. Mr. Fundmoney, who has not been present at any of these meetings because he was on a series of conference calls with other investors, eventually comes by to check in on Mr. Gator. Mr. Gator informs Mr. Fundmoney that the review process is progressing as planned and then requests to meet with the Chief Compliance Officer. Mr. Fundmoney goes away again and then sends in the Chief Compliance Officer by himself, as the firm had done with all of the other operational professionals. The Chief Compliance Officer, Stick Ler, then enters the room and the interview process begins. As the interview proceeds, Mr. Gator apologizes for having to ask what might be some seemingly obvious questions, and he knows that Stick is probably bored with having to sit through "all of these due diligence meetings investors are performing these days," and that Mr. Gator will do his best to move things along. Mr. Gator is adept at rapport building in this way and Stick takes a deep breath, because he feels he can finally relax with an investor who won't grill him during the due diligence process.

Unbeknownst to Stick, Mr. Gator is actually quite a shrewd operational due diligence analyst. He has devoted a great deal of time preparing for the operational due diligence process. Mr. Gator has even hired a third-party investigation firm to conduct background investigations on several key individuals at the private equity firm under review. As a result of these reviews, Mr. Gator has learned that two individuals who work at the firm also happen to serve on the boards of different associations and privately held companies. With this information in hand and Mr. Gator's knowledge of interview techniques and question design, he has a variety of ways in which he can bring this issue up with Mr. Ler.

One option would be to ask the question directly. This exchange might go something like this:

Mr. Gator: Is it true that private equity employees A and B maintain positions on boards of associations and companies outside of this private equity firm?

Stick Ler: Um, if that's what you have found, then, I believe so yes.

This is a closed question that produces a singular response. Stick has even tried to build himself some wiggle room in this regard with the "I believe so" language. In this exchange, the investor, Mr. Gator, has confirmed the information provided by his background investigation firm but little else.

A second option would be to introduce the subject via a series of closed and open questions and then see how Stick responds:

Mr. Gator:	Could you describe to me your basic duties as Chief Compliance Officer?
Stick Ler:	I conduct a number of different tasks all of which relate to compliance. Monitoring of regulatory filings, ensuring the compliance manual is up to date, employee trading, etc.
Mr. Gator:	Thanks. Can you tell me a little more about the compliance manual?
Stick Ler:	Yes, it's all fairly standard policies relating to employee trading, gifts policies, conflicts of interest. Is there anything specific you want to know?
Mr. Gator:	What about outside business activities—does compliance monitor those?
Stick Ler:	Yes, according to our compliance policies and procedures, employees are required to preclear any outside business activities with the compliance department before engaging in them. Also, on an annual basis they have to let us know if any outside activities have changed.
Mr. Gator:	Thanks, that's very helpful. So do you as chief compliance officer maintain a record of any such activities?
Stick Ler:	Yes, that part of my job.
Mr. Gator:	Does anyone at the firm currently have any such outside activities or sit on any boards?
Stick Ler:	No, the register is blank.

Okay, so now we not only have a different response but we have an interesting situation. If an investor has independent knowledge that employees of the firm sit on the boards of companies it can mean one of three things:

1. The third-party investigation firm made a mistake.
2. Stick is lying.
3. Stick is incompetent.

While background investigation firms do make mistakes, for the purposes of our example we will assume it to be true that the employees of the private equity firm do actually currently sit on the boards of companies and associations. So why did Stick not reply in the affirmative? Perhaps Stick was unsure as to the answer. In that case, perhaps, the more honest response would have been something like, "I'm not sure, I'll have to check and get back to you." Perhaps Stick felt the need to agree with Mr. Gator. After all, it seems Stick wasn't too sure of the answer and he perhaps thought the better answer would be to show that everyone at the firm is focused on their job and employees do not sit on any outside boards. Either way it does not bode well for Stick and the private equity firm. Additionally, our prospective investor, Mr. Gator, now has to get comfortable that this was perhaps a minor oversight by Stick and that it is not representative of endemic operational problems throughout the firm. In either case, the operational due diligence process will certainly be lengthened and may likely result in a decision not to invest.

Readers may be thinking to themselves, "Well, certainly I don't want to invest in a private equity fund with operations personnel who potentially lie or are incompetent, but how can such a situation result in losses to me as an investor in a particular fund?" Returning to our example, consider if Stick had made this misstatement not to a potential investor but perhaps to a regulator conducting an on-site examination of the firm. Uh-oh. Misstatements to regulators can result in sanctions, fines, and even the potential shutdown of the entire firm. While this is only an example, such meta data acquired during the interview process can have a definite signaling effect regarding a private equity fund's operational strengths. This meta data is generally observable if an investor is on the lookout for it and employs the appropriate interview and question design techniques to observe such data. This aim of this book is not to provide in-depth analysis of interview techniques or question design, but investors seeking to enhance their operational due diligence processes should at the very least be aware that such techniques exist and are potentially available to them as another tool to enhance their due diligence arsenal.

Combining Interview Techniques and Question Design Tactics: Backdooring

Earlier in this chapter, we alluded to a concept known as *backdooring*. The term comes from the world of computer science and can be defined as a hole in a security system that was intentionally left behind by a system design.[4] We can alter this concept slightly to fit the context of operational due diligence. When an investor is interested in obtaining an answer to a particular question or obtaining a certain piece of operational risk information, sometimes a fund will comply and in other cases a fund may outright refuse to provide certain pieces of information. In other cases, a private equity fund may attempt to distract an investor by providing platitudes meant, in part, to make the investor believe that the question has been answered when it actually has not.

When faced with noncompliance, an investor has to make a choice as to how to surmount this information barrier. When presented with an information barrier, an investor may be able to get around the barrier rather than attempt to go straight through it. This is where the concept of *backdooring* comes into play. Consider a situation in which an investor is attempting to locate a list of the names of certain software applications utilized at a particular firm. There are a number of reasons why an investor may be interested in such information, such as the need to determine whether the private equity firm is utilizing best in class or subpar systems. In response to such a request, the private equity firm may simply attempt to placate the investor with a generic reply to the effect of, "We use a variety of third-party and proprietary applications." This doesn't really get the investor very far toward accomplishing their goal of obtaining the firm's list of software applications to the level of detail required. Employing a *backdooring technique* might yield this information.

Consider, for example, if an investor, after effectively being shut down by the previous reply, could later in the due diligence process ask a question to the equivalent of, "Have there been any recent system upgrades to note?" In providing the answer to this question the private equity firm is likely to reveal more details regarding particular systems than they would have previously. This might be particularly true if the questions are posed to two different individuals. So the investor relations employee at the private equity firm may be more prepared with canned prepackaged replies to the first question as opposed to, say, an information technology employee answering the second question. This is not to imply that the investor relations employee is in any way smarter or more adept in dealing with due diligence requests as compared to the information technology employee. Rather, the point is that the information technology employee at the private equity firm may in fact be more focused and open to discussing technology-related issues, as compared to an investor relations employee. Continuing our example, what about when discussing the posttrade process an investor sheepishly asks for the name of the system where trades are booked? This could then open a door by which an investor can gain further insight into the names of systems utilized at the firm. When considering employee interview techniques and question design tactics, investors should consider relatively straightforward techniques, such as backdooring, to circumvent information barriers and keep the operational due diligence process moving forward.

Visiting Portfolio Companies and Real Estate Properties

While we are on the subject of on-site visits by an investor to the office of a private equity firm, it is also worth considering a potential other type of on-site visit that an investor may consider. This relates to investors performing due diligence on the underlying holdings of the private equity fund themselves.

If an investor is approaching a newly forming private equity fund that is currently in its infancy and still effectively just a legal shell, these companies may have slotted a certain pipeline of investment in which it is anticipated that such funds, once raised, will be allocated. In certain cases, particularly from an investment due diligence perspective, it may be worthwhile for a potential investor in the fund to consider performing an on-site visit to the potential portfolio company as well. Such visits may offer insight from an operational perspective as well. For example, some considerations can include:

- How is it anticipated that the fund will accept capital from the private equity firm?
- What type of reporting can the private equity firm anticipate to receive from the portfolio company?
- What operational controls and procedures are in place at the private equity firm to prevent fraudulent activities?

The last question in this list raises a noteworthy point regarding instances of fraud in private equity firms. In addition to concerns investors may have regarding instances of fraud at the private equity fund management level, both investors and private equity funds must also be conscious of fraud at a private equity fund's portfolio companies. Recent studies have suggested both that such fraudulent activity occurs and that private equity managers remain concerned about such fraud.[5]

In the case that at a particular stage of the due diligence process a firm pipeline of portfolio companies is not yet established, or an investor for one reason or another may not want to visit portfolio companies that are only anticipated to be in the portfolio, or perhaps the management of such firms is not compliant with only potential investor inquiries, an investor instead may choose to take a page from the document requests list methodology previously outlined and instead conduct an on-site visit of a portfolio-holding company that resides in a similarly managed but already existing private equity fund, if such a fund is managed by the firm. Once again, as with the document requests methodology, although such an existing portfolio company in a historical fund is not an exact match to the fund under development, such an on-site visit can still provide valuable insights into the private equity fund's operational connections and oversight of such portfolio companies.

Such anticipated portfolio holdings on-site visits can also be particularly of interest with regard to real estate funds. In those cases, more so than simply visiting an office in which a particular anticipated portfolio company operates out of, an investor can go actually visit the building and/or land. Furthermore, if an investor really desires to do so, they could even attempt to hire independent experts to search land records, perform valuation work or land surveys, and so on. This type of spot-check audit may give a particular investor a great deal more conviction than merely hearing a private equity manager describe a particular property or show an investor a picture of it. This is not to imply that investors should perform full-blown audits of existing or potential portfolio holdings of every private equity fund they invest in. Rather, investors should be conscious of the fact that performing additional due diligence on portfolio holdings, either actual or anticipated, is an option in the due diligence process. Such additional due diligence may assuage any concerns of investors in certain regards, or provide additional insights.

Understanding Private Equity Jargon: Keep It Simple, Stupid

When it comes to document requests or anything else during the operational due diligence process, a key phrase from the world of sports comes to mind: KISS—keep it simple, stupid! Real estate, in some instances even more so than private equity, is replete with its own lexicon of legalese and esoteric jargon. There is a tendency among investors to get lost in this land of jargon. As with most industries, the specific terminology is steeped in history, has been developed over time, and for practical purposes actually can add real value to discussions among those in the know.

For example, to the average non–Latin speaking average Joe on the street, explaining that "the onshore vehicle is pari-passu to the offshore" might not mean much. This short sentence conveys a number of different concepts. First, it means that there are two fund vehicles being offered for a particular investment strategy. Second, we know that one of them is domestic in nature. "Domestic" typically means from the same jurisdiction as the fund management company or investor. Third, we can further deduce that based on context, the domestic vehicle is in relation to our average Joe (e.g., the domestic investment vehicle would be the most appropriate for Joe). Fourth, we know that there is another investment vehicle in addition to the domestic vehicle.

We further know that this vehicle is an offshore vehicle. An offshore vehicle is a fund that is generally more appropriate for investors who reside outside of the previously mentioned domestic jurisdiction. Finally, we know that both the domestic and offshore funds or investment is managed in a pari-passu manner. Pari-passu means in substantially the same manner and most likely under the guidance of the same investment personnel. Everything we have just covered is certainly a mouthful. Therefore, for practical reasons, the technical term pari-passu is preferred to the longer translations of the full term. Investors can think of these terms as being similar to courtroom stenography. The same meaning is conveyed, only in shorthand form.

The point of our discussion is to illustrate that investors may often be faced with such shorthand during the operational due diligence process. Often a fund manager may not be trying to hide anything by using this industry jargon, rather they are just using these generally accepted, commonly used terms in the private equity industry to communicate in direct terms. When faced with such terms, investors should not be afraid to take immediate action to stop an operational due diligence review cold in its tracks, raise their hands, and ask questions. This cannot be repeated often enough.

Investors cannot begin to collect operational risk data and then analyze and even monitor such data when they do not even speak the language. In other words, without completely understanding the terminology being used, both in a generic sense as well as in the context of any particular usage being considered, investors are proceeding headfirst into a blinding due diligence snowstorm. The further they proceed without a basic understanding of the terms, the worse it gets.

Unfortunately, at this stage in the game, investors must take a close look at not only their own internal operational due diligence processes but also at their goals in performing operational due diligence. No one likes to admit that they do not understand something. It is at this point worth taking a moment to distinguish between the terms ignorance and uninformed.

No one likes to admit that they are ignorant of anything, and certainly not in the context of sophisticated private equity due diligence activities. An investor who does not understand something, albeit an obscure term, an abbreviation, or even an operational due diligence process employed at a firm, is not ignorant—they are merely uninformed. An investor who is ignorant is one who does not inquire about an issue that they might not understand. Most investors are not ignorant; they are uninformed. Uninformed investors should not be apologetic about being uninformed. On the contrary, a private equity fund is asking for the opportunity to manage their money and in the context of operational due diligence process there is certainly no such thing as a stupid question. Any fund manager who attempts to make an investor feel foolish for asking a question, however basic it may be, frankly does not deserve the opportunity to manage the investor's money.

ASSET RAISING AND THE USE OF PLACEMENT AGENTS AND THIRD-PARTY MARKETERS

Another area that investors might not necessarily think to include in their core review process, but that generally finds its way into expanded review processes, is any relationships that a private equity firm may have with individuals or groups that assist the firm in raising fund capital. Such groups are typically quite common in other areas of the alternative investment industry, such as hedge funds. Private equity firms may also utilize such groups for a variety of reasons. Not to sound like a commercial for the placement agent industry, however, some firms may feel it is a better use of their time, energy, and resources to focus primarily on what investors are paying them to do—manage the funds. By utilizing third-party marketing firms a private equity manager may be able to stick to their knitting, so to speak, and hone their focus on the task of managing money rather than raising it.

In other cases, a private equity firm may have its own internal fund-raising arm via in-house investor relations or marketing teams. In such cases, the use of placement agents may be beneficial to the fund to both broaden the reach of any internal efforts as well as to provide access to markets that, for one reason or another, may otherwise not be easily accessible to the private equity firm. An example of this that investors may sometimes come across would be a U.S.–based private equity firm utilizing the services of a placement agent to raise capital from sovereign wealth funds based in overseas regions such as the Middle East.

There is nothing inherently wrong with such a relationship. Indeed, by utilizing third-party marketing firms, private equity firms may be able to capitalize on certain fund-raising opportunities that would otherwise not be available to them. However, the placement agents are not facilitating such fund-raising efforts out of the kindness of their hearts. They, of course, get paid for their efforts.

The payment to these third-party fund-raising entities can sometimes be referred to under the euphemism of a fund rebate or a sales charge. This term is typically the more polite way of referring to what others might call a kickback. Regardless of what a private equity firm and their placement agents call such a practice, it is effectively a percentage of the fee that is paid to the placement agent based on the amount of capital that a private equity investor subscribes to such a fund.

For example, let's say that a capital-raising organization has a private equity firm (The Jason Group) in the process of raising a new fund. The target amount of capital to be raised for the first close is $700 million and the first close is anticipated to occur in three months. Despite their best efforts, The Jason Group's team of internal marketers has had difficulty gaining access to the Blackacre state pension fund. The Jason Group feels their new fund, an infrastructure fund, would be a good fit for the Blackacre state pension fund mandate to reinvest in the economy and infrastructure of America. At a cocktail party, The Jason Group's Chief Investment Officer (Mr. Alpha Beta) is introduced to J.M. Wellington III, head of distribution at a placement agency known as Capital Intro Associates. J.M. informs Mr. Beta that he could perhaps be of assistance in making an introduction because they have just hired the recently retired former controller of the state pension fund, Dom Telonge, to serve as an adviser to Capital Intro Associates. An agreement is struck the next day and, lo and behold, after several meetings the Blackacre state pension fund agrees to invest $100 million in The Jason's Group infrastructure fund. Similar to the way that many accident lawyers who frequently advertise on TV are not compensated unless they are successful, Capital Intro Associates also does not earn its keep unless they raise money. In this case, they were successful. Let's say that the rebate (aka, sales charge) that they are paid is 0.50 percent. That means that for their efforts J.M. Wellington III and his firm are entitled to $500,000.

One question that investors should ask themselves is, "Who ends up paying this $500,000?" The answer is generally that it depends. It may seem logical that the private equity firm should bear the cost of raising this capital. However, depending on the language in the offering memorandum for the fund, the fund for which the capital is raised may have to bear a portion or all of this expense. This is an example of an area that investors must dig into, with regard to such placement agency relationships.

Another point worth highlighting from the example relates to the way in which certain introductions or relationships are made. In the example, Capital Intro Associates, the placement agent, has recently hired the former controller of the state pension fund, Dom Telonge. While not to imply any sort of impropriety, another area that investors should investigate is so-called paying a fee or providing favors in exchange for securing capital commitments from investors. These practices, which for the most part are illegal, are called *pay-to-play*, or sometimes referred to as *pay-for-play*, practices. In the example, Capital Intro Associates hiring Dom Telonge would not likely be viewed as a pay-to-play violation since Mr. Delong has since retired from the Blackacre pension fund. However, if Mr. Telonge had indeed still been employed at the state pension fund and was given, say, $20,0000 or a box seat at the Superbowl, and then the Blackacre state pension fund just happened to allocate to The Jason Group fund, this would trigger pay-to-play concerns.

In response to a series of scandals surrounding pay-to-play violations, the legal and regulatory landscape for fund-raising, particularly from public pension plans, has becoming increasingly difficult for both fund managers and third-party marketers to navigate. Some states in the United States have taken action in this regard. An example of such a law is known as Assembly Bill 1743. This bill was passed in 2010 in California and directly affects the ability of hedge funds and private equity firms to raise capital in the state. The law came into effect on January 1, 2011. This law directly affects the activities of placement agents by who solicit funds from California's two largest pension funds—the California Public Employees' Retirement System (CalPERS) and the California State Teachers' Retirement System (CalSTRS). Specifically, placement agents must both register as lobbyists and may no longer receive incentive fees for securing commitments from the pension funds. This law also has potential ramifications for the direct marketing efforts at private equity firms who deal directly with the pension funds as well. The impetus behind this legislation is an attempt to curb the pay to play efforts that have received increased attention as of late. New York has entirely banned placement agents from attempting to place funds at the state's Common Retirement Fund. Illinois and New Mexico have also recently instituted similar rules.

The *New York Times* had reported that the move at CalPERS came about in part after scandals occurred, when Alfred Villalobos, a former employee turned placement agent, was accused of lavishing gifts on pension officials to steer public dollars to favored money managers.[6] Registering as a lobbyist places restrictions on placement agents' activities, including the inability to make campaign donations. Additionally, as lobbyists, placement agents will have to limit and disclose gifts, report certain expenses annually, and take an ethics course every two years. Fund-raising from public plans has become even more complex and burdensome for both placement agents as well as fund managers because certain ambiguity surrounds those who have to register as lobbyists, and there are confidentiality concerns surrounding enhanced disclosure requirements.

At the federal level, the U.S. Securities and Exchange Commission, in an attempt to broaden the scope of regulation surrounding potential pay-to-play violations, has even instituted rules under the Investment Advisers Act of 1940 that prohibit investment advisers from providing advisory services for compensation to a government client for two years after the adviser or employees make a contribution to elected officials or candidates.[7] This rule also prohibits advisors, which can include private equity firms, from agreeing to provide payment to a third party, such as a placement agent, for solicitation of advisory business from any government entity unless the solicitation agents themselves are registered broker-dealers or registered investment advisers who are themselves subject to pay-to-play restrictions.

Furthermore, a private equity firm must also take care to ensure that the marketing efforts of placement agents not only comply with restrictions such as increasing pay-to-play regulations, but also with a host of other state, federal, and international regulations. One example is the antibribery provisions of the Foreign Corrupt Practices Act. The recent actions in this area perhaps signal an indication that the U.S. Securities Exchange Commission and the Department of Justice will increase enforcement action with regard to private equity funds.[8]

While the relationships of private equity funds with all of their third-party service providers should be an important focus during the operational due diligence process, the recent increase in the rigorousness of regulation surrounding fund-raising efforts should cause investors performing due diligence to focus more intently on this topic going forward. Investors may want to consider what additional legal and compliance resources a fund manager is planning to devote in order to comply with these new rules. In order to prevent being invested in a fund that ends up on the front pages due to pay-to-play scandals, investors may also want to take stock of all of a private equity fund's existing and legacy third-party marketing and placement agent relationships in order to determine any potential ways in which a hedge fund may be exposed to regulatory noncompliance either by the fund itself or via association with these service providers before any potential regulatory fines may be imposed.

CASH MANAGEMENT AND CONTROLS

Some investors consider cash to be one of the crucial areas to be focused on in an operational due diligence review. The thinking goes that cash flowing through a private equity firm is effectively the lifeblood of the organization. Without cash to call from investors, invest, or pay bills, there is little concern, the thinking goes, for the rest of the operational infrastructure of a firm. Certain operational due diligence reviews may even take a *follow the cash* approach, whereby the flow of cash from investor subscriptions through to redemptions are tracked.

Over the past several years, a trend had emerged of alternative investment firms seeking to outsource the cash management function in some regard. Part of the reasoning behind this trend is similar to our discussion of the use of placement agents: An alternative investment manager may feel they are capable of placing unencumbered cash into a checking account or in a money market fund; however, some funds may not have the skills, time, or resources to be focused on generating increased return from this cash. In effect, these firms may be leaving money on the table as a result of excess cash sitting around earning lower rates of return.

In addition to generating increased return, cash management may also be of concern for a private equity fund with multiple fund vehicles in different currency denominations. In these cases, cash may be managed to reduce or hedge against certain currency exposures. Many private equity firms may not be focused on the macroeconomic aspects of different developments in currency markets on a daily basis and may rely on third-party cash managers to assist in this area. Furthermore, depending on the strategy of the private equity strategy, third-party cash managers may also provide assistance in the areas of collateral and margin management.

Despite these advantages however, with the recent turmoil in the markets many private equity funds have focused on bringing the oversight of the cash function in-house. As part of the private equity operational due diligence process, investors should approach the cash management function from multiple perspectives. One such approach is to consider the amounts of cash held by the fund. Additionally, investors should focus on the ways in which cash is managed and controlled internally.

In regard to cash management at the private equity fund vehicle level, questions investors should consider include:

- How is unencumbered cash (also called cash on hand) managed?
- Where is unencumbered cash stored?
- What types of instruments are unencumbered cash held in (e.g., treasuries, direct cash, etc.)?
- What rates of return are earned on unencumbered cash?
- How much cash do the funds typically hold?
- How have these cash levels varied over time?
- How much cash is held by counterparties (e.g., prime brokers)?
- If a third-party cash management firm is utilized, how is this process monitored internally by the private equity firm?
- If the fund utilizes a third-party administrator, is a separate cash reconciliation performed by the administrator? If yes, how frequently is this cash reconciliation performed?
- How often is cash reconciled?
- Which individual or department at the private equity firm performs cash reconciliations?

- How are bills of the fund paid?
- If the private equity fund utilizes a third-party administrator, what reviews are performed internally before signing off on a cash transfer?
- If the fund utilizes a third-party administrator, does the administrator require the private equity firm to send copies of invoices from third-party vendors with any wire transfer requests?
- How are margin requirements managed?
- What is the cash-reconciliation process?

Additionally, as part of the operational due diligence process, investors would also be well-advised to be cognizant as to the policies within a private equity fund organization to control the movement of cash. Diagnosing not only the policies and procedures but the overall nature of the control environment can be an important, and sometimes tricky, aspect of the cash oversight process to gauge. In particular, during the operational due diligence process investors should consider addressing the following issues:

- How is cash moved within the organization?
- What wire transfer controls are in place?
- How are bills of the management company paid?
- Who has authority to move cash within the organization?
- Are there multiple signatories required to move cash?
- Are there situations where only one individual has authority to grant signatory approval?
- Are there different levels of cash signatories (e.g., an A list and a B list)?
- Do different movements of different amounts of cash require different levels or numbers of cash signatories?
- How are signature approvals granted? (i.e., electronically, via a physical form, etc.)
- Who ensures that the correct number of signatures is received?
- Is there an appropriate segregation of duties internally within the private equity fund as well as third-party oversight into the cash movement process?
- Can approval signatures be granted remotely or can cash transfer instructions only be granted via certain computers (e.g., via a secure key card device reader attached to computers)?

By taking the time to focus on such cash management issues, investors can gain a more detailed understanding of the seriousness with which a private equity firm approaches the issue of cash management. Areas such as the nature of the control environment of a private equity firm's cash management function can have a signaling effect as to how other, perhaps less perceived, important operational issues are addressed throughout the firm.

BUSINESS CONTINUITY AND DISASTER RECOVERY

In recent years, due to increased concerns related to terrorism, as well as what seem to be increasingly strong weather-related events such as hurricanes, earthquakes, flooding, and snow storms, business continuity planning (BCP) and disaster recovery (DR) have increasingly come into the scope of investor operational due diligence reviews. The operational risks related to BCP/DR can come from within the private equity firm itself or they may be exogenous in nature and the result of events from outside the private equity firm.

It is worth pausing for a moment to consider the two terms *business continuity* and *disaster recovery*. Such terms may be synonymous in the minds of both private equity firm's and investors. This is logical in some sense because a disruption in the normal functions of a private equity firm's operations can involve activation of plans related to continuing operations (i.e., business continuity) as well as restoring any lost data or functionality due to the business disruption (i.e., disaster recovery). These terms are certainly related but distinct concepts.

Business continuity refers to a private equity firm's ability to continue to function in the event of a business disruption. Disaster recovery, on the other hand, relates to a private equity firm's capabilities to restore itself after a disaster event to the point where it was before the disaster occurred.

In the minds of certain investors and private equity firms, BCP/DR planning may not be considered to be as important as in another type of fund manager, perhaps a hedge fund, which trades more frequently. This is not necessarily a correct belief. The thing about business disruptions or disaster type events is that they do not necessarily advertise when they are going to occur. So, for example, let's say that something happens, such as an office fire, that prevents access to a private equity firm's office. If this fire happens to occur during a particularly busy time operationally for the fund, say in the middle of an annual audit or during a capital call period, then the impact of such an event can be just as severe, if not more severe, than a fund that trades very frequently.

Disaster events need not be as large scale as a building fire; they can be as limited as a wall electrical outlet becoming overloaded and cutting power to a server. In general, as outlined earlier, investors can classify the events that lead to business disruptions as either exogenous, coming from outside the firm, or endogenous, internal to the firm. Examples of exogenous events include terrorism, weather-related events (hurricanes, floods, etc.), and power failures. Types of endogenous events include hardware malfunction and employee error (e.g., an employee accidentally deleted essential files, leading to a business disruption).

The design of a private equity firm's business continuity and disaster recovery plan seeking to address these exogenous and endogenous risks can be handled by a multitude of different groups within a private equity organization. Some firms may have a single or multiple BCP/DR committees. One advantage of these committees is that they are often staffed by employees from multiple departments throughout the firm. This is an important point to note as business continuity and disaster recovery planning spans all areas of the organization. Successful implementation of a BCP/DR plan requires the coordination of these different functions in order to keep the organization functioning as a whole. Other firms may hire third parties to design their BCP/DR plans. Many funds turn to their information technology departments to design and maintain the BCP/DR plan for them.

In order to ensure that their planning efforts are appropriate, some firms have recently begun to work with specialized consultants to evaluate their BCP/DR plans. The benefit of utilizing such BCP/DR consultants is that they add a degree of objectivity to the planning process and can avoid such things as the technology bias that may result from a third-party service provider utilizing technologies its staff is more familiar with rather than the best technology available.

Some private equity firms may also pursue certification of their BCP/DR plans. There are a number of BCP/DR certification programs that typically vary by region. These programs can be formal certifications or merely adhere to a series of guidelines published by organizations. Examples of such certifications are summarized in Exhibit 4.5.

EXHIBIT 4.5 Example Business Continuity and Disaster Recovery Guidelines and Standards

Country / Region	Guideline/Standard
United Kingdom	British Standards Institution (BSI), BS 25999
North America	ASIS/BSI BCM.01:2010 Business Continuity Management Systems
Global	International Organization for Standardization (ISO) ISO/PAS 22399:2007 Guideline for incident preparedness and operational continuity management
North America	National Fire Protection Association NFPA 1600: Standard on Disaster/Emergency Management and Business Continuity Programs
Australia	Standards Australia HB 292-2006

In evaluating the BCP/DR plans and functions of a private equity firm, questions investors should consider include:

- Does the firm maintain written BCP/DR procedures? If yes, what is the scope of such procedures?
- Has the firm customized its business continuity and disaster recovery plans or is a generic plan in place that may not address the particular operational aspects of the firm?
- Are any written BCP/DR plans structured around industry certifications or guidelines?
- Do BCP/DR plans cover multiple scenarios including inaccessibility of the firm's offices?
- Do BCP/DR plans provide for coverage of plans for outages of telephony and Internet loss?
- Who is in charge of updating the plans?
- Are employees provided with contact information for each employer in a manner that is not dependent on the firm's systems functioning properly (e.g., a laminated calling-tree card)?
- Data backup and restoring:
  - What are the firm's data backup capabilities?
  - Is data backed up in multiple locations and via multiple media?
  - Is data stored on-site, off-site, or both?
  - Is a separate backup facility maintained for data storage?
  - Has the firm performed test restores from any backups?
  - How long would it take the firm to perform a data restore for system critical functions in the event of a disaster event?
- Backup power:
  - Are uninterruptible power supplies (also uninterruptible power source [UPS] or battery/flywheel backup) in place? If yes, are UPSs available for desktop PCs and servers?
  - How long do UPSs provide power for?
  - Does the firm have backup power–generation facilities? If yes, what type of generator (e.g., diesel, natural gas) is utilized?
  - Who is responsible for maintenance of such devices?
  - If backup power-generation capabilities are in place, does the firm own such devices exclusively or are they shared among other firms?
- Does the private equity firm have a gathering location in the event of a business disruption?
- Does the private equity firm maintain a separate facility from which employees may continue operations? If yes, how many seats are in such locations?

- Has the private equity firm ever had to activate its BCP/DR plan? If yes, what happened?
- Who at the firm is in charge of plan activation? How is plan activation communicated to employees?
- If the private equity firm has multiple offices, how are these offices supposed to coordinate with each other in the event of a business disruption in either location?
- Testing:
  - Are the plans tested? If so, how often?
  - Are BCP/DR plans tested solely from a technology perspective or are personnel tests employed as well?
  - When was the most recent test?
  - What were the results of the test? Were any material issues noted? How have these issues been addressed?

By taking care to incorporate an assessment of BCP/DR functionality into the operational due diligence process, investors can develop a better understanding of how a firm may continue to function in the event of a disaster event. Investors should focus their attention in particular not only on the design of such plans but on testing as well. The best business continuity and disaster recovery plans in the world are effectively useless if employees are not aware of what steps to take when such an event occurs.

UNDERSTANDING THE TRADE LIFE CYCLE PROCESS

Despite the fact that private equity may trade less frequently as compared to other alternative investment strategies such as hedge funds, this does not mean that investors should attempt to seek comfort in these relatively lower trade volumes. Although trading volumes may be lower, each trade is likely more significant. Therefore, even minor errors in trade processing for a relatively low trade volume could result in large-scale losses. Exhibit 4.6 shows a sample trade flow life cycle chart from idea generation through to reconciliation.

Additionally, for a private equity fund that hedges positions or currency, more active trading may occur in these segments of the portfolio as well. An example of a typical trade process for positions and securities that may be engaged in for the more frequent trading activities of a private equity fund is outlined in Exhibit 4.7.

Regardless of the frequency with which trades are executed, investors should attempt to gain an understanding of the trade flow process. Such an understanding is critically important so that an investor can appropriate

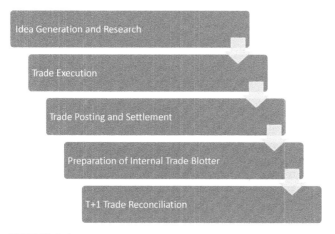

EXHIBIT 4.6   Sample Trade Flow Life Cycle

assess if there is any room for error or manipulation in the process. Some key issues investors should consider in analyzing the trade life cycle process for private equity firms include:

- What is the anticipated trade volume of the newly formed private equity fund under review?
- What types of instruments are traded?
- What is the average trade volume of the firm's funds historically? How has this volume changed over time?
- Who has authority to place trades?
- Do traders have responsibility for marking these trades?
- Is the firm adequately staffed to handle such volume?
- What is the trade documentation process?
- If a blotter is used, who has final authority to review the blotter?
- What oversight is there internally within the hedge fund over individuals with trading authority?
- How are trades executed?
- How are trades allocated among different funds?
- Who determines what opportunities will be allocated among the firm's funds?
- Are allocations based on any sort of predetermined allocation ratio? If so, how frequently is this ratio reset?
- What is the trade confirmation process? What percentage of confirmations are electronic versus paper confirmations?

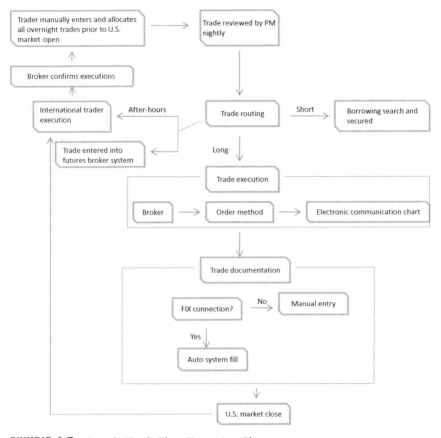

EXHIBIT 4.7 Sample Trade Flow Execution Chart

- Do counterparties, for such instruments as swaps, provide daily position reporting?
- Depending on the instruments traded, are there dedicated individuals within the firm who focus on certain types of reconciliations that may require special expertise (e.g., bank debt)?
- What happens in the event of a trade break?
- How frequently are position reconciliations performed?
- How are trade breaks investigated?
- Is there a hard deadline by which all trades must be reconciled?
- Does the third-party custodian hold custody of all the fund's assets or does the hedge fund hold custody of any assets?

- Are reconciliations performed internally by the private equity firm by a third-party administrator, or both?
- What trading systems are utilized? How are these systems integrated with other systems at the firm, such as the fund accounting system?

When investors take care to gain an understanding of the trade flow life cycle, they are more likely to gain a fuller understanding of a firm's entire operational infrastructure. This is because many of a private equity firm's other operations processes are centered around the trading processes. Therefore, investors can accrue multiple benefits by incorporating a review of trading processes and procedures into their operational due diligence processes.

LEGAL, COMPLIANCE, AND REGULATORY RISKS

In Chapter 3, we introduce a number of questions investors may want to ask with regard to legal and compliance-related matters. Due to new legislation in this regard, the legal and compliance area is one that has received increased attention from both regulators in recent years. As such, when discussing legal and compliance-related risks, it is also beneficial to include a discussion of regulatory related risks:

- What regulators are the private equity firm registered with?
- Has the private equity firm filed for any exemptions with any of regulatory agencies?
- When was the last on-site audit of the private equity firm by any regulator?
- Has the private equity firm received any inquiries from regulators or had other contact with them?
- Please provide the detail of any ongoing regulatory action?
- Can you provide a summary of all historical regulatory audits and the firm's response to such audits?

The legal and compliance function at a private equity firm is generally overseen by a chief compliance officer (CCO). In some firms the CCO role may either be filled by an individual dedicated toward compliance or shared among other responsibilities. Many investors are under the misconception that individuals who work in compliance-related roles are lawyers. This is not the case. Compliance, while related to the law, is a distinct skill set that may or may not require knowledge of legal aspects to perform. Working in a compliance role however, is not necessarily the equivalent of practicing law (e.g., no legal license is required). In many firms the General Counsel of the private equity firm, or someone else with a legal background, may also be the individual responsible for the compliance function, but such a background is not a necessity. As indicated earlier, many private equity firms will engage the services of external counsel for a variety of different functions. Typically, depending on the nature of the vehicles offered, most firms have onshore and offshore counsel.

The role of the compliance function has evolved over time. In the early years of the hedge fund industry, compliance personnel traditionally focused on investment-related compliance. That means ensuring that any required regulatory filings were completed in a timely manner and ensuring that a private equity firm was not in violation of any particularly pertinent restrictions contained in the offering memorandum, such as certain trading restrictions or risk limits. In the modern private equity context, today the modern CCO maintains a number of different functions including both investment and noninvestment issues related to a number of areas, including human resources, anti-money-laundering compliance, electronic communication monitoring, and workplace ethics.

In recent years, due to increasing scrutiny by regulators and the increasing complexity of financial industry legislation, many private equity funds, in addition to external legal counsel, have also begun to employ the services of third-party compliance consultants. Depending on the expertise of the compliance consultant as well as the scope of the engagements, compliance consultants provide a variety of services, including establishing a firm's initial compliance program, assisting with ongoing compliance training, and the conducting of mock audits, often modeled after an actual regulatory examination. Indeed, many compliance consultants used to work for regulatory agencies.

Compliance consultants can also provide private equity firms with continual advice after an initial compliance program is established. Some private equity firms may also hire compliance consulting firms to assist with ongoing compliance training. Compliance consultants can be a valuable resource to many private equity firms. This is particularly true when such firms monitor and are involved on a day-to-day basis with new regulatory developments. In performing a review of the use of such third-party compliance consultants during the operational due diligence process, investors should take care to determine the extent of the use of such consultants. A firm may be tempted to lean too heavily on such firms, while sacrificing the benefits of complementing the work of these firms with internal oversight. A compliance consultant can never substitute for internal oversight. A compliance consultant will not be at the firm on a daily basis and have the same degree of involvement in daily firm activities as a CCO or other in-house employees will have. Investors should gauge how the firm fosters a culture of compliance through the development, enforcement, and ongoing training of compliance policies and procedures.

When investors perform operational due diligence on the legal and compliance functions, they should attempt to gain an understanding of not only the firm's internal legal and compliance functions, but also the ways in which the firm interacts with regulators and third-party compliance consultants if applicable. Through this combined understanding a private equity firm will gain a more detailed understanding of the way in which the firm approaches and maintains a culture of compliance at the firm.

INSURANCE

As we indicated earlier, performing a review of a private equity firm's insurance coverage can also provide valuable insights into the operational strength of an organization. Private equity firms that maintain appropriate insurance coverage are signaling that they not only take business planning seriously, but also plan for contingencies as well.

There is no standard list of required coverage necessary for private equity funds to maintain. Indeed, in most instances, insurance coverage is not required by any laws or regulators but instead is driven by a combination of investor demands and a firm's own desires. Indeed, in practice, there is no consensus that insurance should be carried at all. Insurers themselves disagree about the need to offer coverage to private equity firms. To clarify, insurers are in the business of insuring things and at the right premiums they would likely insure against most risks. The challenge for private equity firms seeking to obtain such coverage is whether or not it is prohibitively expensive. On the other hand, insurers may not be comfortable with the levels of risk, and potential magnitude of losses, associated with private equity funds.

Investors should take care to examine not only the types of insurance coverage maintained by a firm and fund, but also the amounts of such policies and the identity of carriers. The standard types of insurance coverage maintained by private equity firms and funds and includes errors and omissions (E&O), directors' and officers' liability coverage (D&O), general partner liability coverage, and employment practices liability coverage.

Investors performing operational due diligence should also take measures to evaluate which parties are covered by these policies. The typical parties covered by insurance policies are the underlying investment vehicles, the private equity firms themselves (e.g., portfolio manager), the general partners if there is a limited partnership vehicle, the investment manager and directors, officers, employees, and any related partners of the above-mentioned parties.

Some private equity investment vehicles go beyond these basic levels of coverage. Additional coverage types that may be maintained typically include so-called key person insurance. Investors performing such reviews of this coverage should take care to evaluate to whom these policies are made payable as well as who is paying the premiums on the policies.

In reviewing insurance coverage, investors must also take steps to be conscious of any specific policy exclusions that may preclude coverage for certain events. Examples of some commonly used exclusions include claims by regulators, claims arising from violation of anti-money-laundering rules, and bankruptcy of a firm. Investors should be on the lookout for substantially broad exclusion language that would prevent a private equity fund from filing a claim. Examples of such language could be "in the event of market volatility" or "failure to perform as expected," which are often difficult to file claims for. Investors should also consider if a private equity firm has opted to self-insure until policy premiums become more cost effective.

TECHNOLOGY AND SYSTEMS

When performing an operational due diligence review, it is advisable that an investor gain an understanding of a firm's information technology infrastructure during the operational due diligence process. In the modern private equity firm, technology is a critical component of many other core operational processes. Certain more technically inclined private equity trading strategies would effectively not be able to function without technology. The primary software programs utilized by private equity firms include those that facilitate the following functions:

- Trading systems and platforms
- Fund accounting
- Customer relationship management (CRM)
- Portfolio and risk management systems
- Data retention
- Electronic communication monitoring software

There should be equal, if not more, consideration paid to a private equity firm's hardware platforms, including desktop PCs and servers. Investors should take measures to understand whether a firm has taken care to design its hardware program in a way that it considers not only the immediate needs of the firm, but can support future firm growth as well and is scalable.

An issue related to technology and systems includes the operational risk area of information security. Maintenance of the security of proprietary data is of crucial importance to private equity firms. While a private equity firm may maintain certain compliance policies that prevent employees from sharing sensitive information outside the firm, private equity firms have often gone a step further and taken a number of technological and physical security measures. From a software perspective, many funds have begun to more closely monitor employees' Internet activities, e-mail, and personal trading activities via electronic surveillance systems. Specifically in regard to e-mail, firms tend to monitor e-mail correspondence for both message content and the types of files sent. Electronic communication surveillance can also extend to remote-access devices such as BlackBerries and cellular phones. Many private equity firms also ban the use of external hardware devices, such as zip drives, so as to prevent people from walking out the door with proprietary information literally in their pocket.

In terms of information security, private equity firms also may maintain employee activity logs and file downloads. Through this increased monitoring, private equity firms have the ability to detect leaks, in the event information or files go missing or end up in the hands of the competition. While such procedures may border on approaching an Orwellian Big Brother dystopia, for better or worse such information security measures are realities of working and investing in the modern digital world.

The following is a summary of certain information security questions investors should consider utilizing to begin an analysis of a private equity firm's approach toward information security:

- What are the firm's information security defenses?
- What kinds of firewalls are in place?
- Does the firm, either itself or via a third-party provider, perform penetration testing?
- Does the firm, either itself or via a third-party provider, perform social network–type penetration testing?
- Does the firm log employee network activity?
- Has the firm taken any steps to monitor employee usage profiles to monitor for unusual computer usage or director access?
- Is the use of remote storage devices such as zip drives permitted?
- How often are employees required to change their network passwords?

TAX PRACTICES

The area of a private equity firm's tax practices may be one that is often obscured primarily by concerns of tax avoidance. Said another way, most investors may not feel they need to evaluate a private equity fund's tax practices in much detail as long as the fund does not generate negative tax consequences for them. Furthermore, an investor may believe that such concerns are better left for their lawyers and accountant to advise them on, rather than to integrate such concerns into the operational due diligence process. While such concerns are practical, there are a host of other tax-related issues that are operationally relevant to a private equity firm that investors must consider. One example of this would be the host of employment-related taxes that a U.S.-based private equity firm is required to pay as an employer. These include Medicare and Social Security tax and federal and state unemployment taxes. If a private equity firm is deficient in paying such taxes, there could be material consequences for the firm.

Before proceeding with some common tax implications for investors it is worth noting that this analysis is focused primarily on the tax implications as applicable under U.S. accounting standards of generally accepted accounting principles, also known as U.S. GAAP. There are a host of other tax considerations and implications for investors in non-U.S.-based firms that may operate under differing tax regimes such as IFRS, which we discuss in more detail in Chapter 7.

Returning to the tax implications an investment in a private equity firm may have for investors, one area of concern is whether a private equity fund generates unrelated business taxable income (UBTI). UBTI may be thought of as the tax on income that federal income tax-exempt entities, such as charitable organizations, are generally required to pay. Any such income that falls under UBTI is that which is unrelated to the business deemed as the primary business normally carried out by the tax-exempt organization. An example of this would be a pension fund, whose primary business is managing pension investments, operating a construction company. That being said, UBTI does not typically include dividends, gains for the sale of capital assets, or interest. There are a number of specific situations under which a private equity fund may generate UBTI. This is generally considered disadvantageous to tax-exempt investors due to the additional tax implications. Private equity investors should inquire whether a private equity fund has ever generated UBTI and what steps a fund has taken to ensure UBTI will not be generated in the future.

Another tax concern for private equity investors relates to investments made by non-U.S. tax-exempt investors surrounding effectively connected income (ECI). Non-U.S. (i.e., foreign) investors are not generally required to file U.S. tax returns. The exception to this rule is where they have ECI that is based on the active conduct of a U.S.-based business. It is important to note that the conduct must be active. Passive investments do not generally give rise to ECI. An investment made by a non-U.S. investor in a private equity firm's vehicle of a limited partnership nature may generate ECI for a foreign investor. To prevent such negative tax consequences, many foreign investors elect to invest in private equity funds via offshore blocker corporations. Foreign tax-exempt investors should be conscious of any developments in tax law that may have potentially negative tax consequences for them.

During the operational due diligence process, investors should take measures to review tax-related issues to ensure that a private equity fund has proper tax planning procedures in place. Such reviews should also encompass any trends of potential changing legislation in differing tax regimes so that investors will not incur undue taxes as a result of an investment in a particular private equity fund.

DIAGNOSING AND MITIGATING REPUTATIONAL RISK

Before investing in a private equity firm, a concern prevalent in most investor's minds relates to the issues of reputation risk. This sometimes amorphous operational risk category can be difficult to define. Some investors may focus on this category solely from a more hard-line perspective of inquiring whether a private equity manager has ever been arrested for financial crime. Others may broaden the scope of such inquiries to determine if a manager has even been sued or has any negative media relating to them. In many instances investors will engage third-party background investigation firms to perform such reviews. Some key considerations and questions investors may want to consider regarding background investigations and reputation risk management include:

To ask the private equity manager regarding reputation risk:

- Is the private equity firm willing to provide an investor with the necessary release forms and permissions to conduct a background investigation?
- If not, is this a threshold issue that in the investor's opinion would render the firm not investible?
- How does the private equity manager respond to open-ended inquiries such as, "Are there any reputational issues that we should be made aware of?"

Questions to consider when evaluating a background investigation firm:

- How does your fee structure work?
- Are different fees charged for private equity as opposed to other asset classes? If so, why?
- If the background investigation firm has already performed work on an individual or private equity firm, will it resell this work? If yes, is such work available at a discount?

- Is all the background investigation work performed by the private equity firm itself or are subcontractors utilized?
- What is the firm's process for non-U.S. investigations?
- How are searches that may require translation services (e.g., non-English language searches) performed?
- How long do new investigations typically take?
- What is the scope of background investigations performed? Do such investigations include:
  - Previous employment history verification
  - Education background verification
  - Address history
  - Professional certifications verification
  - Litigation searches, civil and criminal
  - Arbitration and disciplinary action archives of regulators
  - Reviews of media and news articles
  - State and federal regulatory searches
  - Uniform Commercial Code, bankruptcies, judgments and liens, and research
  - Research into affiliated entities
  - Review of historical business and regulatory filings
  - Property records

Another consideration with regard to background investigations relates to the issue of on whom background investigations are to be performed. All investors would likely generally agree that the General Partner should be investigated as well as the portfolio manager or managers of the funds. Beyond that there are a number of different approaches that can be taken. The three primary models that are generally utilized in practice are:

1. *Equity ownership model.* An investigation should be performed on all those who have equity ownership in the management company of the private equity firm.
2. *Investment decision-making-authority model.* Background investigations are performed on those individuals who have authority to make investment decisions and act (i.e., trade) on such decisions.
3. *Risk-control model.* Background investigations are performed on all individuals, both investment and noninvestment focused, who control risk within an organization. These can be the portfolio managers and head traders, as well as the chief financial officer (CFO), chief compliance officer (CCO), chief operating officer (COO), and chief executive officer (CEO).

Investors must also consider the issue of when during the operational due diligence process should such investigations be ordered. There is no single correct answer to this question. Due to the expense involved in ordering such investigations as well as the order of investor's different operational due diligence processes, timing may vary. Some investors may order the investigation early on in the process to prevent them from expending effort on further due diligence if an issue will be uncovered during the background investigation that could be considered to be a deal killer. Other investors may view the background investigation process as the final hurdle that a private equity manager must overcome after all other due diligence, both investment and operational, is substantially complete.

CONCLUSION

This chapter provides an overview of additional operational due diligence techniques that can be employed to expand a basic operational due diligence process. This discussion begins with providing a comparison of the core versus an expanded analysis processes. This chapter next covers additional considerations that can be incorporated into a more comprehensive expanded operational due diligence process. Additional considerations include compensation structures and the manager's investment in the funds. This chapter next provides an overview of the benefits of incorporating interview and question design techniques into the operational due diligence process. Finally, this chapter provides an overview of certain areas where common red flags may be present during the operational due diligence process, including service provider reviews and cash management controls. Once an investor has established a strong core operational due diligence program, expanding the review process can increase not only the depth, but also the quality and effectiveness of such due diligence reviews.

NOTES

1. See Davis Polk and Wardwell, "Management Equity Arrangements in Private Equity Transactions Part II: Compensatory Equity Awards," January 26, 2009. Available at: http://www.davispolk.com/1485409/newsletters/privateequity/pe_20090122.htm
2. See Charles Yeschke, *The Art of Investigative Interviewing: A Human Approach to Testimonial Evidence* (Butterworth-Heinemann, 2003), 72.
3. See Nathan Gordon and William Fleisher, *Effective Interviewing and Interrogation Techniques, Third Edition* (Academic Press, 2011).

4. See Jeff Rutenbeck, *Tech Terms: What Every Telecommunications and Digital Media Person Should Know* (Focal Press, 2006).
5. See "Private Equity Investors Are Concerned About Fraud; Many Would Pay a Premium for . . . ," September 10, 2008, www.reuters.com/article/2008/09/10/idUS136482+10-Sep-2008+BW20080910.
6. Azam Ahmed, "New California Lobbyist Law Upsets Hedge Funds," *New York Times Dealbook*, January 14, 2011.
7. U.S. Securities and Exchange Commission, "17 CFR Part 275, Release No. IA-3043; File No. S7-18-09, RIN 3235-AK30," www.sec.gov/rules/final/2010/ia-3043.pdf.
8. See Thomas Fox, "Private Equity and the FCPA," January 3, 2011, www.lexisnexis.com/community/corpsec/blogs/corporateandsecuritieslawblog/archive/2011/01/03/private-equity-and-the-fcpa.aspx.

CHAPTER 5

Valuation Techniques, Methodologies, and Standards

Valuation is one of the areas that Limited Partners (LPs) tend to focus their efforts on during the operational due diligence process. Understanding and diagnosing operational risk in the valuation process is certainly an area that may be fraught with considerable operational risks. Investors who take care to appropriately understand not only the valuation methodologies employed by a particular private equity fund but also the ways in which such theories are put into practice will also likely gain insights into other areas of a firm's operational risk exposures. This further highlights the central area of private equity fund valuation, as many other operational functions may be affected in addition to fund marks such as reporting, information technology platforms to handle pricing fees, and the potential use of service providers in the valuation process. This chapter provides an overview of the private equity valuation landscape and considerations that LPs must consider in approaching the private equity fund valuation process.

LIMITED PARTNER DISTINCTION BETWEEN FUND LEVEL AND PORTFOLIO COMPANY VALUATION APPROACHES

Investors performing operational due diligence on a private equity fund can approach the subject of valuation from two different regards. The first such consideration regarding valuation is the way in which the private equity firm will calculate a value for the portfolio itself. This valuation is utilized to determine the fund's overall performance and how an investor's return on investment is calculated. The second consideration relates to the ways in which a private equity firm will value the fund's holdings. It is this second valuation consideration to which the majority of investors dedicate their operational due diligence efforts.

VALUATION CONSIDERATIONS FOR NEWLY FORMED FUNDS

Investors, performing operational due diligence on a newly formed private equity fund that has yet to begin any investment activity, do not have any historical fund specific valuation evidence from which they can assess whether appropriate valuation methodologies are followed. In these cases, investors can look to the valuation procedures employed in vintage funds or similarly managed funds overseen by the private equity firm, if any such funds were historically managed.

Additionally, despite the fact that a fund has not been actively trading, investors can still take measures to evaluate the anticipated valuation processes and procedures that a private equity fund anticipates employing once investing activity begins. Such valuation guidance will likely be memorialized in several documents that a firm maintains. These can include the offering memorandum and due diligence questionnaires. Additionally, many private equity firms may also maintain separate valuation policies and procedure documents that may spell out the ways in which valuations are calculated on a more detailed basis.

INTRODUCTION TO VALUATION

The operational due diligence process presents investors with an opportunity to understand the methodology choices employed by private equity firms. Some General Partners (GPs) and even LPs may be inclined to imply that private equity fund valuation is a straightforward process. Indeed, your author has come across some GPs who argue that LPs should just effectively write a check to the GPs when the fund is first formed and, at least from a valuations perspective, they should not be overly concerned with valuations on any annual basis, never mind a quarterly one. This mentality is supported by the longer-term nature of private equity funds as compared to more liquid investments, such as hedge funds. A longer-term investment however, does not mean that investors should simply put their hands up and turn a blind eye to oversight of the fund until the fund is approaching the end of its term. This is particularly true in the area of valuation.

While a GP may prefer not to be bothered with the so-called inconvenience of ongoing valuation work, such continual process review and ongoing valuations have investment benefits for the actual management of the private equity portfolio and for investors, as well. Investors should be wary of any GP that pushes back on valuation frequency and transparency in this regard. Indeed, as the discussion in this chapter outlines, many private equity industry self-promulgated valuation standards as well as more general accounting standards suggest, or in some cases require, that a GP devote increased resources to providing such additional oversight to investors in this regard. Additionally, private equity firms that increase reporting frequency and rigorousness of their own fund valuation procedures may reduce the burden for the LP to perform more detailed due diligence at certain times on the fund's valuations. Additionally, this will likely reduce the time and resources that LPs may be required to devote to providing transparency or justifications of their own valuation processes and procedures.

GIPS STATEMENT ON PRIVATE EQUITY

The CFA Institute created and administers a series of fund calculation and reporting standards that are utilized throughout the asset management industry across multiple asset classes and fund types. These standards are collectively referred to as Global Investment Performance Standards (GIPS).[1] GIPS has produced a series of guidance statements on standards interpretations and guidance statements regarding different aspects of fund reporting and transparency. Relevant to our present discussion, these guidance statements include a *Guidance Statement on Real Estate* and *Guidance Statement on Private Equity*.

The GIPS standards are designed to provide a fund's prospective clients with the information needed to evaluate a fund's performance figures. The GIPS guidance with regard to private equity fund valuation outlines that the notions of fair value that are utilized in the GIPS provisions as applicable toward private equity are similar to the concepts of fair value utilized in international accounting standards.

The GIPS guidance in this regards also points out the difficulties in valuing private equity investments has resulted in a number of different attempts at more globalized valuation methodology harmonization through the work of private equity industry groups such as the British Venture Capital Association, the European Venture Capital Association, and the U.S. Private Equity Industry Guidelines Group. It should be noted that the GIPS Private Equity Valuations principles are not meant to replace any regional valuation guidelines but rather to support such methodologies via high-level valuation guidelines.[2]

The GIPS private equity guidelines provide guidance with regard to methodology and performance-reporting standards that a private equity fund can employ. In this regard, the GIPS standards also outline formulas that can be utilized to calculate a fund's internal rate of return, commonly referred to as IRR. Examples of the formulas that the *Guidance Statement on Private Equity* standards outline include the calculation of the annualized IRR, calculated as follows:

$$V_E = [V_B \times (1 + r_{IRR})^{TD/365}] + \sum_{i=1}^{I} [CF_i \times (1 + r_{IRR})^{t_i/365}]$$

where V_B = value of the investment at the beginning of the measurement period
  V_E = value of the investment at the end of the measurement period
  CF_i = cash flow i (positive values for inflows and negative values for outflows)
  i = number of cash flows (1, 2, … I) during the measurement period
  r_{IRR} = annualized internal rate of return
  t_i = number of calendar days from the day when the cash flow i occurred to the end of the measurement period
  TD = total number of calendar days within the measurement period

Additionally, the GIPS private equity guidance outlines that firms with less than one year of performance since inception must present a nonannualized since inception IRR that is calculated utilized the following formula:

$$R_{IRR} = [(1 + r_{IRR})^{TD/365}] - 1$$

where R_{IRR} = nonannualized internal rate of return
  r_{IRR} = annualized internal rate of return
  TD = total number of calendar days within the measurement period

Investors approaching a private equity fund's performance reporting and valuation processes can utilize guidelines such as GIPS to evaluate the valuation methodologies employed. By developing an understanding of such standards, limited partners will have benchmark methodologies against which to compare valuation and performance reporting approaches. Even if a private equity firm does not adhere to GIPS reporting standards, familiarity with such standards can provide useful guidance in evaluating a private equity firm's approach toward valuation and performance reporting in this regard.

IPEV GUIDELINES

Through a collaborative effort of private equity industry participants, the private equity industry over the years has promulgated different guidelines with respect to valuation guidance. One fairly prevalent standard is the *International Private Equity and Venture Capital Valuation Guidelines*, which are generally referred to as the IPEV guidelines. These guidelines provide a methodology framework that a private equity fund may seek to utilize when evaluating and reporting the value of its investments. Compared to the GIPS guidance, the IPEV guidelines are focused primarily on valuation and not on performance reporting standards.[3]

A concept central to the IPEV guidelines is the notion of *fair value*. The IPEV standards define fair value as "the price at which an orderly transaction would take place between market participants at the reporting date." This can be contrasted with the likely discounted amount that a private equity fund would realize should it be forced to exit a position in a distressed sale situation or a forced liquidation.

The IPEV guidelines further outline that, regardless of the valuation methodology employed, the so-called Enterprise Value utilized by a private equity fund to value portfolio companies should follow several measures including:[4]

- Adjust the enterprise value for surplus assets or excess liabilities
- Deduct from the revised Enterprise Value any financial instruments that may rank in priority ahead of the next highest ranking instrument of fund in the event of a liquidation
- Allocate the relevant enterprise value among the firm's relevant financial instruments

The IPEV guidelines also outline guidance with regard to a number of commonly utilized valuation methodologies. These valuation methodologies are summarized in Exhibit 5.1 and are discussed in more detail in the following sections.

Price of Recent Investment

The *price of recent investment* approach effectively can be equated to valuing a position at cost. The IPEV guidelines outline that this methodology is generally most frequently employed in start-up, seed, and early-state valuation situations. Over time the accuracy of such valuations tends to decrease. While the price of recent investment, or at-cost, valuations may be appropriate in the short term after a position is acquired by a private equity fund, the

EXHIBIT 5.1 Overview of Valuation Methodologies as Applicable to Common Company Types

Valuation Methodology	Common Use
Price of recent investment	Start-up, seed, and early state
Multiples	Established business: identified, maintainable income stream
Net assets	Property holding companies, investment business such as fund of funds, whose fair value is derived primarily from the assets held as compared to net earnings.
Discounted cash flows or earnings (of underlying business)	Both established and early-stage portfolio companies
Discounted cash flows (from the Investment)	Underlying private equity fund investment soon to be realized or pending floatation of underlying portfolio company
Industry valuation benchmarks	Limited uses

IPEV guidelines outline a number of reasons why over time the continued use of such valuations are not an accurate representation of a position's fair value. These reasons can include the fact that the transaction may be part of a forced sale and that different rights in investments may attach to portfolio investments.

There is no fixed amount of time after which the use of this price of recent investment methodology is no longer effective, and substantial discretion is afforded to the GP or, perhaps, a third-party valuation consultant as applicable. In determining whether a change in the fair value of a position has occurred, oftentimes the GP or valuation agent may employ a so-called *milestone analysis approach*, for early-stage investments. Often, when different milestones in the growth of a portfolio company are achieved, it presents an opportunity for the private equity firm or valuer to determine whether a new valuation should be performed. The IPEV guidelines describe a number of different factors that are likely to be included under this milestone analysis approach in reaching a decision as to whether to revalue a position. Examples of typical valuation milestones are analyzed in Exhibit 5.2.

Multiple Valuation

The *multiple* valuation methodology focuses on the earnings of a portfolio company. The IPEV guidelines outline that, in general, this method is

EXHIBIT 5.2 IPEV Guidelines Commonly Accepted Milestones for
Early Development Stage Companies

Financial Measures

Revenue growth	Cash burn rate
Profitability expectations	Covenant compliance

Technical Measures
Phases of development
Paten approvals
Testing cycles

Marketing and Sales Measures

Customer surveys	Testing phases
Market share	Market introduction

appropriate for valuing established businesses with identified income streams. This methodology may also be utilized for an early-stage firm's applying revenue multipliers to estimate position valuation. The IPEV guidelines also outline that the multiple valuation approach can be employed when companies possess both positive and negative earnings. In the case of negative earnings, the negative earnings cannot generally be sustained for extended periods of time. For short-term negative earnings, the IPEV guidelines state that such negative earnings are permissible as long as they can be normalized to identify a positive level of maintainable earnings. The IPEV guidelines state that a number of different earnings multiples may be employed including a price/earnings multiple (P/E), enterprise value/earnings before interest and tax (EV/EBIT), and depreciations and amortization (EV/EBITDA).

Net Assets

The *net assets* valuation methodology concentrates on determining the value of a portfolio company with a focus on the value of the net assets of the portfolio company. The IPEV guidelines outline that net assets valuation methodology is appropriate for businesses such as property holding companies and investment businesses, such as funds-of-funds, whose fair value is derived primarily from the assets held as compared to net earnings. The net assets methodology may be most appropriate for companies that are producing low profit levels, such as the example included in the IPEV guidelines of a loss-making company.

Discounted Cash Flows or Earnings (of Underlying Business)

The *discounted cash flows or earnings (of underlying business)* methodology focuses on calculating valuations based on the expected value of future cash flows. This methodology is appropriate for both established and early-stage portfolio companies. Specifically, the IPEV guidelines outline that the present value of expected futures cash flows or the present value of expected future earnings can be utilized with this methodology. This methodology also incorporates an assumption as to the terminal value of the underlying business of the portfolio company.

This terminal value for the underlying business is compared to the terminal value of the investment itself, which is not utilized under the discounted cash flows or earnings (of underlying business) methodology. A number of different inputs and methodologies may be utilized in calculating terminal values, including Ohlson Logit regression models.[5] The guidelines further outline that due to the flexibility of the private equity firm or valuation agent in making detailed cash flow forecasts and the requirement for a terminal value estimation, this method may have drawbacks that may result in "insufficiently reliable" fair values.

Discounted Cash Flows (from the Investment)

The *discounted cash flows (from the investment)* methodology focuses around utilizing the discounted cash flow model to those cash flows that are to be expected from the investment that the private equity fund itself makes. The IPEV guidelines outline that the use of this methodology may be appropriate in situations where an investment is soon to be realized or the flotation of an underlying business is expected. Similar to the risks of utilizing the *discounted cash flows or earnings (of underlying business)* methodology, the *discounted cash flows (from the investment)* methodology requires both cash flow forecasts and terminal value assumptions and estimations that may result in unreliable valuations.

Industry Valuation Benchmarks

The *industry valuation benchmarks* methodology focuses on the utilization of benchmarks in the valuation process. Specifically the IPEV guidelines outline that this method employs the use of industry-specific benchmarks to assist in valuation. Examples provided by the IPEV guidelines include benchmarks such as price per subscriber for cable TV companies or price per bed for companies that operate nursing homes. The IPEV guidelines caution that the benefits of using the *industry valuation benchmarks* methodology are limited to certain circumstances and that the use of such benchmarks is likely to be more beneficial to the private equity firm or third-party valuer as a common-sense check of values that are calculated via other previously referenced methodologies.

Other IPEV Guidance

In addition to the previously referenced valuation methodologies, the IPEV guidelines also provide guidance with regard to the valuation of secondary transactions and in calculating adjustments to a fund's net asset value. The guidelines also present some considerations that can be utilized in determining appropriate valuations to be employed in different insider funding rounds, distressed market transactions, bridge financing, mezzanine loans, rolled-up loan interest, and indicative offers. Finally, the IPEV guidelines also provide guidance with regard to the impact that the structuring of a private equity investment may play in influencing valuations. Some common clauses that the IPEV guidelines outline have an influence on such valuations including antidilution clauses, ratchet clauses, convertible debt instruments, and commitments to follow-on investments.

FAS 157

Statement of Financial Accounting Standards 157: Fair Value Measurement, sometimes referred to as SFAS 157 or FAS 157, is an accounting pronouncement that was issued by the Financial Accounting Standards Board (FASB) of the United States. Since taking effect on November 15, 2007, FAS 157 has had a major impact on the reporting of valuations of positions held by private equity funds. FAS 157 was enacted in an effort to increase harmonization of fair value reporting standards and methodologies. Specifically, the following excerpt from the Financial Accounting Standards Board's Summary of Statement No. 157 outlines the reasons for issuing this statement on fair value measurements:

> *Prior to this Statement, there were different definitions of fair value and limited guidance for applying those definitions in GAAP. Moreover, that guidance was dispersed among the many accounting pronouncements that require fair value measurements. Differences in that guidance created inconsistencies that added to the complexity in applying GAAP. In developing this Statement, the Board considered the need for increased consistency and comparability in fair value measurements and for expanded disclosures about fair value measurements.*[6]

In particular, FAS 157 has sought to accomplish three primary goals:

1. Create a uniform definition of fair value.
2. Establish a fair value measurement framework under generally accepted accounting principles (GAAP).
3. Broaden the disclosure requirements for those fair value observations.

FAS 157 paragraph five is commonly known as FASB ASC 820. FASB ASC 820 defines fair value as "the price that would be received *to sell* an asset or paid to transfer a liability in an orderly transaction between market participants at the measurement date" (emphasis added).[7]

This sale price can be thought of as the exit price of a position. This represents a significant departure from the previous general thinking that fair value was the price a private equity fund would pay to acquire an asset (e.g., cost or entry price).

It is important to note this distinction between the use of sale price versus cost. Different private equity funds may use different reference marks when determining the exit price of a position. Additionally, certain firms may feel it is appropriate to apply discounts based on factors such as illiquidity of a particular portfolio holding. Furthermore, contingent on a number of factors, including timing of the calculations and the types of assets involved, entry prices and exit prices can differ substantially.

FAS 157 provides a framework for fair value measurement that categorizes assets into three distinct categories that are commonly referred to as levels. Each level correlates to the ease or certainty with which the value of an asset may be obtained. Specifically, assets that fall into the Level 1 category are those whose prices are easily available in the market. An example of a Level 1 asset would be a stock traded on the NASDAQ or New York Stock Exchange. Level 2 assets are those whose prices are not readily observable but whose valuations are based on observable inputs of similarly traded assets. An example of a Level 2 asset would be the common stock of a public company restricted from sale under Rule 144. Level 3 assets are those whose values are not observable in the market. Examples of Level 3 assets include certain mortgage-linked assets, private equity investments, and certain long-dated options.

FAS 157 requires private equity fund managers to provide specific additional disclosures regarding valuation methodologies. As outlined earlier, for private equity funds the bulk of a private equity fund's holdings will be classified as Level 3 assets. FAS 157 outlines that for Level 3 assets, private equity funds had to make more disclosures than were previously required. Specifically, Level 3 assets private equity funds are now required to disclose details such as a description of the input used to determine the mark, and the information utilized to develop this. An example of this disclosure would be, "For Level III investments, the Funds value the investments primarily using a discounted cash flow methodology."

For private equity funds, the biggest implication has not necessarily been in regard to the requirements to classify assets into the different FAS 157 levels. Instead, arguably the biggest impact that FAS 157 has had on the private equity industry has been that it has forced private equity funds to focus on the issue of valuation on a more frequent basis. It is not that private equity funds did not necessarily have to outline both the cost and fair value of positions in audited annual financial statements, but rather that FAS 157 has increased the scrutiny paid to this issue by LPs and fund auditors alike. With this increased focus, FAS 157 has continued to promote an increased movement toward valuation transparency and disclosures made by private equity funds. This has benefited LPs during the operational due diligence process because they have additional clarity and another series of data points that they can examine during the operational due diligence process.

Despite the benefits of FAS 157, many LPs still struggle to maintain the appropriate level of information required to fully assess a GP's fair valuation process.[8] These difficulties have caused frustration among LPs regarding their own reporting and valuation requirements. An example of this relates to FASB Accounting Standards Update No. 2009-12, which is commonly referred to as ASU 2009-12. This is somewhat ironic because measures such as ASU 2009-12 were intended to expedite fair value determinations. Others in the private equity industry have simply referred to FAS 157 as "stupid" and as a measure that "injects a ton of false precision and costs" into the process.[9] Investors must seek to balance the drawbacks of FAS 157 with the benefits of additionally transparency and oversight that it provides.

USE OF THIRD-PARTY VALUATION CONSULTANTS

Regardless of the required or self-driven valuation policies followed by a particular private equity fund, the actual valuation work of a private equity firm may be performed completely internally, by the in-house resources of the fund, or via a combination of external and internal resources.

Some private equity firms may argue in favor of performing solely in-house valuations for a number of different reasons. One example that a proponent may raise is that it is not cost-efficient to have a third-party valuation consultant involved. Third-party valuation consultants can be retained under a number of different fee arrangements. Examples of such fee arrangements can include retaining a third-party valuation consultant on a project-by-project basis, such as when a new portfolio asset is first acquired or sold, or on a retainer basis to perform a certain fixed number of valuation reviews on a fixed time schedule, such as annually. Depending on the scope of the review services performed, as well as the size of the actual positions being valued in certain cases, the argument against utilizing a third-party valuation consultant may gain support when a comparison of the trade-off of the cost to the private equity fund versus the value of the actual position is taken into account. For example, if a third-party valuation firm charges $25,000 in order to value a position, but the entire position was acquired by the private equity fund at a cost of only $10,000, then it does not make good economic sense for the fund to expend more on the valuation of such a position than the position may actually have been acquired for or may be worth upon exit of the position.

Continuing our example, consider the same position with a $10,000 acquisition cost. Now assume that over time the value of the position significantly increased to $75,000. This may still be only a small percentage of the overall fund's portfolio. What if the asset was worth $150,000 or $250,000? Would a $25,000 third-party valuation fee be worth the expense? The answer to this question is subjective. There is no single correct ratio or trade-off of expenses versus cost that a fund necessarily adheres to. To the contrary, the decision of the private equity fund to utilize third-party valuation consultants is often a subjective one that varies on a position-by-position basis. The actual or perceived liquidity of such positions may also have a strong influence on such decisions. When a position becomes more difficult to value due to illiquidity, a private equity fund may have less confidence in internal valuations. In these cases, the decision of a GP to utilize a third-party consultant to assist in valuations may be more than a simple calculation of cost versus expense, because the firm may not be overly confident of its own valuation work or may simply want to confirm its own internal work via a third-party opinion.

Outside of these considerations, and based on their own valuation policies, a private equity fund may not provide itself with the option of not utilizing such consultants above certain fund assets under management (AUM) thresholds. For example, a private equity fund may have a policy where any position that is more than a fixed percentage of the overall portfolio at the time of purchase requires a third-party valuation to be performed. Firms may also implement ongoing valuation requirements for positions that continue to be of a certain size at fixed intervals.

Consider for example, a fund that makes an investment in an underlying portfolio company. At the time of purchase assume that the position represents 9 percent of fund AUM. Let us further assume that this fund maintains a valuation policy that requires a third-party valuation consultant

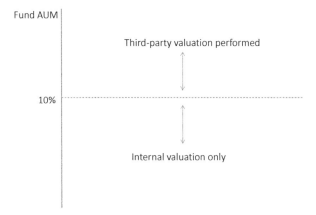

EXHIBIT 5.3   Sample Assets under Management
Threshold for a Private Equity Firm to Use Third-Party
Valuation Consultants

to perform an independent valuation of positions that at the time of acquisition are 10 percent or more of fund AUM. Therefore, this 9 percent position does not meet the assets under management threshold and at this stage would not be required to undergo a third-party valuation. This relationship is summarized in Exhibit 5.3.

Continuing our example, let's also assume that the fund's valuation policies outline the position that an increase in size to over 10 percent of fund AUM requires a third-party valuation. If the position subsequently increases in size from 9 percent to 11 percent, then according to this policy the fund must now utilize a third-party valuation consultant to perform a valuation. When such policies are in place a number of questions are raised as to when such valuations are to be performed.

For example, it would not likely make sense for the fund to engage a third-party valuation consultant to perform a valuation of a position that is 11 percent of the portfolio if the private equity fund anticipates perhaps that the position may decrease in size again to below the 10 percent threshold in a short period of time. It is also worth noting that most private equity firms provide themselves with enough discretion in certain regards so that they have the flexibility to make such determinations. Furthermore, such valuation policies may provide flexibility regarding the timing of the valuation of such positions. For example, if the position due to a supposed increase in value rose from an anticipated 9 percent to 11 percent of the fund's assets under management at the beginning of the first quarter, then the private equity firm, which for our example may have been used to performing semi-annual position valuations, may not be inclined to have such a valuation performed off-cycle. As the earlier discussion demonstrates, the presence of seemingly detailed valuation policies and procedures may also provide the GP with certain discretion in this regard. When investors perform operational due diligence on the valuation processes of a private equity firm under review, they should inquire as to the scope of services and the use of such consultants. Some questions that investors could pose include:

- Does the fund use valuation consultants regularly?
- If not utilized for every position in the fund portfolio, with what frequency are such consultants utilized (e.g., asset threshold level or position size levels, etc.)?
- Are several different third-party valuation consultants utilized?
- If multiple consultants are utilized, are they specialized by asset type or generalists?
- What steps has the fund taken to ensure that cherry-picking of valuation consultants valuations is not a risk?
- Are consultants changed with any frequency?
- What is the scope of valuation work performed by these consultants?
- Do third-party valuation consultants perform on-site visits to portfolio companies to assist in the valuation process?
- Will the fund share a copy of such valuation work with investors?
- Is third-party valuation work shared with the fund's third-party administrator?
- What work does the fund's auditors perform in reviewing or confirming these third-party valuations?
- Are third-party valuation consultants providing actual values, ranges of values, positive assurance of values, or negative assurance?
- What are the plans to resolve a conflict, if the GP disagrees with the mark of the valuation consultant?

VALUATION OUTPUT PROCESS DOCUMENTATION

In terms of valuation, one consideration that LPs should take into account during the operational due diligence process is the way in which a private equity firm documents the outputs of the valuation process. To clarify the documentation being referenced in this discussion is not the valuation policies and procedures that outline the so-called rule by which a private equity firm intends to value its portfolio holdings. It should also be noted that the output documentation being referenced is not that which is required to be produced as part of any audit work or regulatory reviews. Rather, in this case, the documentation being referenced is that which a private equity firm, adhering to the previously referenced policies and procedures, may produce in conducting valuations in accordance with these valuation rules. Indeed, a private equity firm's valuation policies and procedures may outline certain specific valuation output process requirements. In other instances, the valuation policies and procedures may not necessarily outline a requirement that a private equity fund produce any sort of valuation output documentation, but rather leave this to the broad discretion of the GP.

Due to this broad flexibility, investors may encounter a wide variety of different methods by which a private equity firm attempts to document the results of their valuation processes. For example, some private equity firms may only produce documentation, such as a valuation memorandum, when a position is acquired. Other private equity funds may opt to produce a valuation memorandum when a position is exited. Still other firms may seek to produce such valuation memorandum when an event occurs that they feel will materially affect the fair value of a fund holding.

Another option is for a private equity firm to produce valuation memoranda with a certain specified frequency (e.g., quarterly) regardless of whether or not any valuation-type events occur. These options are not exclusive of each other. A private equity firm may opt to produce valuation memorandum at intervals based on any of the previously referenced intervals or via some other alternative methodology. Furthermore, a private equity may produce internal valuation documentation in coordination with the work of any third-party valuations that may have been performed. For example, a private equity firm may have a policy of employing a third-party valuation agent for new positions but the firm may produce its own internal valuation memoranda when valuation events occur throughout the life of a held asset. When approaching an analysis of the valuation process employed by a private equity fund, investors should inquire about the frequency with which any such valuation memoranda are prepared.

Another consideration regarding the frequency of such valuation memoranda is what information is contained in such memoranda. For example, for a newly acquired position a private equity firm may produce more extensive valuation memoranda that may leverage off the GP's own initial due diligence work on the portfolio position, as compared to other valuation situations. There is no set format by which a private equity firm must document the output of its internal valuation process. Indeed, as outlined earlier, outside of any audit or regulatory requirements, a private equity fund does not need to produce user-friendly documentation as to how valuations were calculated. As such, due to this lack of uniformity, investors should inquire as to the format of any valuation documentation produced. For example, does a private equity fund's valuation memorandum provide an overview of qualitative factors such as the market environment as relevant to the asset and comparisons with other industry competitors that may influence an asset's fundamentals? In certain instances, as outlined earlier, a third-party valuation agent may be utilized. It is likely that the work of the third-party valuer will be more extensive in certain regards than a private equity firm's own internal valuations. In these situations, investors should inquire as to how private equity firms compensate for any such valuation scope discrepancies when calculating and documenting valuations on their own accord.

VALUATION COMMITTEE REVIEW SCOPE

If a private equity fund does produce internal valuation memoranda, investors should also inquire as to how such memoranda are utilized. Are they simply thrown in a drawer or does the firm employ active discussions around the points raised? In certain cases, a private equity firm may also maintain a distinct internal valuation committee that is responsible for reviewing, and in some cases approving, any valuation memoranda. If a valuation committee is maintained by a private equity firm, investors should attempt to gauge the rigorousness of such valuation committee reviews.

One way investors can begin this process is by first reviewing the makeup of the valuation committee. If the committee consists solely of investment personnel then there is a greater potential for a conflict of interest in the valuations committee reviews of any values struck or the approval of valuation memoranda by the valuation committee. Rather, it is considered best practice for a private equity firm to have as members of the valuation committee representatives of different departments throughout the firm.

Examples of departments that may be commonly represented include legal and compliance, fund operations, and risk management. With an understanding of the makeup of the valuation, committee investors can next inquire as to the frequency by which any review of valuations, or associated valuation memoranda, occur. This may be an indication of how seriously the firm views the role of such a committee. For example, if the valuation committee meets only once a year, this does not suggest vigorous valuation oversight, as compared with one that convenes valuation committee meetings on a monthly basis.

ADDITIONAL LIMITED PARTNER VALUATION CONSIDERATIONS

A private equity hedge fund's policies and procedures related to valuation should undergo careful scrutiny as part of the investor due diligence process. A LP's proprietary approach to hedge fund operational due diligence should encompass a multifaceted review of private equity valuation procedures. Investors should take steps to ensure that their operational due diligence process also evaluates what checks and balances, if any, are in place to ensure consistency and independence in determining valuations. In addition to those considerations outlined as part of the evaluation process of a private equity fund's valuation procedures, some key questions investors should consider include:

- What steps has the GP taken to ensure independence in the pricing process?
- Where do the majority of pricing inputs come from?
- How is an appropriate price determined if a discrepancy exists among pricing inputs? Is an average taken? Are the highest and/or lowest price discarded? Who makes these determinations?
- Does the fund maintain an internal pricing committee?
- What role does the administrator play in the pricing process?
- Is the administrator, independently of the private equity manager, corresponding with any trading counterparties? If so, what data is shared among these organizations?

CONCLUSION

This chapter provides an introduction to valuation techniques, methodologies, and standards employed by private equity funds. It is advisable that LPs approach the operational due diligence process armed with a familiarity with valuation policies and procedures as well as the relevant private equity industry guidelines and any accounting or regulatory requirements regarding valuation processes or disclosures. Additionally, LPs should take care to review the relevant internal valuation policies and procedures that may have been created by a particular private equity fund under review. These policies can often provide useful insights during the operational due diligence process, as to a particular private equity firm's approach toward valuation. Despite their apparent detail, such policies often afford the GP significant discretion. Such discretion may be limited in part by the use of third-party valuation agents. However, LPs should take care to vet such relationships and determine the scope and extent to which such external valuers are utilized. Valuation can be an opaque subject for many investors. Yet a comprehensive operational due diligence review should attempt to pull the curtain back and provide transparency of both process and actual valuation practices employed by a private equity firm.

NOTES

1. GIPS is a registered trademark of the CFA Institute.
2. CFA Institute, *GIPS Guidance Statement on Private Equity*, 2010, www.gipsstandards.org/standards/guidance/develop/pdf/gs_private_equity_clean.pdf.
3. *International Private Equity and Venture Capital Valuation Guidelines*, August 2010 Edition, www.privateequityvaluation.com/documents/International_PE_VC_Valuation_Guidelines_Sep_2009_Update_110130.pdf.
4. Ibid.
5. See Alice Lee, *Financial Analysis, Planning, and Forecasting: Theory and Application, Second Edition* (World Scientific Publishing Co. Pte. Ltd., 2009).
6. Summary of Statement No. 157, www.fasb.org/st/summary/stsum157.shtml.
7. Financial Accounting Standards Board, "*Statement of Financial Accounting Standards No. 157, Fair Value Measurements,*" 2008, www.fasb.org/cs/BlobServer?blobcol=urldata&blobtable=MungoBlobs&blobkey=id&blobwhere=1175820931833&blobheader=application%2Fpdf.
8. Nicholas Donato, "LPs Struggle with Fair Value Auditing," *PE Manager*, May 3, 2011, www.privateequitymanager.com/Article.aspx?article=60844&hashID=99B088427D9E0715489A2BDFC8FC6E546A548C90.
9. Jason Mendelson, "FAS 157 Is Stupid," *Venture Beat*, January 15, 2009.

CHAPTER 6

Legal Due Diligence

Early on in the history of private equity, investors did not perform much, if any, operational due diligence. In recent years, in part driven by losses due to poor operations in funds and outright fraud in others, investors have begun to recognize the benefits of operational risk assessment in private equity funds. These moments of enlightenment, whether driven by a true desire to actually make more informed investment decisions or driven by a once bitten, twice shy reaction caused by bad experiences with poor operational infrastructures in the past, is a positive development for both private equity investors and fund managers alike. As Justice Louis Brandeis once famously said, "Sunlight is the best disinfectant," and with the increased transparency that is required by a well-developed and properly implemented operational due diligence program, private equity investors will hopefully make better-informed operational choices when selecting a private equity fund.

OPERATIONAL DUE DILIGENCE SPECIALISTS VERSUS GENERALISTS

While increased acceptance of operational due diligence is commendable, it presents investors and private equity allocators, such as private equity funds-of-funds and consultants, with a series of challenges. In addition to carrying out the actual review and monitoring work entailed in a private equity operational due diligence program, professional allocators in particular must now make certain decisions as to the structure and resources to be allocated toward operational due diligence.

One decision that must be made in designing the structure of an investor's operational due diligence function is the balance between specialization and generalization. Operational due diligence on private equity funds is a multidisciplinary exercise. This is a point worth repeating. To conduct a thorough assessment of the operational risks of a private equity fund, an investor needs to have the ability to employ analysis techniques from a myriad of different skill sets. These skill sets pull from a variety of different fields of practice including the law, accounting, and information technology. Within each of these broad categories of practice are a panoply of subcategories of related disciplines. Certainly, no single individual can be an expert in each of these areas. This is particularly true when it is taken into account that each of these areas is an evolving field. The law related to private equity funds is continually changing, based on new court decisions and revisions to existing regulations. Similarly, new accounting pronouncements may affect the way in which funds account for certain positions or the way information is presented in financial statements. Information technology evolves at what seems to be an exponentially increasing speed, particularly in the arena of alternative investments. When designing an operational due diligence program, an investor may think it better to plan in favor of specialization as opposed to a more generalized approach.

This intuitive response, however, may not be the best course that investors could take in designing an operational due diligence program. Let's consider the example of a specialist in the field of law. Of course, saying that a particular individual is a specialist in a field as broad as the law is, in and of itself, a generalization. It is equivalent to saying that someone is a specialist in medicine. There are myriad subspecialties within the field of medicine. If you had a broken leg you might not be inclined to go to a general internist but instead to a specialist such as an orthopedist. In the same way, if you slipped and broke your leg in a grocery store you will likely need a completely different attorney than if you are seeking assistance reviewing an offering memorandum of a private equity fund. As such, selecting an appropriate specialist who is capable to assist in the appropriate manner is a crucial element of any specialization program.

While specialists may be a valuable asset in the operational due diligence process, particularly for investors who may not possess the core competencies in a particular operational risk area, overspecialization can be detrimental to the operational due diligence process. One reason for this is that when different specialists are engaged, an *information silo* effect may result. Information silos in the context of an operational due diligence review reflect a scenario where different specialists remain focused on their respective segments of the operational due diligence review. The downside of these information silos is that there is typically a lack of communication among specialists. As such, information found in one operational risk segment that may be relevant to another segment may not be shared appropriately or be considered in a broad-enough context, making it difficult for an investor to connect all of the appropriate operational dots to fully vet certain latent cross-sectional operational risk factors.

This chapter will focus on key considerations investors should keep in mind when evaluating the legal environment in which a private equity firm and fund operates, as well as reviewing common legal documents. This chapter will also provide an overview of trends in private equity fund legal documentation. Investors who do not have a legal background may consider leveraging off the work of legal specialists, such as external legal counsel or operational due diligence consultants whose staff consists of individuals with legal backgrounds, to assist them in navigating this field of the operational due diligence process.

COMMON PRIVATE EQUITY FUND STRUCTURES

Most private equity firms are organized via a combination of partnership entities. At the head of these entities is typically the General Partner (GP). The GP is the managing partner of a private equity company. As indicated in Chapter 1, the GP is not typically a single individual but rather a legal entity that is organized by the private equity firm's principals to oversee the management of a private equity fund.

Sitting below the GP entity is the private equity fund itself. Private equity funds are typically organized via a structure known as a Limited Partnership. Sitting below the private equity entity itself are the portfolio companies that are the investments held by the private equity fund. Feeding into a private equity fund are investors in the fund. Investors in a private equity fund are commonly referred to as Limited Partners (LPs). This name comes from the fact that many private equity funds are organized as limited partnerships and therefore the investors that subscribe (i.e., invest) in those funds are LPs. Exhibit 6.1 provides an overview of a typical private equity legal structure.

In some instances, a private equity fund will have an intermediary level entity known as the Manager or Investment Advisor between the general partner and investors, which technically may serve as the manager of a particular private equity fund. An example of a private equity structure including such an entity is outlined in Exhibit 6.2.

UNDERSTANDING THE PRIVATE PLACEMENT MEMORANDUM

As private investment vehicles, private equity maintains a specialized series of common charter documents. These charter documents may vary, contingent on different jurisdictional regulatory requirements. Generally, the charter documents outline a number of the material terms and risk factors

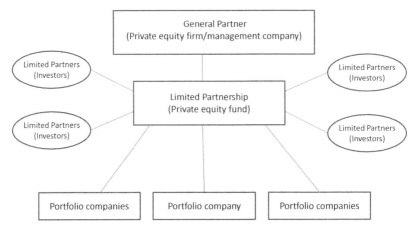

EXHIBIT 6.1 Diagram of Typical Private Equity Legal Structure

associated with a potential investment in the private equity. The most notable, and generally most detailed, of these charter documents is the *offering memorandum* (OM).

This controlling document outlining the major risks and terms of a particular fund is also sometimes referred to as the *private placement memorandum*, which is sometime referred to in abbreviated form as the *PPMs*.

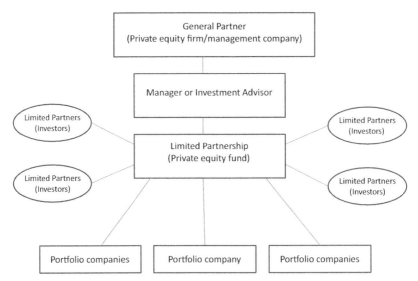

EXHIBIT 6.2 Diagram of Typical Private Equity Legal Structure with Manager/Investment Advisor Layer

Regardless of the moniker employed, there are several key considerations that should be at the forefront of any investor's mind when approaching a review of this document.

Simply because the private equity fund is likely to be the most information-packed and longest document investors will likely review during the operational due diligence process, reviewing such documents does not replace the need to read other documents collected during the operational due diligence process.

In beginning to review the private placement memorandum, investors should be conscious of what the key roles of this document are. For the purposes of this text we will refer to these key roles as the 3C's of private placement memorandum: *central, controlling,* and *core.* Each of these concepts is outlined in more detail in the sections that follow.

Central

PPMs Are Described by Many Other Due Diligence Documents Many of the other documents that comprise the battery of documents that investors should request, collect, and review during the private equity operational due diligence process are descriptive documents. That is, they attempt to boil down or digest the often cumbersome and disclaimer-ridden legal jargon of the PPM into more investor-friendly nonlegalese. A good example of this may be an already prepared descriptive due diligence questionnaire assembled by a private equity manager. As is commonplace today, many of these due diligence questionnaires (DDQs) will detail the key terms of a private equity investment vehicle's offering. While the actual decisions about the setting of levels for items such as management fees resides with the actual management personnel of the firm itself, such decisions are first memorialized in a particular private offering investment vehicles offering memorandum.

Incorporation by Reference Another example of the central role played by the private placement memorandum in the operational due diligence process is the way in which many other documents will not only describe the offering memorandum but also incorporate the document by reference. To clarify, "incorporation by reference" occurs when the document an investor is reading at a particular time, such as an audited financial statement, refers to a second document. In an operational due diligence context, the onus is effectively on the investor reading the first document (e.g., the audited financial statements) to pause midsentence and review the other referenced (e.g., second) document.

As this description of the process may have intimated, this can be somewhat cumbersome and confusing. This is particularly the case when an investor is performing operational due diligence on a firm or particular private equity fund with which they are just starting to gain familiarity during the initial stages of the due diligence process. Further complicating the issues and adding additional roadblocks to the process is when, continuing our example, the document being referenced itself will reference yet another document. Even worse, from an investor's operational due diligence perspective, is the situation where the referenced document does not even attempt to incorporate other documents by reference but simply contains a general disclaimer or couching language that, as may be the case for private placement memoranda, effectively states that the document being reviewed is not a complete statement of all of the terms of the private placement memorandum and the investor should consult the investment management firm. It may even contain a passing reference or halfhearted recommendation that an investor should refer to yet other documents (and in some cases may not even provide an enumerated list of those other documents). This incorporation by reference approach, while it may possess strong legal footing and a sound theoretical backing and potentially prevents the combination of all legal documentation into a single voluminous omnibus document, also creates a difficult terrain that investors must be equipped to navigate when first considering how to approach private placement memorandum analysis in the context of the broader operational due diligence process.

Controlling

In the law, there are two related concepts that are relevant to our discussion of private placement memorandum, particularly when considered from the perspective of an investor seeking to balance the operational due diligence process with a private equity firm's desire to raise capital via marketing efforts. The first such concept is known as parole evidence. Parole is commonly utilized as an adjective interpreted to mean "oral."[1] The parole evidence rule is a common law principle that outlines that a party is generally prohibited from introducing external oral evidence that supplements or contradicts a contract. For the purposes of this discussion, the PPM can be thought of as the legal contract entered into between the investor and the private equity fund. In this context, the PPM can be viewed as controlling because any other statements or marketing puffery do not generally control. If a dispute arises, the offering memorandum will be the primary document that may be looked at by courts. This is not to imply that other documents may not come into play; however, certainly the PPM of a fund will be crucial.

A second related concept is the so-called four corners rule. This states that when ambiguity is present in a contract, or PPM for the purposes of our discussion, the interpretation of such ambiguity should be determined only by looking to the document itself.[2] The term *four corners* refers to a nondigital document (i.e., a rectangular piece of paper) that contains four corners. The point of this rule, which sometimes may produce admittedly harsh results in interpreting document ambiguity, is that the document itself is the controlling factor and extrinsic evidence should not be considered.

Core

For the reasons just described, the private placement memorandum is arguably one of the most important documents that should be collected during the operational due diligence process and is one of a core cadre of documents around which the rest of the document collection and review should be built. Understanding the importance of the core nature of this document is crucial for investors to acknowledge during the operational due diligence process.

Onshore versus Offshore Considerations   The material terms of most charter documents for offshore and onshore vehicles are oftentimes analogous. For onshore vehicles, the OM is sometimes referred to as an *offering circular*, and as a *private placement memorandum* for offshore vehicles. Due to the structures of onshore and offshore entities, there will be differences with regard to the nature of disclosures between onshore and offshore OMs. For example, an offshore OM will typically contain information regarding the vehicle's board of directors, which would not be applicable, and therefore not contained, in the onshore OM.

Private Placement Memorandum Review Process   As noted earlier, a private equity fund's interests are offered to limited investors subject to certain terms and conditions. The PPM describes these basic terms and conditions. Items described in the PPM include a private equity vehicle's trading strategies, and provides descriptions of the fund's management team. In addition to the basic descriptive functions served by this document, the primary purpose of the OM is to detail a series of disclosures to potential investors. These disclosures include the terms of the shares in the private equity vehicle, tax aspects, information about third-party service providers utilized by the private equity vehicle, and subscription and redemption terms.

COMMON DOCUMENT RISK ASSIGNMENT TERMS

Regardless of the specific domicile of each private equity vehicle, such as the distinction between onshore or offshore, private equity OMs generally contain a series of standard risk assignment terms. Examples of these common risk assignment terms include which entities will be responsible for investment making decision authority, which entities will be responsible for day-to-day management of the fund, any key person clauses, and the roles to be played by service providers as opposed to the fund vehicle itself.[3] It is important for the reader to understand the potential interaction of these other risk assignment terms with these indemnity and exculpatory clauses. The interaction of such clauses within the total framework of the investment and operational due diligence process can have marked impact on the total risk assessment of a private equity manager and, at a minimum, should be considered as part of any best practice due diligence process.[4] Two such common document risk assignment terms relate to the concepts of exculpation and indemnity.

EXCULPATION AND INDEMNITY

Each risk assignment term, as well as a host of other intricacies contained in an offering memorandum, is replete with its own unique considerations and intricacies. Investors do not necessarily need to be familiar with the full scope of legal intricacies related to each term or risk assignment in the offering memorandum. However, when reviewing such terms investors would be well advised to look below the surface. A full understanding of certain issues is necessary in order to determine which items are relevant and which may be ignored or given less importance. Oftentimes a specialized practitioner in a particular field, such as accounting or the law, will possess more detailed knowledge in this regard. As outlined earlier, such specialization can add value but investors must not sacrifice overspecialization for a lack of continuity of operational risk factor identification throughout a particular review.

In order to introduce the reader to the level of detail with which certain items may be considered, we will proceed with a detailed review of the terms of *exculpation* and *indemnity*. While these concepts of exculpation and indemnity are just two of the common risk assignment terms contained in the offering memorandum of a private equity fund, this example will provide readers with the type of detailed understanding a specialist may possess. Furthermore, such an understanding can also be useful for investors seeking to recover from losses in the event of a fund failure. Finally, we will provide an overview of trends based on the research of Corgentum Consulting.

Definitions and History of Exculpation and Indemnification

The terms *indemnity* and *exculpatory* have a long history of uses in many contexts outside of both private equity and securities law in general. The concepts of indemnity and exculpation have their roots in insurance law.[5] Examples of early uses of these terms include a diverse series of areas ranging from the development of Saxon law to maritime law and twentieth-century construction contracts.[6] Before beginning our analysis of exculpatory and indemnity clauses in a private equity context, it is useful to first develop an understanding of the uses of such clauses in a broader context. In an investment context, the uses of indemnity and exculpatory clauses in modern private equity OMs draw many similarities to uses in mutual fund prospectuses, particularly in offshore jurisdictions.[7]

While concepts of indemnity and exculpation are both principally related to the assignment of liability, differences are present with regard to the nature and uses of such clauses. *Black's Law Dictionary* defines the term exculpate as, "to free from blame or accusation." An exculpatory clause, in its most generic sense, is a contractual provision that relieves a party from liability resulting from a negligent or wrongful act.[8] Exculpatory clauses have a long history of use in trust and estate law.

While exculpatory clauses provide relief from liabilities, the core focus of indemnity provisions is to provide compensation for damages.[9] *Black's Law Dictionary* defines indemnification as "a duty to make good any loss, damage, or liability incurred by another."[10] In order to clarify the meaning of indemnification it is useful to analyze the nature of the "duty" described in the *Black's Law* definition. The "duty" or obligation to indemnify is a voluntary obligation.[11] The fact that this obligation is voluntary differs from a legal obligation to compensate that may arise. Somewhat clarifying the voluntary nature of this obligation is that an indemnity clause is further defined as "a contractual provision in which one party agrees to answer for any specified or unspecified liability or harm that the other party might incur."[12] A review of the case law, discussed in more detail later, will demonstrate how knowledge and the voluntary nature of fund director's indemnity provisions, plays a key role in liability apportionment.

Uses of Indemnity and Exculpatory Clauses in Private Equity Offering Memoranda

In private equity, OMs indemnity and exculpatory clauses may serve several purposes. First, these terms serve a risk assignment function by outlining the nature and scope at which the fund vehicle itself will be indemnified and will be responsible for exculpatory relief. Second, the risk assignment terms of the OM often outline the responsibility of not only the fund itself but also related entities such as the General Partner or the Investment Manager. In addition to affiliated entities, these clauses can also provide guidance regarding any liability between the fund itself and service providers such as the fund's administrator. With regard to the fund administrator, it should be noted that indemnity and exculpatory terms are typically first outlined in the services agreement signed between the private equity vehicle and the administrator. A fund administrator is a firm that is typically responsible for processing investor's subscriptions and for calculating the value of the investor's holdings. A summary of the indemnity and exculpatory provisions of the fund administration agreement is then typically provided in the private equity OM.

Approaches to Indemnity in Private Equity Offering Memoranda

Private equity PPM's indemnity clauses can be classified into two primary categories based on the entities involved. The first series of indemnification provisions focus on what can be described as "internal" indemnification provisions. Before analyzing internal indemnity clauses, we must outline some of the common entities described in the PPM. The three most common entities are those previously mentioned in this chapter and outlined in Exhibit 6.3.

These "internal" provisions focus on indemnification among various affiliated entities and individuals associated, either directly or indirectly, with the private equity fund. A typical internal private equity OM provision typically outlines that the Partnership will indemnify the General Partner, the Management Company, their respective affiliates, and the respective members, partners, shareholders, officers, directors, employees, agents, and representatives thereof for liabilities incurred in connection with the affairs of the Partnership.

The second series of indemnification provisions can be described as "external" indemnification provisions. These external provisions focus primarily on the relationship between a private equity investment vehicle and a service provider, such as an administrator. In these external indemnification provisions, the administration agreement typically outlines that the administrator will not be liable to the Partnership or its LPs and will be indemnified at a certain exemption standard outlined in more detail later.

EXHIBIT 6.3   Common Private Equity Private Placement Memorandum Entities

Entity Name	Entity Explanation	Notes
Partnership	The Partnership is commonly referred to as the onshore fund	This is generally equivalent to the "Fund" in offshore vehicles
General partner	Typically a limited liability company (LLC) which has overall responsibility for the management, operations and investment decisions made on behalf of the Partnership.	None
Management company	Typically a limited partnership (LP) that provides various management services to the Partnership.	This same entity also commonly performs the duties of an entity commonly known as an "Investment Manager" in offshore documents.

Focus of Exculpation Clauses in Private Equity Offering Memoranda

Unlike indemnity clauses, exculpatory clauses in private equity OMs are generally completely internal in their focus. That is to say, exculpation provisions tend to focus solely on the relationship between affiliated private equity entities and persons rather than between the private equity and third-party service providers. A typical exculpatory clause will generally provide that neither the General Partner nor its affiliates shall be liable for costs and expenses from mistakes of judgment or any action or inaction that a person reasonably believes to be in the best interest of the Partnership. These provisions also typically go on to outline that the General Partner will not be liable to any losses due to such mistakes, action, or inaction as well as costs, expenses, or losses except for those above certain minimum exemptions.

Prohibitions against Broad "Hedge Clauses"

A *hedge clause* is a type of disclaimer that attempts to absolve the writer from the responsibility for any accuracy of information obtained from otherwise reliable sources.[13] Effectively, a hedge clause indicates that the writer believes the information to be accurate and that reasonable care has been used to ensure accuracy, but if it is not accurate the writer made a reasonable effort so they should not be held accountable.[14] These clauses are typically seen in market letters, security research reports, or other printed matter having to do with evaluating investments. Such hedge clauses may also be contained in private equity OMs or investment advisory agreements with clients. These clauses can be combined with other indemnity or exculpatory provisions or standalone hedge clauses.

In the United States, we can begin our analysis of hedge clauses at the federal level. The focus of a federal review of hedge clauses is guided in large part by the test outlined in the *Securities and Exchange Commission Release No. 40-58*, which states that, "the anti-fraud provisions of the Securities and Exchange Commission statutes are violated by the employment of any legend, hedge clause, or other provision which is likely to lead an investor to believe that he has in any way waived any right of action he may have . . . "[15]

From a federal regulatory perspective, supported by a series of repeated holdings separate from SEC statutes, it has been shown that hedge clauses have little, if any, legal effect as a protection from liability arising from misstatements.[16] This comports with similar notions from non-U.S. case law, which outlines that any exculpatory or indemnity clause will be ineffective in the presence of knowing dishonest or reckless disregard of duty where fraud is present. Some further guidance on this issue comes from the Heitman SEC No-Action Letter.[17]

At issue in Heitman was whether the use of hedge clauses and related client indemnification disclosure in investment advisory agreements constitutes fraud under Sections 206(1) and 206(2) of the Investment Advisers Act of 1940 (Advisers Act).[18] While the SEC did not outline a bright-line prohibition against hedge clauses in its response to Heitman, the letter effectively stated that the determination as to whether a particular hedge clause was in violation of the 1940 Act was contingent upon the specific facts and circumstances. The Heitman letter further outlined several criteria that could be used to aid in making this determination, including the form and content of the particular hedge clause (e.g., its accuracy), any oral or written communications between the investment adviser and the client about the hedge clause, and the sophistication of each client.

In the United States, in addition to registration with potential required registration with federal securities regulators, such as the SEC, National Futures Association, and the Commodity Futures Trading Commission, investment advisors may need to register within particular states as well. Depending on the particular laws of each state, certain states may have more or less rigorous requirements and rules regarding investment advisors. With regard to alternative investment advisors in different states, based potentially on a deeper understanding and focus on alternative investments, states that have been found to be particularly knowledgeable about private equity include Colorado, Utah, California, and Washington.[19]

One area of focus at the state level has been restrictions on the use of hedge clauses, particularly regulating the ways in which private equity managers have sought to limit the liability of partners and members, particularly those organized as partnerships or limited liability companies. In Washington, for example, several limitations exist regarding the use of hedge clauses.[20]

These restrictions include that a hedge clause may not provide that a client waives compliance with state or federal securities laws, as well as prohibitions against overly broad hedge clauses.[21] Furthermore, a broadly drafted indemnification provision may be deemed to be impermissible in Washington.[22] Other states maintain similar prohibitions against the use of overly broad hedge clauses. For example, the Connecticut Department of Banking has outlined that the antifraud provisions of the Connecticut Uniform Securities Act may be triggered by overly broad hedge clauses.[23]

Exceptions to Exculpatory and Indemnity Clauses

Exculpatory and indemnity clauses in private equity and OMs often contain language that serves to create exemptions to these clauses. In general, five standard exemptions to such terms are typically raised as defenses by investment managers, service providers, and fund directors once a fund failure or substantial loss occurs. These five most commonly raised exceptions are actual fraud, fraud, willful fraud, willful default, and gross negligence.[24] We can begin our analysis of this exemption by starting with a grouping of fraud-related exemptions.

Actual Fraud, Fraud, Willful Fraud, and Willful Default

Black's Law Dictionary defines actual fraud as "A concealment of false representation through a statement or conduct that injures another who relies on it in acting."[25] Other terms used to represent actual fraud include *fraud in fact*, *positive fraud*, and *moral fraud*. Seeming to focus on the morality aspect associated with actual fraud, other sources define actual fraud as involving elements of personal dishonesty and reckless disregard for duty.

Most of the case law surrounding questions of actual fraud focuses on the honesty and intentions of the parties. In the arena of investment management, issues of actual fraud and fraud have been primarily litigated in jurisdictions either directly based upon, or with strong roots in, British Law. One of the most litigated issues in this context surrounds the relationship between accessory liability and both actual fraud and fraud. Regarding the question of the assignment of liability, the pertinent series of cases that will be focused on relate to the context of either a trust or fiduciary relationship. In these series of cases, the general fact pattern involves several common elements:

- The perpetration of fraud or actual fraud.
- An assignment of agency or a requirement of oversight by a third-party, such as a fund director, who is not the direct perpetrator of the fraud.
- A genuine lack of knowledge, or reckless disregard, of the fraudulent actions of the perpetrator.
- A loss of funds as a result of the fraud.

Accessory Liability and Dishonesty   The central question courts have been posed with based on the previously described general fact pattern of occurrences is to opine as to the culpability, if any, of these agents or third parties. One such leading case, *Royal Brunei Airlines Sdn. Bhd. v. Tan*, was decided by the Privy Council court of the Asian State of Brunei Darussalam.[26] In *Royal Brunei* the court addressed accomplice liability for third parties in relation to fraud. The court held that in a case of actual fraud, dishonesty is required for accessory liability in breach of trust for a fiduciary.[27] In this case, the court further outlined that the test for honesty should be objective rather than subjective. Paraphrasing the court, *Royal Brunei* outlines an objective test of honesty that effectively boils down a question of, knowing what they knew, would an honest person have done what they did? To utilize this test, however, it first requires a working definition of honesty, which in a moral framework may be inherently subjective. The *Royal Brunei* court offers the following guidance in this regard:

> *In most situations, there is little difficulty in identifying how an honest person would behave. Honest people do not intentionally deceive others to their detriment. Honest people do not knowingly take others' property. Unless there is a very good and compelling reason, an honest person does not participate in a transaction if he knows it involves a misapplication of trust assets to the detriment of the beneficiary. Nor does an honest person in such a case deliberately close his eyes and ears, or deliberately not ask questions, lest he learn something he would rather not know and then proceed regardless.*

Following the Royal Brunei decision, the uniform application of the objective test of honesty had been called into question in lieu of a subjective hybrid test.[28] More recent interpretations suggest that the courts have reaffirmed the application of the objective test toward dishonesty.[29]

Knowledge Requirements Turning away from tests that focused solely on the honesty requirement, other cases have focused on the degree and type of knowledge held by the individual in relation to the fraud. An example of one such leading case is *Baden v. Societe Generale*.[30] *Baden* outlined five categories of knowledge a fund director or other affiliated individual may possess in relation to a fraud. They include (1) actual knowledge; (2) willfully shutting one's eyes to the obvious; (3) willfully and recklessly failing to make inquiries that an honest person would have made; (4) knowledge of circumstances that would indicate the facts to an honest and reasonable man; and (5) knowledge of circumstances that would put an honest and reasonable man on inquiry.[31] It is worth recognizing, however, that the five categories of knowledge outlined in *Baden* incorporated the idea that a person would be deemed to have knowledge if they failed to make any inquiries subject to an honest and reasonable person standard.[32]

Director Liability and Dishonesty Expanding on the inaction element of the knowledge requirement in *Baden*, courts have also focused on the relationship between honesty, knowledge, and proactive fund director action.[33] One leading case in this area is *Barlow Clowes International Ltd (In Liquidation) v. Eurotrust International Limited*.[34] In *Barlow*, the fund directors were found liable, despite indemnity provisions, because of their payments to the fund, even though the payments were made with not dishonest intentions.[35] The court in *Barlow* further held that it was not necessary for the directors to know or understand the precise involvement of different individuals in the fraudulent activity.[36]

Gross Negligence Shifting focus away from honesty and knowledge requirements of directors in relation to fraud, other cases have focused on the roles of investors who invested in mismanaged investment programs, which subsequently ended up in insolvency. One such recent leading case is *San Diego v. Amaranth*.[37] In *San Diego* the San Diego County Employee's Retirement Association (SDCERA) alleged that by mounting up fund losses in excess of $6 billion, the fund recklessly ignored risk management controls and lied about trading strategies.[38] SDCERA also asserted claims for gross negligence, breach of fiduciary duty, and breach of contract.[39] The court, in ruling in favor of Amaranth, concluded that the OM and subscription agreement provided to SDCERA outlined the risks associated with the fund

EXHIBIT 6.4 Other General Indemnity and Exculpatory Exemptions

Other Exemption Term	Other Variations and Related Terms	Definition
Malfeasance	Willful malfeasance, misfeasance	A wrongful or unlawful act
Negligence	Willful negligence	The failure to exercise the standard of care that a reasonably prudent person would have exercised in a similar situation
Bad faith	N/A	Dishonest of belief or purpose
Misconduct	N/A	A dereliction of duty; unlawful or improper behavior

and that, coupled with the indemnity provisions in the OM as well as the fact that SDCERA was a sophisticated investor, insulated Amaranth. This ruling illustrates an example where the negligence indemnity exemptions outlined in the OM provided a firm and directors with protection despite both alleged inaction (e.g., poor management oversight) and proactive actions (e.g., lying about trading strategies).

Other Exemptions   In addition to the five standard indemnity and exculpatory exemptions, private equity OMs may contain a number of other exemptions. These exemptions will be outlined in more detail in the empirical analysis section. It should be noted that these other exemptions may either be used in conjunction with the five standard exemptions or independently. Some of the other general exemptions as well as their definitions are outlined in Exhibit 6.4.

It should also be noted that other exemption terms not included in Exhibit 6.4 but also found in private equity OMs include dishonesty and misfeasance.

Liability Releases

Courts in multiple jurisdictions have relied on precedent relating to the role and liability of traditional corporate director laws to decide cases in which directors serve on the boards of alternative investment management companies and funds.[40] There is a long history of case law from multiple jurisdictions that demonstrates that directors of a corporation may be exposed to liabilities resulting from corporate losses.[41] Many jurisdictions historically provided for releases from liability for investment fund directors. These liability releases often came in the form of indemnity and exculpatory clauses in fund offering documents. In the early 1900s courts in many jurisdictions upheld such director releases of liability.[42]

In this context, one of the central questions that has arisen in regulatory frameworks and litigation is whether directors maintain a responsibility to engage in proactive monitoring and supervision of the corporation.[43] In the United Kingdom, for example, Section 205 of the Companies Act of 1948, which has since been recodified in Section 232 of the Companies Law 2006, has implications designed to, at a minimum, keep directors on their toes due to the threat of prohibitions against total releases from liability.[44] In the United States, a series of shareholder derivative actions resulting from convictions of corporate wrong doing provides guidance in this area. Relevant to this discussion, one of the first such landmark cases was heard by the Delaware Supreme Court in 1963. The case was *Graham v. Allis-Chalmers Mfg. Co.*[45] In *Graham*, the court rejected the notion that directors maintained an obligation to implement a so-called system of watchfulness to ferret out wrongdoing. The court clarified that corporate directors were affirmatively entitled to rely on the honesty and integrity of their subordinates absent any suspicions they may have otherwise.[46] The *Graham* court clarified that under such a situation liability would only potentially occur if a director had such a suspicion and took no action. This pronouncement by the court came to be known as a "red flag" test under which directors could assume that all was well unless they came across a red flag.

In analyzing the liability assignment implications of indemnity and exculpatory clauses, it is important to consider these clauses not in isolation, either individually or as a bundled group, but rather in the context of other legal doctrines that address liability assignment. Such analysis is supported by the case law in this area, as courts presented with numerous liability issues have had to address them in the context of multiple legal doctrines. In particular, one such example of this is the application of the *ultra vires* doctrine toward director liability.

Ultra vires is defined as beyond the scope of power allowed or granted by a corporate charter or law.[47] A leading recent case in this area decided by the appeals court of Jersey in the Channel Islands is *Viscount of the Royal Court of Jersey v. Shelton*. In *Shelton*, the court outlined that in the absence of a jurisdictional provision, which would render a particular indemnification provision void, such a clause in a company's articles of incorporation would allow a director to escape most liability from losses, assuming that the director did not act with dishonesty.[48] *Shelton* also outlines a situation where an indemnity clause was present without an exculpatory clause. The court held that, via a principal of circularity of action, the indemnity clause itself will have the effect of an exculpatory clause because there is no cause of action against a party whom a person is liable to indemnify in respect for the same matter.

In Pari Delicto and the Wagoner Doctrine in Fraud Defenses

In cases involving instances of fraud, in which investors in private equity typically suffer losses, the fraud is not generally uncovered until after the losses have occurred to some degree.[49] When litigation follows, often questions arise as to who bears responsibility for the fraud. Additionally, as the losses may exceed the remaining assets of the firm, indemnity and exculpatory principles often are litigated in a bankruptcy context. Recently such scenarios have come to fruition during the global economic crisis of 2009 both in private equity and other corporate contexts.[50]

The *in pari delicto* doctrine can be defined as the principle that a plaintiff who has participated in wrongdoing may not recover damages resulting from the wrongdoing.[51] In bankruptcy proceedings in cases where a fraud has occurred, the *in pari delicto* doctrine is often used as a defense to insulate service providers, management, or fund directors from liability by imputing liability to both the corporation and any individual actors.[52] Some critics have raised the argument that this imputation of equal fault and subsequent escaping of liability relies on misapplication of the *in pari delicto* doctrine in conjunction with traditional agency principals.[53]

The *in pari delicto* doctrine is often not utilized in isolation as a defense to fraud imputation to service providers and directors. A common legal principle that factors into a court's analysis and application of these fraud defenses includes the Wagoner doctrine. The Wagoner doctrine originates from the rule outlined by the Second Circuit in *Shearson Lehman Hutton Inc. v. Wagoner* that "a claim against a third party for defrauding a corporation with the cooperation of management accrues to creditors, not the guilty corporation."[54] In certain instances, the *in pari delicto* doctrine is referenced interchangeably with the Wagoner doctrine. However, other sources draw distinctions between the two.[55] There is a divergence of opinion among different United States circuit courts as to the interpretation of both *in pari delicto* and the Wagoner doctrines. A recent ruling by the United States Court of Appeals for the Eight Circuit has called into question certain aspects of the Second Circuit's original interpretation in Wagoner.[56] Such interpretations, however, may still give rise to *in pari delicto* defenses. Also factoring into the use of these doctrines as defenses, are a number of exemptions including the "innocent insider" doctrine and the "adverse interest" exemption.

As a recent New York Supreme Court decision in *Bullmore v. Ernst & Young Cayman Islands*, fund directors may not be able to rely on indemnity and exculpatory clauses to provide protection from claims arguing imputation of fraud to them in bankruptcy contexts where *in pari delicto* and the Wagoner doctrine come into play.[57] As *Bullmore* demonstrates indemnity and exculpatory provisions may rely not only on the active or inactive nature of a fund director, but also on the nature of any communication between the fund's service providers and the directors.

TRENDS IN INDEMNIFICATION AND EXCULPATION CLAUSES

Now that we have established an understanding of the basic uses and standard exceptions to the exculpatory and indemnity clauses in private equity and private equity offering memoranda, we can next review the results of a Corgentum Consulting study of a proprietary data set of these private equity offering memorandum. The purpose of this analysis is to facilitate a clearer understanding of trends in the drafting of private equity offering memoranda.

Predata Analysis Hypotheses

Before an analysis of the Corgentum Consulting data set was performed, based on professional experience performing operational due diligence reviews of private equity, three distinct hypotheses were in place. First, it was predicted that a certain minimum level of standard risk inclusion and exception language would be present among the OMs included in the data set. Furthermore, above this minimum baseline standard it was predicted that significant diversity would emerge in regard to the type and nature of exceptions included. Second, it was predicted that a private equity vehicle's investment strategy would have no material effect on drafting trends in exception language for both indemnity and exculpatory clauses. Finally, the third hypothesis that was present in the predata analysis stage was that exception drafting trends for indemnity and exculpatory clauses would be influenced more by the primary legal counsel utilized by the private equity fund, and which may have drafted the OM as opposed to other jurisdictional concerns such as fund domicile.

EXHIBIT 6.5   Detail of Private Equity Vehicle Incorporation Jurisdictions Included
in the Data Set

Jurisdiction of Incorporation	Percent of Managers Included in the Data Set
Delaware (United States)	37%
Cayman Islands	22%
Bahamas	19%
Guernsey	1%
Isle of Man	3%
Jersey	4%
British Virgin Islands	14%

Overview of Data Set

Jurisdictional Considerations of Private Equities Included in This Study
No domicile or jurisdictional restrictions were in place for a private equity
fund to be included in the data set. A globally diverse cross-section of private equity was included in this study as there were not any domiciles or
jurisdictional restrictions. The two most popular jurisdictions of incorporation for the private equity vehicles included in this study were Delaware
(United States), at 37 percent for onshore vehicles, and the Cayman Islands,
at 22 percent for offshore vehicles. Exhibit 6.5 shows a summary of the
jurisdictions of incorporation for the private equity vehicles included in this
study.

Multiple Versions of Offering Memoranda   In the course of the life cycle
of private equity investment vehicles, multiple iterations of offering memorandum for the same vehicle at different points in time may be generated.
Generally, subsequent iterations of a particular investment vehicle's offering
memorandum are drafted to reflect changes in an investment vehicle's legal
structure, offering terms, fees charged, or more generally to reflect global
changes within an organization. Indeed, during the course of this study, 34
percent of the data set of offering memoranda had at least one instance of
prior issuance at a previous time period. In such cases, the most current
version of such offering memoranda in the data set was analyzed.

***Pari Passu* Investment Vehicles**   The data set of private equity vehicle
OMs utilized in this study contained approximately 61 percent OMs that
were managed *pari passu*. To clarify, this would be a pair of OMs, one
of which was for the onshore OM private equity vehicle and one for the
offshore vehicle.

EXHIBIT 6.6   Detail of Legal Entities of Private Equity Vehicles Included in the Data Set

Legal Entity and Structure Types	Percent of Managers Included in the Data Set
Limited Liability Corporation	48%
Limited Partnership	38%
Unit Trust	11%
Others*	3%

*Others refer to private equity vehicles that employed legal entity and structure types that were strategies not included in the above categories. Examples of such structures would be so-called exempted corporations under different jurisdictional regimes.

Legal Entities and Structures   As referenced earlier, the set of offering memoranda utilized for this empirical analysis included private equity vehicles organized under a wide variety of corporate structures including limited liability corporations, limited partnerships, and unit trusts. Furthermore, the private equity vehicles that comprise the data set were further organized as either standalone individual funds or alternatively under a wide variety of multifund structures, including iterations of master-feeder structures. Exhibit 6.6 provides a summary of the legal entities included in the data set.

Language Omission and Multiple Document Revisions over Time   During the course of the analysis of the offering memoranda of the funds included in this study, one trend that emerged was the phenomenon of language omissions. Language omission refers to instances where language in the OM concerning one of the particular factors analyzed in this study was omitted entirely from a private equity investment vehicles' particular OM. Comporting with notions of drafting consistency, among similarly managed private equity investment vehicles managed by the same private equity management organization, such language omissions were universally consistent among documents drafted at or about the same time period when comparing onshore and offshore vehicles. Approximately 3 percent of the OM vehicles included in the data set represented some characteristics of language omission. To compensate for these, exogenous sources—outside of the offering memorandums themselves—were utilized to replace the omitted language. It should be noted that in all cases for the OMs included in the data set, indemnity and exculpatory provisions were included.

Dispersion in the consistency of language omission tended to increase when the onshore and the offshore vehicle of a private equity investment vehicle offering memoranda were drafted at different time periods. In these multiple versions cases, as outlined earlier, the most recent version of the

OM was selected. Surprisingly, such dispersion tended to occur regardless of whether the same legal counsel that had drafted the original document also completed the subsequent document update, or another legal counsel performed the update.

In certain instances, the inclusion of language to address a particular topic that may have been completely unaddressed in a previous OM for a particular private equity investment vehicle may have been motivated by exogenous factors. These factors may have included a change in the law within a particular jurisdiction, or even more universally, a general change in the market perception of certain risk factors that bore more common inclusion in subsequent offering memoranda drafts, but patently did not merit similar inclusion across all private equity vehicles at the time.

Other Considerations It should also be noted that a minimum requirement of private equity vehicles to be included in the data set was that a private equity vehicle would have been managed for a period of not less than one year as of the date of the offering memorandum. Separately managed or customized account structures were not included in this study. There were no minimum firmwide assets under management (AUM) requirements on either a firmwide strategy level or vehicles' level basis to be included in this study.

Data Preparation

The first step in preparation of this data set for analysis was to gather and review the private equity vehicle OMs. In this state the OMs were reviewed with a specific focus on compiling data on three primary categories: indemnity and exculpation provision exemptions investment strategy, jurisdiction of incorporation, and legal counsel. Additionally, other data were compiled on the descriptive categories (e.g., firmwide AUM, vehicle jurisdiction of incorporation, etc.). After all the relevant information was logged and coded, the next step of the review involved a statistical and trend analysis.

Trend Analysis and Implications

Standards/Levels of Indemnification All of the private equity offering memoranda included in the Corgentum study contained some language related to indemnification and exculpation. Typically, the language specifies that the fund has agreed to exculpate and indemnify the investment manager, general partner, principals, affiliates and their partners, directors, officers, and employees against losses and liability in the event that their actions do not meet certain liability thresholds. More specifically, these

EXHIBIT 6.7 Indemnification and Exculpation Standards in Private Equity Offering Memoranda*

Indemnification/Exculpation Standard	Percentage of Offering Memoranda Included in Study
Willful malfeasance	41%
Malfeasance	12%
Gross negligence	78%
Willful negligence	61%
Negligence	42%
Willful default	24%
Bad faith	84%
Misconduct	34%
Fraud	81%
Actual fraud	24%
Willful fraud	17%
Dishonesty	54%
Misfeasance	4%

*Standards, and associated percentages, included are not mutually exclusive. All the offering memoranda analyzed in this study contained at least two indemnification and exculpation standards included in the table.

liability standards are typically categorized along more specific striations including malfeasance and negligence. Exhibit 6.7 summarizes the results of this analysis.

Comparing the data in Exhibit 6.7 to the first hypothesis, it is apparent that certain indemnity and exculpatory exemptions were more consistently utilized. These included bad faith (84 percent), fraud (81 percent), gross negligence (78 percent), willful negligence (61 percent), dishonesty (54 percent), negligence (42 percent), and willful malfeasance (41 percent). We can now compare this to the five standard exemptions referenced by much of the literature in this area and outlined earlier in this chapter (e.g., *actual fraud, fraud, willful fraud, willful default, and gross negligence*). This comparison demonstrates that portions of the five outlined standard exemptions comport with the data set, as gross negligence and fraud are in the top of the standard exemptions. Furthermore, while negligence is not specifically listed in the five standard exemptions for the purposes of this discussion we can group both negligence and willful negligence under the so-called umbrella category of gross negligence, as they are both variations of negligence. Turning to the remaining leading exemptions in the data set, the analysis suggests that perhaps, based on the limited sample of this data set, bad faith, dishonesty, and willful malfeasance should be added to the list of standard exemptions.

Returning to the first part original hypothesis, above the minimum baseline level of exemptions it was predicted that significant diversity would emerge in regard to the type and nature of exceptions included. When analyzing the data, it seems that indeed beyond the core exemptions previously discussed, little clustering or other terms existed. The closest cluster outside of the largest core exemptions in the data set was misconduct (34 percent) followed by a significant drop-off of approximately 24 percent and 17 percent for incidences of fraud, actual fraud, and willful fraud, respectively.

Additionally, 23 percent of the private equity offering memoranda reviewed in this study contained a provision for indemnification and exculpation in the event the above listed parties (including the General Partners and/or the Investment Manager) acted with the reasonable belief that an act (or omission) was in the best interests—or at least not opposed to the interests—of the fund.

Exemption Trends within Strategies and Geographic Location   Now that we have developed an understanding of trends of indemnity and exculpatory exemptions within the data set, we can cross-reference these within each of the defined strategies to see if any trends are noticeable. Exhibit 6.8 presents a summary of the exemption and strategy data within each data set. It should be noted that in Exhibit 6.8 the sum total of each row equals the total percentage of each exemption outlined. For example, the sum of the "Malfeasance" row across each strategy is 12 percent, which equals the incidence of the Malfeasance row in Exhibit 6.7.

In reviewing the cross-referenced data, several noticeable trends emerge. Beginning with the Venture Capital strategy, this category exhibited the highest percentages in the willful malfeasance, willful default, and gross negligence exemption category. Similarly, the LBO fund strategy exhibited the highest percentages in the willful negligence exemption category, and tied with the "Mezzanine" fund category within the bad faith exemption category. Exhibit 6.9 presents a summary of the private equity strategies which lead each exemption category.

Returning for a moment to the second predata analysis hypothesis it was predicted that a private equity vehicle's investment strategy would have no material effect on drafting trends in exception language for both indemnity and exculpatory clauses. These data seem to contradict this hypothesis as certain strategy exemptions did consistently lead certain categories. That being said, it seems more research may be necessary to test the validity of certain indemnity and exculpatory exemptions being closely associated

EXHIBIT 6.8 Indemnity and Exculpatory Exemptions Cross Referenced by Private Equity Strategy

	Venture Capital	LBO Fund	Mezzanine Fund	Distressed Debt	Real Estate Funds	Hybrid	Others
Willful malfeasance	18%	2%	4%	4%	2%	7%	4%
Malfeasance	2%	1%	4%	5%	0%	0%	0%
Gross negligence	33%	23%	14%	4%	1%	2%	1%
Willful negligence	14%	19%	10%	2%	3%	11%	2%
Negligence	1%	11%	9%	2%	14%	4%	1%
Willful default	14%	1%	5%	0%	1%	1%	2%
Bad faith	15%	22%	22%	15%	4%	1%	5%
Misconduct	5%	7%	4%	2%	14%	2%	0%
Fraud	5%	17%	14%	8%	22%	12%	3%
Actual fraud	2%	4%	5%	7%	1%	4%	1%
Willful fraud	0%	0%	14%	1%	0%	1%	0%
Dishonesty	1%	2%	4%	2%	22%	10%	13%
Misfeasance	0%	0%	1%	0%	2%	0%	1%

EXHIBIT 6.9 Private Equity Strategy Leaders within Each Indemnity and Exculpatory Exemptions Category

Exemptions	Strategy Category Leader
Willful malfeasance	Venture capital
Malfeasance	Distressed debt
Gross negligence	Venture capital
Willful negligence	LBO fund
Negligence	LBO fund
Willful default	Venture capital
Bad faith	Tie between venture capital and mezzanine fund
Misconduct	Real estate funds
Fraud	Real estate funds
Actual fraud	Distressed debt
Willful fraud	Mezzanine fund
Dishonesty	Real estate funds
Misfeasance	Real estate funds

EXHIBIT 6.10   Indemnity and Exculpatory Exemptions Cross Referenced by Jurisdiction

	Delaware	Cayman Islands	Bahamas	Guernsey	Isle of Man	Jersey	British Virgin Islands
Willful malfeasance	6%	2%	4%	4%	3%	1%	21%
Malfeasance	2%	1%	0%	4%	1%	2%	2%
Gross negligence	9%	11%	11%	14%	9%	11%	13%
Willful negligence	0%	8%	14%	15%	24%	0%	0%
Negligence	1%	17%	12%	8%	3%	0%	1%
Willful default	5%	4%	6%	2%	5%	0%	2%
Bad faith	34%	1%	1%	12%	2%	12%	22%
Misconduct	12%	4%	4%	4%	5%	3%	2%
Fraud	34%	3%	12%	1%	15%	7%	9%
Actual fraud	1%	2%	1%	3%	0%	17%	0%
Willful fraud	1%	2%	2%	3%	0%	6%	3%
Dishonesty	8%	14%	17%	4%	11%	0%	0%
Misfeasance	1%	0%	0%	1%		0%	2%

with certain investment strategies. We can next perform a similar analysis to cross-reference strategy exemptions with jurisdictional information. This analysis is summarized in Exhibit 6.10.

Similar to the methodology employed in the private equity strategy cross-reference analysis, it should be noted that in Exhibit 6.10 the sum total of each row equals the total percentage of each exemption outlined. Reviewing the jurisdictional cross-referenced data, several trends are observable. Beginning with the onshore jurisdiction of Delaware, this category exhibited the highest percentages in the exemption categories of willful malfeasance, bad faith, misconduct, and fraud, and tied with Guernsey for misfeasance. In comparison, the second most popular jurisdiction among the private equity vehicles included in the data set, the Cayman Islands, exhibited the highest percentage in only one exemption category, dishonesty. Exhibit 6.11 presents a summary of the jurisdictions, which led each exemption category.

Furthermore, this analysis suggests indemnity and exculpatory drafting trends that may be representative of the perceived risks associated with different private equity strategies. This analysis still leaves several unanswered questions, which require further research. For example, why would a

EXHIBIT 6.11 Jurisdiction Leaders within Each Indemnity and Exculpatory
Exemptions Category

Exemptions	Jurisdiction Category Leader
Willful malfeasance	Delaware
Malfeasance	Guernsey
Gross negligence	Guernsey
Willful negligence	Isle of Man
Negligence	Bahamas
Willful default	Bahamas
Bad faith	Delaware
Misconduct	Delaware
Fraud	Delaware
Actual fraud	Jersey
Willful fraud	Jersey
Dishonesty	Bahamas
Misfeasance	Tie between Delaware and Guernsey

private equity fund adhering primarily to a venture capital strategy be more
or less susceptible to an actual or perceived risk from willful malfeasance,
a category in which it exhibited the highest incident percentage in the data
set, as opposed to negligence? Furthermore, an investor could make the argument that if a private equity manager adhering to a particular investment
strategy felt the need to include the relevant indemnity and exculpatory exemption within each category based on a perceived or actual risk of a higher
incidence of this occurrence (e.g., willful malfeasance), why should the private equity manager benefit from indemnification and exculpation at the
investor's expense? Said another way, when drafting these exemptions, does
the private equity manager or their attorney know something the investor
does not? In an attempt to answer this query, an analysis was performed
to see if any indemnity and exculpatory exemption trends developed when
cross-referenced with legal counsel used to draft the OMs.

**Variations among Offering Memoranda when the Same Legal Counsel
Was Utilized** The private equity investment vehicles included in this study
utilized a wide variety of different U.S. domestic and offshore legal counsel to draft OMs. These law firms ranged from small practitioners to large
multinational firms. Surprisingly, analysis of the data indicated that variations existed among certain terms of the offering memoranda of different
private equity organizations that utilized the same legal counsel. Beyond
basic indemnity and exculpatory and strategy and fund specific differences,
these variations were also in place among the offering memoranda analysis

factors not included in the scope of this study, such as key person clauses. The presence of such variations was most apparent among *pari passu* funds.

When comparing this to the third predata analysis hypothesis, regarding the possibility that exception-drafting trends to indemnity and exculpatory clauses would be influenced more by the interests of the primary legal counsel utilized by the private equity rather than by geographical concerns, it seems that this initial hypothesis was not wholly correct. As indicated earlier, just because two different private equity vehicles have their OMs drafted by the same legal counsel, it appears there is less of a tendency for the same law firms to utilize boilerplate OMs in drafting indemnity and exculpatory exemption terms. Furthermore, it seems that when comparing these differences to the jurisdictional cross-reference data, there is a stronger link among certain exemption terms to different jurisdictions than to any specific legal counsel. This perhaps may be two different regulatory regimes in each onshore and offshore jurisdiction that would potentially influence drafting exemptions or, as intimated, due more to the bespoke drafting nature of these OMs to the particularities of each private equity manager.

Indemnification and Exculpation Study Conclusions

The analysis in this paper confirmed two of the three original preanalysis hypotheses. First, the data analysis confirmed that a certain minimum level of standard risk inclusion and exception language would be present among the OMs included in the data set. Second, the analysis confirmed the prediction that a private equity vehicle's investment strategy would have no material effect on drafting trends in exception language for both indemnity and exculpatory clauses. The third preanalysis hypothesis did not prove to be wholly correct as OM indemnity and exculpatory drafting trends did not demonstrate a greater influence from the legal counsel that was employed than from geographical concerns.

The data analysis also supported the notion that, beyond a certain core set of terms and disclosures, the analysis of OMs in the data set demonstrated that a private equity fund via its legal counsel has a great deal of discretion in not only crafting the terms that dictate the economics of the particular investing relationship (e.g., management and performance fees), but also regarding the terms of indemnity and exculpatory provisions. The conclusions further suggest that perhaps, based on the limited sample of this data set, bad faith and willful malfeasance should be added to the list of five standard exemptions.

By developing a further understanding of benchmark indemnity and exculpatory exemptions, investors may then be able to use these data in several ways. First, investors can incorporate these data as an aid in their preinvestment due diligence process. By comparing the indemnity and ex-culpatory exemptions contained in the OM of a private equity vehicle under consideration to the data in this study, or perhaps based on a larger data set utilizing the analysis framework outlined in this study, an investor could develop an exception report to alert for any possible due diligence red flags. Furthermore, once a decision has been made to allocate to a particular private equity vehicle, investors could use this benchmark data to demonstrate to a private equity manager that the drafting standards of a particular OM do not comport with drafting trends. Therefore, investors may be able to utilize these data to negotiate side letters or more favorable investment terms.

OTHER LEGAL DOCUMENTS CONSIDERATIONS

In addition to the PPM, during the operational due diligence an investor should request a number of different legal documents. These documents may include items such as subscription documents, articles of association, and the limited partnership agreement. In reviewing each of these legal documents, in addition to terms such as indemnification and exculpation, investors should take care to vet a number of different considerations and terms. The following is a summary of questions and issues investors should consider in evaluating these issues:

Key Person Clause
- Does the fund maintain a key person clause?
- If so, which individuals are named?
- If multiple individuals are named, does the key person clause require a triggering activity to occur to both individuals (i.e., an "and" clause) or to either individual (i.e., an "or" clause)?
- Does the key person clause contain a notice-only provision?
- What is the scope of any key person clauses? (e.g., death, incapacity, etc.)
- Does the key person provision provide for penalty-fee redemptions?

Carried Interest
- How is the subject of carried interest approached?
- Are waterfall distribution or other similar schemes employed?
- Does carried interest follow a return-all-capital-first approach?
- Is a deal-by-deal approach applied to carried interest?
- Are any so-called gross-up provisions included in the documents?
- Are any carried-interest escrow structures employed?

Other Considerations

- In reviewing the legal documents, does the investor have a good understanding of advisory and transactional fees?
- What disclosures are contained regarding fees?
- What is the timing of fee and expense collection and recovery and distributions?
- What is the timing of fee collection and recovery?
- Are any fee-sharing arrangements in place?
- What are the general partner's potential liabilities for clawback obligations?
- Is there any language that limits the ability of the GP to offer fee discounts?
- Does the PPM contain language related to manager reserves?
- What types of conflicts of interest are discussed in the PPM? Are there self-dealing or advance-consent provisions?
- Do the legal documents for the fund contain no-fault divorce termination provisions as well as allowing for termination for cause? By supermajority? By simple majority?
- Do the legal documents contain any jurisdiction specific language that may present unique risks or other implications that an investor must consider?

CONCLUSION

In conclusion, this chapter provides an introduction to some of the considerations that investors should take into account when approaching the legal due diligence portion of an operational due diligence review. As this chapter outlines, merely reading such documents and taking them at face value is not sufficient in a thorough operational due diligence review. Investors can utilize research in this field, such as the Corgentum Consulting study that this chapter mentions, as well as their own experience to develop perspective regarding legal documentation trends. Additionally, investors evaluating a private equity firm and fund's legal documentation may consider utilizing a combination of specialists, such as external legal counsel as well as operational due diligence consultants, to bolster internal efforts.

NOTES

1. See Bryan Garner, *A Dictionary of Modern Legal Usage* (Oxford University Press, 1987).

2. See Steven Emanuel, *Emanuel Law Outlines: Contracts* (Aspen Publishers, 2010).
3. Vinh Quang Tran, *Evaluating Private Equity Performance* (Hoboken, NJ: John Wiley & Sons, 2006), 245.
4. The Private Equity Journal, Excerpts from the *Guide to Sound Practices for Funds of Private Equity's Managers*, 2.1 (AIMA, 2009).
5. "Exculpatory Clauses: The Historical Impact of Common-Carrier Law and the Modern Relevance of Insurance," *The University of Chicago Law Review* (vol. 24:2, Winter 1957, 315, 317.
6. See Henry Hallam, *History of Europe During the Middle Ages*, vol. 3 (The Colonial Press, 1899), 210; see Deutscher Nautischer Verein, *History of Indemnification of German Private Property at Sea out of the French War Indemnity* (Oxford University 2006), 119; see Justin Sweet and Jonathan J. Sweet, *Sweet on Construction Industry Contracts: Major AIA Documents* (Aspen Publishers, 1999), 630.
7. House of Commons Treasury Committee, *The Run on the Rock Fifth Report of Session 2007–08*, vol. II (Parliamentary House of Commons, 2008), 257.
8. *Black's Law Dictionary*, 8th ed. (2004), 608.
9. A. N. Yiannopoulos et al., *Admirality and Maritime Law* (Beard Books, 2006), 485.
10. *Black's Law Dictionary*, 8th ed. (2004), 783.
11. Jessie Scott, *Insurance —A Complete Guide* (Othello, 2008), 9.
12. *Black's Law Dictionary*, 8th ed. (2004), 783.
13. John Downes and Jordan Elliot Goodman, *Barron's Finance and Investment Handbook*, 6th ed. (Barron's Educational Series, 2003), 469.
14. David Logan Scott, *Wall Street Words: An A to Z Guide to Investment Terms for Today's Investor*, 3rd ed. (Houghton Mifflin Company, 2003), 176
15. SEC Release No. 40–58 (April 18, 1951), Fed. Sec. L. Rep. (CCH) ¶ 56, 383–6.
16. Louis Loss et al., *Fundamentals of Securities Regulation* (Aspen Publishers, 2003), 1026.
17. Heitman Capital Management, LLC, SEC No-Action Letter, *2007 SEC No-Act.* LEXIS 159 (February 12, 2007).
18. Cillian M. Lynch, "SEC Issues No-Action Letter on the Use of "Hedge Clauses" in Investment Advisory Contracts," *Stradley Ronon Fund/Adviser Alert*, May 2007.
19. John R. Hewitt and James B. Carlson, "Securities Practice and Electronic Technology," *Law Journal Press*, 2006, 9–11.
20. State of Washington Department of Financial Institutions Securities Division, *Notice to Private Equity Manager Regarding the Use of Partnership and LLC Agreements to Satisfy the Written Investment Advisory Contract Requirements* (September 28, 2006), 2, www.dfi.wa.gov/sd/pdf/notice_hedge_fund_sept_28.pdf.
21. Washington Administrative Code, 460 WAC §§ 24A-220(19) (2008).
22. Revised Code of Washington, RCW 25 §§ 15.040(1)(a) (2001).

23. Connecticut Department of Banking, *Investment Advisers Cautioned on Use of Hedge Clauses*, (May 1991), www.ct.gov/dob/cwp/view.asp?a = 2252&q = 299222.
24. Christopher Russell, "Briefing Exculpation and Indemnity Clauses," Ogier Client Briefing, June 2008.
25. *Black's Law Dictionary*, 8th ed. (2004), 685.
26. *Royal Brunei Airlines Sdn. Bhd. v. Tan* [1995] 2 AC 378.
27. Charles Mitchell, "Dishonest Assistance in a Breach of Trust," www.ucc.ie/law/odg/messages/051011h.htm.
28. *Twinsectra v Yardley* [2002] 2 AC 164 (HL).
29. *Dubai Aluminium v. Salaam* [2002] 2 AC 164 (HL).
30. *Baden v. Societe Generale* (1983) [1993] 1 W.L.R. 509.
31. Alastair Hudson,. "Knowing Receipt," 30, http://cw.routledge.com/textbooks/9780415497718/podcasts/podcast30.pdf, outlining the five types of knowledge requirements discussed in *Baden v. Societe Generale* (1983) [1993] 1 W.L.R. 509.
32. Alastair Hudson, "The Impact of *Barlow Clowes v. Eurotrust* on Dishonest Assistance," available at www.alastairhudson.com/trustslaw/BarlowClowesNote.pdf.
33. Compare *Twinsectra Ltd. v. Yardley* (200) UKHL 12, explaining that a lawyer who assisted a lender in defrauding a bank was not liable because he had no knowledge of the fraud; and *Grupo Torres v. Al-Sabah* (2001), outlining that a lawyer who was a director of a company was found guilty of blind-eye dishonesty; with *Brinks Ltd. v. Abn-Saled* [1996] CLC 133, describing that an accomplice defendant must actually have assisted in the fraud to be liable; and *Agip (Africa) Ltd. v. Jackson* (1990) 1 Ch 265, explaining that accountants were liable for knowing assistance by participating in fraud.
34. Gary Watt, *Todd and Watt's Cases and Materials on Equity and Trusts* (Gary Watt 2007), 531, explaining that the court in *Barlow Clowes International Ltd. (In Liquidation) v. Eurotrust International Limited* (2006) 1 All ER 333, Privy Council, focused on the relationship between honesty and proactive knowledge.
35. Mohamed Ramjohn, *Text, Cases and Materials on Equity and Trusts*, 4th ed. (Cavendish Publishing Limited, 1995), 300.
36. Philip R. Wood, *Principles of International Insolvency* (Sweet & Maxwell Limited, 2007), 754.
37. Jenny Strasburg, "Amaranth Asks Court to Dismiss San Diego Fund Lawsuit" (update 3), *Bloomberg*, June 7, 2007.
38. Jenny Strasburg, "Amaranth Sued by San Diego, Warns of Refund Delays" (update 3), *Bloomberg*, March 30, 2007.
39. Winston and Strawn LLP, *San Diego County Employees Retirement Association v. Nicholas Maounis, Charles Winkler, Robert Jones, Brian Hunter, and Amaranth Advisors* (2010), www.winston.com/index.cfm?contentID= 154&itemID=2793.
40. Michael Greene and David Dobbyn et al., "Ireland," in *Directors' Liability: A Worldwide Review*, eds. Alexander Loos et al. (2006), 293, 294.

41. See, for example, *Charitable Corporation v. Sir Robert Sutton* [1742] EngR 115; (1742) 2 Atk 400; 26 ER 642, explaining that directors can be found liable for inactivity.
42. See *Re Brazilian Rubber Plantations and Estates Ltd.* [1911] 1 Ch. 425.
43. Mark J. Loewenstein, "The Corporate Director's Duty of Oversight," *The Colorado Lawyer* 33, May 1998, 27.
44. Seamus Andrew & Niall Goodsir-Cullen, *Accountability of Cayman Islands Directors*, RECOVERY, Autumn 2007, at 36 (explaining the progression of director liability release regulation from Section 205, Companies Law 1948 which is the predecessor section to Section.
45. 188 A.2d 125 (Del. 1963).
46. Edward P. Welch et al., *Folk on the Delaware General Corporation Law: Fundamentals* (Aspen Publishers, 2009), 259.
47. *Black's Law Dictionary*, 8th ed. (2004), 1559.
48. Ian M. Ramsay, "Liability of Directors for Breach of Duty and the Scope of Indemnification and Insurance," *Company and Securities Law Journal* 5:3 (1987).
49. Jerry W. Markham, *A Financial History of Modern U.S. Corporate Scandals: From Enron to Reform* (M.E. Sharpe, 2006), 441.
50. Robert Bernstein and Jeffrey Gross, "Circuit Explores 'Wagoner' Rule on Corporate Management Fraud," *New York Law Journal*, March 5, 2009.
51. *Black's Law Dictionary*, 8th ed. (2004), 807.
52. Steve Jakubowski, "*In Pari Delicto* and a Jurisprudential House of Cards," *The Bankruptcy Litigation Blog*, January 14, 2010.
53. Catherine E. Vance, "*In Pari Delicto*, Reconsidered," *American Bankruptcy Institute Journal* XXVII:9, November 2009.
54. See *Shearson Lehman Hutton, Inc. v. Wagoner*, 944 F.2d 114 (2d Cir. 1991).
55. Robert A. Schwinger, "Law vs. Equity: Second and Third Circuits Diverge on 'In Pari Delicto,'" *New York Law Journal*, July 2010.
56. "Defense of *In Pari Delicto* Does Not Affect Trustee Standing," *Bankruptcy Case Blog*, http://stjohns.abiworld.org/node/26#_ftn4 (March 19, 2009), explaining that the Eight Circuit's decision in *Moratzka v. Morris* (*In re Senior Cottages of America*), 482 F.3d 997 (8th Cir. 2007) delineated the issue of standing and defenses that bolsters the standing of a trustee to pursue fraud claims.
57. Alejandra Kim, "Judge Bars Suit Alleging Negligence by Private Equity Accountants," *New York Law Journal*, July 10, 2008, explaining that the decision in *Bullmore v. Ernst & Young Cayman Islands*, 20 Misc. 3d 667, 861 N.Y.S.2d 578, 582-83 (N.Y. Sup. Ct. 2008) found that directors were not innocent because they had ceded control to the fund and it would have been impossible for them to take action if Ernst & Young had alerted them of fraudulent activity.

CHAPTER 7

Financial Statement Due Diligence

Investors are becoming increasingly aware of the importance of document reviews during the private equity operational due diligence process. One of the most important sets of documents that investors should collect, analyze, and monitor are a private equity fund's audited financial statements. Audited financial statements provide a historical snapshot into the financial life of a private equity fund and can serve as a valuable source of information during the due diligence process. Before investing with any private equity fund manager, investors should take steps to analyze and understand the information contained in these documents. To fully capitalize on the information learned during a review of a private equity fund's audited financials, these reviews should be incorporated into the larger operational due diligence process.

Financial statement analysis is a useful tool that investors have in their operational due diligence arsenal to detect and evaluate a variety of operational risk factors that may be present at a private equity firm and fund. Before delving into a discussion of these techniques, it is first useful to gain an understanding of what is contained in a fund's audited financial statements. We will begin this discussion by considering the role of the group preparing them—the auditors. Auditors or audit firms are engaged by the management of a private equity fund to provide an accounting of the fund. Auditors conduct their work subject to a number of different audit standards as outlined in the following sections.

AUDIT STANDARDS

Audit standards are effectively a set of benchmark rules or guidelines by which an auditor should perform their audit. Generally accepted auditing standards (GAAS) are principles meant to be utilized by auditors so that they can produce financial statements that allow them to prepare audits in a manner that comports with the professional standards of the accounting industry.

There are two general types of audit standards that are employed in private equity audited financial statements. Sitting on top of all of these considerations are notions of any relevant jurisdictional choices and governing country or state laws that may be applicable as well.

U.S. GAAS

The first standard has its origin in the United States and is called U.S. Generally Accepted Auditing Standards (U.S. GAAS, or simply GAAS). Under the guidance of the American Institute of Certified Public Accountants (AICPA) standards, U.S. GAAS is divided into 10 standards, which are further subdivided into three groups: General Standards, Standards of Field Work, and Standards of Reporting.[1]

Depending on the type of audit engagement, these rules can become quite complex and granular in nature. Complicating the matter further, depending on the type of audit engagement, the controlling audit standards rules and relevant guidance can come from a wide variety of sources. In the United States, the two major sources of authority in this regard are the AICPA and the Public Company Accounting Oversight Board (PCAOB). Depending on the type of audit, guidelines may come into play such as those from the Government Accountability Office's Government Accounting Standards outlined in the so-called Yellow Book.

The AICPA has a long history of issuing guidance to the accounting profession with regard to audit standards dating back to the early 1900s. Despite this history, the AICPA did not formally establish the ASB until 1978. The next major development in the recent U.S. history of audit standards came about as a result of the passage of the landmark Sarbanes-Oxley Act of 2002, the Public Company Accounting Oversight Board was created. The PCAOB developed its own series of standards and interpretations for the audit of public companies. Many of the PCAOB rules were based on ASB standards. Indeed, the PCAOB utilized the ASB rules as its temporary rules during 2003. Based on the establishment of the PCABO the AICPA has since designated the PCAOB guidance as the leading authority with regard to the generally accepted audit standards for public companies. The ASB standards are generally the point of reference for audits conducted of private companies.[2] Pronouncements made by the ASB are referred to as Statements on Auditing Standards (SASs).[3]

ISA

Outside of the United States, the primary audit standards utilized are so-called International Auditing Standards (ISAs). ISAs were developed and are issued by the International Federation of Accountants (IFAC) via the

International Accounting and Assurance Standards Board (IAASB). The history in the development of ISAs was rooted in the desire to progress toward more uniformity in global accounting standards. It dates back to 1977 when approximately 50 countries joined together to found the IFAC.

ACCOUNTING STANDARDS

Now that we have provided an overview of the guidelines for auditors in preparing the financial statements (e.g., GAAS and IAS), we can next discuss the accounting standards in place. The accounting standards in place directly influence the format in which an investor will likely encounter financial statements during the operational due diligence process. There are two primary formats utilized to present financial statements: GAAP and IFRS.

Generally Accepted Accounting Principles (GAAP)

GAAP is "a technical accounting term that encompasses the conventions, rules, and procedures necessary to define accepted accounting practice at a particular time."[4] In other words, GAAP is the umbrella term for one type of the general format in which financial statements will be presented. It is worth noting that, in a private equity context, this does not mean that all GAAP financial statements contain exactly the same categories of information with different numbers filled in for each different private equity fund as applicable. Variation among GAAP statements is perfectly acceptable depending on certain choices made by the auditor and the management company and the type of statements being produced.

An example of this relates to the Statement of Cash Flows, discussed in more detail further on. Under the guidance provided in a pronouncement from the Financial Accounting Standards Board (FASB) Accounting Standards Codification (ASC), a fund can be exempt from the GAAP statement of cash flows requirement. Specifically according to the Statement of Financial Standards (SFAS) 102 (FASB ASC 230-10-15-4), a fund can be exempt from the GAAP statement of cash flows requirement if it adheres to the following criteria including:

- During the period, substantially all of the enterprise's investments were highly liquid (for example, marketable securities, and other assets for which a market is readily available).
- Substantially all of the enterprise's investments are carried at market value.

- The enterprise had little or no debt, based on the average debt outstanding during the period, in relation to average total assets.
- The enterprise provides a statement of changes in net assets.

In countries that utilize GAAP, there can be variations on the type or format of GAAP utilized. Examples of this include U.S. GAAP and U.K. GAAP.

International Financial Reporting Standards (IFRS)

Next to GAAP, the second major format for accounting statements is what is known as International Financial Reporting Standards (IFRS). IFRS are principles-based standards that comprise a series of historical standards. In particular, IFRS includes two sets of standards issued before 2001: International Accounting Standards (IAS) and Standing Interpretations Committee (SIC).

IAS can differ from GAAP not only in the format in which financial statements are presented but also in the rules governing the way in which positions are accounted for. So returning to our Statement of Cash Flows exemption example, under IAS 7 there are no specific exemptions provided for smaller entities because the Statement of Cash Flows is viewed as a required statement. This can be contrasted with the guidance provided in the Financial Reporting Standard No. 1 (FRS 1) in the United Kingdom under U.K. GAAP, which does provide for Statement of Cash Flows exemptions for small entities. As these examples illustrate, it is essential for an investor to be conscious of the audit standards and presentation forms of the accounting standards.

It is also worth noting that some funds in the past may have produced financial statements in a modified format (non-GAAP or non-IFRS) depending on the jurisdiction and the fund's preference. However, it is not likely that in the current environment, and particularly in light of the movement toward convergence discussed in more detail in the next section, that investors would be willing to provide capital to such funds without audited financial statements routed in GAAP or IFRS.

Movement toward Convergence

In order to level the global playing field and facilitate more uniform comparison of financial statements globally, for the past several years both the FASB and IASB have been pursuing a convergence of IFRS and GAAP standards. Additionally, the SEC has also been considering incorporating IFRS into the U.S. financial reporting system.[5] Regardless of whether full convergence of the standards takes place in the short term, it is likely that in the long term there will be a continued movement toward the convergence of GAAP and IFRS. It should also be noted that the financial statement analysis techniques that this chapter describes can for the most part be utilized under IFRS, GAAP, or any variations thereof. The techniques do not include the finer points of IFRS and GAAP distinctions (such as the previously mentioned example regarding Statement of Cash Flow reporting exemptions), as such discussions are best left for another book. Rather, now that we have laid a framework of the basic fundamentals of private equity financial statements audit and accounting standards, we can begin to delve into the practical applications of how investors can go about interpreting such statements to facilitate their operational risk assessment of a private equity fund.

OTHER FINANCIAL STATEMENT FORMATS

In certain cases, particularly for funds located outside the United States, there may be cases when audited financial statements are presented in a format of that other then GAAP or IFRS. This is also sometimes seen among real estate funds when a manager for example would elect to present fund performance according to methodologies and formats promulgated by an organization such as the European Association for Investors in Non-listed Real Estate Vehicles (INREV). In these cases a fund manager may also present IFRS financial statements alongside these non-IFRS statements.

Audited Financial Statement Presentation Formats

As just indicated, some funds may employ different methodologies in outlining the format of private equity funds financial statements. Audit firms may have a particular form that they use with their clients. Other firms may alter the format slightly on a case-by-case basis. Of course, these variations may be driven by changes in the accounting pronouncements or standards to be employed, which may require the inclusion or omission of certain pieces of information or disclosures. However, in this case, reference is being made more to the fact that certain audit financial statements, by the discretion of the private equity firm and the auditors, may present a single year's financials in each audit. This is the common practice. Still some other firms may opt to include year-over-year financial statements. The same audit firm may even utilize multiple formats for different funds. Investors should consider these different formats when designing a plan to review audited financial statement.

Audit Materiality

Audited financial statements from a private equity fund manager are a key tool that should be utilized by investors in performing comprehensive operational due diligence. Often these statements contain a wealth of information about not only the financial position of a particular fund throughout a fiscal year, but also regarding any elections made by the fund, expense levels, and the overall opinion of the auditor of the financial statements. These opinions are typically classified into two groups: qualified and unqualified. Unfortunately the danger associated with these qualifications is that an unqualified opinion is often thought to mean that everything is okay, whereas it can in fact reveal that everything is not okay, and that more due diligence required. This "everything is okay" mentality can often provide investors with a false sense of security. Many investors do not take the time to understand what exactly an auditor is recommending with an unqualified opinion. Effectively, with an unqualified opinion an auditor is stating that the financial statement contains no material misstatements. But who determines what is material and what is not? Above certain minimum standards, the auditor does. This materiality level is often set during the design of the audit plan, which also contains a number of opportunities for the auditor to make certain discretionary judgments. With all these qualifications and caveats it is understandable that confusion persists regarding audits.

Academic research in the field of accounting demonstrates that an auditor's judgments with respect to materiality are not solely formulaically driven by mathematical calculations of, for example, a percentage of trade volume. Instead studies have suggested that materiality judgments are significantly impacted by a panoply of qualitative factors, including client integrity, culture, and even level of moral judgment.[6] There are no hard rules by which materiality levels or set.

Stated another way, as crazy as it may seem to an investor who relies on audits to inform their opinions about a private equity fund's financial condition, it may be perfectly acceptable within accounting standards for an auditor to make certain mistakes and misstatements as long as the audit is within the materiality level for the financial statements as a whole. In defining performance materiality, ISA 320 outlines as much by stating that an auditor in setting the materiality level should do so with the intent to reduce "to an appropriate low level the probability that the aggregate *uncorrected and undetected misstatements* exceed materiality for the financial statements as a whole" (emphasis added). Translation: Audit work that is not correct or contains misstatements is fine as long as it does not pass the invisible line of materiality.

This concept of audit materiality is often counterintuitive to what most investors believe the work of an auditor to be. Auditors do not necessarily tick and tie every single position held in a fund. From the auditor's perspective they may not even want to do this. The more work an auditor has to do, the more time it takes. As the old adage goes, time is money. Auditors at the end of the day are not the customers of investors, but of the private equity firms and funds that ultimately sign their paychecks. As such, while they want to still make a profit, they also want to keep the client (e.g., private equity manager) happy as well. Exorbitant audit fees, which may ultimately reduce the pool of capital available to compensate private equity managers and deal teams, do little to foster goodwill in this relationship. Furthermore, if the auditor charges a flat fee for their work, then it may be even less in an auditor's economic interest to expend the additional resources necessary to go through each individual trade. To pause for a moment, the purpose of this discussion, lest it should be misinterpreted, is not to malign auditors or the accounting profession. Auditors, generally, do fine work that is of great value to both the private equity firm and investors alike. Besides, there are no secrets between the private equity fund management and the auditors as to what work will actually be performed. The scope of the auditor's work is detailed in a series of places, including the engagement letter between the auditors and the private equity firm/fund as well as in documents such as audit plans that auditors are required to prepare. This is all, of course, in conjunction with the previously discussed GAAP and IFRS rules.

One of the more interesting questions in the context of an operational due diligence process, which investors may ask when faced with analyzing the audited financial statements of a particular fund, is at what materiality level was the audit conducted? One may think that based on all of the disclosures and legalese it would only be logical that, of course allowing for the discretion of the auditor to factor in both quantitative and qualitative factors in setting this materiality level, that this seemingly harmless piece of information would be disclosed somewhere in the folds of the audited financial statements. Perhaps in plain view in the opinion section proceeding the financial statements? Maybe deeper in the financial section in a footnote to one of the statements? Perhaps in a more esoteric location, ensconced between the boilerplate legalese about a new accounting pronouncement and related party transaction disclosures? No. Nowhere in the audit financial statements of a private equity firm will you find this information disclosed. Furthermore, the author would hazard a guess that most private equity fund managers, and even their chief financial officers or chief operating officers who liaise with the auditors and supervise audit progress would not be apt to volunteer this information. Perhaps they are uninformed of such minutia of the audit? Or, to give funds the benefit of the doubt, they, just like the auditors, do not wish to call attention to the issue of materiality. To drive the point home even further, it would be almost unheard of for an investor to have the veritable temerity to inquire as to how audit materiality levels may have changed or evolved on a year-to-year basis. Sadly, in the new world of supposed increased transparency and the willingness of funds to demonstrate their operations prowess, the marketplace has not yet exerted enough pressure on private equity fund managers to commonly reach such levels of disclosure.

Additional Audit Considerations

In reviewing the audited financials of a private equity fund, an investor is likely to run the risk of being overwhelmed by a barrage of disclosures and disclaimers. Such confusion can result in investors placing too much reliance on the shoulders of the auditors, while forgoing an independent operational due diligence review of a private equity fund manager. Consequently, it is important that investors overcome several commonly held misconceptions regarding auditor attestations and the work auditors actually perform. Some of the more commonly held misconceptions regarding the work of auditors include:

- An audit consists of a detailed review of every position taken by a private equity fund.
- There is no discretion among auditors in designing and implementing an audit plan.
- All auditors set the same scope of audit and materiality levels consistently.
- Auditors must perform on-site visits with each private equity fund manager they audit.
- Auditors must perform a detailed review of private equity fund's counterparties and service providers.

While an auditor may adhere, either in part or fully, to the items listed, investors must remember that, above minimum standards mandated by the accounting profession, auditors maintain a certain amount of discretion in designing and implementing an audit plan. Depending upon the nature of the audit engagement, best practice may dictate that different private equity fund strategies and fund structures require more audit scrutiny than others. One point for investors to consider is whether a private equity fund's auditor adheres only to minimum mandated guidelines or goes above and beyond to minimize not only audit risk but to also detect operational risk. The fact that certain accounting rules may not have caught up to a particular private equity fund practice should not serve as an escape hatch for an auditor seeking to dodge the responsibility of broadening the scope of a review or increasing the level of materiality employed in an audit.

While a private equity fund investor may not be able to uncover certain items regarding a specific audit plan (e.g., level of materiality utilized in a particular audit), it still behooves investors to attempt to ask questions about the audit process and methodology. Going beyond the financial statements in this regard will often provide additional insights into both the quality and comprehensiveness of the auditor's work. Additionally, and almost more importantly, investors will likely gain perspective into the involvement and level of oversight exerted by the private equity fund manager on the audit process.

CONSIDERATIONS THAT ARE UNIQUE TO PRIVATE EQUITY AND REAL ESTATE FINANCIAL STATEMENTS

In the vast majority of cases, investors performing initial operational due diligence on a private equity fund will be faced with a scenario in which the fund itself has not yet been in operation. Indeed, it is during this initial capital-raising period that a private equity fund is likely to receive the greatest number of requests to deal with investors' operational due diligence inquiries. The other scenario is when a fund has already raised some capital but may be seeking to raise additional capital in order to reach a previously anticipated size set by the fund manager, perhaps in order to fully fund the portfolios planned investments. While these situation are admittedly much less frequent than operational due diligence opportunities during the initial fund-raising period, an investor may come into a fund once it has begun operating. Each of these cases present investors with a different series of operational due diligence opportunities and challenges. Furthermore, regardless of whether the private equity fund in consideration has been up and running before an investor begins to perform operational due diligence on the fund, investors will also need to consider the history of the fund management company as well as whether the fund has historically managed, or currently manages, other funds. By taking all of these factors into consideration, investors will be able to make smarter allocation decisions.

The Vintage Fund Advantage

In the parlance of the private equity world, borrowing not unashamedly from the world of wine, the "vintage date" or "vintage year" of a private equity fund refers to the year in which the fund began its operations or making investments. Some reasonable people may consider it to be the year that the private equity fund was opened for business. However, to confuse matters, many private equity practitioners may refer to this as the year in which the fund was "closed." Closed in this case does not mean that the fund was closed (i.e., shut down operations) but instead indicates the end of the fund-raising efforts of the fund. To provide some context in the fundraising stage, a fund may use the term *open*, as in open for new investment, and various degrees of the term *closed*, often with a modifier before it, to indicate the relative status of the fund's openness toward accepting additional capital from investors. Examples of this can include "soft closed," which means that a fund is only accepting capital from existing investors or people who are far along in the due diligence process, or "hard closed," which means the fund is not accepting any new capital from investors. During the initial fundraising periods many private equity funds may throw these terms around, perhaps to instill a sense of urgency among investors on the fence or those who are dragging their feet with respect to due diligence efforts. As such, the definition and applicability of these terms can vary from fund to fund.

For the purposes of our discussion, now that we have introduced some of this admittedly confusing terminology, we have laid the groundwork to discuss *vintage funds*.

One way to think of a vintage fund is to equate it to a sequel of a popular movie. Hollywood studios typically produce a sequel based on audience interest and demand to see more of their favorite characters and to continue the initial story. The sequel is generally even more of a big budget blockbuster than the first film. The same is true of private equity vintage funds. Assume that the first fund successfully raised money and generated profits. Seeking to capitalize on this momentum, the private equity management company has decided to raise another fund. In comparison to the first fund, this second fund is set up at a point later in time than the first fund. Therefore, this second fund has a new and different vintage than the first fund. This is where the term *vintage fund* comes from. In practice, these funds are typically established over a period of subsequent years while the predecessor funds are still in operation.

Often these vintage funds will effectively be managed in a modified *pari-passu* format to the predecessor funds. In addition to adhering to similar investment philosophies, these funds will also generally have similarities in regard to not only the management company overseeing the funds, but the personnel responsible for managing the funds as well. These similarities will also play into operational considerations, as vintage funds are almost always serviced on a fund management company's same internal operational platforms and by the same operations personnel who previously services, or are still servicing in the case of a fund that is currently still making and managing investments, the predecessor fund.

From an operational due diligence perspective the fact that a private equity firm has previously managed a vintage fund can provide investors with a significant advantage as compared to similar firms that had not managed vintage funds.

When an investor first approaches a private equity fund as part of the operational due diligence process as previously described, one of the key documents that should be requested are the financial statements of the fund. If the fund has yet to begin making investments and is still only in the capital-raising stages, then the fund has not yet been through an audit cycle and therefore, there are no audited financial statements for investors to review. This presents a bit of a chicken-or-the-egg scenario. On the one hand, a prudent investor would not want to invest in any fund for which they cannot review the audited financial statements. On the other hand, if the fund is brand-new, then there are no audited financial statements to review. One of the goals of operational due diligence is to facilitate the investment process and not to stop the investor's ability to make investments cold in its tracks based on such logistical constructs. Besides, if every investor could not invest in a fund without reviewing the financial statements, then no new funds would ever raise any money.

Faced with this issue, what is an investor still seeking to perform operational due diligence on audited financial statements to do? One way to proceed is to review the audited financial statements of the vintage fund.

To play devil's advocate for a moment, a skeptical prospective investor may ask: Why should I bother reviewing the financial statements of a different fund that is not the fund I am considering investing in? This is a fair question that bears addressing. The following is a partial list of reasons why reviewing such financial statements is advantageous:

- If you do not review vintage year statements, or other financial statements for other funds as available as discussed in more detail further on, then there is nothing else to review.
- Vintage fund statements are the next closest available match/option to the fund you will be considering.
- Reviewing the audited financial statements can provide insight into several areas of fund operations as well as the scope, quality, and timeliness by which audits will be generally conducted. These pieces of information can give a prospective investor in a private equity fund some perspective on how such items will be handled similarly for the fund they are considering investing in.

What is an investor to do if faced with the often-common scenario of there not being a previously managed vintage private equity fund? The "new" fund may either be a fund from an established private equity firm that is pursuing a new strategy or just a brand-new fund started by a new firm.

In the former case, if the firm has managed other private equity funds in the past, it is still worth an investor's time to examine these other statements. Of course, vintage fund statements would be preferable; however, there are no such statements available in this scenario. Audited financial statements from other funds, even if they are managed by a completely different investment team at the same private equity firm, can still provide valuable insights into the firm's relationship with the auditor and the general quality with which such audits are performed.

If a private equity firm has, indeed, operated similar funds in the past, this presents investors with a distinct opportunity for data-gathering that a brand-new firm with no prior fund history cannot offer. Certainly, investors will be more drawn to a private equity firm with a prior established track record. After all, it may seem as if it is only common sense to believe that if a firm has already started and managed, or is in the process of managing, a fund, then they have learned from this experience and will be better suited at least operationally than a brand-new fund. These overly broad generalizations, however, are made only by foolhardy investors without the time and resources to properly vet a private equity firm. Of course, there may be certain institutional operational capacities and processes that have been developed and refined in the establishment of the first fund managed by a firm, but this does not remove the onus on the investor to thoroughly vet the operational risks of each fund on an individual basis. Merely resting on the laurels, operational or otherwise, of a manager in the place of proper due diligence is a dangerous game of Russian roulette that eventually will not end well when the manager who the investor did not perform operational due diligence on causes an operational blow-up.

UNDERSTANDING FINANCIAL STATEMENT SECTIONS

When an investor approaches the audited financial statements of a private equity fund for review as part of the operational due diligence process, it is useful to obtain a basic understanding of each of the different common sections that are present.

Opinion Letter

The opinion letter section of the financial statements is sometimes referred to as the independent auditors report. This letter is typically addressed to the Limited Partners of a private equity fund.

The opinion letter may then contain language that, in effect, attempts to disclaim liability in this regard by stating something to the effect of "These financial statements are the responsibility of the fund's management." The opinion letter will next state the audit standard employed as well as a brief standard disclosure as to what an audit entails. Finally, at the conclusion of the letter the auditor will express an opinion as to whether the financial statements, in their opinion, fairly represent the financial position of the fund.

Investors who begin to review private equity statements with any frequency may begin to feel their eyes glaze over while perusing the often cookie-cutter pieces of such statements. However, the one area that is often overlooked in such statements is the letterhead. Investors should first check to see whether the logo in the letterhead for the audit firm actually matches the corporate logo of the auditor. If financial statements have been fraudulently manufactured or manipulated, then the logo might not match.

A second item that investors should look for in the letterhead is the name of the audit entity that is actually performing the audits. For offshore funds, the audit entity listed in the letterhead will likely be an offshore affiliated entity of the parent onshore audit entity. For onshore funds, a domestic entity will likely be listed. A final consideration with regard to letterhead relates to the address of the audit firm. This can often provide insight into the way in which a private equity firm interacts with the auditor. If a private equity firm is located in New York but their auditor, or, at least, the audit office listed in the letterhead, is in Austin, Texas, investors may want to consider discussing this with the private equity firm. For example, does the auditor not perform on-site visits? Or perhaps the New York–based private equity firm maintains a relationship with the Austin, Texas, office because of a legacy relationship with an audit partner. Investors can often gain useful insights by reviewing such seemingly minor details found in the financial statements and following up with the private equity fund regarding such issues.

OTHER FINANCIAL STATEMENT SECTIONS

In addition to the opinion letter, the audited financials for a private equity fund may contain a number of different sections that are outlined in the following sections.

Statement of Assets and Liabilities

The Statement of Assets and Liabilities is also known as the balance sheet. This financial statement will provide a summary of assets, liabilities, and partner's capital.

Statement of Operations

The Statement of Operations, Assets, and Liabilities is also known as the income statement. The income statement will generally provide a summary of any gains allocations from affiliated entities, as well as a summary of income and expenses. Investors can utilize the information contained on this statement to facilitate an analysis of fund expense allocations.

Statement of Cash Flows

The Statement of Cash Flows provides a summary of cash flows from operating and investing activities. This financial statement typically details the movements of cash throughout the fund including net increase in partners' capital from operations, and any reconciliation adjustments, details of proceeds from sales, and details of purchases of investments. Additionally, the Statement of Cash Flows will typically outline any cash flows from financing activities as well as any cash and cash equivalents held by the fund.

Statement of Changes

The Statement of Changes is sometimes referred to as the Statement of Changes in Partners' Capital. This statement will typically outline changes in the contributions and withdrawals of the General Partner and Limited Partners over a particular period, which is typically annually. The Statement of Changes will likely also detail the allocation of net increase in partners' capital from operations on a pro rata basis.

Schedule of Investments

The Schedule of Investments is typically presented in condensed format in audited financial statements. The Schedule of Investments, if included, may be presented as either a standalone financial statement or as part of the financial statement notes. The Schedule of Investments may group investments by sector, region, or other methodology. This schedule may be presented in a number of different formats that may include the cost of each portfolio asset, the market value of each asset, and the percent of fund capital represented by each portfolio asset.

Financial Statement Notes

Despite the fact that they are often contained at the very end of the document, the notes accompanying financial statements are key components of the financial statements themselves.

Because of their informative value, one approach toward analyzing the financial statements worth considering may be to read the notes first before digging into the relevant sections of the financial statements themselves. Throughout the financial statements you will often see references made to the notes. In some audited financial statements the auditors make reference to the financial statement notes on almost every page of the preceding statements. Some statements can be quite curt, such as "See accompanying notes."

Other auditors may try to be at bit more cordial with references to the effect of, "The accompanying notes are an integral part of these financial statements." Regardless of the terms in the approach utilized, the notes can be gleaned by investors for valuable information. When incorporated into a larger operational due diligence review of a private equity fund, the information not only from the financial statement notes but the entire financial statement review can further facilitate investors in the quest to separate the wheat from the chaff and navigate the often seemingly insurmountable tsunami of documents that may overwhelm even the well-intentioned investor who approaches the process without a plan.

A few words of caution are advisable before an investor tucks into the financial statement notes. First, in a manner similar to the offering memorandum (Chapter 6 discusses this in detail), the financial statement notes are replete with legal platitudes, cover language, ambiguously perplexing disclosures, employment of reference by incorporation, and a whole host of other devices that make them not easily digestible. Even to the trained eye, such as a Certified Public Accountant in the United States or a Chartered Account outside of the United States, translating these notes into nonlegalese may be somewhat of a challenge.

Part of the benefit of performing operational due diligence as a regular practice for all of an investor's prospective and actual private equity investments is that with each subsequent review, investors begin to build up an internal database of knowledge. As such, any investor who has done this will begin to gain some level of familiarity with both the format and general content of the various sections of audited financial statements. The same is true for the analysis of the notes contained in the audited financial statements of private equity firms. So what exactly is contained in the financial statement notes? There are seven main areas that are covered.

1. **Organization and Business.** This section generally contains an overview of the basic history and details of the fund. To begin with, this section may include an overview of when the fund was incorporated and commenced operations. It is worth noting that these are often two different dates. A fund is often incorporated for legal purposes on a date before operations actually begin.

2. **Summary of Significant Accounting Policies.** In this section, the auditors will typically refer to the accounting standards that are employed with language to the effect of "These financial statements have been prepared in conformity with U.S. generally accepted accounting principles (U.S. GAAP) and all amounts are stated in U.S. dollars." This section may also include a variety of subsections highlighting significant accounting policies including: cash and cash equivalents, due from brokers and unsettled transactions, investment transactions and related income, valuation of investments, securities purchased under agreements to resell, use of estimates, indemnifications, income taxes, foreign currency, and new accounting pronouncements.

3. **Investments.** This section will provide an overview of the type of investments held by the fund. The investments section may also detail certain risk exposures the fund may have, including credit risk, market risk, and off-balance-sheet risk.

4. **Commitments and Contingencies.** In this section the details of any commitments to affiliated entities and other third-party firms is generally stated such as a cash deposit that may serve as a collateral line of credit.

5. **Related Party Transactions.** This section of the audited financial statement notes will typically outline any transactions that a private equity fund may engage in with other funds or the General Partner including fee-sharing arrangements.

6. **Financial Highlights.** The financial highlights section is where certain information and ratios relating to the fund are typically presented by the auditor. This section typically begins with an outline of total return for the fund for the period covered during the financial statements. The financial highlights section next typically contains a number of ratios, including investment income ratio and expense ratios. These ratios are typically calculated based on monthly average net assets during the year.

7. **Subsequent Events.** This section of the audited financial statements typically outlines the details of any accounting changes as well as subscriptions and redemptions of which the fund has been notified for period following the end of the audit period.

Financial Statement Due Diligence Considerations: Why Can't I Just Ask the Auditor?

The reader may pose the question. "Well, if the private equity fund manager won't talk, why don't I just ask the auditor?" Stated politely, the answer to that is "Good luck." Investors performing operational due diligence on private equity funds will quickly realize by perhaps their second or third review that most auditors give the impression that they live in a constant state of paranoia. Auditors do not like to or want to speak with investors. Your author would like to believe it is not because they are not proud of their work. No rather, the common logic is that the auditors will point their finger at their lawyers who have advised them not to talk. Indeed, auditors may also seek to blame investors who have suffered fund losses and sued auditors, claiming in part that they materially relied on their audits and because the auditors [*insert reason here*] (e.g., didn't do their job, were reckless, were negligent, etc.). Regardless of the merits of such suits and whether the auditors may or may not be liable, the fact of the matter is that this has resulted in auditors constructing a virtual wall of silence around themselves. One of the challenges in performing operational due diligence is for investors to figure out how to penetrate this fortress, and obtain even the smallest glimmers of transparency.

To see this in action, we can consider the service provider confirmation process that Chapter 3 outlines. Unless instructed otherwise by a private equity firm, an investor will typically seek to confirm a fund or firm's relationship with an auditor. Typically this initial confirmation is attempted by e-mail message or phone call. When such requests are made, the vast majority of auditors will simply not respond. To borrow from the legal profession, this is a technique known as stonewalling. The auditors likely figure that if they do not even acknowledge the investor's request they are off the hook from any investor being able to claim that they relied on anything that they may have communicated to the investor outside the audited financial statements, all of which have been likely scrubbed by their attorneys.

Now what is an investor supposed to do? Forget about delving into discussions related to audit materiality levels or any actual questions about the audited financials that you may want to ask of an auditor, rather than the private equity fund themselves. At this stage in our example, an investor is still merely trying to confirm the relationship between the auditor and the private equity fund or firm.

During this process the private equity firm in question, perhaps responding to requests from the auditors, may set up a number of roadblocks to what could be a simple and seamless process. The first of such hurdles could be that the private equity firm will not provide investors with the specific details of whom to contact at the audit firm. An example of how this can occur would be disclosures in a firm's prepared due diligence questionnaire that lists certain contact details regarding service providers. When it comes to the auditor, however, the due diligence questionnaire will merely list the name of the firm in question and a vague statement such as "details available upon request" or "please contact the firm for further information." This then requires the investor to contact the fund to obtain the details, which, as outlined in more detail later, the private equity firm will not directly provide.

A second technique employed by private equity firms in attempting to skirt the actual independent audit confirmation issue would be to point out that, in the case of a vintage fund arrangement where the same audit firm is being engaged for the new fund, the previous audits were produced by the auditor on their letterhead. Despite the current state of the post-Madoff world, a private equity fund may, feigning naiveté, sheepishly pose the question, isn't that sufficient? Plainly, no. As a long list of historical frauds throughout the alternative investment world have demonstrated—Sam's Israel Bayou hedge fund comes to mind—letterheads can be forged and audit firms may even be entirely made up.

Having jumped through this hoop, a private equity firm may next attempt to quell any investor concerns by producing a recently dated and signed engagement letter from an auditor, once again on letterhead, for the proposed work on the new fund. This is not sufficient, either. The point that many private equity funds may often miss and which is worth highlighting to investors is the importance of independence in the relationship confirmation process. If the information being used to confirm the relationship with a private equity firm is provided to an investor by that same private equity firm, then, stated plainly, the confirmation is not independently obtained.

The way in which most audit confirmations proceed beyond this point varies. One way they may proceed is that oftentimes an investor must insist that they need independent confirmation of the firm's relationship with the auditor. If this is the first time the fund has dealt with such a request, the private equity firm themselves, without the investor being involved, will typically contact the auditor and convey the request. The auditor will next likely provide a confidentiality agreement and liability release for the investor to sign. This is also sometimes accompanied by a second similar confidentiality agreement and release whereby the private equity firm releases the auditor from liability. This dual release system can often be quite cumbersome for both investors and the private equity firms to navigate. Additionally, if investors prudently have external legal counsel review these documents before executing them, this can add additional expense and significant delay in the operational due diligence process timeline. Finally, once all these releases are in place the auditor may only send the investor a letter, full of the standard disclosures and legalese, which confirms the relationship but denies just about everything else you could think of in regard to the oversight and work of the auditor.

With this background, it is worth noting that in certain instances auditors may actually reply to investor's inquiries the first time they are made. These replies can range from basis e-mail confirmations to an actual phone conversation. While there may be very valid reasons for auditors and private equity firms to establish certain safeguards that may lead to an unintended result and encumber the investor operational due diligence process, ultimately the onus is on the investor to put in the effort to confirm auditor relationships.

This seems a bit ridiculous when you think about it. Consider the following example: you are considering purchasing a home. You go to the bank to obtain a mortgage. The bank tells you that they will extend a mortgage to you but only after you have the home inspected by a certified engineer. Eager to get the mortgage, you go out and hire the inspection engineer. The engineer conducts the home inspection and produces a report, in which he states based on the home inspection guidelines issued by the Counsel of Almighty Home Inspectors that in his opinion the report fairly shows that there are not material issues with the home. He even signs and stamps it with his official stamp. You then eagerly go to the bank with your report. The bank reviews it but has a few questions about some of the conclusions made by the inspector and wants more information. They call the inspector (his phone number is listed on the opinion page of his report). A week goes by and the home inspector does not return the bank's phone call. You are still waiting to hear if the bank will approve your mortgage and inquire as to the status. The bank tells you that they attempted to contact the home inspector but he hasn't replied. You angrily call up the home inspector and ask why he hasn't returned the bank's phone calls. The home inspector explains that he has had a problem in the past with banks suing him and requires them, and you, to sign a 30-page confidentiality agreements and releases before talking to anyone. Furious, you remind the home inspector that he was hired by you, you pay his bill, and at the end of the day it would be only common courtesy for you to get on the phone with the bank. He refuses. Frustrated, you walk away and decide to buy a different house. This example is a bit equivalent to the way some audit firms deal with their private equity clients and the frustrations investors face when dealing with such firms. Investors should be prepared to deal with such challenges during their operational due diligence processes, and develop strategies to overcome these hurdles so as not to stall their reviews.

UNDERSTANDING FAS 157

In reviewing audited financial statements of a private equity fund an investor is likely to come across FAS 157 breakouts. FAS 157 was first implemented in November 2007. FAS 157 created a framework for categorizing valuations. Valuations are supposed to be categorized into one of three categories according to the inputs utilized to value each position. The higher the level, the less readily observable market prices and, therefore, the position is generally more thinly traded and thought to be more illiquid. When it was first implemented as an accounting rule, it was supposed to initially have a big impact on the alternative investment industry. Level 1 assets are those with readily observable inputs. Level 2 assets are those with no directly observable prices themselves, but those assets do have price inputs that are based on them (e.g., an interest-rate swap whose components are observable points—like a Treasury bond).

The Level 3 Anathema

Finally we come to Level 3 assets. These are supposed to be assets with no readily observable inputs. There is a general stigma against Level 3 assets—both private equity firms and investors seemingly want to avoid them at all costs. Why? Well, for starters there is the perception of the market premium placed on liquidity. Whether or not you agree that the desire for enhanced liquidity is rational—the fact of the matter is that when given the choice, most groups, private equity funds, and investors would generally prefer the more liquid asset.

Private equity funds in particular do not like Level 3 assets. When FAS 157 was first implemented in the private equity firm's 2008 audited financial statements, there was much hesitation among auditors and private equity funds alike regarding how to classify those assets with questionable inputs or uncertain levels of illiquidity. Many auditors took a conservative hard-line approach and classified these questionable assets and liabilities as being in Level 3. While investors may have been originally unhappy to learn that a private equity fund that they thought may have been more liquid than the FAS 157 levels in the audited financial statements suggested, at least investors took some comfort in knowing that the auditors had most likely been conservative in their approach to level classification.

Where Are We Now? A Floating FAS 157 Standard

Flash-forward a few years to the present, and the FAS 157 level classification system has reached a tipping point that threatens to render level classification virtually useless. What has happened is that private equity firms have recently rediscovered an important fact—the auditor works for them, and they are not too subtly reminding auditors of this fact. Unhappy with their assets being classified as Level 2 or Level 3, many private equity funds have continually argued with their auditors over the past few years that certain assets inputs are really observable and that they should be moved up from one level to another. This has resulted in the gradual transition of assets from Level 3 to Level 2 and from Level 2 to Level 1.

Part of the transition may justifiably come from auditor's increased comfort with the FAS 157 rules over time, coupled with enhanced guidance from the author of FAS 157 the Financial Accounting Standards Board (FASB). But FASB guidance and auditor knowledge levels aside, it would not be unreasonable to hazard a guess that the increased private equity fund pressure toward auditors to recategorize assets and liabilities as being more liquid has something to do with it. After all, if a private equity fund and an auditor cannot agree, a private equity fund can always threaten to switch auditors or split up their audit work for different funds among multiple audit firms.

While many auditors may publicly portray the image that they would not consider compromising their standards at the beck and call of private equity funds for issues such as FAS 157 level classification, it seems as if the auditors have found some wiggle room in which to operate with regards to FAS 157. Auditors now seem comfortable in kowtowing to private equity fund requests for FAS 157 level reclassification as long as they have a leg to stand on, albeit a shaky one, in the form of some sort of observable input. The problem is that an input that was once not readily observable when FAS 157 was first implemented has now entered a gray area of observability, which the auditor uses to level-up assets and keep the private equity fund as their paying client.

Further complicating the issue is that many private equity funds have begun creating their own FAS 157 classification systems that they use to distribute FAS 157 statements to investors throughout the year. Some private equity fund administrators have also gotten into the FAS 157 business and begun providing classification guidance as well. Reconciling these levels to any FAS 157 levels in audited financial statements can yield an interesting glimpse into potential differences in classification methodologies. Furthermore, by analyzing FAS 157 levels over time an investor could begin to understand how classification levels may have changed over time.

Operational Due Diligence Insights into FAS 157 Today

Detailed operational due diligence can provide useful insights into these types of issues. Often, yellow or red flags, such as a virtually captured auditor, inconsistencies in valuation methodologies, and overly optimistic statements about liquidity, come to light when analyzed in the context of a comprehensive operational due diligence review. Such analysis can be time-consuming but may yield some useful insights into any latent operational risks that may be present in a fund.

CONCLUSION

This chapter provides an overview of some of the techniques investors may consider employing when performing due diligence reviews of a private equity fund's financial statements. This chapter also introduces several issues and concerns investors may want to focus on in conducting these reviews. In summary, some key questions that investors may want to ask themselves when designing the financial statement review component of their private equity operational due diligence program can include:

- For how many years should you collect audited financial statements? Since inception?
- How do you analyze and track fund expenses? Are operational expense levels appropriate as compared to other *pari passu* funds?
- Are audits being completed according to previously established timelines? How can you locate evidence of this?
- Does the auditor perform any additional audit, tax, or testing services?
- How have the audited financials changed year over year?
- Has the fund's auditor remained consistent since inception? What about the primary office from which the audit is conducted?
- Does your review of the audited financial statements agree with both your review of other fund documentation (e.g., offering memorandum, due diligence questionnaire) as well as manager statements?
- Have you been able to receive independent confirmation, either formally or informally, from the auditor that they indeed perform audit work for the fund(s) under review?
- Are all audits, including historical ones, on appropriate letterhead from the auditor?
- What is the nature of the relationship between the auditor and the fund administrator? Has the auditor visited the fund administrator's offices?
- How do you monitor things such as related party transactions and cash levels?
- Are there any related or affiliated funds audited financials that you should review even though you are not considering investing directly in these other funds?

NOTES

1. See George Georgiades, *GAAS Practice Manual 2009: Current SASs, SSAEs, and SSARSs in Practice* (CCH, 2008).

2. See Louis Braiotta Jr., *The Audit Committee Handbook*, 5th ed. (Hoboken, NJ: John Wiley & Sons, 2010).
3. See Vincent M. O'Reilly, *Montgomery's Auditing*, 12th ed. (Hoboken, NJ: John Wiley & Sons, 1999).
4. See Barry J. Epstein, *Wiley GAAP: Interpretation and Application of Generally Accepted Accounting* (Hoboken, NJ: John Wiley & Sons, 2010).
5. "AICPA Recommends SEC Allow Optional Adoption of IFRS by U.S. Public Companies," August 17, 2011, www.aicpa.org/Press/PressReleases/2011/Pages/AICPARecommendsSECAllowOptionalAdoptionofIFRSbyUSPublicCompanies.aspx.
6. See Gary Previts, *Research in Accounting Regulation*, vol. 20 (Oxford, UK: JAI Press, 2008).

CHAPTER 8

Distinguishing the Assets Class: Real Estate–Specific Concerns

S ome private equity investors may consider real estate to be a distinct asset class that has very little if any relation to private equity funds. Indeed, if investors approach the subject with any private equity fund manager themselves, they are likely to hear a long litany of reasons regarding why the two asset classes are different. Others may draw more similarities between the two types of investments. From the investor's perspective it is easy to see from where such similarities arise. Both investments in real estate and private equity require a longer-term investment horizon as compared to perhaps more liquid asset classes such as hedge funds. Additionally, both private equity and real estate funds tend to invest in more illiquid positions, as compared to hedge funds.

From the perspective of an investor seeking to perform operational due diligence on both private equity and real estate funds, accompanying these shared illiquidity characteristics are similarities in approaches to valuing illiquid assets as well as fund structures.

Despite such similarities it is important for investors not to approach operational due diligence reviews of both private equity and real estate funds with a blanket approach. Such a universal approach may result in a homogenized approach that diminishes some of the particularities regarding each asset class. This chapter provides an introduction to certain issue-specific factors relating to performing operational due diligence on real estate funds.

REAL ESTATE TRADE FLOW PROCESS

When beginning the operational due diligence process on a real estate fund, it is often helpful for Limited Partners to begin the process with obtaining an understanding of the investment research and trade flow process by which a particular real estate fund invests. An understanding of such a process is particularly useful due to the different types of unique asset classes related to real estate. For example, different funds may invest in a wide range of property types including commercial, residential, and agricultural property types.

SAMPLE REAL ESTATE PROCESS

In order to provide the reader with an oversight of a typical process in this regard, we will walk through such a process in more detail for a sample real estate fund, which we will refer to as RE Fund, that invests in commercial real estate.

Initial Research

RE Fund maintains a research team that consists of three individuals: Mr. A (Fund Manager) and two research analysts. In vetting potential opportunities for the funds, this team utilizes a combination of in-house economic forecasts as well as a variety of third-party research sources.

Sector Analysis

The fund's management team defines the characteristics of commercial real estate assets into three different sectors: city centers, shopping centers, and supermarkets. The firm utilizes an internal matrix methodology to identify and monitor these characteristics. This commercial matrix is utilized when considering new investments for the RE Fund as well as for selecting properties for disposition or redevelopment. To facilitate the quality of data utilized in the matrix, the management team for the fund seeks to maintain ongoing dialogues with agents and retailers to monitor market conditions.

Feasibility Study

A feasibility study is generally conducted for all new deals. As part of this process, new investment opportunities are appraised via a process that includes consideration of the real estate asset under review. If after this initial screening a property is still deemed to be acceptable, a more detailed report is prepared for the firm's progress review committee.

Analysis Tools

To facilitate further portfolio analysis, the fund management team will utilize two proprietary applications. One application focuses on commercial property analysis opportunity vetting. The second application allows for asset analysis and portfolio construction. The first application is utilized to focus on the identification and monitoring of real estate assets via a scoring system. When scoring a property, the management team assigns different weights to different indicators across economic, real estate, market, and retail experience factors. The second application tool is utilized to identify and benchmark real estate assets with a focus on identifying and tracking local market asset performance over time utilizing an analysis of a variety of performance indicators.

Acquisition Plan and Committee Review

Once a potential investment has been identified, the RE Fund manager creates an acquisition plan for investments. These plans include an analysis of several areas including research, legal, tax, compliance, accounting, reporting, and technical asset management. The plans are reviewed by an appointed controller.

In addition to these proprietary tools, the firm also performs competitive analysis for each asset. The combined results of these efforts are listed in an annual review of hold or sell analysis for the funds, which feeds the development of a three-year business plan for the portfolio. The analysis includes a review of plans to acquire a new square footage once the properties under development have been completed.

Technical Due Diligence

RE Fund also maintains a technical due diligence department consisting of four individuals. This group is responsible for overseeing the work of internal efforts and third-party firms that perform technical due diligence on properties. The type of technical due diligence performed include reviews of building construction, fire systems, and soil analysis to detect the presence of any potentially dangerous materials.

Property Acquisition

Once the final due diligence review is complete and all the appropriate approvals have been obtained, RE Fund will then proceed with the acquisition of the property. This process includes the drafting and completing of all relevant purchase documentation. To ensure the limited liability of each property, a holding vehicle is usually created for each property. It should be noted that the fund will not be permitted to invest more than 18 percent of the net asset value of the fund into real estate assets that are subject to development or are held vacant pending development. Generally, at the time of the acquisition capital will be drawn down from investors to facilitate the purchase.

Logging of the Purchase and Sale of Assets

Once a real estate asset has been purchased, an application is submitted to the accounting department for the creation of a project code in the RE Fund's systems. The entire purchase process from project initiation to the purchase of an asset is administered through a series of operational checklists. For projects that involve real estate that is yet to be built, the construction process will also be monitored according to a fixed format.

In the event a real estate asset is to be sold, a sales proposal is prepared. After review and approval by the acquisition and sales manager, the asset is put on the market. The business unit then provides the corresponding documents relating to the sale to enterprise system. Specifically, the required documents are a completion statement and a sales agreement. Once RE Fund receives these documents, the data is reviewed by at least seven individuals from the valuation group. Similar procedures are in place for managing systems which includes digital storage of documents. The enterprise management system is also utilized for making index-linked calculations and logging any rental increases for each contract.

Use of Third-Party Developers

In the past, properties for the funds have been sourced by RE Fund via forward purchase agreements, which are structured on a turnkey basis. RE Fund has utilized several different third-party developers to facilitate these agreements and an affiliated entity, RE Fund Development, to oversee construction and leasing arrangements. It should be noted that the responsibility to perform due diligence on third-party developers lies primarily with the fund's portfolio manager.

Property Management

Once the asset managers have negotiated the specific deal terms, the process moves over to RE Fund's property management team. The property management group first ensures that the specific details of each property and tenant have been logged into the firm's enterprise system. The daily work of property managers focuses on a variety of different tasks, which the team has divided into the following areas:

- **Administration and risk management.** This involves inputting new information into the enterprise system as well as the property management function, which serves as the first line of risk management defense. This function also includes maintaining required governmental paperwork such as health, safety, and fire risk assessment certificates with the relevant governmental authorities.
- **Financial control.** This function involves overseeing all income and expenditure flows including rent collection.
- **Tenant occupancy.** This involves overseeing that properties do not sit vacant and maintaining good contacts with tenants.
- **Market information.** Includes managing and collecting relevant market information with respect to tenants and properties.

The property management function is also responsible for overseeing that appropriate insurance coverage is maintained for each property. Bids are received from a number of different entities. Building insurance is assessed on a quarterly basis as part of the oversight work of external valuation agents. Insurance coverage on buildings is maintained across a number of standard areas including fire, water, and general liability. The asset manager also maintains a certain amount of discretion as to whether they feel certain types of coverage should be in place, such as for a historical building.

RE Fund outsources the management of property to a number of third parties to support the group's internal efforts. Two examples are:

- **Shopping Center Management.** Daily management of the fund's larger commercial properties such as shopping centers malls and other rental properties to a wide variety of third-party firms.
- **Residential Property Management.** The management of residential properties such as apartments is also outsourced to a variety of third-party local specialty firms. In addition to the firms previously outlined, the firm maintains relationships with a number of subcontractors that are on-call for emergency repairs. All costs are benchmarked internally as compared to the costs of similar projects at other properties RE Fund manages throughout the United States. For any large repair or maintenance expenditures, there is an internal process that requires different offers to be received from several vendors.

Post-Deal Management

After a property has been acquired, RE Fund conducts ongoing monitoring of the property. This includes an ongoing review of the tenant's credit quality. On a biannual basis, the RE Fund's Investment Committee conducts a full review of each fund's portfolio. Additionally, on a quarterly basis the fund's board will review an investment management status report on the portfolio.

As a result of this ongoing monitoring, RE Fund may recommend the implementation of management initiatives. Examples of these initiatives can include property refurbishment or the renewal of a tenant's lease. These initiatives are subject to the approval of the firm's Investment Committee.

Credit Research

Throughout the deal sourcing and review process, the fund manager leverages off of the expertise of the fund's credit team. The credit team is a centralized resource that provides credit analysis to many different funds throughout the funds, including the firm's fixed-income products. As part of their analysis, the fund's credit team reviews a number of factors including the overall creditworthiness of a particular tenant and an analysis of the predictability of cash flows. The results of this credit analysis are a recommendation and relevant commentary from the credit department that are shared with the fund managers. Portfolio managers are automatically alerted when any changes in credit recommendations by the fund's credit team for relevant companies are issued. Often these recommendations are supplemented with discussions between the fund managers and the credit team.

As the description outlines there are a number of different stages during the private equity investment process, each of which has different operational risk considerations which investors must consider during their operational due diligence reviews.

REAL ESTATE VALUATION

Real estate valuation is a complex and daunting task to approach, especially for investors seeking to perform operational due diligence. As with each different private equity fund has different investment considerations, so too does the real estate asset class have similar unique considerations for each fund. With real estate, similar to the common approaches utilized to value certain types of assets, there are generally some similarities in the valuation of common types of assets. During the operational due diligence process, investors should develop an understanding of the valuation approach and methodologies employed by the real estate fund under review. Some of the key considerations regarding real estate valuation are outlined in the following sections.

Sample Fund Procedures

From the perspective of an investor, a real estate fund's internal valuation procedures drive the valuation process. When beginning an analysis of valuation policies and procedures, investors should gain an understanding of the way a fund approaches the valuation process as well the nature of independence in the process. So that the reader may gain familiarity with such processes, the following paragraphs describe a sample fund valuation process for our fictional real estate fund, RE Fund.

It is anticipated that valuations for RE Fund will be performed on a quarterly basis. It should be noted that these valuations are primarily performed by each individual deal team for a particular position. A variety of valuation methodologies are utilized as appropriate, including discounted cash flow analysis (for unstabilized properties), direct capitalization analysis (stabilized properties), comparables analysis, and mark-to-model for residential mortgage-backed securities. The methodology utilized and the results of these valuations are documented in the RE Fund's proprietary valuation memorandum. Accompanying these valuation memorandums are details of financial calculations utilized and any accompanying source documentation relied upon including appraisals, bids/offers, and signed letters of intent.

After initial valuation memorandums are complete, they are reviewed and, if acceptable, approved by deal team leaders. After approval, final valuation details and supporting documentation are uploaded into the firm's data-sharing software. In addition to being uploaded into the firm's systems, deal team leaders sign-off on valuation memoranda. These signatures and hard copies of all valuation memoranda and supporting documentation are stored in a valuation binder.

After all valuations have been uploaded and consolidated for a fund, valuation methodologies and supporting documentation are reviewed for the real estate funds by the managing director for financial management. These reviews include an analysis of the valuation methods applied to ensure consistency of approach as well as discussions with deal team leaders concerning specific deals as required. After this review, if acceptable, valuations are approved by this team.

The next stage in the valuation review process includes a review of valuations by the real estate accounting group. This level of review includes an analysis of any fund costs associated with a particular investment as well as an analysis of valuations of prior quarter valuations and any changes to equity multiples employed. If approved by the real estate accounting group, the valuations then move to the final stage of review.

The final stage of quarterly valuation reviews involves reviews of consolidated executive summaries of valuations. This level of analysis includes a review of position valuations by fund and sector. Trend analysis and any internal rate of return (IRR) changes are also reviewed. Additionally, in the event any specific asset needs to be reviewed in more detail, this would occur as well. If these valuations are acceptable to the team, the final approval of quarterly valuations is provided.

Use of Valuation Consultants

Certain private equity funds may engage the use of third-party valuation consultants to provide independence in the valuation process. Increasingly investors may demand the employment of such consultants to provide oversight and independence in the valuation process. Some funds may utilize the services of a single third-party consultant while others may employ multiple third-party valuation consultants. The use of multiple consultants can provide diversity in the valuation process and different valuation consultants may offer specialized knowledge in appraising certain property types.

It is important for investors to assess how often consultants will perform valuation reviews. During the operational due diligence process, investors should also assess to what standards the private equity fund's valuation consultants may adhere. An example of such standards may be the so-called "Red Book" standards in the RICS Valuation Standards.

During the operational due diligence process, investors should also gain an understanding of the process by which a real estate fund may engage with a valuation consultant.

Sample Valuation Consultant Process

The following is an example of a valuation process for our hypothetical real estate fund, the RE Fund.

The quarterly review process begins with external valuation agents providing RE Fund with a draft valuation of a single value for each asset. These draft valuations are reviewed by RE Fund's valuation group, which is independent of the RE Fund. After the valuation group completes its reviews, a second review is conducted by the individual RE Fund's asset managers Should the RE Fund asset manager have comments, these are communicated to the valuation group, which will review the comments with the appraiser.

After any comments or issues have been investigated and resolved, the external valuation agent will approve the valuation. After the external valuation agent's values have been approved, the internal valuation group prepares a report outlining a reevaluation of all appraisals. Coordinating this process internally from the RE Fund's perspective is the firm's head of finance, who has the ability to challenge any such quarterly appraisals. In the event a challenge is raised, another neutral third-party valuation agent would be brought in to settle any disputes. As part of this monitoring work, the valuation group produces an internal list that includes all real estate projects from the previous quarter and the new values. Where there is a difference of 0.07 percent or greater, then a more detailed report is made that lists why the value changed, and the value has to be approved by the asset manager. Physical sign-offs have to occur on all valuation schedules. On an annual basis, full valuations, which may include on-site property visits, are also performed.

Common Approaches to Valuation

There are a number of common approaches to valuation. These approaches can include the cost approach, the sales comparison approach, and income approach. The cost approach is fairly straightforward and involves holding a position on the cost that a private equity fund paid for a particular asset. The sales comparison approach, which may sometimes be referred to a "comparables approach," focuses on the valuation of similar properties. This can include a review of the prices that similar properties may have commanded. Additionally, in valuing such properties the sales comparison approach may also focus on issues related to regional concerns specific to local jurisdictions.

The income approach focuses on the income generated by a particular property to determine valuations. During the operational due diligence process investors must determine any assumptions that a private equity fund may have made in establishing valuation models under the income approach. These assumptions can include future rates of property occupancy as well as any macroeconomic assumptions such as continuing rates of inflation.

Outside the United States, a number of different regional valuation methodologies may be utilized. Many of those methods are similar to the approaches just mentioned with additional regional considerations included. In the United Kingdom, for example, the following methods may be utilized:

- **Accounts/Profits Method.** This method is utilized for certain residential properties such as motels and eating establishments. These methods

EXHIBIT 8.1   Common Standard Valuation Approaches Organized by Country

Valuation Method/Valuation Organization	Country
Comparable method	United Kingdom
Investments/income method	United Kingdom
Accounts/profits method	United Kingdom
Development/residual method	United Kingdom
Contractor's/cost method	United Kingdom
RICS appraisal and valuation standards	United Kingdom
Uniform Standards of Professional Appraisal Practice (USPAP)	United States
Wertermittlungsverordnung	Germany
Council of Land Valuers	Israel
Japanese Association of Real Estate Appraisal	Japan
The Russian Society of Appraisers	Russia

typically utilize income statements averages from multiple time periods to calculate yields that are utilized in the valuation process.

- **Comparable Method.** This method is similar to the sales comparison approach that, as just mentioned, typically utilizes data from previous sales.
- **Development/Residual Method.** This method is utilized to value vacant land under development.
- **Contractors'/Cost Method.** This method has many similarities to the cost approach, and is typically utilized in evaluating construction costs.
- **Investment/Income Method.** This method is utilized in the valuation process to determine the cash flows generated by rental properties.

Finally, the last valuation method we will discuss are those valuation standards promulgated by the Royal Institution of Chartered Surveyors, which is commonly referred to in the United Kingdom under the acronym RICS. The RICS Valuation Standards is commonly referred to as the Red Book, outlining a number of different standards across property types and property related matters, including commercial property, building surveying, and residential property. Exhibit 8.1 outlines other common standard valuation approaches organized by country.

MONITORING CONFLICTS OF INTEREST

When performing operational due diligence on real estate funds, investors must be conscious of the presence of conflicts of interest. These conflicts of interest can range across a variety of different topics from ethical monitoring, compliance oversight, and deal allocation. The following is a summary of a conflict of interest policy for our hypothetical RE Fund.

The firm maintains a conflict of interest policy as part of its larger firmwide code of ethics policy. On a firm level, RE Fund requires that any action or decision that may result in a conflict, including those among departments and funds or between the firm and an investor, must be reviewed by senior management, the chief compliance officer, or the general counsel. In addition, the firm's policies require the firm to promptly disclose apparent, potential, or actual conflicts of interest.

On a fund level, as part of the review of potential conflicts of interest for the real estate fund, the compliance department oversees any specific conflicts of interest related to who sourced the deal and management responsibility for a particular deal. Additionally, the firm attempts to remove any potential conflicts of interest among real estate personnel by instituting appropriate segregation of duties among individuals and departments as well as multiple levels of intradepartmental review for fund acquisitions and quarterly valuations.

For real estate funds, the firm's conflicts of interest policy also attempts to resolve any potential conflicts that may be in place should multiple real estate funds in addition to the RE Fund which may be interested in the same property. In such an event the deal would be subject to multiple levels of review by compliance and senior management. This review would take into account factors such as which personnel first sourced the deal, and the appropriateness of the property for each fund.

Property Management Considerations

The role of property management for real estate fund is one that should be carefully analyzed by investors during the operational due diligence process for real estate funds. The property management function is often one that, although rooted in what can be thought of as traditional noninvestment-related activities, is more aligned with the investment side of the GP than the operational function. To illustrate, one of the goals of property management is answering questions such as "Will a particular property generate a reasonable return?" and arguably a more urbane concern, such as "Do the real estate holdings of the fund maintain adequate insurance coverage in the event the property is destroyed"? Despite this seemingly uneasy alliance with the investment side of the world, property management may very well slip through the cracks of certain due diligence processes that may be focused on more traditional investment notions, and as such an investor faced with the task of performing operational due diligence on real estate property management may well fall within the domain of the operational due diligence realm.

Property management requires knowledge of multiple disciplines. The areas covered by a property management function can include:

- Collecting rent from tenants
- Determining the appropriate types and amount of property insurance coverage
- Negotiating lease terms with tenants
- Managing the lease renewal process as rebate leases may come due
- Working with brokers to fill property vacancies
- Maintaining common areas
- Emergency property repairs (e.g., fixing a burst pipe)
- Any required environmental remediation (e.g., cleaning up oil that may have spilled on the property)
- Ongoing property maintenance (e.g., landscaping, waste removal, and so on)
- Overseeing the collection of rents from overdue tenants

It is worth noting a few items regarding the previous list. With regard to commercial property with tenants, the property management function also generally must ensure that tenants' spaces are maintained in acceptable condition. This can include ongoing oversight of properties, as well as ensuring that tenants do not overstep bounds with regard to extensive renovations.

Property managers generally also provide oversight with regard to property security. Security for occupied properties includes preventing things such as vandalism. Examples of such property concerns for occupied properties can include providing adequate security at shopping malls to prevent occurrences, such as theft or attacks on patrons, such a muggings in a poorly lit parking lot.

The issue of property security is of particular concern for properties under development or being refurbished. Security on these types of properties is essential to ensure that unauthorized individuals do not access the property. Such property security concerns should be monitored because they can have significant implications for the fund. Although each property holding is typically ring-fenced into a separate legal entity, any such potential insurance claims or litigation resulting from property injuries can at a minimum serve as a distraction for a fund and at worst generate losses for the fund.

With all of these different responsibilities, the role of most property managers at the management company level is to be, as the name suggests, just a manager. If a water pipe bursts and is flooding a particular property, it is not the property manager who typically grabs a wrench and a plunger. Instead the property manager grabs a phone and typically calls a plumber with whom they already have a contract in place to perform such emergency repairs. It is important for investors to understand the diverse roles and responsibilities of a property manager during the real estate operational due diligence process.

Tenant Property Concerns Rent Collection

In properties with buildings, as opposed to vacant properties, real estate holdings that have tenants have a number of unique operational issues that investors should consider during the operational due diligence process. One example relates to the collection of rents from tenants. When private equity funds collect rents, it is important for investors to track the flow of cash from tenants to the fund. Some issues investors may want to consider as part of this process include:

- Does the private equity fund utilize a special agency or vendor to aggregate or collect fund rents?
- Do rents go to separate bank accounts for the fund or are collected rents commingled with other fund cash?

Investors may also want to take into account any issues related to the collection of overdue rents from tenants. Different real estate funds, depending on the property type as well as the general state of the economy, may have different occupancy rates for properties. These factors can influence the magnitude of overdue rents. In these cases, investors should attempt to gauge the ways in which the funds collect any overdue rents during the operational due diligence process. There are a number of different approaches that real estate funds may take in this regard. Generally, interest will be charged on overdue rent, but a real estate property manager may offer a tenant who is behind on the rent concessions such as a waiver of interest if the rent is paid in a timely manner. Additionally, real estate fund managers may also attempt to obtain leverage over tenants to pay overdue rent via the threat of commencement of formal rent collection proceedings or the perhaps less aggressive tactic of involving third-party collection agencies. During the operational due diligence process investors should investigate not only the ways in which overdue rents are collected but the amounts of overdue rents as well.

FRAUD CONSIDERATIONS: MORTGAGE FRAUD AND STRAW-MAN BORROWERS

Investors should also take measures during the operational due diligence process to investigate ways in which the fund managers attempt to avoid exposure to fraudulent activities in real estate transactions. One area where such deal fraud may be particularly prevalent relates to mortgage fraud. Examples of ways in which real estate funds may be exposed to such mortgage fraud risk include through the bundling of investments or via direct real estate investments. In most mortgage fraud situations, there is collusion between the loan originator and the property appraiser.[1] Other groups may also participate in the fraudulent conspiracy, including brokers, title companies, and estate agents. Other related fraudulent mortgage schemes may involve the creation of a straw-man borrower. An example of this would be a transaction in which a real estate fund's holdings are flipped. The straw man would be used to pay an inflated market value for a price that would then feed into a similarly phony inflated appraisal value.

Investors should take measures during the operational due diligence process for real estate funds to review any such questionable legal entities or relationships both at the real estate fund's property holdings level as well as at the firmwide level as well. By developing such an understanding, investors are less likely to be exposed to fraudulent activity in real estate investments.

UNDERSTANDING REAL ESTATE FUND FEES

In addition to standard private equity fund fees, such as a management fee and carried interest, real estate funds may charge a variety of additional fees. During the operational due diligence process, investors should take measures to understand exactly what additional fees, if any, are being charged to the real estate fund under consideration. Such additional fees, while individually small, can add up in aggregate to have a material effect on the investor's rate of return. Not only is it advisable to understand the basic nuts and bolts of such fees, but investors should also consider the methodology behind such fees. Examples of additional fees that may be charged by real estate funds include an acquisition fee, property management fee, an income performance fee, and a forward commitment performance fee. In certain cases a real estate fund may be compared against certain benchmark indices. If a fund metric such as net operating income or performance does not exceed a particular benchmark then a resulting high-water mark may result that the fund needs to clear before this fee is earned. In other situations, such as for acquisition or property management fees, such fees may be tied to individual real estate holdings, as opposed to overall fund performance. In certain instances, the descriptions of certain fee arrangements, particularly in a real estate fund's offering memorandum, can be quite complex. This is particularly true when multiple scenarios under which such fee may or may not be collected are evaluated. For any such complicated or difficult to understand fees, investors should walk through basic fee calculations with the real estate fund to ensure both a basic understanding of fee calculations as well as to determine consistency of approach in such calculations.

PROPERTY HOLDINGS LEGAL CONSIDERATIONS

As with most private equity property holdings, a number of asset specific considerations may come about, many of which are rooted in legal considerations. This is particularly true for real estate funds. However, certain characteristics of property ownership and management are more consistent across different real estate funds than similarities may be across traditional private equity portfolio company holdings companies. An example of this relates to property insurance.

Regardless of whether a real estate fund holds vacant property or property with actual structures built upon it, it is required in virtually every circumstance that the real estate fund will maintain some sort of insurance coverage. Determining not only what coverage types are appropriate, but also the amount of such coverage is not an exact science. During the operational due diligence process, investors should take care to evaluate the methodology utilized by the real estate firm in this regard. Certain real estate firms will utilize a checklist-type approach toward determining what coverage should be maintained at certain properties. In certain instances, depending on the geographical location of different properties certain types of coverage may be mandated (e.g., earthquake coverage in California). Coverage type and amounts may also vary by property type. So for example, it is likely advisable for a shopping mall that may be frequented by shoppers who could trip and fall on the property to have appropriate coverage. This could be compared to an agricultural or more undeveloped piece of property with more restricted access.

Additionally, depending on the nature of activities conducted on a property, insurance coverage may vary as well. For example, a real estate fund that owns property that is used in manufacturing a flammable substance will most likely have increased coverage against fire damage as compared to a nonflammable-substance manufacturing operation. Additionally, the tenants of such property are likely to be required to have certain insurance coverage in place, as well as a condition of tenancy.

During the operational due diligence process, investors should take measures to understand a private equity firm's approach toward determining insurance coverage type and amount. Furthermore, investors should attempt to gauge the way in which underlying tenant coverage is monitored by the private equity firm.

Another related legal matter to consider is the due diligence process that the real estate manager itself performs on the underlying properties. One example of this due diligence can relate to title searches. Typically a private equity fund, or their attorney, will engage a third-party title search firm to perform these searches. While the title search firm may hold liability for any errors, during the real estate fund operational due diligence process investors should take measures to determine what actual title search efforts are being either performed or reviewed at the fund manager level. If a fund completely outsources the function and title issues that come to bear after a real estate fund purchases a property, while the fund may have recourse against the title company, such issues can create potential short-term losses for investors as well as serve as a distraction to fund management.

A third related legal matter regarding properties held by real estate funds involves the ways in which such properties are held by the fund. As outlined previously, many real estate funds do not themselves own the property directly. Rather, a separate ring-fenced legal entity is established whose sole asset is typically the property. This is typically done on the advice of legal counsel to limit the liability of this separate entity solely to issues arising from a particular piece of property. If the property was owned by the fund directly, and large liabilities ensued, the amount of such liabilities could extend beyond the value of the single asset. This would likely result in a situation where the liability claims reached through to the rest of the fund and created large-scale liability exposures. In order to prevent such a scenario, these separate entities are usually established. During the real estate fund operational due diligence process, investors should attempt to gain an understanding of the way in which a fund approaches the ownership of fund property holdings from a technical perspective and determine what legal entities are involved in the process. Such determinations can also provide a deeper understanding of the potential for any conflicts of interest or self-dealing among entities.

CONCLUSION

This chapter provides an introduction to some of the similarities and differences related to the operational considerations investors should take into account when performing operational due diligence on private equity and real estate funds. Real estate is a unique subset of private equity investing that has a number of unique aspects and potential operational risk exposures that investors must take into account during the operational due diligence process. This chapter outlines by example several of the factors investors must consider, including developing an understanding of the real estate trade flow process. Other areas that investors should vet carefully during the real estate operational due diligence process include valuation concerns and the use of third-party valuation consultants, developing an understanding of common approaches to valuation on a global basis, reviewing conflicts of interests present at both the GP and underlying real estate fund property holding level. This chapter also introduces some key areas investors should consider during the operational due diligence process related to fraud oversight in real estate transactions, particularly in regard to mortgages. Finally, this chapter outlines several real estate specific concerns related both to underlying specific property types and fund structures, including tenant rent collection concerns, fund fees, and legal considerations related to fund property holdings. By properly incorporating a review of real estate specific risks into the operational due diligence process, investors are likely to be more aware of the potential for exposures to property specific risks that may be overlooked by investors performing operational due diligence who seek to overlay more generic private equity operational due diligence processes onto the unique real estate asset class.

NOTE

1. Charles Jacobus, *Real Estate Principles,* 11th ed. (Mason, OH: Cengage Learning, 2010).

CHAPTER 9

Putting It All Together: Asset Allocation and Ongoing Monitoring

After an investor has completed an operational due diligence review of a particular private equity fund, they must then come to an operational conclusion. At first glance, this conclusion is binary in nature: a particular private equity fund may either pass or fail a particular investor's operational requirements. This decision necessarily influences the investment decision. For example, if a fund does not pass operational muster, even if a fund is acceptable to an investor from an investment due diligence perspective, the investor will likely not invest in the fund. We are assuming that if an investor bothers to exert the time, resources, and energy required to perform operational due diligence, then he or she will not simply discard the conclusions of this process and proceed blindly with an allocation based solely on investment considerations. Similarly, if a private equity fund's operational infrastructure is strong enough to pass a particular investor's internal operational risk threshold yet does not pass investment muster, we will assume that this investor would not proceed with an investment solely on the operational strengths of a fund.

Yet what about the situation in which an investor has performed both investment and operational due diligence and the fund passes the binary, allocate or not allocate, test on both regards? Another question an investor may consider is how much capital to allocate to this particular fund. While the intricacies of portfolio construction and asset allocation from an investment perspective are better left to other texts, we can consider this question from an operational risk perspective. That is, what if an investor beyond a minimum passing acceptable level of operational risk has different levels of conviction among different private equity funds? Should an investor's level of operational conviction with a particular manager factor into the capital allocation process among multiple private equity funds? This chapter examines this question and discusses ways in which such operational considerations may be included when constructing a portfolio of private equity investments.

INCORPORATING THE RESULTS OF OPERATIONAL DUE DILIGENCE INTO ASSET ALLOCATION

It has been said that asset diversification is the only free lunch you will find in the investment game.[1] However, when diversifying investments it is important to consider factors beyond those generally emphasized, such as purely investment-related risks. It is perhaps even more critical to zero in on the potential increase in Operational Drag that one may take on by investing in a particular firm and diversify that risk accordingly.[2] Operational Drag can be defined as the negative effects of operational risk on the efficiency of an organization. Even though a particular type of firm may seem very attractive, ignoring any due diligence red alerts can result in investment problems that far outweigh any possible benefits.

One who is just setting out on the journey of asset allocation for the first time may be bewildered (and rightly so!) by all of the choices and information that must be processed. The numerical financial aspects of asset allocation have been studied and reported on in great detail, but significantly less attention has been paid to the types of risk whose potential negative externalities can be mitigated by careful due diligence. Recall that complete due diligence is composed of two halves: operational due diligence and investment due diligence. This relationship is outlined in Exhibit 9.1. In the following, an algorithmic framework is developed to handle these sometimes intangible, difficult to quantify elements of asset allocation with an operational risk backdrop.

In Chapter 1, the common private equity operational risk categories are identified. The table of these categories is reproduced for convenience in Exhibit 9.2.

A model will now be developed for minimizing the total operational risk of a portfolio consisting of several private equity funds. Note that this model does not include financial risk. To begin constructing the model, let each of the potential fund investments be identified by X_i, so that each element belongs the set of $X = \{x_1, x_2, x_3, \ldots, x_N\}$. This can all be expressed as $x_i \in X$. Each x_i has an associated risk value, r_i, which is the sum of all the risk values of all the different risk categories (along with any other asset allocation due diligence risk types) presented in Exhibit 9.2. m_j represents each of these risk types. The units of r_i are "risk," which can be measured in,

EXHIBIT 9.1 Complete Due Diligence Is Composed of Two Halves: Operational Due Diligence and Investment Due Diligence

for instance, potential dollar amounts lost due to the operational riskiness of the private equity firm in this category. They are all part of the set $M = \{m_1, m_2, m_3, \ldots, m_L\}$, so that each $m_j \in M$. Each risk type has a corresponding risk amount u_j, where $u_j \in U = \{u_1, u_2, u_3, \ldots, u_L\}$. Note that there is absolutely no restriction that N (the number of potential asset investments) be equal to L (the total number of risk categories).

The r_i equations are considered to be inputs to the operational risk minimization problem. One may then pose the question as to how these equations can be determined. Through the due diligence process outlined thus far in this text, it is possible to assess the contribution of each risk type

EXHIBIT 9.2 Common Private Equity Operational Risk Categories

Risk Category
Cash controls
Trade life cycle processing
Valuation
Transparency and fund reporting
Liquidity management
Technology and systems
Legal and compliance
Counterparty oversight
Quality and roles of service providers
Business continuity and disaster recovery

to the total operational risk of a particular private equity firm. In the most general case, each of the r_i equations is different from all of the others. This is due to the fact that some firms' overall risk may be more strongly affected by a particular risk category than would be the case for others. Each of the r_i can generally be a different function of all of the u_i. Note that the r_i being functions of the u_i means that the u_i variables are present in the r_i equations, but you could be raised to powers or have other mathematical operations performed on them in these equations. For instance, if one is investing in a firm whose strategy is more reliant on technology and systems than other private equity firms, then the technology and systems risk category may carry much more weight than some of the other areas, because this aspect is fundamental to the potential profit that would be earned on the investment.

Determining the r_i equations is a formidable task. It may be nearly impossible to find information related to the various risk categories, and their impact on the overall risk of investment in a particular firm. The operational risk model presented here combines heuristics, data acquired from investigations, and a mathematical framework into a generalized algorithm for quantifying the minimization of total operational risk of an investment portfolio. These r_i equations are critical for both evaluating new potential fund investments and performing operational due diligence on funds already in your portfolio. For instance, if one fund's equation clearly yields higher overall operational risk than that of another firm, it would be important to combine this information with financial data in deciding which of the two firms to invest in.

Let $\bar{R}$ represent the total risk due to all of the x_i, so that $\bar{R} = \sum_{i=1}^{N} r_i$. In order to achieve an optimal due diligence asset allocation, it is desirable to minimize $\bar{R}$. However, in practice, this is not always possible. The operational due diligence risk allocation frontier is defined by all of the possible values that $\bar{R}$ can assume by varying each of the u_j that comprise all of the r_i and, hence, $\bar{R}$. If $\bar{R}$ is a function of only one of the u_j, then the operational due diligence risk allocation frontier is generally a curve in three-dimensional space. In turn, if it depends on two of the u_j, then the operational due diligence risk allocation frontier is generally a surface in three-dimensional space.

Mathematically, the method to minimize $\bar{R}$ is to take the derivative of $\bar{R}$ and equate it to zero (see the Appendix for more details). Now the question that arises regards which variable(s) should be taken to differentiate $\bar{R}$? To be diligent, we should incorporate all of the m_j for each individual risk function r_i. This involves taking partial derivatives of $\bar{R}$ with respect to each of the u_j for each r_i. However, since $\bar{R}$ is a function of both all of the r_i and m_j, it is necessary to take partial derivatives using the chain rule (see the Appendix).

Therefore, the general equation for this set of derivatives would be the following:

$$
\left\{
\begin{aligned}
\frac{\partial \bar{R}}{\partial u_1} &= \frac{\partial \bar{R}}{\partial r_1}\frac{\partial r_1}{\partial u_1} + \frac{\partial \bar{R}}{\partial r_2}\frac{\partial r_2}{\partial u_1} + \cdots + \frac{\partial \bar{R}}{\partial r_N}\frac{\partial r_N}{\partial u_1} \\
\frac{\partial \bar{R}}{\partial u_2} &= \frac{\partial \bar{R}}{\partial r_1}\frac{\partial r_1}{\partial u_2} + \frac{\partial \bar{R}}{\partial r_2}\frac{\partial r_2}{\partial u_2} + \cdots + \frac{\partial \bar{R}}{\partial r_N}\frac{\partial r_N}{\partial u_2} \\
&\ \ \vdots \qquad \vdots \qquad \vdots \qquad \vdots \qquad \vdots \\
\frac{\partial \bar{R}}{\partial u_L} &= \frac{\partial \bar{R}}{\partial r_1}\frac{\partial r_1}{\partial u_L} + \frac{\partial \bar{R}}{\partial r_2}\frac{\partial r_2}{\partial u_L} + \cdots + \frac{\partial \bar{R}}{\partial r_N}\frac{\partial r_N}{\partial u_L}
\end{aligned}
\right\} =
\left\{
\begin{aligned}
0 \\
0 \\
\vdots \\
0
\end{aligned}
\right\}
$$

Since each of the $\frac{\partial \bar{R}}{\partial r_k} = 1$, where $k = 1$ to L, this set of equations can be reduced to the following:

$$
\left\{
\begin{aligned}
\frac{\partial \bar{R}}{\partial u_1} &= \frac{\partial r_1}{\partial u_1} + \frac{\partial r_2}{\partial u_1} + \cdots + \frac{\partial r_N}{\partial u_1} \\
\frac{\partial \bar{R}}{\partial u_2} &= \frac{\partial r_1}{\partial u_2} + \frac{\partial r_2}{\partial u_2} + \cdots + \frac{\partial r_N}{\partial u_2} \\
&\ \ \vdots \qquad \vdots \qquad \vdots \qquad \vdots \qquad \vdots \\
\frac{\partial \bar{R}}{\partial u_L} &= \frac{\partial r_1}{\partial u_L} + \frac{\partial r_2}{\partial u_L} + \cdots + \frac{\partial r_N}{\partial u_L}
\end{aligned}
\right\} =
\left\{
\begin{aligned}
0 \\
0 \\
\vdots \\
0
\end{aligned}
\right\}
$$

In more compact notation, this can be expressed as:

$$
\frac{\partial \bar{R}}{\partial u_k} = 0, \quad \text{for } k = 1 \text{ to } L.
$$

Exhibit 9.3 shows a summary flowchart of the operational risk asset allocation algorithm. This summarizes the process of arriving at the final equation presented above. The result of the algorithm at the right is the

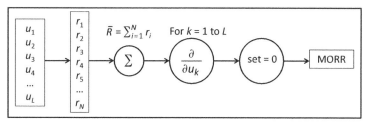

EXHIBIT 9.3 Flowchart of Algorithm for Operational Due Diligence Asset Allocation

Minimum Operational Risk Regime (MORR). This is a set of coordinates in u_j–$\bar{R}$ space that defines the minimum total risk, $\bar{R}$. Given a particular set of risk functions, r_i, the u_j in the MORR are those that minimize the total risk.

If one ponders this, he may encounter the quandary that a lower value of risk in a particular category (such as u_1 = cash controls) may actually increase the total risk, $\bar{R}$. Although this may seem counterintuitive, the issue is resolved when one considers that the risk equations r_i are indicators of the magnitude of the contribution of each of the u_j to the total risk, $\bar{R}$. If one risk type carries significantly more weight than another in one of the r_i equations, then an increase in the one that contributes more to the risk of that private equity firm may outweigh the related decrease in the other category. For instance, if a firm implements stricter cash controls, from the perspective of an investor the operational risk in the human capital category may increase. Previously at the firm, only one signatory approval was required for cash transfers. Now, multiple approval lists with various levels of approval, which are striated by vender and disbursement level, are required. This increased scrutiny necessarily requires more resources, personnel and other, to implement such controls. Focusing solely on the human capital operational risk category in this regard, we can compare the resource drain on human capital with the increased cash control oversight. If cash controls risk contributes more to the risk of a single private equity firm, then an increase in cash controls risk would outweigh a related decrease in human capital risk.

Let's take the simple example of one private equity fund investment and one risk category, such as business continuity and disaster recovery. Therefore, N and L are both equal to 1 in this case. Now define the risk function for the single asset to be $r_1 = \lambda u_1 + 5$ where λ is some dimensionless constant. Therefore, in this situation $\frac{r_1}{u_1} = \lambda$. Since the only nonzero r_i is r_1, $\bar{R} = r_1$. Then, $\frac{\partial \bar{R}}{\partial r_1} = 1$. Therefore,

$$ \frac{\partial \bar{R}}{\partial u_1} = \frac{\partial \bar{R}}{\partial r_1} \frac{r_1}{u_1} = (\lambda) * 1 = 0. $$

This makes sense because, in this case, r_1 is a linear function of u_1, which is minimized when $\lambda = 0$ (see Exhibit 9.4). At $\lambda = 0$, $r_1 = 5$, which is the global minimum of $\bar{R}$. This result could also be obtained if $u_1 = 0$, which is the assumed minimum value that it can have. In other words, if the first term in the r_1 equation, λu_1, is zero, then the $\bar{R}$ function is minimized. Therefore, the MORR is a single point: MORR = $\{(0,5)\}$.

Since the minimum value of r_1 occurs at the point $u_1 = 0$, $= r_1$ has a minimum value of 5, as can be seen from the plot.

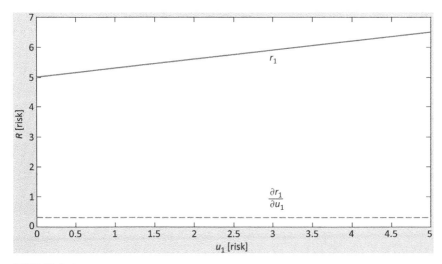

EXHIBIT 9.4 Example 1 Risk Function and Its First Derivative

The risk function and its first derivative for Example 1 are plotted in Exhibit 9.4 for $\lambda = 0.3$. Now a more complex example will be examined. In Example 2, there are three potential investments, but each with different due diligence risk categories. The following is the operational risk paradigm for this particular allocation:

$$r_1 = 2u_1u_2$$

$$r_2 = 2/u_1$$

$$r_3 = 2/u_2$$

$$\bar{R} = \sum_{i=1}^{3} r_i = r_1 + r_2 + r_3 = 2u_1u_2 + 2/u_1 + 2/u_2$$

$$\frac{\partial \bar{R}}{\partial u_1} = 2u_2 - \frac{2}{u_1^2} = 0 \rightarrow u_1^2u_2 = 1$$

$$\frac{\partial \bar{R}}{\partial u_2} = 2u_1 - \frac{2}{u_2^2} = 0 \rightarrow u_2^2u_1 = 1$$

Since none of the u_i variables can be negative (since this would imply negative risk, which is not possible in this model), then $u_1 = u_2 = 1$ in this case. It is now necessary to check that these values of u_1 and u_2 actually minimize $\bar{R}$. The determinant of the 2×2 Hessian matrix must be calculated to achieve this goal. See the Appendix for the mathematical explanation of

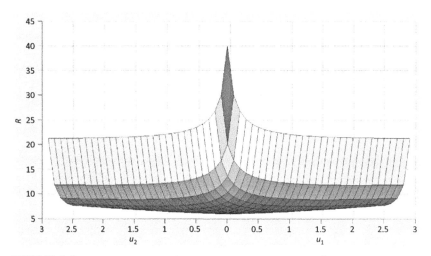

EXHIBIT 9.5   Alternate View of Three-Dimensional Plot of $\bar{R}$ versus u_1 and u_2 for Example 2

this approach. As a result of this method, $M(1,1) > 0$ and $\bar{R}_{u1u1}(1,1) > 0$, so $(1,1)$ is indeed a local minimum of $\bar{R}$.

Exhibits 9.5 and 9.6 present three-dimensional plots of the $\bar{R}$ function in terms of the amount of risk in two different categories, 1 and 2. As mathematically shown above, this function is minimized for $u_1 = u_2 = 1$. For

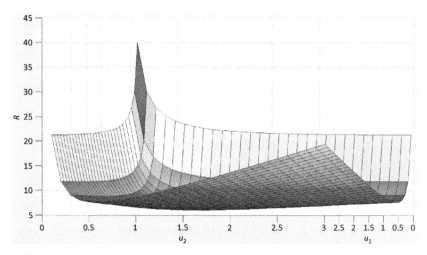

EXHIBIT 9.6   Alternate View of Three-Dimensional Plot of Total Operational Risk versus u_1 and u_2 for Example 2

these values of u_1 and u_2, $\bar{R} = 6$. The coordinate $(u_1, u_2, \bar{R}) = (1,1,6)$ makes up the Minimum Operational Risk Regime (MORR) for this problem. This can also be stated as MORR $= \{(1,1,6)\}$. If the results of the operational risk allocation algorithm yield multiple minimum points, then there will be multiple points in the MORR. For instance, if there were three points in the MORR, then MORR $= \{(u_{1A}, u_{2A}, \bar{R}_A), (u_{1B}, u_{2B}, \bar{R}_B), (u_{1C}, u_{2C}, \bar{R}_C)\}$, where A, B, and C are the point indices. If $\bar{R}$ would have depended on all of the u_j and there were three coordinates at which $\bar{R}$ was globally minimized, then the MORR would look something like MORR $= \{(u_{1A}, u_{2A}, \ldots, u_{LA}, \bar{R}_A), (u_{1B}, u_{2B}, \ldots, u_{LB}, \bar{R}_B), (u_{1C}, u_{2C}, \ldots, u_{LC}, \bar{R}_C)\}$.

In Exhibits 9.5 and 9.6, total operational risk assumes its minimum value of 6 at $u_1 = u_2 = 1$.

This was an example of a total operational risk function that could be analytically minimized relatively simply. However, for a more complicated set of operational risk equations, this process can become significantly more difficult. Numerical methods, such as the Levenberg-Marquardt algorithm, are best suited to such complex minimization problems.

EVOLUTION OF MINIMUM OPERATIONAL RISK REGIME (MORR)

It is now instructive to examine what occurs when the risk functions change for some reason. For instance, operational risk assessments in different categories may vary from year to year, causing the r_i equations to vary. In general, the risk equations for each private equity investment may vary completely, but to begin let us investigate several simple changes that are easy to understand analytically.

For instance, in Example 2, if any of the r_i increases by a constant, such as 50, then $\bar{R}$ increases by 50 as well. Now:

$$\bar{R} = \sum\nolimits_{i=1}^{3} r_i = r_1 + r_2 + r_3 = 2u_1u_2 + 2/u_1 + 2/u_2 + 50$$

Now the minimum value of $\bar{R}$ is 56 (50 higher than the previous minimum $\bar{R}$), which occurs at $u_1 = u_2 = 1$ (see Exhibit 9.7). This makes intuitive sense: if the risk in any of the individual private equity funds in a portfolio increases by a certain constant amount, then the overall possible minimum risk of the portfolio increases. If, on the other hand, $\bar{R}$ is decreased by 5 from the original value, then the minimum at $u_1 = u_2 = 1$ is decreased to $\bar{R} = 1$ (see Exhibit 9.8). In other words, if the risk in any of the individual

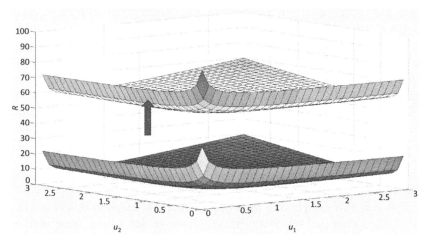

EXHIBIT 9.7 A Pure Translation of Total Operational Risk Upward Increases Its Minimum Value

private equity funds in a portfolio is reduced by a certain constant amount, then the overall possible minimum risk of the portfolio decreases.

It is also possible that the r_i equations remain the same, but that the particular values of the u_j fluctuate over time. This would imply that the importance and risk structure of the various risk categories do not vary for a particular target private equity firm investment, but that the risk in the different categories changes. One could imagine watching the plot in Exhibit 9.6 change over time. For instance, let u_1 refer to the "legal and compliance" risk type and u_2 be the "business continuity and disaster recovery" category. An example of this is shown as a time series in Exhibit 9.9. Since $\bar{R}$ depends only on u_1 and u_2, it makes sense to plot $\bar{R}$ over time, as well. *The (possibly large) fluctuations in $\bar{R}$ over time reinforce the notion that ongoing monitoring is essential in order to maintain appropriate oversight over a fund's evolving operational risk profile.*

As shown in Exhibit 9.9, as u_1 and u_2 vary over time, so does the value of total operational risk for this particular portfolio of private equity funds.

Although we have attempted to create an asset allocation model that facilitates the assignment of quantitative figures to operational risk, such a model is only as good as the subjective choices and preferences of the investor determining the input risk equations utilized in the model. Limited Partners can utilize the operational risk data gathered during the fund operational due diligence process to facilitate such judgments. However, assigning a fixed number to an often qualitative risk factor is where the science of asset allocation meets the art of the discipline. As Albert Einstein aptly noted,

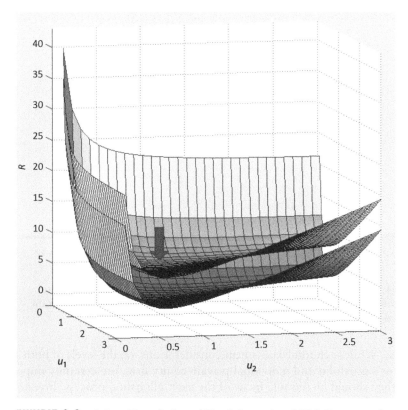

EXHIBIT 9.8 A Pure Translation of Total Operational Risk Downward Decreases Its Minimum Value

"As far as the laws of mathematics refer to reality, they are not certain, and as far as they are certain, they do not refer to reality." Such a notion is fully appreciated when attempting to "put a number" on operational risk exposures present in potential investments in private equity funds.

OPERATIONAL RISK CORRELATIONS TO PORTFOLIO TRANSACTION FREQUENCY

When factoring operational risk considerations into the asset allocation process, investors may be focused on the totality of such risks. Total operational risk is a broad risk category that is made up of many subrisk operational risk factors. Earlier in this chapter, we introduce a model by which total operational risk data can be factored into the asset allocation decision

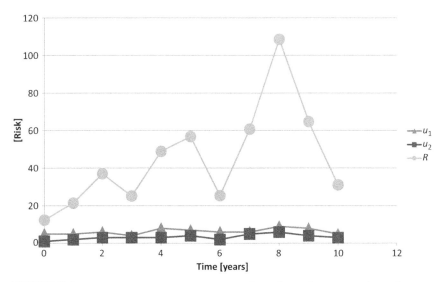

EXHIBIT 9.9 A Time Series Representation: The Values of u_1, u_2, and Total Operational Risk for the Overall Operational Portfolio Risk Function from the Original Example 2

process. While such total assessment considerations, on the levels of both an investor's portfolio and individual private equity firm, are certainly important, they should be the sole focus of the asset allocation process. Investors must also be conscious of these underlying operational risk categories.

An example of such a category is trading or transaction frequency of a fund. *Portfolio transaction frequency* refers to the number of trades executed by a fund during a particular fixed time period, such as on a daily basis. As intimated previously, investors may hold a common misperception that the more frequently a fund trades, the higher the total amount of operational risk in the fund. As such, investors may mistakenly equate the traditionally lower frequency with which private equity trades, as compared to funds that may trade more frequently, such as hedge funds, as representative of lower aggregate operational risk exposures. As the following discussion will indicate, the volume of trade frequency executed by a particular fund, including private equity funds, is not necessarily correlated to total operational risk.

OPERATIONAL LIFT-TO-DRAG RATIO

A concept related to Operational Drag is that of Operational Lift. In aerodynamics, drag is the force that acts in opposition to the thrust of a

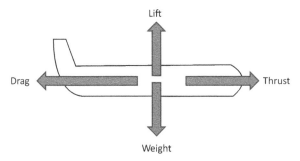

EXHIBIT 9.10 The Forces Acting on an Airplane in
Flight Are Lift, Drag, Thrust, and the Vehicle's
Weight—A Balance of Forces That Also Describes
Operational Lift-to-Drag Ratio

vehicle, such as an airplane. A lift force is created when air flows around
a plane's wings. Lift is what keeps the plane flying and allows it to ascend
in spite of gravity (see Exhibit 9.10). Therefore, maintaining enough lift
force is essential for flight. Operational Lift can analogously be defined as
the positive effects of operational strengths on the efficiency of an organization. Returning to the aerodynamics terminology, the lift-to-drag ratio is
the quotient of the lift and drag forces being exerted on a plane. This ratio
varies with the velocity of the plane. A key objective of aircraft designers is
to achieve a high lift-to-drag ratio to improve efficiency and performance.
Similarly, it should be the goal of any investor to maximize the ratio of
Operational Lift to Operational Drag. Just as the aerodynamic lift-to-drag
ratio varies with velocity and other factors, the Operational Lift-to-Drag
ratio varies from one asset to the next due to its particular characteristics
and history.

The frequency of transactions made by a private equity fund is not a
reliable indicator of operational risk. Private equity funds trade less than,
for instance, hedge funds due in part to the different strategies employed
by each. However, this neither increases nor decreases the probability that
investing in that particular asset will add to Operational Drag. Investors
should not fall prey to the notion that the lower frequency of transactions
performed by private equity companies implies that they create less operational risk. Although the types of risk may vary between hedge funds and
private equity companies, for example, equal amounts of operational risk
may still be involved in both classes of investments. This can be seen by calculating the correlation between transaction frequency and the Operational
Lift-to-Drag ratio.

Mathematically, the correlation between two data sets can be calculated from the following formula:

$$r_{xy} = \frac{\sum_{i=1}^{n} (x_i - \bar{x})(y_i - \bar{y})}{\sqrt{\sum_{i=1}^{n} (x_i - \bar{x})^2 \sum_{i=1}^{n} (y_i - \bar{y})^2}},$$

where r_{xy} is the correlation between the data sets x and y, x_i and y_i are the ith data points in each set, and $\bar{x}$ and $\bar{y}$ are the means of the x and y data sets. r_{xy} can also be expressed as the ratio of the covariance to the product of the standard deviations of the two data sets. The covariance, which is an indication of the extent to which variables increase (or decrease) jointly, is the expected value (mean) of the product of $(x_i - \bar{x})$ and $(y_i - \bar{y})$. The correlation can range between –1 and 1. Positive correlations mean that as one variable increases, the other does as well, while negative correlations imply that an increase in one variable results in a decrease of the other. A correlation of zero means that there is no clear trend between the two variables. In other words, the two variables are uncorrelated.

In correlation terminology, trading frequency and the Operational Lift-to-Drag ratio are uncorrelated. This can be seen from the following plot (Exhibit 9.11), which shows hypothetical data for a particular set of private equity companies in a portfolio. Each firm makes a particular number of

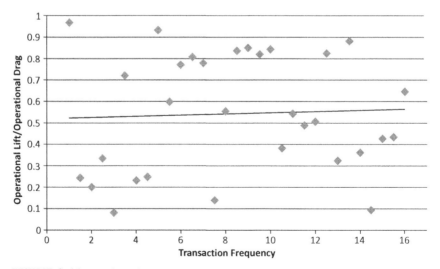

EXHIBIT 9.11 A Plot of a Private Equity Fund's Operational Lift-to-Drag Ratio as a Function of Its Trading Frequency

transactions each year, indicated on the abscissa. The ordinate displays the Operational Lift-to-Drag ratio associated with each firm. A linear trendline was determined for the data, and is plotted as the solid black diagonal line in Exhibit 9.11. The R^2 value, which is the square of the correlation, r_{xy}, for which the equation was provided above, determines the "goodness of fit" of this trendline to the actual data. For this data set, the R^2 value is about 2 percent. Since R^2 can take on values only between 0 and 100 percent, this R^2 value indicates that a linear trendline does not accurately represent this data. This is because there is a weak correlation (near 0) between the two plotted variables, which are the transaction frequency and the Operational Lift-to-Drag ratio. Another way of thinking about this is that visually it is difficult to discern any patterns in the data. For variables that have a correlation with an absolute value close to 1, clear patterns (either increasing or decreasing) are exhibited. As is clear from Exhibits 9.11 and 9.12, this is not the case for transaction frequency and the Operational Lift-to-Drag ratio.

As shown in Exhibit 9.11, it is clear that the data points do not form an easily discernible pattern, and hence can be considered uncorrelated. This means that there is no direct relationship between a fund's transaction frequency and Operational Lift-to-Drag ratio.

As shown in Exhibit 9.12, as transaction frequency increases, the Operational Lift-to-Drag ratio remains constant, meaning that these two variables are uncorrelated.

As the discussion above has outlined in general, there is not an easily discernable correlation between fund trading frequency and the total

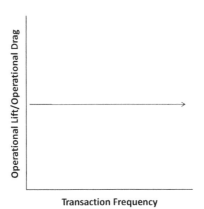

Transaction Frequency

EXHIBIT 9.12 A Simplified Diagram of the Trendline of Operational Lift-to-Drag versus Transaction Frequency Data

operational risk of a fund. From an operational due diligence perspective, Limited Partners should therefore look beyond preconceived notions that simply because of lower traditional trading volumes, there is less operational risk in private equity funds. Investors can therefore use these results to be more objective in this regard when distinguishing between operational due diligence resources allocated to performing reviews of funds with different trading frequencies. Additionally, by overcoming any potential deficiencies in operational due diligence resource allocations among funds of different trading frequencies, investors will be able to not sacrifice scope or depth of reviews when conducting operational due diligence reviews of private equity funds.

Since trading frequency has no net impact on any individual private equity fund's Operational Lift-to-Drag ratio, then the overall risk of the portfolio is also unaffected by trading frequency. By the probabilistic properties of an expectation function (or mean), since the expectation of the contribution of trading frequency to each fund's risk is zero, then the expectation of the impact of trading frequency on the whole portfolios risk is also zero. In light of this, the equations developed in the previous section still hold true even in the presence of varying trading frequencies among different funds that may be held in an investor's portfolio.

NEGOTIATING PRIVATE EQUITY SIDE LETTERS

This chapter so far provides an overview of considering the results of the operational due diligence process into the asset allocation process for private equity funds. Once the asset allocation percentages have been established, however, an investor actually needs to commit capital to a private equity fund. This is typically done via a document known as a subscription document. Before subscribing to a fund and committing capital, investors may have some items that they may want attempt to negotiate with the fund. This is where the concept of a side letter comes in. A side letter is a document that alters the terms that a so-called regular Limited Partner would have when subscribing to the fund. These terms may be items such as additional fund fees, or they may involve items such as fund transparency.

Before investing in a fund, some Limited Partners may have a standard policy of attempting to negotiate side letters by asking for certain terms such as a *most favored nations clause*. Under a most favored nations clause, sometimes referred to as an *MFN* or *MFN clause,* a Limited Partner is entitled to get the best treatment possible among all Limited Partners. Other investors may be more selective in their negotiation of side letters. Such side letters are often negotiated by Limited Partners at the conclusion of the due diligence process. As such, during the operational due diligence process investors may note certain issues that they may table with an intention of negotiating around such operational issues in a side letter.

A common example of an operational risk that investors may attempt to address in a side letter relates to key person risk. For example, a private equity fund's offering memorandum may contain a key person clause that provides only for notification in the event of the departure, death, or incapacitation of the fund's portfolio manager. A Limited Partner may be unhappy with the extent of this provision. Perhaps the Limited Partner in our example prefers a key person clause that not only provides for notification to Limited Partners in the event a key person event occurs regarding the fund's portfolio manager, but that also allows for additional notifications if the General Partner's (GP's) Chief Investment Officer departs the firm. This may not be of material concern to other Limited Partners (LPs), but the role of the Chief Investment Officer is particularly important to the LP in our example. The LP may attempt to negotiate a side letter that requires the GP to provide notification to the LP in the event of the departure of this individual.

In certain instances, an LP may have several operational items that they wish to negotiate for in a side letter. As with any negotiation, the LP must be prepared to compromise with the GP. In these instances, an investor may be able to leverage information obtained and the overall experience that the LP may have had during the operational due diligence process. Consider for example, an investor approaching an investment in a vintage fund. Further assume that this LP was not invested in the previous vintage fund. To assist this investor in the operational due diligence process, perhaps the LP in our example requests transparency into the portfolio of the vintage fund. Let us further assume that despite several requests from our LP, the GP agrees only to provide a summary of the top five holdings.

Now let us fast-forward to the end of our LP's due diligence process on the current vintage fund. In this case, our investor may have several issues that they wish to negotiate in a side letter with the GP. Let us assume that one of these items relates to portfolio transparency. Perhaps the GP in this example anticipates providing quarterly reporting updates on the portfolio. Our LP, however, wishes to have more frequent transparency, perhaps monthly. While the GP may object to providing this transparency, the LP can gently remind the GP that they had refused to provide the requested level of transparency during the LP's earlier operational due diligence process, and at the time the LP effectively gave them a pass and decided to invest anyway. Of course, there is no guarantee that such negotiation tactics may bear any fruit, but this does not mean that they should simply be disregarded. Oftentimes the side letter negotiation process may be left for the LP and GP's lawyers to work out. However, the LP's lawyer may not be cued in to the give and take that may have occurred during the operational due diligence process. LPs should consider integrating the experiences and results of the operational due diligence process into such side letter negotiations.

ONGOING MONITORING: OPERATIONAL DUE DILIGENCE MONITORING FOR PRIVATE EQUITY FUNDS

Why Bother Performing Ongoing Monitoring on Private Equity Funds?

After the initial allocation to a private equity fund investors are effectively left with two options with regard to operational risk. The first choice is to do nothing more. This is a bad choice. The second option is to perform additional ongoing operational monitoring. This is the preferred choice for several reasons. First, an LP has already devoted a significant amount of time and resources toward developing an understanding of a private equity fund's operational infrastructure. With this detailed understanding in place, the investor has effectively constructed a road map by which operational risk can be monitored throughout the life of the fund. After such an investment of resources and energy, simply throwing the operational road map aside does not make much sense.

Some may raise an argument that states something to the effect of, "What is the point of ongoing operational due diligence on a private equity fund, if LPs have their capital effectively locked up for the life of the fund?" There are several responses to such arguments. One response is that, if an investor does not perform ongoing operational due diligence and a private equity manager happens to be perpetrating a fraud that may have its roots in manipulating operational procedures, such as cash flow throughout the organization, the investor is not likely to either catch the fraudulent activity or uncover any red flags or signals that may cause concern. Readers who do not believe that such events are possible are encouraged to see Chapter 11.

Putting fraudulent activity aside, a second response to the argument against performing ongoing monitoring relates to the role of the advisory board. As Chapter 10 discusses, LPs who sit on the advisory board of a private equity fund who uncover continued or new operational problems during the ongoing operational due diligence monitoring process may have the ability to take direct action with the GP regarding such issues.

Finally, a third response that we will consider regarding objections to performing ongoing operational due diligence monitoring relates to the issue of feedback and a concept that we will call *reverse signaling*. Giving them the benefit of the doubt, we can assume that GPs are not interested in conducting fraud. Furthermore, we will assume that some GPs are actually interested in adhering to operational best practices in their operations. If this is the case, then they may actually be interested in hearing feedback from LPs who conduct ongoing operational due diligence on funds that they manage. This feedback may be particularly useful from LPs that engage in *operational benchmarking*. (Chapter 12 discusses this trend in operational due diligence in detail."

Additionally, this feedback regarding operational practices may be of particular use to GPs from LPs that allocate to many different private equity funds, such as a private equity fund of funds. Even if such LPs may not hold seats on the advisory board of a particular fund, GPs may be open to hearing this feedback and improving operations accordingly.

The concept of signaling is introduced in Chapter 3. Signaling effects with regard to operational risk of a private equity firm refers to the presence of indicators that themselves are not necessarily demonstrative of operational risk, but which should alert investors as to the need for further inquiries for the presence of operational risk. An example that was previously outlined would be the signaling effects of a private equity fund that held self-custody of assets. Another example would be a private equity fund that engaged in numerous transactions with affiliated entities. These transactions with affiliated entities themselves are not necessarily inherently operationally risky but the presence of such transactions raises the specter of potential conflicts of interest and self-dealing.

A related concept to signaling and signaling effect is *reverse signaling*. In the context of operational due diligence of a private equity firm, reverse signaling refers to the concept whereby an LP's actions and due diligence inquiries send a signal to the GP. To illustrate by example, consider a private equity firm that raised capital and was closed to new investors in 2007. Next consider the discovery of the Bernard Madoff scandal in 2008. The role of custody, and self-custody in particular, was one of the litany of operational issues noted in the Madoff postmortem.

As a result of the *Madoff Effect* that we mention in Chapter 1, by which investors tend to tailor their operational due diligence around recent frauds, in the post-Madoff environment many private equity investors, many of which also invest in hedge funds, began to inquire more closely regarding the custody relationships of private equity funds. For investors already invested in a private equity fund, such as those in our example, if they had been resigned not to perform ongoing operational due diligence, they perhaps were content not to inquire in detail about such relationships with heightened scrutiny. Other LPs however, may have taken the opportunity to inquire more closely regarding a private equity fund's custodial relationships. Furthermore, many of these LPs may have expressed their dissatisfaction with this relationship due to the generally cautious attitude toward such self-custody arrangements in the post-Madoff era.

Through these enhanced due diligence efforts the LPs were in effect sending a signal to the GP that they at a minimum were more concerned about potential operational issues surrounding the firm's self-custody relationship. This is an example of a reverse signal. If the investors actually discussed these concerns with the private equity fund, this would be an example of feedback. If a GP receives a number of reverse signals from LPs via these ongoing due diligence efforts, the GP may be more inclined to take action to remedy such issues.

Furthermore, if the LPs provide feedback on top of these reverse signals, there is an increased likelihood that this momentum could bring about change. In our example, the LPs could perhaps suggest that the GP engage a third-party custodian for the remainder of the life of the fund or, perhaps more practically, the GP should engage a third-party custodian for the next vintage fund for which they raise capital. If an LP invested in the previous 2007 is interested in investing in this vintage fund, and maintaining a long-term relationship with the GP, then, perhaps, their reverse signals and feedback communicated regarding operational issues during the previous 2007 fund may have additional positive ramifications regarding future funds as well. Furthermore, if such changes in future funds are not applied universally to all LPs, those LPs that communicate reverse signals and provide feedback may be in a better position to negotiate favorable side letters for the new fund.

How Often Should Ongoing Monitoring Be Performed?

Once an LP has been convinced of the benefits of ongoing monitoring of private equity funds from an operational due diligence perspective, they must next consider the question of how frequently such monitoring should be performed. There is no single correct answer to this question. In practice, different LPs opt to conduct ongoing monitoring with different frequencies. A general rule of thumb is to perform ongoing operational due diligence—typically an on-site operational risk reviews—approximately every 12 months. The frequency with which LPs conduct such ongoing monitoring may also depend on whether or not they serve on the advisory board of a fund, as well as if they have any other sorts of communication with the fund on a regular basis.

Ongoing Remote Monitoring Techniques

Limited partners can utilize a number of different techniques to facilitate ongoing fund monitoring. These can include remote operational monitoring techniques. Remote operational due diligence monitoring refers to when an LP conducts surveillance and intelligence gathering that can be performed outside of the on-site visit. LPs can employ a variety of methods to monitor operational risk exposures including *media monitoring, litigation and regulatory monitoring,* and *GP communication monitoring.*

Media monitoring can range from basic Internet monitoring via automatic alerts that are typically freely offered by multiple services such as Google alerts. Such free services provide LPs with a way to organize and monitor multiple media searches. A drawback of such free services is that they do not necessarily cover the types of media that may be relevant to a particular search. Furthermore, such free searches do not necessarily screen for false positives or relevance. For a fee, there are a number of more sophisticated and comprehensive tools in the marketplace that can be more useful to facilitate investors' ongoing monitoring efforts.

Litigation monitoring refers to the notion of checking to see if a private equity fund, employees, or affiliated firms are suing someone or being sued. LPs can monitor such activity electronically utilizing legal databases such as Lexis-Nexis or Westlaw. In certain instances, court filings may not be updated on these databases. In such cases, physically visiting a court and searching its records may be the only way to effectively monitor a lawsuit, especially when its progress is of a time-sensitive nature. It is also worth noting that the benefits of litigation monitoring can become significantly diminished in countries that are either not as litigious as the United States, where cases frequently are settled between parties out of court, or in countries where court filings may be more likely to be kept confidential.

Regulatory monitoring refers to the concept of monitoring any required regulatory filings that a private equity fund may be required to make on a continuing basis. Monitoring can typically be accomplished by LPs via the relevant regulator's websites.

GP communication monitoring refers to an LP's review of any ongoing monitoring produced by a private equity fund. This information can be in the form of annual reports or quarterly investor updates. There is no one uniform format that GPs follow in distributing such information. Certain GPs may include organizational updates or other operational details in these communications. LPs can monitor such communications for insights or signals of any changes in the operational risk profile of the fund.

If as the result of any of these ongoing monitoring efforts operational risks are noted, or signals are raised that require further inquiry, investors may consider ramping up the frequency of their on-site ongoing operational due diligence reviews to further vet such issues.

CONCLUSION

This chapter provided an overview of incorporating the results of the operational due diligence process into the asset allocation process. Limited Partners should consider operational risk considerations when designing an asset allocation program consisting of private equity funds. This chapter introduced a sample model in this regard including the concept of the Minimum Operational Risk Regime. Incorporated into this discussion was an analysis of operational risk correlations to portfolio transaction frequency and the related concepts of Operational Drag and Operational Lift. This chapter then outlined some of the considerations that Limited Partners should take into account with regard to side letters. Finally, this chapter covered the benefits of ongoing operational due diligence monitoring for private equity investments and outlined techniques for remote operational monitoring. Limited Partners can further enhance the value of their initial operational due diligence reviews on private equity funds by factoring the results into the asset allocation process and via well planned and executed ongoing monitoring techniques.

Mathematical Concepts

The purpose of this Appendix is to clarify certain mathematical concepts introduced earlier in this chapter. Each of these concepts is outlined in more detail in the following sections.

THE DERIVATIVE

A derivative is defined as the rate of change of one variable with respect to another. For instance, in physics, the derivative, or rate of change, of the position of an object is its velocity. In other words, velocity is the *rate* at which position varies with time. When one launches a rock vertically into the air, it will stop moving when it reaches the peak of its trajectory (see Exhibit 9A.1). At this point, its vertical speed is zero. In other words, at the instant that it reaches its peak, its position is not changing, and hence the derivative of position is zero at that moment.

Therefore, it becomes apparent that by setting the velocity of an object equal to zero, it is possible to find the time at which the object reaches its maximum vertical position. The following set of equations define this problem:

In the following, x denotes height, $\dot{x}$ is velocity, and $\ddot{x}$ is acceleration (an overdot indicates a derivative with respect to time). First, let the acceleration, $\ddot{x}(t) = a$ and the initial velocity of the projectile be $x(t \doteq 0) = v_0$. Then,

$$x(t) = x(t = 0) + x(t \doteq 0)t + \frac{1}{2}\ddot{x}(t)t^2$$

$$\dot{x}(t) = v_0 + at$$

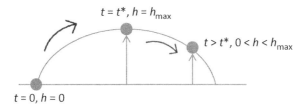

EXHIBIT 9A.1   Illustration of Derivative Using
Example of a Rock Projectile

Setting the last equation equal to zero yields the time, t^*, at which the projectile reaches its maximum height:

$$v_0 + at^* = 0 \rightarrow t^* = -\frac{v_0}{a}$$

t^* is the time at which the projectile reaches its peak. The sign is negative because the upward velocity and acceleration oppose each other and thus have opposite signs (if up is defined as the positive direction, then v_0 is positive and a is negative).

A similar argument would apply to a marble rolling through a bowl. At the very center (bottom) of the bowl, the marble has reached its lowest point, and its vertical speed is temporarily zero, since it is switching from upward to downward motion, or vice versa. Again, the derivative of position with respect to time, or speed, equals zero here. In this case, as opposed to the example of the vertical projectile, a minimum in height was found rather than a maximum. Setting the derivative equal to zero will determine the value of a local minimum or maximum at a specific point.

THE CHAIN RULE

Let y, w, and x be variables. If y is a function of w, and w in turn is a function of x, then the formula for the derivative of y with respect (in Leibniz notation) to x is:

$$\frac{dy}{dx} = \frac{dy}{du} \cdot \frac{du}{dx}$$

This formula is sufficient to understand the discussion in the text. A more detailed derivation of the chain rule is beyond the scope of this book.

THE SECOND PARTIAL DERIVATIVE TEST

The second partial derivative test is implemented to assess whether a function's critical points are in fact maxima, minima, or saddle points. A critical point is one at which a function is either nondifferentiable or has a derivative of zero. We will ignore the former case because all of the functions considered herein are "well-behaved," meaning that they are defined everywhere for independent variables with values of zero or larger. As shown in the text, critical points are found by equating partial derivatives of a function with zero. To check the nature of the critical point(s), the second partial derivative test involves calculating the determinant of a 2×2 Hessian matrix for a function f, denoted by $M(x,y)$, where x and y are the independent variables and f is the dependent variable as shown as follows:

$$M(x, y) = \begin{vmatrix} f_{xx}(x, y) & f_{xy}(x, y) \\ f_{yx}(x, y) & f_{yy}(x, y) \end{vmatrix}$$

The subscripts of f denote the variables with respect to which partial derivates of f are calculated. Two subscripts represent a second partial derivative. The following rules define the nature of a critical point with $x = a$ and $y = b$.

1. If $M(a,b) > 0$ and $f_{xx}(a,b) > 0$ then (a,b) is a local minimum of f.
2. If $M(a,b) > 0$ and $f_{xx}(a,b) < 0$ then (a,b) is a local maximum of f.
3. If $M(a,b) < 0$ then (a,b) is a saddle point of f.
4. If $M(a,b) = 0$ then the second derivatives test is inconclusive.

This process is now carried out for Example 2 in the text of Chapter 9:

$$\frac{\partial^2 \bar{R}}{\partial u_1^2} = \frac{4}{u_1^3}$$

$$\frac{\partial^2 \bar{R}}{\partial u_2^2} = \frac{4}{u_2^3}$$

$$\frac{\partial^2 \bar{R}}{\partial u_1 \partial u_2} = 2$$

$$\frac{\partial^2 \bar{R}}{\partial u_2 \partial u_1} = 2$$

$$M(1, 1) = 4/1^3 {}^* 4/1^3 - 2^* 2 = 12 > 0$$

$$\frac{\partial^2 \bar{R}(1,1)}{\partial u_1^2} = 16 > 0$$

Since $M(1,1) > 0$ and $f_{xx}(1,1) > 0$ then $(1,1)$ is indeed a minimum.

NOTES

1. Henry Smith, "Diversification: The Only Free Lunch?," *FT Mandate*, April 2010.
2. See Jason Scharfman, *Hedge Fund Operational Due Diligence: Understanding the Risks* (Hoboken, NJ: John Wiley & Sons, 2008).

CHAPTER 10

Boards, Committees, and Activism

After a new private equity fund has been established from a legal per- spective the General Partner will go through a fundraising period during which capital allocations are sought from third-party investors. At this stage, after the fund has already been established as a legal shell, many of the key decisions related to items such as fund terms have already been decided by the GP and memorialized in the core fund documentation such as the offering memorandum for the fund. While in certain cases the GP may be open to revising such documentation based on investor feedback received during the due diligence process, in general most of these basic fund terms and decisions have been effectively set in stone.

PRIVATE EQUITY FUND ADVISORY BOARDS

One common feature of private equity funds that is quasi–set in stone at the time of the forming of most funds relates to a fund governance committee that is commonly known as an advisory board.

An advisory board is a board that typically consists of several represen- tative investors who provide advice to the GP regarding the management of a fund. There is no requirement, legal or otherwise, that a private equity fund must maintain an advisory board. In reality, most private equity fund advisory boards' roles focus more on fund governance than they do on the role as consigliore. This makes sense because in effect they are supposed to be providing advice to the GP or fund manager that they have hired because of their supposed expertise in not only picking profitable portfolio holdings, but also in running a fund in general. As such, in this context a private equity advisory board can be viewed more as focused on minding the store, which is funded with their own capital, rather than providing actual advice with regard to fund management. Such a distinction may be a semantic one; however, because the role of the advisory board is to act in the best interests of their own investments—which are necessarily aligned with the role of the fund as a whole, since the private equity fund consists of the members of the advisory board's own capital.

DIFFERENT TYPES OF ADVISORY BOARDS: LIMITED PARTNERS VERSUS PURE ADVISORS

As just indicated, in most cases, the advisory board of a private equity fund consists of representatives of several different Limited Partners. There is no finite size that advisory boards must consist of. In practice generally, advisory boards consist of three or five LPs but may go up to nine members. It is also worth noting that it is generally considered best practice for an advisory board to consist of an odd number of members to facilitate any dispute resolution and tie breaking. Advisory boards will typically meet at least once annually but may meet more frequently, contingent upon fund policy and any changes throughout the year that may occur in the management of the fund. Generally, the LPs on the advisory board will be some of the larger investors in the private equity fund. These larger investors may often demand a position on an advisory board as a requisite to their investing in a private equity fund. Therefore, in these cases an advisory board consists of investors in the private equity fund.

The term advisory board is also sometimes employed to refer to a board that does not consist of investors in the fund. For the purposes of this text, we will refer to such board members as *pure advisors* because they are not advising on a fund that manages capital that they themselves have invested in the fund. Rather, these pure advisors are simply providing guidance and advice to the GP regarding the management of the fund, and they are not themselves typically invested in the fund. It should be noted that similar to the board of directors of an offshore hedge fund vehicle, these pure advisors are not providing such advice out of the goodness of their hearts, but rather for compensation. As such, the advisory board members are effectively employees of, or at the very least consultants to, the fund.

The background of such individuals can often be quite varied. Some GPs may seek to construct such advisory boards with pure advisors with certain asset-specific or regional knowledge. Other private equity firms may select certain pure advisors for their knowledge of larger global or macroeconomic trends that may influence the fund's portfolio. Still others may attempt to place established individuals with renowned reputations on the board. This latter example highlights the dual roles that some of these advisory boards play. In some cases, a GP may seek to utilize the makeup of its advisory board as a marketing device to demonstrate the quality of individuals who serve as advisers to the fund. There is nothing inherently wrong with utilizing the biographies or backgrounds of these pure advisors in fundraising. However in such situations potential LPs should, during the operational due diligence process, inquire as to whether the fund has employed such pure advisors simply as a ministerial marketing device or whether the GP and private equity fund managers are actually interested in the advice of these pure advisors.

It should also be noted that, as referenced earlier, these advisers are compensated generally by the private equity fund itself, as opposed to the GP. Investors should also inquire into the levels of compensation paid to these pure advisers. A well-respected pure adviser with a highly regarded reputation may not necessarily serve on an advisory board for a particularly reasonable rate. In these cases, the GP may feel that the expense is worth it. Such motivation may not lie only in the potential advice that such a pure advisor may give but also in the additional capital that this pure advisor being associated with the fund may be able to raise. In this case, the potential for a conflict of interest arises where the GP may select an adviser that would help him or her to raise more capital, and the GP is compensated in part based on the size of the fund via management fees. However, the expenses borne by the fund to pay for this advisor's compensation may not particularly have an appropriate trade-off effect for the individual LPs, particularly when this pure advisor has not at the end of the day been employed because the GP or portfolio managers are particularly interested in this individual's advice.

A final consideration regarding the makeup of such pure advisor advisory boards relates to the number of boards such individuals may serve upon. Some pure advisors may only be professional advisors. In many cases, these individuals have long work histories and take the pure advisor role after retirement. Others may work for firms whose sole purpose is to serve on the boards of funds. In both cases, it is a real possibility that an individual can serve on the boards of multiple funds. There is no single bright-line rule as to how many boards an individual may serve on, although the number of boards can sometimes border on the absurd (e.g., over 50). In these cases, when analyzing the multiple hats worn by such board advisors, investors should question, as part of the operational due diligence process, whether it is reasonable to expect this pure advisor board member to devote a sufficient amount of time to advising the private equity fund.

ONGOING OPERATIONAL DUE DILIGENCE MONITORING ADVISORY BENEFITS

In the context of an investor's operational due diligence review of a private equity fund, after the initial operational due diligence review is complete an

LP will then reach some sort of operational conclusion as to whether or not to allocate to a private equity fund. This operational conclusion will, of course, be tempered with appropriate investment allocation considerations, as well. Assuming that after shaking the Magic 8 Ball of due diligence, the readings indicate that all signs point to yes, and the decision is made to allocate, investors should simply not disregard all of the hard work they put into the due diligence process. Rather, a number of benefits can be garnered from ongoing monitoring as well. These ongoing benefits can translate through to LPs from both the investment and operational perspectives.

From an operational perspective such ongoing monitoring can provide an investor with a particularly unique voice if they sit on a private equity fund's advisory board. This is one of the key reasons that it is advisable for investors to seek advisory board seats whenever possible. A private equity advisory board may be privy to certain pieces of information that may not be actively shared with other LPs. In fact, the other LPs have given consent, either actual or implied via waiver, for the GP of the private equity fund to have the authority to let those LPs that serve on a private equity fund's advisory board to have certain representative decision making authority with regard to acting on this information as well. For an LP that has performed extensive operational due diligence before investing in a private equity fund, who now sits on an advisory board, the oversight afforded to the advisory board can serve to substantially benefit the larger pool of LPs in just as a meaningful way as the investment oversight or approval authority the advisory board may carry out, if not more so.

For example, consider an LP who, during an initial operational due diligence review in the preinvestment stage, noted operational concerns regarding the frequency of cash reconciliations performed by the fund. Despite these concerns, the LP allocated funds to the private equity firm. Let us further assume that this private equity fund maintains an advisory board and that the LP in our example, has a seat on this advisory board. In this role as an advisory board member, the LP need not only perform the perhaps more ministerial roles such as approving valuations or casting a vote with regard to certain decisions asked of the advisory board.

This LP can also utilize his role on the advisory board to proactively monitor the way in which a fund continually deals with such operational issues. Remember, this investor's interaction with the private equity fund is not limited solely to their role as an advisory board member. This LP is also an investor in the fund. As such, this LP should feel perfectly free to conduct ongoing operational due diligence reviews of the private equity fund. The difference between this LP and other LPs is that the LP in our example also has a seat on the fund's advisory board. While it would be nice to believe that a GP of a private equity fund would be receptive to each LP's concerns or suggestions, both operationally related and otherwise, in practice they may not. When an LP has a seat on an advisory board, they not only have more direct access to the GP but, perhaps more importantly, they have a forum by which to communicate with other LPs who are advisory board members as well. This is another significant advantage that is available to advisory board members who are LPs. Other LPs who are not on a fund's advisory board might not have a forum, such as an advisory board meeting, through which to communicate with other investors; furthermore, they may not even know the identity of other LPs.

In such cases, an LP with concerns regarding certain operational risks revealed during the ongoing operational due diligence monitoring process may not be able to discuss such concerns with other LPs who are invested in the same private equity fund. As such, an investor may only be able to express his or her concerns to a GP. Unfortunately, such concerns may fall upon deaf ears and the GP may not have any reason to make the operational improvements required to address any deficiencies that may have developed or become exacerbated throughout the life of the fund. Contrast this with an LP who sits on a fund's advisory board. In that case, the LP not only has more of a direct line of communication with the GP, but also and perhaps more importantly, the ability to work with other LPs.

In this case, if an LP conducts their own ongoing operational due diligence reviews and has operational concerns, they can share these with other advisory board LPs. If these other LPs agree, they can then approach the GP of the private equity fund with these concerns through a more unified voice of not only multiple LPs but also through the formal role of the advisory board. Concerns that are voiced in this way are more likely to get not only the attention of the GP, but perhaps motivate the GP to implement actual operational changes as well.

BALANCING THE ROLE OF INNER CIRCLE VERSUS BROADLY REPRESENTATIVE ADVISORY BOARDS

An advisory board can also serve a number of practical functions, as well. An example of this relates to the ability of the advisory board to act with authority on behalf of the larger pool of LPs, some of whom may be completely unrepresented on the advisory board. This is often useful from a standpoint of efficiency. It is oftentimes much faster and more efficient for the GP to deal directly with the smaller group of advisory board members as opposed to the whole group of all LPs. An example of how this would function in practice could relate to the granting of certain waivers to the GP by the advisory board. These waivers could include waivers of certain investment policies, waivers regarding certain potential conflicts of interest, or waivers regarding diversification guidelines.[1]

While these efficiencies may both expedite fund decision making and reduce the ongoing burden to be involved in the daily management or governance decisions of a particular fund in other circumstances, advisory boards may not be so representative of the larger base of all LPs. Interestingly, this representative role can vary not only by private equity investment strategy but by region as well. For example, U.S. and European venture firms may generally score high marks when it comes to keeping all investors informed of fund developments through the advisory board. However, European buyout firms may limit information flow to only the key group of the inner circle of LPs who are fortunate enough to sit on a fund's advisory board.[2]

ADVISORY BOARD CRITICISMS: CROWDING OUT, POWER AGGREGATION, AND REDUNDANT BOARD LAYERS

Certain investors may not desire a private equity fund to maintain an advisory board at all. In these cases, the LPs may view the role of an advisory board as inefficient and redundant. Furthermore, they may view the advisory board as hampering the flow of communication to all investors. As discussed in more detail in this section, these investors may feel that the advisory board concentrates certain decision-making authority in too few LPs while effectively crowding out the smaller LPs. In these cases, the larger LPs may not agree with a limited grouping of power at the top.

Additionally, depending on the role of LPs themselves, certain LPs may view the role of private equity boards as placing an additional onus on their already overtaxed governance responsibilities. For example, LPs who manage capital on behalf of other investors, such as a private equity fund-of-funds, may be in a situation where they have their own advisory board. This relationship is summarized in Exhibit 10.1.

In these cases, the LPs, such as the private equity fund of funds in our example, may already be subject to governance and oversight by LPs who invest in the fund it manages itself. These advisory board members may therefore express their opinions and oversight to the GP of the private equity fund of funds. The GP of the private equity fund of funds may feel this oversight is sufficient and, therefore, they may not want the burden, or responsibility, of having to act in a governance role as an advisory board member by switching from GP of their own private equity fund of funds to an active LP as an advisory board member. From an operational due diligence perspective, LPs at the private equity fund of funds level should

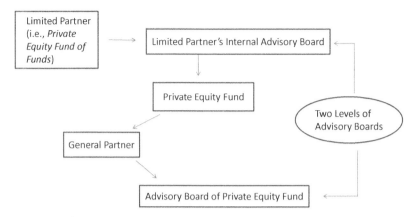

EXHIBIT 10.1   Example of Redundant Advisory Board Layers

be cautious of the signaling effect of GPs who express such objections to serving as advisory board members of underlying portfolio private equity funds. While such advisory board members at the underlying portfolio fund level does present an additional time commitment, this is in part why they are being compensated by investors, to not only make initial selections of underlying private equity funds but also to provide ongoing oversight and management of the portfolio of these funds.

Having the GP serve in their LP capacity as a member of the underlying LP advisory board is an effective way to perform such responsibilities. Indeed, as outlined later, depending on the type of underlying private equity fund, as well as the geographic region in which such funds operate, LPs that do not serve on a fund's advisory board may be at a disadvantage because of the uneven distribution of information from the private equity fund's GP through to LPs, which tends to favor advisory board members.

INFORMATION FLOW CONSIDERATIONS FROM UNDERLYING PORTFOLIO GENERAL PARTNER TO LIMITED PARTNERS

Additionally, when the GPs who allocate to other private equity funds seek to abdicate responsibility of governance and oversight to other LPs who serve on a private equity fund's advisory board, these investors may be responsible not only for a general dereliction of duty but also with regard to certain fiduciary obligations to appropriately report to their fund's own LPs on the performance and activities of the underlying portfolio companies'

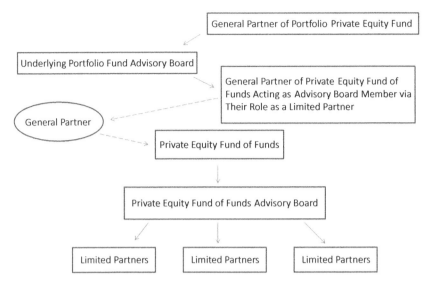

EXHIBIT 10.2   Example of Information Flow When a General Partner of Private Equity Fund of Funds Serves as Both Limited Partner and General Partner

activities. Furthermore, by not serving on the advisory board of the underlying portfolio company's fund, these GPs of the private equity s may make it more difficult for Limited Partners to comply with their own reporting and disclosure requirements due to a dearth of sufficient information from the underlying portfolio company to the ultimate end private equity fund of fund LPs. The typical flow of information from the underlying portfolio fund GP level through to the LPs of the investment allocator, such as a private equity fund of funds, is summarized in Exhibit 10.2.

Advisory boards often maintain a significant amount of authority with regard to approving certain fund activities. One core function that is often granted to the advisory board is the approval of the GP's valuation of a private equity fund's investments.[3]

LIMITED PARTNER DUE DILIGENCE CONSIDERATIONS FOR A PRIVATE EQUITY FUND OF FUNDS

Continuing our discussion of a private equity fund of funds, it is also worth considering the unique due diligence requirement that may be performed by an LP that allocated to a private equity fund of funds. In the same way

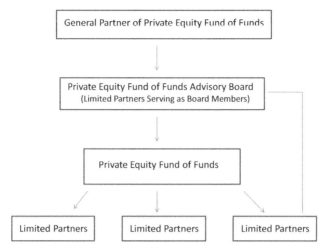

EXHIBIT 10.3 Dual Role of Certain Limited Partners on Private Equity Fund of Funds Advisory Board

that a private equity fund of funds may serve on the advisory board of an underlying private equity fund, so too may an investor serve on the advisory board of a private equity fund of funds. This relationship is summarized in Exhibit 10.3.

In much the same way that LPs investing in a regular private equity fund should perform operational due diligence, so too should such operational due diligence be performed by LPs when considering an investment in a private equity fund of funds. Similarly, when LPs sit on an advisory board of a private equity fund of funds, they can also express opinions regarding operational concerns that may have been raised during either the initial or ongoing operational due diligence process. It is worth highlighting some of the key considerations that LPs should consider when performing operational due diligence on a private equity fund of funds, some of which are unique to this fund structure, as opposed to performing due diligence on a direct private equity investment fund.

When performing operational due diligence on a private equity fund of funds, an additional layer to the due diligence process should incorporate a review of the quality, nature, and framework of the due diligence function in place at the private equity fund of funds. As an example, four commonly utilized operational due diligence frameworks include a dedicated framework, a shared framework, a modular framework, and a hybrid framework. This review should encompass a review of the resources allocated by the private equity fund of funds to the due diligence function. Additionally, this review should include an analysis of the process utilized to perform an initial due diligence review as well as the process and frequency for ongoing monitoring.

Additionally, it is part of the initial and ongoing due diligence processes for an investor to conduct a review of any underlying private equity funds that a fund of hedge funds may have a large exposures to. This review of the underlying private equity should include a review and analysis of documentation from the underlying private equity manager. This documentation analysis may be accomplished via documentation collected directly from the underlying hedge fund manager, from the private equity fund of funds manager, or from underlying fund service providers. The review of the underlying private equity fund manager may involve utilization of due diligence techniques as previously described, including:

- Evaluating the investment strategy of the underlying private equity fund manager
- Evaluating the operational infrastructure of the underlying private equity fund manager
- Reviewing the quality and appropriateness of the underlying private equity fund's service providers

The operational due diligence process undertaken by an LP at the private equity fund of funds level should also encompass a determination of the manner, types, and frequency of information that are generally being transmitted between the underlying private equity fund manager and the private equity fund of funds. It should be noted that this information would be in addition to the types of information obtained by the private equity fund of funds during the initial and ongoing due diligence process of the underlying fund manager.

For example, this information could include performance estimates of an underlying private equity fund manager, various types of risk data such as an underlying manager's exposures to certain sectors or markets, and updates on operational information. As part of this analysis, an LP performing due diligence would generally consider not only the level of transparency afforded to the fund manager, but the way in which the private equity fund of funds verifies this data and utilizes this data to perform ongoing monitoring of the underlying private equity fund. Finally, an LP should review and analyze the information provided by the underlying private equity fund to the private equity fund of funds. As such, when an LP that sits on the advisory board of a fund of hedge funds, they should take into account the information obtained from these additional operational due diligence techniques to further enhance their active role as an advisory board member.

ADDITIONAL PRIVATE EQUITY ADVISORY BOARD CONSIDERATIONS

By the time a fund is up and running and accepting capital from investors, the basic terms of the fund generally have been established. These terms can include basic fees charged by the fund as well as a number of other provisions that are activated or triggered only either when certain events happen or upon the decision of the LPs. An advisory board of a fund may serve a crucial role in making sure that the GP strictly adheres to such provisions, as well as assisting in coordinating efforts among other nonadvisory board LPs to trigger certain events. Some of these key provisions are outlined in the following sections.

No-Fault Divorce and Associated Provisions

In many cases the LPs of a fund want the ability to undo the fund by ending the fund's ability to acquire new assets and forcing liquidation of existing holdings. This is the point of a *no-fault divorce clause*. A related provision is the *no-fault removal of the GP clause* that allows LPs to remove the existing GP and install a new one. Another related provision is the *no-fault free of commitments provision* that simply suspends the acquisition period of the fund to allow LPs to put the brakes, perhaps just temporarily, on the ability of the GP to continue acquiring portfolio positions.

This is of course contrary to the goals of GPs that want LPs to continue the life of a fund, so that they can continue to generate fees, as well as to stay in power as GP of the fund. To balance these competing interests in practice, many no-fault divorce provisions require a supermajority to be enacted. Since the advisory board of a fund is typically made up of those LPs with the largest investment in the fund, the advisory board would likely play a crucial role in voting toward the activation of this clause.

Limitation on Liability

As outlined earlier, advisory boards that consist of LPs, as opposed to pure advisors, serve two basic functions. First, they are generally supposed to represent the best interests of the larger pool of LPs, including those that do not have advisory board seats. Second, they are supposed to serve as advisors to the fund in terms of how to proceed in certain situations including portfolio management advice. Advisory board LP members however, do not want to be liable to other LPs for mismanagement of the fund. As such, advisory boards will often request that the GP absolve them from technical legal liability for management and control of the fund. Typically the advisory board will request such an opinion in the form of a legal opinion.[4]

Key Person Provisions

A *key person provision*, sometimes referred to as a *key man provision*, at its most basic level outlines that in the event of the departure of a key employee of the GP, such as a portfolio manager, investors will at a minimum be notified. In certain situations, key person provisions will not only provide LPs with a notice of the triggering of a key person event but also offer them a redemption window. In most cases, when any sort of redemption window is provided, no penalty fees are charged to LPs.

Key person provisions may be further expanded to include not only the departure of employees but also to include a number of other terms, including the death of a key individual, incapacity of a key individual, or the lack of material involvement with the business for a specific period of time for a key individual. Another twist on key person provisions may be that once a key person event is triggered, the GP may not be permitted to engage in new acquisitions for a specified period of time subject to approval by the majority of investors or the private equity fund's advisory board. Furthermore, a key person provision could provide that the GP would have to liquidate the fund, subject to approval of the investors or the fund's advisory board. It should be noted that in the above examples, we have referred to a key person clause as being activated in relation to a singular key individual. These situations can be changed to reflect multiple key individuals as well. When multiple key individuals are involved, different scenarios exist.

For example, let us consider a private equity firm with two coportfolio managers: Mr. A and Mr. B. One such key person scenario may be an "or" key person clause. Under an "or" key person clause, the clause would be activated in the event of the departure (or death, incapacity, or lack of material involvement for a specified period of time, should it be applicable as outlined earlier) of either Mr. A *or* Mr. B. A second scenario would be an "and" key person clause. Under this "and" key person clause, the key person clause would be triggered only if *both* Mr. A and Mr. B departed the firm. From the perspective of an LP, "and" key person clauses are thought to be less advantageous because of their more restrictive manner as compared to "or" key person clauses.

The advisory board can have a material role in monitoring the activities of the GP in the event a key person event occurs. Furthermore, the advisory board may be the best advocate for the larger pool of LPs who do not have advisory board seats in monitoring any new acquisitions or fund liquidations during a key person event.

CONCLUSION

This chapter provides an introduction to the factors investors must consider when approaching operational due diligence upon a private equity fund's advisory board, including the different types of advisory boards that may be present at a private equity fund. We also provide an overview of some basic considerations LPs should consider when serving on an advisory board of a private equity fund. While there may be a number of advantages that may accrue to an LP serving on an advisory board, there may also be a number of potential drawbacks. This chapter also provides an overview of the benefits of ongoing operational due diligence monitoring in an advisory board context as well as considerations of information flow from the GP of an underlying portfolio through to LPs. We then outline an overview of LP due diligence considerations for private equity fund of funds, and the role that such considerations may play in the context of an LP's role on an advisory board. Finally, this chapter outlines additional private equity advisory board considerations, including the role of the advisory board in interacting with no-fault divorce provisions and key person provisions.

NOTES

1. See James Schell, *Private Equity Funds: Business Structure and Operations* (New York: Law Journal Press, 2004), 9–10.
2. See Guy Fraser-Sampson, *Private Equity as an Asset Class*, 2nd ed. (Hoboken, NJ: John Wiley & Sons, 2010).
3. James M. Kocis, *Inside Private Equity: The Professional Investor's Handbook* (Hoboken, NJ: John Wiley & Sons, 2009).
4. Ibid.

CHAPTER 11

Case Studies and Scenarios

When reviewing a private equity firm's operational data, there are often a number of grey areas that come to the surface as part of the review process. Depending on where a particular investor's operational threshold lies, plus numerous other factors, rational investors can come to different allocation decisions. The purpose of this chapter is to provide some perspective to Limited Partners when they are approaching these operational crossroads by outlining several case studies and scenarios an investor may be presented with when conducting an operational due diligence review. This chapter begins by outlining the details of historical private equity frauds. We then proceed with a discussion of several hypothetical situations. All situations and persons described in these scenarios are purely fictional and solely for demonstrative purposes.

CASE STUDIES

Many Limited Partners (LPs), General Partners (GPs), and others involved in the private equity industry, such as service providers, may in general have a perceived notion that their industry is virtually immune from large-scale losses as a result of fraud. Fueling such concerns could be the lack of Madoff-type events in recent memory, which produce sensationalist headlines and widespread global losses. A review of recent history in this regard, however, presents a stark comparison to notions that private equity functions in a moral vacuum in which fraud cannot survive. Fraud and losses due to primarily operational reasons has been shown to exist on both sides of the private equity investing spectrum. Recent studies concerning private equity managers' experiences with fraudulent activities at underlying portfolio companies suggest that fraud is certainly present at these firms. Similarly, and perhaps more notably from the Limited Partner's perspective, are brazen fraudulent activities at the General Partner level, which have resulted in large-scale losses for private equity investors in the funds that these organizations manage.

Case Study 1: Danny Pang and $700 Million PEMGroup Fraud

Danny Pang was born in Taiwan on December 15, 1966, and came to the United States as a youth and later enrolled at the University of California, Irvine. Pang ostensibly exemplified the great American success story, from working hard as a Taiwanese immigrant, to graduating from a university with an MBA, to building a career at Morgan Stanley until he was senior vice president, and to starting his own firm.

Pang became a partner at Sky Capital Partners venture-capital firm in the 1990s, investing some of his family's money.[1] In 1997, Pang was fired from Sky Capital by President and CEO Michael Hsu, who later said in an interview that Pang "stole my personal money" by getting Hsu to set up a brokerage account and then using some of the cash for himself. In June 1997, Hsu wrote in an e-mail to the *Wall Street Journal* that Pang "stole $3 million from an investment escrow account by faking signature[s] of mine and [the] CEO of our investment target."[2] According to Hsu, when Pang was confronted he said that he "just needed the money." Hsu claimed that he did not report the theft to police because it was an embarrassing internal scandal and Pang's family, which was a big investor in Sky Capital, asked him not to report it. Hsu says Pang traveled to Taiwan and confessed the theft to Sky Capital's board and that he had recovered about two-thirds of the stolen money by seizing Pang's share of the venture-capital firm. In an interview, Hsu said Sky Capital fired Pang.

Danny Pang also had some issues in his personal life. In 1993, shortly after a lavish engagement party at the Ritz Carlton Hotel in Laguna Beach, his fiancée Elaine Fan refused to marry him because she found out that he had a live-in girlfriend.[3] Pang then married his girlfriend Janie Louise Beuschlein, a stripper whom he had met at a club that he frequented.

Pang lived a lavish lifestyle in upscale Newport Beach, California, with his wife Janie Pang and their children. While Pang appeared to be a polished business executive in public, everything was not peaceful at home. In court records, police reports detail how they were called to the home at least four different times.[4] Janie Pang accused her husband Danny Pang of ongoing domestic violence and expressed fear that Pang might "kill her." Additionally, while the police were there, Mrs. Pang accused Mr. Pang of stealing money from her parents, breaking her nose, and forcing her to withdraw large sums of cash for her husband to use on women, gambling, and alcohol. However, police never arrested Pang and no criminal charges were ever filed.

In May 1997, Mrs. Pang hired a private investigator who reported to her that Mr. Pang had been out with another woman.[5] Shortly after confronting her husband over the phone about the investigation while he was away on a business trip, a clean-cut elegantly dressed man with a briefcase arrived at the door asking for her husband. After being let in by the maid and speaking briefly with Mrs. Pang, he pulled out a semiautomatic pistol. The terrified maid rushed the Pangs' children out the back door as the gunman chased Mrs. Pang through the home. Within minutes, the killer found Mrs. Pang, who tried to hide in her bedroom closet, and fired several .380-caliber rounds, killing her on the day of her fourth wedding anniversary.[6]

Pang claimed that since he was away, he was not connected to his wife's murder, although he was widely believed to be connected to Asian crime rings and to have hired a hit man to kill his wife to avoid a messy divorce. In 2001, Mrs. Pang's son from her first marriage sued Mr. Pang over Mrs. Pang's $750,000 life insurance policy.[7]

In 2001, Pang founded, and named himself the chief executive of, the Private Equity Management Group and Private Equity Management LLC, or PEMGroup, based in Irvine, California. In 2004, PEMGroup raised its first round of funding by selling their products through six local Asian banks, including internationally known Standard Chartered Bank, EnTie Commercial Bank, Bank Sino Pac, Cosmos Bank, Hua Nan Commercial Bank, and Taichung Commercial Bank.[8] Banks trusted Pang because he presented an aura of success as an accomplished Taiwanese-American executive, with a history of educational and business accomplishments, while hosting lavish parties in luxury suites at top hotels and flying around the globe in private jets. Standard Chartered sold about US$221 million worth of PEMGroup securities, EnTie Bank sold US$52 million, Bank SinoPac sold US$146 million, Cosmos Bank sold US$48 million, Hua Nan sold US$205 million, and Taichung Bank sold US$70 million.[9]

In 2006, Pang used funds from investors to buy the firm a $15 million private Gulfstream jet, and then later used the jet to take private trips to Las Vegas.[10] Employees stated that on the way home Pang had a briefcase full of cash; he threw $10,000 bundles at them, the same way he threw money to the Las Vegas showgirls.

The *Wall Street Journal* published an article on April 15, 2009, questioning Pang's credentials and alleging that his firm had been fraudulently stealing millions of dollars from investors since 2003. Within a day, the SEC seized control of PEMGroup, which was believed to be valued at $4 billion.[11] Shortly after the article was published, it was reported that Pang had his lawyer draft an agreement with an employee who worked with the *Wall Street Journal* offering to pay the employee $500,000 for saying that their statements was false.[12]

In the SEC's complaint filed in April 2009, it charged Pang of defrauding investors of hundreds of millions of dollars by fraudulently offering securities from his two firms.[13] The SEC alleged that Pang misled investors about the face value of investments in real estate timeshares and life insurance policies. The complaint states that PEMGroup violated Section 17(a) of the Securities Act of 1933, Section 10(b) of the Securities Exchange Act of 1934, and Rule 10b-5. Investors believed that Pang's firms would purchase life insurance policies from senior citizens and invest the money in real estate timeshares.

According to the SEC complaint, over 16,000 Taiwanese investors were sold securities (debentures) under the assumption that they would be guaranteed a 5.25 percent to 7 percent annual rate of return paid semiannually.[14] While investors were guaranteed principle and interest on their investments by Pang, he committed fraud by paying old investors with new investor money, essentially running a Ponzi scheme. Additionally, the firms forged insurance documents to further mislead investors that they carried $108 million of insurance when they carried only $31 million, and claiming that returns were "guaranteed."[15] Lastly, the firm misrepresented Pang's credentials, including falsifying his education and employment history. Additionally, PEMGroup was later charged by the SEC for illegally structuring financial deals to evade currency-reporting requirements.

In a press release from the SEC, Rosalind R. Tyson, Director of the SEC's Los Angeles Regional Office, states, "Pang's alleged use of phony credentials and false insurance coverage to guarantee his investments underscores how critical it is for investors to exercise due diligence before entrusting their savings to promoters."[16] Simple due diligence would have raised several red flags that Pang was a fraud. He falsified his resume. According to university records, which many investors did not seem to have checked, Pang enrolled only for a single summer term, in 1986, and never received the degrees he claimed. Additionally, Morgan Stanley has no record of Pang ever working there.[17]

While the SEC continued their investigation in September 2009, Pang was rushed to the hospital and died of an overdose of medication. His death at age 42 was ruled a suicide by the police department, although his family still protests that he had a heart condition.[18]

Case Study 2: John Orecchio and the $24 Million AA Capital Fraud

While cases of fraud at private equity firms may seem rare, the brazen fraud committed by John Orecchio should be a prime example that public and private pension fund managers investing in private equity should keep in mind. While the scope of this fraud may seem relatively small, the common theme of lack of attention to detail regarding operational due diligence for private equity firms will continue to be a growing and ongoing concern.

John Orecchio earned his undergraduate degree from the University of Notre Dame and earned an MBA from Northwestern University's Kellogg School of Management.[19] Orecchio's notable employment history included working at Hitachi Capital America as a managing director. He also obtained his Chartered Financial Analyst (CFA) certification. He went on to serve as a managing director in the Leveraged Finance Group at Bank of America (which had resulted from a merger with Continental Bank), where he was responsible for the financing of a diverse portfolio of buyout transactions typically sponsored by a private equity firm. Orecchio later became a managing director of Bank of America Capital Corporation, a subsidiary of Bank of America Corporation. In this position Orecchio was responsible for the day-to-day management with one other manager of a $5 billion private equity fund investments portfolio and was a member of the firm's Investment Committee.

Orecchio was a married father of three, and he and his family lived in the Chicago suburb of Arlington Heights in a modest home.[20] He was a well-connected financier and in 2000, when AA Capital Partners was spun out from ABN Amro, he became the cofounder and CEO.[21] At that time, AA Capital had millions under management, which were invested in special direct investments such as casinos and record labels, as well as private equity funds. The private equity fund managed by AA Capital managed money from the pension funds of six different unions between 2001 and 2006.[22] Orecchio solicited union pension investments through heavy lobbying, including offering luxury seats at sporting events, extravagant wining and dining, and lavish gifts. Orecchio's firm also made payments to the groups led by former mayor of Detroit Kwame Kilpatrick in exchange for these groups introducing AA Capital to union bosses.[23]

In August 2003, according to the SEC report, Orecchio began a relationship with a woman who performed at a Detroit strip club.[24] Orecchio began to live a double life, plundering investor accounts to finance an extravagant lifestyle that included driving a Bentley, luxury suites at sporting events, trips on private jets to tropical and exotic destinations with his young mistress, then "fiancée," and a stable of thoroughbred racing horses.[25]

According to the SEC's complaint, a majority of investors' money ($126 million) was kept in the firm's private equity funds, but at least $68 million was kept in cash in client's trust accounts. The firm asked clients to put millions of dollars in trust accounts for discretionary spending, such as capital calls. [26]Around May 2004, Orecchio convinced his CFO Mary Beth Stevens to give him a "tax loan," which over time turned into over

20 different loan disbursements to his personal accounts of approximately $5.7 million of investors' money.[27]

The SEC complaint also noted that during an Ernst & Young independent audit of the 2004 financial statements for the funds, the lead accountant took the CFO's word that Orecchio used the funds for a "tax loan," although there was no supporting documentation, such as the terms of the loan, to prove that the fund transfers were loans.[28] Additionally, the SEC's Division of Enforcement and the Office of the Chief Accountant later charged the lead accountants with improper conduct, citing that they neither failed to confirm the CFO's statements that Orecchio made tax payments for the loan amount to the IRS, but also failed to confirm the loan and repayment plan with Orecchio in person.[29] Additionally, the complaint stated that the Ernst & Young audit team failed to discuss the loan with their colleagues who prepared the tax filings for the AA Capital fund or their affiliated Private Equity funds.

In 2006, the SEC began investigating AA Capital's boutique firms' association to unions. The complaint states that Orecchio and AA Capital defrauded investors by misappropriating funds for personal use, including funds for a Detroit "Strip Club" and a horse farm in Michigan.[30] Additionally, the complaint alleges that AA Capital failed to keep the proper documentation, books, and filings as required of a registered advisory firm. The SEC filed numerous violations against AA Capital and Orecchio, including violating Advisers Act (204 & 206), and seized control of the firm's assets.[31]

On July 21, 2009, Orecchio was charged by the U.S. Department of Justice with one count of wire fraud and one count of embezzling funds owned by an employee pension benefit plan.[32] The combined charges carried a maximum penalty of 25 years in prison plus fines. The filing charges that while acting as the investment manager at AA Capital, Orecchio was accused of making repeated "capital calls" from the $169 million of pension funds he managed. It was alleged that he converted over $24 million to his personal accounts and personal investments, instead of using the funds for his investors' investments, fund management fees, or other conventional overhead expenses.

In June 2010, Mr. Orecchio pleaded guilty and was given a nine-year, four-month sentence for his actions.[33] In addition, he was required to pay restitution of more than $26 million in addition to a $50 million civil judgment that was awarded in a civil suit to the U.S. Department of Labor.[34] Earlier that year, in January 2010, AA Capital's CFO and Chief Compliance Officer Mary Beth Stevens settled with the SEC over charges that she violated the Advisors Act and aided and abetted the misappropriation of funds by Orecchio.[35] The settlement required Stevens to pay disgorgement of $79,583.50, including prejudgment interest of $22,472.24, and civil penalties of $50,000 to the Securities and Exchange Commission in five installments, but she was not required to admit guilt. Additionally, Orecchio's partner, Paul Oliver, and cofounder of AA Capital was also charged by the SEC and was required to pay disgorgement of $49,786, prejudgment interest of $7,979, and a civil penalty of $75,000 to the SEC. Additionally he was not allowed to be affiliated with any investment advisor for 12 months. Lastly, in June 2010 the Department of Labor reached a deal with AA Capital's insurance providers, including Indian Harbor Insurance and Federal Insurance, to recover $7.8 million worth of investor's funds.[36]

Case Study 3: PalmInvest €30 Million Fraud

In 2005, two Danish businessmen, Danny Klomp and Remco Voortman, started the PalmInvest fund in Hilversum in the Netherlands. They put together a professional advertising campaign with television commercials, print advertisements, and brochures to convince over 400 investors to give them a minimum of €50,000 each for real estate bonds.[37] The bonds guaranteed a 9 percent return on property investment in Dubai for real estate investment and development in Palm Jumeirah.[38] Investors were told that their money would be used to purchase apartments and villas on the man-made palm-shaped islands in Dubai.

In January 2008, 90 investigators seized documents and luxury goods during a raid of eight offices, five homes in the Netherlands, and one home in Monaco.[39] The real master developer, a fellow called Nakheel who was responsible for the three palm-shaped islands being built off the emirate's coast, issued a statement shortly after the raid saying that they had never heard of PalmInvest and later filed legal action against the firm.[40] Investigators arrested five employees with charges of participating in organized crime, money laundering, and embezzlement. At least part of the cash was used to fund advisors' lavish lifestyles including luxury homes, cars, jewelry and watches, travel, and clothing.[41] Both founders were given sentences of 3.5 years in jail as well as being banned by the court from working as financial advisors for five years.[42] In 2010 and 2011, auctions of the fund managers' luxury goods and homes were held to help recoup some of the money lost by investors.

Case Study 4: Chartwell Partner Embezzlement Scheme

In 1992, Todd Berman and a partner founded Chartwell Investments, a private equity firm based in New York.[43] Todd Berman earned his undergraduate degree from Brown University and an MBA from Columbia University Graduate School of Business.[44] According to the U.S. State's Attorney's Office documents of 1999, Berman created several investment companies using a combination of his own personal, his partner's, and an investor's funds to create Chartwell Investments to manage the investment firms in the portfolio.[45] The firm made equity investments in companies such as PlayCore Holdings, which made playground equipment, Richard Childress Racing, and Morris Material Handling. [46] Berman sat on the board of directors for the firms and helped with strategic direction and management. In turn, Chartwell received a management fee from each of the firms in the portfolio plus expenses. For example, in the SEC filings for Morris Material Holdings, the summary documents include the following language detailing the Chartwell Management Consulting agreement:

> *The Company has entered into a management consulting agreement with Chartwell Investments Inc. pursuant to which Chartwell Investments Inc. provides the Company with certain management, advisory and consulting services for a fee of $1.0 million for each fiscal year of the Company during the term of the agreement, plus reimbursement of expenses. The term of the management consulting agreement is 10 years commencing at the Recapitalization Closing and is renewable for additional one year periods unless the Board of Directors of the Company gives prior written notice of nonrenewal to Chartwell Investments Inc.*[47]

According to the U.S. State's Attorney's office documents, starting in 1999 Berman set up a loan agreement between the funds to transfer money out of investor's funds and firm funds for operating expenses.[48] Over a series of 18 months from 2001 to 2003, Berman misled his partner and investors by fraudulently transferring funds to his personal banking accounts.[49] Additionally, according to the SEC complaint he altered financial statements and told the firm's third-party accountants not to tell anyone about the transfers. Berman fraudulently collected additional funds by billing the portfolio companies for his personal expenses in addition to Chartwell's expenses.[50] These personal expenses included a trip around the world, renting private jets, helicopters, and cars, and staying in luxury hotel rooms.

In 2003, Berman was charged by the Justice Department of embezzling $3.6 million from his partner and firm, which included over 600 personal expense reimbursements.[51] Berman could have received a maximum prison sentence of 20 years, but pleaded guilty in 2004 and was sentenced to five years in prison.[52]

Case Study 5: Dutch Real Estate Fund Steals €200 Million

In 2006, the Philips Pension fund's direct real-estate portfolio PREIM was worth €1.34 billion, and the entire Philips Pension fund was valued at €14.5 billion according to the fund's annual report.[53] In 2006, the direct real estate investments yielded 10.5 percent. However, the fund fell 1.6 percent short of its goal, and reported an overall return of investment of only 4.9 percent.[54]

According to the ANP press agency, a company spokesperson from Philips stated, "the company started an internal investigation into 'irregularities in reporting' by its pension fund and PREIM last year"[55] The firm's growing suspicions centered on the sale of unprofitable or less-profitable real estate transactions, which led to a forensic investigation by the firm. Additionally in early 2007, a division of Rabobank called Rabo Real estate group began its own investigation into the actions of the firm Bouwfonds, prior to their acquisition of the company.[56]

Between 2006 and 2007, the police investigated the irregularities; investigators taped over 70,000 telephone conversations and used secret surveillance at meetings. According to a public prosecutor, "The case came to light when a tax inspector checked out one of Cees Hakstage's [former director at Rabobank's property development arm, Bouwfonds] receipts."[57] It was also reported that the tax inspector ". . . asked questions but did not get a clear answer. He then came across a money trail that led to more dubious bills."[58]

In November 2007, 67 people were arrested in over 50 raids in three different countries including Belgium, the Netherlands, and Switzerland, which were conducted by more than 600 police officers.[59] The two main suspects in the case were the director of Bouwfonds and the head of Philip's PREIM fund, who was accused of charges such as forgery, money laundering, and participating in a criminal organization.[60]

According to prosecutors, the fraud involved surveyors accepting bribes in exchange for undervaluing property, which was sold to a business connection, and then was sold again for the full market value. The profits from the deals were divided among the players instead of going to the Philip's pension funds investors.[61] After the arrest, the prosecutor stated, "We think that the suspects have received substantial amounts for awarding and processing large building projects and large property transactions, possibly involving dozens of millions of euros."[62] The investigation uncovered that the fraud was believed to have been going on since 1995, and most likely was able to continue for so long because the firm's regulators did not pay close enough attention to the division's weak performance.[63] The combined fraud is expected to have cost over €250 million euros, with the Philips pension fund having lost at least €150 million and Rabobank having lost €100 million through Bouwfonds.[64]

To illustrate the fraud, consider that one firm that was allegedly involved was the property company Celonstate. According to a public prosecutor, they "bribed a former director of PREIM, the real estate management subsidiary of the pension fund. They bought property from PREIM for too low a price, and allegedly paid the former director's company indirectly €5.4m in return."[65]

Many of the defendants settled their cases and agreed to pay millions of euros back to the Philip's pension fund as well as to the justice ministry. Additionally, many of the settlements included mandatory community service or a short stint in jail. Last, while many of the settlements included paying back the pension fund, Philips filed many additional civil lawsuits against a majority of the conspirators. In 2008, Philips pension fund began to reduce their real estate portfolio, and sold 15 percent of their assets to the Dutch real estate fund Vesteda for approximately €200 million and to Njeuwe Steen for over €142 million.[66]

Case Study 6: Onyx Capital Advisors

Onyx Capital Advisors was founded in 2006 by Roy Dixon Jr., and was headquartered in Detroit, Michigan. Dixon's longtime friend Michael Farr, a former NFL player for the Detroit Lions, received Onyx investor funds for his three small businesses.[67] In 2007, three Detroit pension funds invested $23.8 million into the Onyx Capital Advisory Fund I, LP ("Onyx Fund") startup private equity fund.[68] The agreements for the fund included capital calls, as well as additional fees including an annual management fee of 2 percent of capital in the fund or $500,000 payable quarterly.

On April 22, 2010 the SEC charged Dixon, the fund, and Michael Farr of stealing more than $3 million from the fund. The SEC's security fraud complaint alleged that shortly after the pension funds joined the fund, Dixon and Onyx Capital Advisors took $2.06 million from the Onyx Fund for advanced management fees. Additionally, Farr transferred an additional $1.05 million to his own personal businesses.[69] According to the SEC complaint, Dixon withdrew management fees at will between 2007 and 2009, overcharged funds for fees, and double-billed the funds for certain fees.[70] Merri

Jo Gillette, the Director of the SEC's Chicago Regional Office, stated that "Farr assisted Dixon by making large bank withdrawals of money ostensibly invested in Farr's companies, and together they treated the pension funds' investments as their own pot of cash."[71] Furthermore, Onyx Capital tried to hide the scheme from investors by withholding tax returns and altering investor reports and financial statements.

The SEC securities fraud complaint also accuses Dixon and Onyx Capital Advisors of misleading and making false statements to potential clients. For example, when a fund expressed concern over Dixon's lack of experience with private equity funds, he sent a letter on behalf of the firm to one of the pension funds, falsely stating that the joint owner of Onyx Capital had extensive experience evaluating private equity investments, and that he would devote all of his efforts to the Onyx Fund. The letter went so far as to contain a forged signature of an individual that freelanced for the firm but had never been employed by Onyx Capital Advisors.[72] While it appears that a settlement, plea, or other deal has not yet been arranged, the SEC's fraud complaint asks the court to compel the defendants to "disgorge their ill-gotten gains and pay prejudgment interest and civil penalties." Additionally, the pension funds involved with the Onyx Fund are also filing separate lawsuits for damages.[73]

Case Study 7: Allianz Bribery

In 2010, the *Wall Street Journal* reported that the SEC was investigating Allianz SE, one of Europe's largest insurance companies. According to Allianz's 2010 Annual Report, the firm had a presence in approximately 70 countries, and served over 76 million customers with comprehensive insurance and asset management products. As of year-end 2010, its total assets under management were reported to be €1,518 billion.[74]

In September 2010, U.S. and German authorities were notified by company personnel from Allianz and Manroland that their internal investigation of payments made to groups without consent was an ongoing issue.[75] These included incidents in which payments were made without proper documentation. In November 2010, the SEC requested documents from the firm regarding one of the firm's private equity holdings.

Allianz had owned a majority stake in a German printing company called Manroland AG since 2006. Manroland AG is the world's market leader in offset web printing and one of the leading printing manufacturers.[76] The SEC began its investigation under the Foreign Corrupt Practices Act (FCPA) regarding potential bribery payments made by a Swiss subsidiary of Manroland.[77] Under the Foreign Corruption Practices Act, companies with

U.S. interests are forbidden from paying bribes to foreign officials to win business.

While Allianz is a European firm, it was listed on the New York Stock Exchange until October 2009 and therefore falls under the FCPA regulation.[78] The investigation reviewed whether the Swiss bank account held by Vostra SA received money from Manroland from 2002 to 2007 to pay bribes to a Swiss subsidiary. Additionally, outside council is reviewing additional undocumented transactions across the globe that may be bribes, believed to total more than $10 million.[79] This is the first incident of the SEC investigating a private equity firm's affiliate actions overseas under FCPA. This probe may break new ground in the United States' enforcement of the foreign bribery laws as the SEC has never charged a private equity firm based on the conduct of a foreign private company in its portfolio. However, at this point no charges have been filed.

HYPOTHETICAL SCENARIOS

Scenario 1: "From Russia with Love": Are Country-Specific Political Risks Valid Concerns?

The Baritone family amassed a great fortune at the turn of the century, which was safely monitored by the steward of the family from generation to generation. In 1998, three brothers assumed the responsibility for the family's money for the first time and were given complete control of the family's estate. The family held several dozen hotels throughout Europe and a fleet of luxury car dealerships, with the total estate valuing over €3.95 billion. Many financial advisors, hedge funds, venture capitalist, inventors, and developers solicited the three brothers daily at their mansion in London.

As the family had always been in the hospitality business, the brothers are considering whether to invest 30 percent of their sizable fortune with one of the largest private equity companies in France, Le Mette Bas. Specifically, the brother's investment in the Le Mette Bas fund would focus on developing luxury vacation property, retail entertainment complexes, and other forms of commercial property throughout Eastern Europe.

The private equity firm has historically always focused on many small projects throughout Europe, but has heavily lobbied the Baritone brothers to invest their funds in their most ambitious projects in Russia. If the brothers fund the projects, the fund would allocate 50 percent of the funds to their resort property development along the Chukchi Sea, and the other 50 percent to time-share property development in the resort town of Bravania.

While the brothers have been taught by the stewards of the family that when considering investing in certain countries, specific consideration needs to be given to the political climate and risks of a country, they feel that the fund managers at Le Mette Bas are well-versed in the risks they are taking. That said, one of the Baritone brothers still has some doubts about the validity of the fund's practices, so they set up another meeting with the managers.

During the meeting with the Le Mette Bas private equity fund, the brother asks what kinds of operational due diligence the private equity firm performs on portfolio companies. The fund's managers go on to explain a list of operational checks and ongoing monitoring that the funds perform on the portfolio companies. However, from this discussion the eldest Baritone brother learns that the portfolio companies do not use Western accounting standards and that because of ongoing issues with graft, the portfolio companies are not subject to strict regulatory oversight.

As the financial returns look extremely solid, the two younger brothers are pushing the eldest brother to overlook the lax regulation and nonexistent compliance mandates for the portfolio companies. However, throughout the course of the meeting the brothers also learn that the Le Mette Bas private equity fund itself has several Russian national officials and other close ties to the government serving on the boards of the portfolio companies and that a previous employee worked for the government prior to joining the firm. Lastly, according to the most recent financial documents, at least 40 percent of the funds for these projects were recently raised from a state-run pension fund, which creates additional operational concerns for the brothers about the possibility of strict oversight of the portfolio companies by the Russian government if these ties are broken in the future.

With all these operational concerns, should the Baritone brothers invest 30 percent of their family's fortune in the Le Mette Bas private equity fund?

Scenario 2: "The Tax Man Cometh": Thinking about Tax Regimes, Unintended Tax Consequences, and Offshore Havens

The Danbeer family has all their income invested in growing their business call centers in the Boise, Idaho, area, which act as the customer call centers for many Fortune 500 companies. While the call centers have been growing, the Danbeer family is increasingly concerned that the U.S. government's current trajectory will lead to more burdensome regulation and taxes for their business. Therefore, in 1999, the Danbeer family decided to sell their business for $400 million and retire to Naples, Florida.

The family decided to invest their money in a number of investment vehicles, including a private equity fund called Notaxico that is registered in the tax haven of Groto, but invests in mid-sized companies in Asia. The

Danbeers are told by the private equity manager that the fund is registered in Guernsey to minimize the tax consequences for their primarily U.S.-based investors. As the Danbeers were unfamiliar with offshore tax regulation, they decided to discuss the matter with the members of their country club to get their opinion.

The Danbeers decided to trust Notaxico's managers that they will not be taxed on the income from the fund and invest $100 million. However, by not consulting an accountant and lawyer, the Danbeers failed to realize that any income or dividends paid by Notaxico from their portfolio companies in Asia would be taxed. The Danbeers failed to realize that the United States federal government, regardless of the tax status of the fund, taxes all offshore income and capital gains that are paid to U.S. citizens. Regardless of the fact the Notaxico's private equity firm was a foreign corporate entity, the Danbeers were still liable for $15 million worth of income taxes for payments made by the fund in 2002, when they tried to repatriate the funds back to the United States. The Danbeers were furious at themselves for failing to understand the tax consequences of Notaxico's action overseas, and at the fund managers for leading them to believe that the tax haven of Groto would protect their earnings.

Additionally, Notaxico failed to inform investors that if the fund's registration was transferred to a country with an income tax equal to the United States or to a country that had a tax treaty in place with the United States, they would still owe taxes. In this instance, while the Danbeers may have been eligible to collect a tax credit in the United States by paying at least $15 million worth of taxes to another sovereign nation, they would still have paid taxes to someone.

While the U.S. federal government will almost always tax your income regardless of where or how you make it in the world, many investors work with highly specialized accountants to try to avoid it. Many U.S. investors postpone the payment of the taxes by sheltering their income overseas by using tax havens, manipulating Subpart F rules, or setting up Controlled Foreign Corporations (CFCs), but such actions can lead to unintended tax consequences.

Scenario 3: "Spider Mites and Timber": Learning about Asset-Specific Risks and Risk Management Approaches

Murry Oakland is considering diversifying his investments by investing $50 million in the GreenTree private equity fund in Burbank, California. The fund is a traditional timber investment management organization (TIMO) fund that invests in land in the Northwestern United States and focuses on several species of trees that is used for lumber and paper. A majority of the high-end lumber from the oak and redwood trees is exported for furniture making, while the rest is shipped to facilities throughout the United States and Canada. The fund's marketing team provided all the typical documents to Oakland, including a generic operational due diligence questionnaire that reviewed the firms buying procedures, portfolio manager bios, financials, and pertinent legal documents.

Oakland knows very little about commercial lumber or trees, but is fairly confident that the fund will generate the returns he desires. However, knowing very little about this industry, Oakland decides to contact the fund's manager about visiting the forestland that he would be investing in, so he can see the trees himself. Oakland takes his private jet up to the largest plot of trees owned by the fund and takes a hike with his dog Buddy and the head lumberjack, Paul.

While he is out on the land, Paul tells him about the different acres of trees that they walk through and about the longevity, temperament, and almost everything Oakland would ever want to know about the types of trees. Paul tells Oakland about how he is very happy that this season's trees are healthy, but alludes to problems in the past with another tree farm that had fungus, fire, and termites, all within 19 months of each other. While Oakland feels that his investment would be well taken care of by the tree staff, he has some additional concerns about how the fund handles disaster events such as fire and infestations, so he schedules a meeting with the fund's manager.

At the meeting, the fund's manager reviewed the business continuity and disaster recovery plan for the firm. They also discussed how the fund creates valuation models for trees and land plots, including how they value stunted, damaged, or dead trees. Additionally, the manager reviews an example of a time when spider mites severely damaged 20 acres of American oak trees. The manager explained that the mites were similar to ticks, and that they bred and spread rapidly and were almost impossible to remove. However, he reassured Oakland that preventive measures were now in place to aggressively check for mites and that monthly pesticide applications were performed at all of GreenTree's tree farms. Oakland walked out of the meeting feeling overwhelmed, and concerned that he knew nothing about spider mites or trees besides what he had learned in the past few weeks.

Do you believe that Oakland understands the risk behind his investment in the GreenTree TIMO fund? Would you have taken the same approach as Oakland to operational due diligence or would you gather more information about these types of investments before committing? If you were unsure about the risks, would you hire an outside consultant before investing your personal money?

Scenario 4: "Reconciling with Delay": Understanding the Operational Implications for Low Frequency Trading and Large Exposure Strategies

Sophia Robins has traditionally invested in hedge funds and funds of funds in the past, but would like to consider investing a portion of the profits from her media empire in a private equity fund. She reaches out to two different private equity fund managers who come to her estate in Aspen, Colorado, and formally present the benefits of their funds. However, while there seem to be many similarities between hedge funds and private equity funds, Ms. Robins realizes during the course of vetting the funds that the term of private equity investments are substantially longer than she is used to.

She is uncomfortable with the fact that the private equity funds only make a few trades a year, and that her losses could be much larger than a missed trade opportunity from a traditional high frequency hedge fund. While she is used to losing small fractions of the portfolio during trading, she is unsure about the highly illiquid nature of private equity investments and the five-year minimum lockup that the private equity funds are requesting. Additionally, Ms. Robins's investment consultant is concerned that the small startup private equity funds that were selected by Ms. Robins before he was hired do not meet his standards regarding operational practices and procedures. He is concerned that the private equity firms lack proper infrastructure, back-office personnel and well-documented policies and fund documents that he would typically like to see before advising a client to invest $10 million of their money.

Should Ms. Robins make an exception for the lack of standards and procedures for the private equity firms? What would make you comfortable with giving a private equity firm's investment manager $10 million of your money for the next five years?

Scenario 5: "Snowball Effect": Can One Minor Issue Create a Larger Problem?

Kiekie Baron is considering investing $5 million in the Silver Mirage private equity fund in Reno, Nevada. While the fund looks like a solid investment, during the operational due diligence review, Baron's independent consultants run a series of standard background checks on the key principals of the fund. One of the checks uncovers that a department head was charged with a misdemeanor criminal activity. Consequently, during a meeting, the Silver Mirage managers reveal that the employee failed to notify the fund about the arrest. While the employee had not been sentenced yet for the changes, the employee claims that the whole thing is a giant misunderstanding and that his lawyer expects the charges to be dropped in the next couple of months. Additionally, the fund claims that they were unaware of the charges as the company's preemployment screening came back clean, because the charges occurred after the initial date of hire.

The Silver Mirage private equity fund maintains a code of ethics that states, "Employees shall advise compliance immediately if they become involved in or threatened with litigation or an administrative investigation or proceeding of any kind, or are subject to any judgment, order or arrest." This senior employee's violation of the policy leads to additional questions about the funds' employees potential for additional Code of Ethics violations, damage to the fund's reputational risk, and additional questions regarding the culture of compliance within the firm. In addition, this could lead to potential issues with ADV disclosures, the need to update policies and procedures regarding blatant disregard of compliance procedures and lead to problems with personnel turnover. Lastly, Mr. Baron asks the fund if they plan to notify existing and new investors regarding this compliance issue, and they note that they will waive his first six months of management fees if they can "keep the breach between the people in this room only."

These issues will cause an elongated due diligence process, and can lead to a reduce investment or no investment. Exhibit 11.1 provides a summary of these facts.

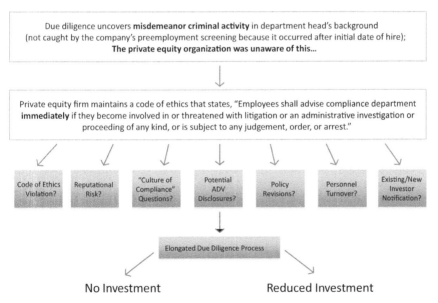

EXHIBIT 11.1 Snowball Effect: Can One Minor Issue Create a Larger Problem?

If you were Mr. Baron would you keep your investment the same, reduce it, or refuse to invest?

Scenario 6: "Little Things": Do Multiple "Small" Operational Issues Matter?

Maxine Park is considering investing $100 million in the Slacker Diamond private equity fund. However, during the operational due diligence review, Mrs. Park's operational due diligence team uncovers a number of small operation issues, which include:

1. Negative media coverage of the funds' employees, which leads to questions about the level of preemployment screening and additional reputational risks.
2. Inefficient use of legacy administration and additional potential problems with a lack of service provider oversight.
3. Extended delay in Geneva implementation that is caused by a lack of operational planning.
4. No offsite business continuity or disaster recovery ("BCP/DR") or disaster recovery site, which indicates a lack of input from the IT department into organizational planning.
5. No internal valuation committee and a board comprising only affiliated board members, which indicates a lack of independent operational oversight.
6. A Chief Compliance Officer ("CCO") who is unaware of outside business directorships, which may indicate that employees are not required to report to the COO or that the firm's policies are not being enforced.
   - Additionally this may show that there are additional Code of Ethics violations by junior personnel, or that there is a culture of noncompliance or outdated policies.
7. High personnel turnover, which may indicate issues with the firm's compensation structure or issues with the retention planning for employees.
   - Additionally, this may lead to problems with information security or enhance other underlying issues.

These minor issues can lead to larger questions about the financial stability of the funds, scalability of the business, and if there are sufficient internal checks and balances. Exhibit 11.2 provides a summary of these issues.

In addition, they could lead Mrs. Park and other potential investors to consider if there is appropriate oversight from senior management, and if

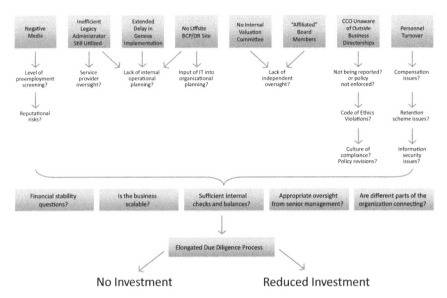

No Investment   Reduced Investment

EXHIBIT 11.2   Example of Multiple "Small" Operational Issues

different parts of the organization are communicating and cooperating as needed.

So many additional "minor" issues will cause an elongated due diligence process and can lead to a reduce investment or no investment. If you were Mrs. Park would you keep your investment the same, reduce it, or refuse to invest?

Scenario 7: "The Next Miracle Drug?": Is a Manager's Claim to Be the Best Source to Value Illiquid Unrealized Profits Valid?

Joe Cowstoy is considering investing in a private equity firm in Albuquerque, New Mexico, called Vitrablife, which is focused on health-care investing. Vitrablife focuses on investing in portfolio companies that are developing innovative drugs that are awaiting approval by the FDA. As part of the valuation process, the private equity fund tries to evaluate future revenue streams from these drugs.

In a meeting with the fund's marketing consultant, Cowstoy asks what valuation methods they follow, and he is initially referred to the offering memorandum for the fund. After Cowstoy reads the documents, he notes a reference that the fund uses "standard market practice" approaches.

Cowstoy finds this language extremely vague and calls the fund's manager to inquire about what they actually do to calculate the valuations. The fund's manager claims that the fund is a member of the Future Pharmaceutical Association of America (FPOAA), and that the fund follows the standard market valuation procedures implemented by the group. Cowstoy tries to find out about this association, but cannot discover anything about it on the Internet. He decides to ask the fund's manager about this FPOAA, and after phrasing questions in multiple ways and asking multiple questions, he realizes that the firm is the only member of this association.

Do you think Vitrablife did anything inappropriate when answering Cowstoy's questions? Is okay that Vitrablife invented their own methodology for valuation? Would you be okay with a manager giving you the runaround, especially when your question is about something as serious as valuation? Do you still want to invest in the fund?

Scenario 8: "Too Much of a Good Thing": The Importance of Understanding and Monitoring Conflicts of Interest and Deal Allocation Considerations

The Gutra pension fund is consider investing $20 million of their investor's funds in a traditional private equity firm called Little Stone based in Blarney, Ireland. After reviewing the funds' documents and speaking with the investment team, the investment team notices that there are no set rules or guidelines for the ways in which investments are allocated among the firm's funds. While the Little Stone funds are making money and they have made a lot of good deals among the funds, the Gutra pension fund is concerned that the allocation balance could drastically shift in the future.

The Little Stone private equity firm manages multiple real estate funds, some of which have similar investment mandates, including investing in retail property. When Little Stone's managers come across several new deals, which may be appropriate for more than one fund, there are no written policies in place to determine how the managers will allocate the deals among the funds.

While the fund's managers claim that they do not need written policies, Gutra's operational due diligence team is concerned that the lack of formal policies to avoid conflicts of interests raises red flags. Furthermore, there is concern that there is potential for cherry-picking deals from one fund to another, and that the firm has not demonstrated that the allocation policies are fair. Additionally, as the Little Stone private equity firm is in the process of launching another new fund, for which the same type of retail properties would also be appropriate, they are interested in how the fund will deal with the allocation balance between three funds.

Little Stone's managers indicate on a conference call that they are considering writing a formal allocation policy for the fund, but at the earliest, it might be ready next year. Additionally, the fund managers are given vague answers when Gutra's ODD team asks the following questions:

- Is there a fixed trade allocation ratio, or is it determined ad hoc?
  - If there is a fixed ratio and how often is it set, or is it done on a deal-by-deal basis?
- How often is the fixed ratio reset?
  - Is risk management or other departments such as legal and compliance involved with resetting the ratio?

With the previous questions still unanswered, do you believe that Gutra should invest with any of the Little Stone funds?

NOTES

1. Mark Maremont, "Highflying Financier Faces Questions over Fund Empire," April 16, 2009, www.marketwatch.com/story/highflying-financier-faces-questions-2009-04-15
2. See Mark Maramount, "The Talented Mr. Pang," *Wall Street Journal*, November 21, 2009, 18–19.
3. "The Life and Loves of Danny Pang," *New York Magazine*, published November 23, 2009, http://nymag.com/daily/intel/2009/11/danny_pang_2.html.
4. "The Unsolved Murder of Janie Louise Pang," *Wall Street Journal*, published April 15, 2009, http://online.wsj.com/article/SB123976601469019957.html.
5. See Mark Maremount, "The Talented Mr. Pang," *Wall Street Journal*, November 21, 2009, www.wsj.com/article/SB100014240527487042043045745458032807770320.html.
6. "The Unsolved Murder of Janie Louise Pang."
7. "And the Title for Most Insane Alleged Fraud of 2009 (So Far) Goes to...," *New York Magazine*, April 15, 2009, http://nymag.com/daily/intel/2009/04/and_the_title_for_most_insane.html.
8. Crystal Hsu, "FBI agents Arrest Taiwanese Financier Danny Pang," *Taipei Times*, www.taipeitimes.com/News/front/archives/2009/04/30/2003442403.
9. Ibid.
10. "And the Title for Most Insane Alleged Fraud of 2009."
11. "SEC Freezes Assets of Financier Danny Pang," April 27, 2009, www.sec.gov/news/press/2009/2009-89.htm.

12. "And the Title for Most Insane Alleged Fraud of 2009."
13. "Securities and Exchange Commission vs. Private Equity Management Group, Inc. et al.," www.sec.gov/litigation/complaints/2009/comp21013.pdf.
14. Ibid.
15. Residual Value insurance Declarations, www.wsj.net/public/resources/documents/hcc_policyOne_090415.pdf.
16. "SEC Freezes Assets of Financier Danny Pang."
17. Maremont, "The Talented Mr. Pang."
18. Maremont, "Highflying Financier Faces Questions."
19. Bloomberg Businessweek, "AA Capital Partners." http://investing.businessweek.com/businessweek/research/stocks/private/person.asp?personId=67584&privcapId=1609483&previousCapId=8388529&previousTitle=Ranch%20Capital,%20LLC.
20. Jason Grotto, "Investor Lived Dual Life on Plundered Cash," *Chicago Tribune*, June 16, 2010.
21. Bloomberg Businessweek, "Looking Out for Number One," October 30, 2006, www.businessweek.com/magazine/content/06_44/b4007006.htm.
22. Ibid.
23. Paul Egan, "Suspect in Corruption Inquiry Says Union Official Got Favors," *The Detroit News*, October 27, 2009.
24. "United States District Court Northern District of Illinois Eastern Division, United States Attorney Charges John A. Orecchio," filed September 8, 2006, www.justice.gov/usao/iln/pr/chicago/2009/pr0722_01a.pdf.
25. Litigation release No. 19826 by the *SEC v. AA Capital Partners, Inc. and John A. Orecchio*, U.S.D.C. N.D. Ill., Civil Action Number 06 C 4859, filed September 12, 2006, www.sec.gov/litigation/litreleases/2006/lr19826.htm.
26. Bloomberg Businessweek, "Looking Out for Number One," October 30, 2006.
27. United States of America before the Securities and Exchange Commission Administrative Proceeding File No. 3-13553, July 17, 2006.
28. Litigation release No. 19826 by the *SEC v. AA Capital Partners, Inc. and John A. Orecchio*, U.S.D.C. N.D. Ill., Civil Action Number 06 C 4859, filed September 12, 2006.
29. Ibid.
30. Ibid.
31. United States District Court Northern District of Illinois Eastern Division, United States Attorney Charges John A. Orecchio, filed September 8, 2006.
32. United States Attorney's Office, "Investment Advisor," July 22, 2009, www.fbi.gov/chicago/press-releases/2009/cg072209.htm.
33. Jason Grotto, "Man Gets 9 Years for Embezzlement," *Chicago Tribune*, July 17, 2010.
34. Ibid.
35. Administrative Proceeding File No. 3-13553, *SEC v. Mary Beth Stevens*, January 5, 2010, www.sec.gov/litigation/admin/2010/ia-2973.pdf.
36. Timothy Inklebarger, "Labor Department Gets More Money from AA Capital," *Pensions & Investments*, June 22, 2010.

37. Andrew White, "Dutch Duo Jailed for $36m Dubai Property Fraud," Arabian-Business.com, April 22, 2010, www.arabianbusiness.com/dutch-duo-jailed-for-36m-dubai-property-fraud-157771.html.
38. Rob Corder, "Dutch Police Bust Palm Scam," ArabianBusiness.com, January 21, 2010, www.arabianbusiness.com/dutch-police-bust-palm-scam-53014.html.
39. Elsevier, "Massale FIOD-inval vastgoedfonds Palm Invest," January 21, 2010, in Dutch only, www.elsevier.nl/web/Nieuws/Laatste-24-uur/154896/Massale-FIOD-inval-vastgoedfonds-Palm-Invest.htm.
40. Suzzanne FentonStaff, "Dubai Nakheel Takes Legal Action against PalmInvest" *GulfNews*, January 22, 2010.
41. Rob Corder, "Palm Fraudsters Lived Playboy Lifestyle," ArabianBusiness.com, January 22, 2010, www.arabianbusiness.com/palm-fraudsters-lived-playboy-lifestyle-122060.html.
42. DutchNews, "Palm Invest Swindlers Jailed for 3.5 Years, Both Are to Appeal," April 22, 2010, www.dutchnews.nl/news/archives/2010/04/palm_invest_swindlers_jailed_f.php.
43. Edgar Online, "Excerpt from a S-4 SEC Filing, Filed by Morris Material Handling, Inc., on 5/13/1998," http://sec.edgar-online.com/morris-material-handling-inc/s-4-securities-registration-business-combination/1998/05/13/section22.aspx.
44. Bloomberg Businessweek, "Executive Profile Todd R. Berman," August 1, 2011.
45. United States Attorney Southern District of New York, "Founder of Chartwell Managers Pleads Guilty in U.S. Court to Stealing More Than $3.6 Million," December 6, 2004, www.justice.gov/usao/nys/pressreleases/December04/bermantddplea.pdf.
46. Ibid.
47. Edgar Online, "Excerpt from a S-4 SEC Filing, Filed by Morris Material Handling, Inc., on 5/13/1998."
48. United States Attorney Southern District of New York, "Founder of Chartwell Managers Pleads Guilty."
49. Bloomberg Businessweek, "Looking Out for Number One."
50. United States Attorney Southern District of New York, "Founder of Chartwell Managers Pleads Guilty."
51. Bloomberg Businessweek, "Looking Out for Number One."
52. United States Attorney Southern District of New York, "Founder of Chartwell Managers Pleads Guilty."
53. IP Real Estate, "Philips Scheme Dismantles Real Estate Portfolio," December 11, 2007, www.ipe.com/realestate/philips-scheme-dismantles-real-estate-portfolio_26487.php?searchfor=philips fraud.
54. IP Real Estate, "Philips Fund Fraud Brings Calls for Transparency," November 16, 2007, www.ipe.com/news/Philips_fund_fraud_brings_calls_for_transparency_26050.php.
55. Ibid.

56. Rabobank, "Interim Report 2010 Rabobank Group," http://2009. annualreportsrabobank.com/downloads/Real_estate_hjv10.pdf.
57. DutchNews, "Property Sector Fraud Trial Kicks Off," November 17, 2009, www.dutchnews.nl/news/archives/2009/11/property_sector_fraud_trial_ki.php.
58. Ibid..
59. DutchNews, "Massive Property Development Fraud Case Comes to Trial at Last," March 3, 2011, swww.dutchnews.nl/news/archives/2011/03/massive_property_development_f.php.
60. IP Real Estate, "Director Arrested in Philips Pensions Fraud," November 19, 2007, http://ipe.com/realestate/director-arrested-in-philips-pensions-fraud_26074.php?categoryid=1035.
61. IP Real Estate, "Philips Fund Fraud Brings Calls for Transparency."
62. Ibid.
63. DutchNews, "Property Fraud Costs Philips, Rabobank €250m," November 4, 2009, www.dutchnews.nl/news/archives/2009/11/property_fraud_costs_philips_r.php.
64. Ibid.
65. IP Real Estate, "Philips Scheme Reclaims Millions."
66. IP Real Estate, "Cost of Fraud Triples for Philips Fund," August 4, 2008, www.ipe.com/news/Cost_of_fraud_triples_for_Philips_fund_28738.php.
67. Bloomberg Businessweek, "SEC Alleges Fraud in Handling of Pension Money," April 22, 2010, www.businessweek.com/ap/financialnews/D9F8D3B80.htm.
68. Case 2:10-cv-11633-DPH-MKM Document 1, "U.S. Securities and Exchange Commission v. Onyx Capital Advisors, Llc, Roy Dixon, Jr., and Michael A. Farr," Filed 04/22/10, www.sec.gov/litigation/complaints/2010/comp-pr2010-64.pdf.
69. U.S. Securities and Exchange Commission Litigation Release No. 21500, "Sec Charges Private Equity Firm and Money Manager for Defrauding Detroit-Area Public Pension Funds," April 23, 2010, www.sec.gov/litigation/litreleases/2010/lr21500.htm.
70. Case 2:10-cv-11633-DPH-MKM Document 1, "U.S. Securities and Exchange Commission v. Onyx Capital Advisors, Llc, Roy Dixon, Jr., and Michael A. Farr," Filed 04/22/10.
71. Jonathan Oosting, "SEC: Former Lion Mike Farr, Partner Stole More Than $3M from Detroit-Area Pension Funds," Mlive.com, April 22, 2010, www.mlive.com/newsF/detroit/index.ssf/2010/04/sec_former_lion_mike_farr_part.html.
72. Case 2:10-cv-11633-DPH-MKM Document 1, *U.S. Securities and Exchange Commission v. Onyx Capital Advisors, Llc, Roy Dixon, Jr., and Michael A. Farr,* filed 04/22/10.
73. Justia Dockets & Filings, *General Retirement System of the City of Detroit et al. v. Onyx Capital Advisors, LLC,* http://dockets.justia.com/docket/michigan/miedce/2:2010cv11941/248682/.
74. Allianz Group, "Annual Report 2010," March 18, 2011, www.allianz.com/static-resources/en/investor_relations/reports_and_financial_data/annual_report/ar2010/v_1301386895000/ar2010_group.pdf.

75. Joseph Palazzolo, "Corruption Currents: US Probing Allianz for Possible Bribery—Sources," *Wall Street Journal*, December 22, 2010.
76. Manroland website, "Company," August 22, 2011, www.manroland. com/com/en/company.htm.
77. Palazzolo, "Corruption Currents."
78. Ibid.
79. Ibid.

CHAPTER 12

Trends and Future Developments

T he private equity industry is constantly evolving. Depending on the state of the economy, different types of strategies or funds may be in vogue one year and then shunned the next. Some may feel that from an operational perspective, this change occurs at a slower pace than the supposedly fast-moving investment side of business. Both private equity investing and private equity operations are in flux. Private equity operational risks in particular, because of the evolving nature of the private equity industry as well as an environment of increased regulatory scrutiny, have undergone significant changes in recent years. This chapter provides an introduction of certain trends and anticipated future developments in this space. It is important for investors to understand and anticipate such trends so that their operational due diligence processes do not become stale, but rather adapt to appropriately review the continually changing nature of private equity operational risk.

USE OF THIRD-PARTY ADMINISTRATORS

The issue of fund administrator is one that has evolved in recent years across different parts of the investment industry. These changing attitudes have had a direct impact on the services offered by administrators. A private equity firm, when launching a new fund, has two primary options for fund administration: self-administration or third-party administration.

In self-administration, a private equity management company makes the determination that it will perform administration services for the fund it is managing. An example would be an instance in which administration services are carried out by the General Partner or via an affiliated entity. In many cases, a private equity firm opting for self-administration may create an entity that performs several services (e.g., custodial) for affiliated funds, including administration.

The second option is third-party administration. As previously mentioned in this book, third-party administrators generally offer two types of core services : fund accounting and shareholder servicing. A myriad of different services are offered by third-party administrators in addition to those previously outlined, including performing enhanced investor reporting and valuation oversight.

With an understanding of the two primary administration options we can now discuss trends in the administration space as applicable to private equity funds. Historically, certain private equity funds, as compared to their hedge fund counterparts, have relied more heavily on self-administration of funds. Those funds that have historically self-administered point to a number of different functions of this self-administration framework that they feel are beneficial for both GPs and Limited Partners.

First, a private equity firm that supports self-administration may feel that significant cost savings may be realized by self-administering. Effectively, this argument relies on the notion of taking from one hand and giving to the other. In such cases, rather than spend fees on third-party administrators, a private equity fund expends its own resources to self-administer the fund. In these self-administration cases, particularly when the GP has established an affiliated entity for the purposes of self-administration, the private equity fund may charge fees to the fund for such services. Such fees are not likely to be utilized as a profit center for the affiliated, or in-house, self-administration entities, but rather to cover the costs of administration. Many critics of self-administration may point out, in criticism of this model, that administration is an industry where economies of scale can be recognized. A private equity firm that self-administers the funds it manages, even one with multiple funds, is unlikely to realize the cost savings and process efficiencies that a large administrator will manage. Furthermore, third-party administrators in the private equity industry, as in most other asset classes, generally charge fees on a sliding scale as a percentage of the fund's assets under management. In these cases, from the LP perspective, those in support of third-party administration may argue that on a prorated basis across the entire spectrum of fund expenses the trade-off of benefits with non-self-administration may tip the scales in favor of third-party administration.

A second argument that a GP may raise in favor of self-administration is a feeling that a third-party administrator is unnecessary because in many cases it is duplicative. From an operational perspective, it is generally considered to be a best practice for a fund to shadow the work of the administrator internally. A GP may argue that such duplicate efforts are unnecessary. After all, they may argue, "Why can't a fund perform the traditional fund administration fund work correctly once, rather than have it performed twice?" In this regard, those who are against such self-administration models may cite the fact that the whole point of a private equity firm producing parallel books and records is not solely a duplication of effort. Rather, when a private equity firm parallels the work of a third-party administrator a number of benefits accrue to both the GP and LPs. First, a private equity firm that shadows the work of an administrator is likely to be more involved in, and familiar with, the work that is actually being performed by the administrator. In such cases, a signaling effect is also present. The third-party administrator will know that the private equity firm is watching their activities more closely as compared to a private equity firm that is not cognizant on a more granular basis of such work. This increased frequency of oversight also has ramifications for the frequency of communication between the private equity firm and the third-party administrator. A private equity firm that is running parallel fund books is likely to engage in more of an ongoing dialogue with a private equity firm to discuss any ongoing issues that may come about throughout the administration cycle. With this ongoing communication comes increased oversight and an increased likelihood of a lack of errors in fund accounting production. Such oversight is not generally present when a fund self-administers. As such, those who do not support fund self-administration cite this lack of oversight to be a knock against self-administration.

A fund seeking to support its decision to self-administer may point to the fact that there is generally no requirement, legal or otherwise, that a private equity firm engage a third-party administrator as well. In response to this argument, it may be suggested that a measure of legality or illegality is not necessarily tied to the qualities of best practice or not. Just like financial industry regulation, the net effect of such regulation is oftentimes to create a minimum operational floor, not a ceiling. There is often significant room for improvement above minimum legal or regulatory requirements and operational best practices.

Those investors who do not support self-administration oftentimes cite a number of benefits to be found in employing a third-party administrator. First, there is potential for a conflict of interest in self-administration. Third-party administrators provide a degree of independence that is not available in self-administered funds. Consider the NAV calculation and distribution services often performed by a third-party administrator: By contrast, a GP that self-administers the funds it manages, even via an affiliated entity, lacks this independence to have fund statements independently prepared and distributed to investors.

In reviewing trends in the private equity administration function, investors may have been less insistent in the past in demanding that a fund employ a third-party administrator. Due in large part to the awareness that the potential for conflicts of interest is too great, many LPs have exerted increased pressure on GPs to engage third-party administrators for private equity funds. It is likely that there will continue to be a trend toward private equity firms demanding the use of third-party administrators.

With this trend, LPs must be conscious that all private equity administrators are not created equal. Administrators can vary in the services they offer (i.e., full NAV, NAV-lite, shareholder services, etc.) and the functions performed (i.e., valuation agent, maintenance of official books and records, etc.). Investors may find if they invest in several different private equity funds that even two managers that utilize the same administrator may have completely different opinions and experiences. Such differences may not only relate to more patent investor concerns such as the time it takes to cut the final monthly NAV figures, but the less obvious as well, including which fund has more senior personnel servicing their account. Investors who take care to understand the often-overlooked specifics of a private equity fund's relationship with its administrator can often gain an informational advantage over those who do not—and ultimately reduce their overall operational risk exposures. The following are some key questions investors may want to pose to both private equity fund manager(s) and their administrator(s) as part of the operational due diligence process:

For the Third-Party Administrator

- What is your experience in dealing with the private equity fund strategy of my manager?
- What are your total assets under administration, both firmwide and for this particular strategy?
- Do you perform any other services besides administration? (i.e., sell software, custody, company secretarial, etc.)
- How many individuals are dedicated solely to my private equity manager/fund? How many are shared?
- What has been the annual rate of team turnover on the fund accounting side?
- How often do you hear from my private equity manager? Are they actively involved in the process?
- What pricing sources do you utilize and which instruments are priced via these sources?
- Is there anything in the portfolio that you as the administrator do not price independently?
- Do you have a dialogue with my private equity's auditor?
- How do you receive data from my private equity fund? Do you have direct access to their prime broker systems?
- Is this level of service you provide typical of all your clients?

For the Private Equity Manager

- Have you ever visited your administrator's offices?
- Why did you select your current administrator? What other administrators did you consider?
- When did you last negotiate your administration contract?
- What are your administration fees? Do you feel these fees are competitive?
- Do you provide your administrator with copies of all relevant documentation related to pricing, cash movements, and so on (e.g., copies of invoices to be paid, internally produced valuation memos)?
- What are some things your administrator can improve upon?

INCREASED FOCUS ON MATERIAL NONPUBLIC INFORMATION IN THE UNITED STATES

During the course of a private equity firm's investing activities, they will typically come across a number of different entities in both the public and private space. An example of this may be in PIPE transactions, where the potential for the transmission of material nonpublic information between a public company and a private equity firm is an ongoing risk that both entities must monitor.

The prosecution of Raj Rajaratnam's Galleon Group and associated raids of fund managers' offices by the Federal Bureau of Investigation make it clear that cracking down on allegedly illegal insider trading is a priority in the U.S. government's financial regulatory agenda. This is also highlighted by the increased scrutiny faced by expert research networks in recent times.

Traditionally, many investors have equated the use of material nonpublic information with boiler-room insider trading rings and backroom corporate tipsters. However, many investors may not realize the numerous ways in which perfectly legitimate private equity funds during the course of daily business may come into contact with, either directly or indirectly, data that could be potentially classified as material nonpublic information.

Private equity funds may receive material nonpublic information inadvertently (i.e., an unsolicited fax comes into the firm with questionable insider information or a hedge fund receives an unsolicited email offering material nonpublic information). Alternatively, a private equity manager may be directly exposed to such information during the course of otherwise perfectly legal investment research. This can sometimes happen when a private equity fund makes use of third parties to provide research or perspective on a specific industry or company. In recent years, an industry has blossomed of *expert networks* or *consultant networks* that effectively provide a matchmaker service between industry or company experts and private equity funds.

Expert networks often make the experts agree in advance that they will not disclose material nonpublic information. However, the firms that manage these expert networks themselves are rarely, if ever, on call to ensure that the disclosure of material nonpublic information takes place. Indeed, even if such information were disclosed, it may be difficult for someone without specific knowledge of an industry or company to detect what information is both *material* and *nonpublic* in the first place. It is within this nuanced legal gray area, between legal investment research and material nonpublic information, that the U.S. government and private equity GPs and LPs performing operational due diligence on private equity funds must navigate, while at the same time maintaining a private equity fund's competitive advantages.

The United States has a long history of case law that provides guidance regarding liability, particularly for those with fiduciary obligations, for trading on material nonpublic information.[1] In 2000, the SEC codified rules prohibiting the uses of material nonpublic information under SEC Rules 10b5-1 and 10b5-2. Depending on a hedge fund's interaction with material nonpublic information, a number of defenses may be invoked when allegations of wrongdoing are brought, including an affirmative defense for preplanned trades (the so-called 10b5-1 loophole), use of mosaic theory, a lack of awareness that the private equity fund traded on material nonpublic information, use of information barriers, and the implementation of reasonable policies and procedures to prevent trading on material nonpublic information.

Limited Partner Operational Due Diligence Considerations for Hedge Funds and Material Nonpublic Information

During the operational due diligence process, investors should ask their private equity managers a number of questions in order to diagnose both a fund's potential exposures to the risks associated with material nonpublic information as well as what preventative measures, if any, a GP may have taken to insulate themselves against the liability associated with receiving or trading on such information. Specifically, the types of questions that can be asked include:

Use of Expert Networks

- Does your private equity firm make use of third-party expert networks? If yes:
  - Which expert networks are utilized?

- How frequently are they used?
- Has the private equity firm vetted the procedures in place, if any, at the expert network to prevent the transmission of material nonpublic information?
- Has the private equity firm fund proactively communicated to expert networks that they do not wish to receive material nonpublic information?
- Is the private equity firm's internal compliance department involved in providing training to analysts about what material nonpublic information is and the associated trading restrictions?
- Is compliance involved in random audits of interaction between a hedge fund's analysts and experts?
- Are any restrictions in place regarding what kind of experts may be spoken to?
- Does the firm have a system in place to track all interactions with such expert networks, including which firms and industries were discussed?

Other Third-Party Firms That Provide Information

- Does your private equity fund receive trading ideas or other market intelligence from any other third-party sources, such as smaller niche brokers or law firms? If yes, what types of information does your hedge fund receive from these sources?
- In the case of law firms, does the private equity firm typically steer certain legal work in exchange for deal flow?

Internal Private Equity Fund Procedures

- Does your private equity firm have any explicit policies regarding material nonpublic information (i.e., in the compliance manual or code of ethics)?
- Has the private equity firm internally performed any training with respect to material nonpublic information?
- Does compliance perform any testing or historical trade analysis to track potential uses of material nonpublic information?
- In the event the private equity firm may come into contact with material nonpublic information, does the firm maintain a clear procedure as to what employees should do, including:
  - Procedure to report the source of information and nature of information to compliance
  - Implementation of both a restricted list and blackout periods for trading in such information (perhaps both for the firm's funds and personal account dealing)

Going forward, it is likely that increased attention will be paid in this regard to the scrutiny exercised by regulators and LPs in this area. This trend is likely to continue, particularly for the private equity space, with investments that continue to blur the line between public and private investments.

INCREASED RELIANCE ON AUDIT-TYPE CERTIFICATIONS

With investors focusing with increased attention to operational robustness throughout the asset management industry, fund managers have sought to increase the ways in which they can demonstrate operational quality. Perhaps in acknowledgment of the fact that regulatory-prescribed minimum guidelines are no longer sufficient to satiate the operational demands of many investors, many fund managers have sought certification of their operational control environments.

In the private equity industry, many firms of a variety of sizes and asset levels have sought formal audit certifications of their practices. Prior to the increased focus in these audit certifications, it was commonplace for only large hedge fund service providers such as administrators to undergo such detailed operational review processes. In pursuing these audit certifications, many private equity firms have taken cues from their hedge fund counterparts who have led the charge in pursuing such certifications. Hedge funds themselves were influenced by the audit certifications pursued by many of their own service providers such as third-party administrators who had traditionally pursued certifications, such as the SAS 70 standard.

The Statement on Auditing Standards (SAS) No. 70, Service Organizations, commonly known as an SAS 70 report, is an example of a common audit certification that has been increasingly pursued by private equity firms. The Auditing Standards Board of the American Institute of Certified Public Accountants (AICPA) issues the auditing standards. Technically, today, the majority of such SAS 70 audit firms conduct audits not only in adherence to SAS 70, but also in adherence to the subsequent amendments known as SAS 88, *Service Organizations and Reporting on Consistency*, and SAS 98, *Omnibus Statement on Auditing Standards*. These reports are generally titled "Report on the Processing of Transactions by Service Organizations," but may also be referred to as "Report on Controls Placed in Operation and Tests of Operating Effectiveness," or some variation thereof.

Formally, an SAS 70 can be defined as a report "where professional standards are set up for a service auditor that audits and assesses internal

EXHIBIT 12.1   Common Global Audit Certifications

Country	Standard
United States	Statement on Auditing Standards (SAS) No. 7
Canada	Canadian Institute of Chartered Accountants (CICA) 5970
United Kingdom	Audit and Assurance Faculty Standard (AAF) 01/06
Australia	Guidance Statement (GS) 007
Hong Kong	HKSA Statements Auditing Practice Note 860.2
Japan	Audit Standards Committee Report No. 18
Germany	IDW PS 951

controls of a service organization." SAS 70 reports come in two forms: A Type I report details the auditor's opinion as to the fairness of the presentation of the organization's description of controls as well as the suitability of the design of such controls to achieve the specified control objectives. A Type II report contains all of the information in a Type I report, as well as the auditor's opinion as to whether the specific controls had operated effectively during the period under review. SAS 70 reports have equivalents in other countries as well. In Canada, a report similar to SAS 70 is known as Section 5970. Exhibit 12.1 provides a summary of common global audit certifications.

As indicated earlier, private equity firms and real estate firms in particular have enhanced such audit certifications more broadly in recent years. One trend that has emerged is the increase in global harmonization of such audit certifications. Capitalizing on this trend has been the growing popularity of the International Standard of Assurance Engagements (ISAE) 3402, Assurance Report on Controls at a Service Organization, and its U.S. equivalent SSAE 16. An ISAE 3402 is not meant to replace any country-specific audit certifications, but rather to augment global standards as investors have sought broader control reports assessments that not only focus on internally financial reporting controls but also extend into regulatory compliance, business continuity, and disaster recovery control evaluation.[2] Similar to the SAS 70 the ISAE 3402 report certification is granted in two parts via ISAE 3402 Type 1 and Type 2 reports. Indeed, the SAS 70 was effectively replaced by ISAE3402 and SSAE 16 in 2010, but LP's may indeed still come across the term SAS 70.

As the methodologies related to such certifications continue to be more broadened in scope and harmonized globally, it is likely that private equity firms will continue to embrace such audit certifications, whether it be an act of their own volition or because LPs force them to.

INCREASED USE OF OPERATIONAL DUE DILIGENCE CONSULTANTS

With increased focus on operational quality and operational due diligence in general across the field of private equity, there has been an increasing number of investors who engage the services of a third-party consultant to assist in the operational due diligence process. Capitalizing on this trend, any traditional investment consultants and even investment banking organizations have sought to add "operational due diligence provider" to the list of service offerings. Despite the convenience of such one-stop shopping for both investment and operational advice, many investors have shunned such solutions due to the inherent conflicts of interest that are present when offering both investment and operational advice. Indeed in many cases, investment consultants are compensated based on the investment advice they offer. On the other hand, these investment consultants try not to remind their clients of any such compensation arrangements when they tout the benefits of their operational due diligence processes. Such potentially conflicted advice has found many investors seeking the use of independent operational due diligence advice in the private equity space.

This is a bit of a niche area of the consulting business that many investors have begun to acknowledge. Indeed, Corgentum Consulting, your author's employer, is such a consulting business focused on working with clients to provide independent operational risk reviews of fund managers, including private equity funds. Many clients approach consulting companies with a strong sense of comfort with the investment side but are cautious about the operational due diligence side. Indeed, these clients may lack bandwidth, competency, or desire to build an internal operational due diligence department of their own. Still other clients may maintain their own dedicated operational due diligence departments, and utilize the services of an operational due diligence consultant to augment their existing functions.

Indeed, investors who first begin to consider private equity often take a number of different approaches toward due diligence. Depending on a number of factors, including their own internal resources, institutional capacity, amount of capital to allocate, the nature of alternatives strategies they are considering, and investment horizon, investors generally take one of several paths. Some typical options include:

- Directly investing into the alternatives themselves.
- Utilizing a traditional investment consultant for guidance.
- Investing with a pooled allocator, such as a private equity fund of funds or managed account platform.

Each of these options presents its own unique benefits and challenges however, they do share one common theme—the question of how each of these options approaches due diligence.

Hedge Fund Operational Due Diligence: A Specialized Skill Set

For the sake of simplicity, let us classify due diligence into two broad categories: investment and operational. In much the same way that investment due diligence has become a specialized field, so too has operational due diligence. Over the past several years, operational due diligence has developed into a similarly specialized practice area. Regardless of whether investing directly into a private equity fund, utilizing a traditional investment consultant, or investing with a private equity fund of funds or platform, investors still should consider the benefits that an independent operational due diligence consultant may add.

Complementing the Due Diligence of Traditional Investment Consultants

Operational due diligence consultants work with traditional consultants to complement the investment due diligence work of their traditional investment consultants. As outlined earlier, it is inherently a conflict of interest for the same party offering investment recommendations to similarly offer advice on the operational merits of a hedge fund or private equity manager. Biases are inherently present, based on the investment consultant's opinion as to the investment merits of a manager, and the potential is too great for an investment consultant's operational convictions to be swayed one way or the other. As such, many investors who utilize traditional investment consultants also work with third-party operational due diligence consultants to assist in their reviews of private equity funds.

Gauging Consultant Qualifications and Experience

Investors must take steps to ensure that their private equity operational due diligence consultant possesses the qualifications and experience to conduct thorough operational due diligence reviews. Some questions to ask include:

- Is a multidisciplinary team of professionals utilized or is one area (i.e., accounting or compliance) focused on?
- Does experience exist covering different types of hedge fund strategies in different regions throughout the world?

- Is the hedge fund operational due diligence process institutional in nature?
- Does the hedge fund operational due diligence process evolve over time to adapt to changing industry practices?

Trust but Verify: Due Diligence on the Due Diligence Providers

Investors should perform due diligence on their private equity operational due diligence consultants to ensure that they are not simply checking the box and telling investors to "trust them" that a manager is operationally sound.

This includes not just outsourcing the operational due diligence process but becoming an active participant in the process. The old auditors' adage, "trust but verify," is applicable not only when performing operational due diligence on hedge funds and private equity funds themselves, but also on those performing the due diligence.

Investors ranging from large institutions and professional allocators such as fund of hedge funds to high-net-worth individuals can benefit from employing operational due diligence consultants to augment their own internal efforts, and it is likely that this practice will increase in the future.

POOLING OPERATIONAL DUE DILIGENCE RESOURCES AMONG MULTIPLE LPs

Private equity, particularly in the context of monitoring operational risks, can perhaps best be thought of as the beginning of a long-term relationship. In private equity funds, as compared to more traditional long-only funds or even hedge funds with lockups, an investor allocating their capital investors will be in business with a private equity firm for a period of several years as a result of these long lock up periods.

A number of efficiencies, from cost, time, and resource expenditure perspectives, may be realized if investors, particularly in initial fund closing situations, are fairly limited in number. This may generally be the case if an initial fundraising period is approaching a close and a large amount of capital is being sought from only a handful of investors, each of whom intends to, in the parlance of the private equity world, "write big tickets" (i.e., make large allocations). Rather than each of these big-ticket investors each performing distinct operational due diligence, they could pool resources to conduct a combined review, perhaps via an operational due diligence consulting firm.

Of course it is unlikely that such shared approaches will obviate the need for individual LP due diligence reviews. However, there has been an increasing trend among LPs to develop dialogues in this regard. Indeed, via informal information-sharing or private industry networking events for LPs, there is an increasing trend toward information-sharing of not only investment data, but operational data, as well. Whether or not such shared resource approaches are utilized broadly, the concept of such information-sharing, either formally or informally, is likely to increase.

OPERATIONAL BENCHMARKING

Once the operational due diligence process is complete, an investor is sometimes left facing a problem that they did not have before starting the operational due diligence process. Before beginning the operational due diligence process, an investor likely had some vague notions regarding the investment skill and operational quality of a particular manager, but had little hard data to go on in making a determination on the manager's operational stalwartness. We can fast-forward and compare the pre–due diligence investor, whom we will call I, to the post-operational due diligence investor, whom we will refer to as, I'.

What is the basic core difference between I and I'? Information. If an investor performing operational due diligence in any form gains anything on the journey from I to I', it is basic operational risk data. Utilizing a bare minimum of the techniques described in this book the I' investor, as compared to I, likely knows what happens after a buy or sell decision is made in a particular PE fund. These details could include items such as who executes the trade, how the trade is logged in the firm's systems, what are the firm's trade order and execution systems, and so on. A more sophisticated I' may even know details such as how conflicts of interest are prevented when entering into trading. For example, is there an appropriate segregation of duties among execution, settlement, reconciliation, and even potentially the valuation function? But putting the advanced I' aside for a moment, and returning to our basic comparison of I and our bare minimum I', the latter now has a series of operational data points that he must now analyze. How is this process supposed to be undertaken?

A trend that has recently gained traction as LPs have begun to perform more operational due diligence reviews and amass more operational data is to analyze and mine such data. This has created an area of comparison among private equity funds' operational practices that we will refer to as *operational benchmarking*. This trend of operational benchmarking allows investors to make more informed operational decisions because they have the ability to rely on data, however limited, that provides some insight into which operational practices are employed by a private equity fund's peers.

The overuse of such benchmarking runs the risk of turning the operational due diligence exercise into an exception-reporting process. Just because the bulk of the private equity firms that an investor has previously reviewed to compile their own individual operational risk database adhere to a particular operational practice does not mean that this is representative of more common operational trends. Furthermore, the minority of the participants of an investor's operational dataset may be the group that is adhering to operational best practices. However, an investor focused on exception reporting of deviations from larger trends may mistake such best practices for lesser-used practices. To overcome such potential pitfalls investors can benefit from the use of a third-party operational risk consultant that can serve as an operational best-practice adviser and has already developed fuller operational data sets that can facilitate benchmarking.

Despite the potential pitfalls that may be present, it is likely that investors will continue to embrace a trend of increasing utilization of operational benchmarking techniques to further facilitate operational due diligence reviews of private equity funds.

ILPA GUIDELINES

The Institutional LPs Association (ILPA) is an organization that focuses on LP advocacy. In 2009 ILPA first published a series of Private Equity Principles with a goal of encouraging discussions between LPs and GPs.[3] In January 2011 ILPA released version 2.0 of its Private Equity Principles. The new principles focus on three guiding principles that, as the principles espouse, are essential for a private equity partnership. These principles are:

1. Alignment of Interest
2. Governance
3. Transparency

Additionally, ILPA is leading an effort to create a number of standardized templates to facilitate uniformity and transparency across multiple areas, including capital calls and distribution notices and annual quarterly reporting, as well as portfolio metrics.[4]

It may be argued that the ILPA guidelines place an unnecessary burden on GPs. Some smaller investors may attempt to use the ILPA guidelines as a sword rather than a shield to bully GPs into increased transparency submission. On the other hand, as absurd as it may seem, some other LPs may not even want increased transparency because they, either for regulatory or other reasons, may be forced to disclose the information received from GPs. This out of sight, out of mind attitude may have its place, but it can lead to losses that the LPs could have potentially avoided, or at least would have been warned about had they been otherwise open to receiving such information. These LPs may be left with not only losses, but if they are representing other investors, potentially also with claims of willfully ignoring or recklessly disregarding the truth. Regardless of the arguments for and against the ILPA standards, the trend toward increasing transparency will ultimately be a net benefit for the private equity industry as a whole. Such transparency will also likely continue a trend of investors seeking to better understand private equity operational practices.

FROM SELF-REGULATION TO MANDATORY REGISTRATION

It seems as if there has been a sustained movement among the private equity community toward developing standards and practices with a focus on self-regulation. That is where the standards and practices to which a private equity firm adheres are themselves developed by private equity firms. This can be seen in the development of policy documents such as the Walker Guidelines in the United Kingdom. Perhaps taking a page out of the playbook of the hedge fund community, the private equity community over the past several years has focused on presenting a more organized public face that perhaps coincides with more streamlined and focused lobbying efforts. Such a development has seemingly increased with the threat, and now reality, of increased regulation of the private equity industry via such regulatory developments as Dodd-Frank and Alternative Investment Fund Managers Directive (AIFMD). It seems as if the markets have in effect said "Thanks for the effort, but no thanks," to self-regulation of not only the private equity industry but most financial markets as well.

Oftentimes however, it seems there is a disconnect between these self-developed private equity guidelines and any recently enacted regulatory constructs. Self-regulation rules are generally crafted in such a way as to provide more wiggle room. For example, the Walker Guidelines outlined in part that "a private equity firm should commit to ensure timely and effective communication with employees." While such aspiration policies are admirable, it is unclear exactly what is meant by timely and effective communication. Would communication be timely if it were within one day of the occurrence of an event? What about two weeks? As compared with more rigid regulatory requirements such self-regulatory guidelines tend to be more flexible.

It is worth noting that the goal of this discussion is not to criticize the development of self-regulation. The development of these self-regulations is certainly better than an environment with no regulations at all. However, with the increasingly complex web of heightened global financial restrictions, it is highly unlikely that many private equity firms, regardless of their home jurisdiction or the port of call of their portfolio holdings, will be able to remain unregulated.

IMPACT OF DODD-FRANK ON OPERATIONAL DUE DILIGENCE

The broad impact of the Dodd-Frank Wall Street Reform and Consumer Protection Act has a number of implications for the private equity industry. While the full impact of this legislation is still unfolding, Dodd-Frank has a number of ramifications that will directly influence operational due diligence on both U.S.-based private equity managers and those managers that have a presence in or interact with U.S. markets.

Subsequently, investors will need to revise their approaches toward operational due diligence in order to determine if a private equity manager has reacted effectively to this landmark legislation. Specifically, one area that will be most readily affected is a private equity fund's approach toward compliance. Investors must also consider Dodd-Frank in the context of other recently passed rules such as the SEC's amendments to Rule 206(4)-2 of the Investment Advisors Act of 1940 (the so-called Custody Rule). Other key areas that may be affected include information technology requirements, fund reporting, recordkeeping, and transparency. With the passage of Dodd-Frank, LPs had a number of opportunities to gauge the way in which GPs approached the registration process. The seriousness with which a private equity fund took the regulatory changes may have a strong signaling effect regarding not only their attitude toward ongoing compliance with the law, but also their attitude toward future compliance best practices. As part of the operational due diligence process, LPs could inquire about a number of different items related to the post-Dodd-Frank environment, including:

- What changes has a private equity fund manager made in anticipation of Dodd-Frank passage?
- Has a private equity fund appropriately budgeted for the increased costs of compliance associated with Dodd-Frank?
- With the increased focus on compliance, has a private equity fund spoken to the appropriate service providers (i.e., legal counsel, compliance

consultants, etc.) to ensure that quality individuals and adequate services are dedicated to the private equity fund's account?

- What changes in compliance policies and procedures has a private equity fund undertaken? How have these changes been communicated to staff? How have changes been documented in the firm's compliance manual? If changes have not been made yet, when will they be made?
- If a private equity fund manager was not registered with the U.S. SEC relying previously on an exemption such as Section 203(b)(3) of the Investment Advisers Act, what is their plan for registration?
- If a private equity fund is already registered, will they fall into the category of manager that may need to potentially deregister? If so, are they prepared to deal with local state registration requirements? For example, do they fall into New York or Wyoming Blue Sky threshold exemptions?
- Has a private equity fund developed a reporting and technology infrastructure to meet new requirements?

In conclusion, the passage of Dodd-Frank and related legislation has had a dramatic effect on the ways in which private equity managers approach the issue of compliance and controls. LPs will likely need to monitor compliance, both initial and ongoing, with regulations such as Dodd-Frank on an ongoing basis. This will likely result in a trend of increasing resource allocations both from GPs toward compliance related matters, as well as from LPs toward due diligence resources aimed at vetting compliance with such regulations.

CONCLUSION

This chapter provides an overview of developing trends regarding operational risk in the private equity industry. The trends that this chapter discusses originate not only from external sources such as regulations, but also directly from private equity funds and investors. Often these trends influence all three groups directly. An example of such a recent trend that has repercussions for all three groups is the increased focus on material nonpublic information in the United States. Other examples of trends discussed in this chapter that have more direct effects on the relationship between GPs and LPs are the increased use of third-party fund administrators and increased reliance on audit-type certifications. This chapter also provides a discussion of the increased use by LPs of operational due diligence consultants and the ILPA guidelines. Finally, this chapter provides a discussion of legal- and compliance-related trends, including a trend toward requiring mandatory regulatory registration for private equity funds and the impact of Dodd-Frank. It is especially important for LPs to be cognizant of such trends when developing and maintaining an effective private equity operational due diligence program. By remaining aware, LPs will be more likely to effectively gauge not only how GPs plan for such change, but also how they adapt their operations to address investors' present and future concerns.

NOTES

1. See, for example, *United States v. Carpenter*, 484 U.S. 19 (1987); *United States v. O'Hagan*, 521 U.S. 642 (1997).
2. See Fiona Gaskin, "Goodbye SAS 70, Hello ISAE 3402?," http://download.pwc.com/ie/pubs/pwc_goodbye_sas_70_isae_3402.pdf.
3. Institutional Limited Partners Association, "Private Equity Principles, Version 2.0," January 2011.
4. Institutional Limited Partners Association, "ILPA Publishes Updated 2011 Private Equity Principles and First Standardized Reporting Industry Template to Help Enhance the Private Equity Asset Class Globally," January 11, 2011, http://ilpa.org/index.php?file=/wp-content/uploads/2011/01/Principles-Version-2.0-Press-Release.pdf&ref=http://ilpa.org/principles-version-2-0/&t=1316768530.

About the Author

Jason A. Scharfman is the Managing Partner of Corgentum Consulting, a provider of comprehensive operational due diligence reviews of alternative investments including hedge funds, private equity, real estate, and funds of hedge funds. He is recognized as one of the leading experts in the field of operational due diligence and is the author of *Hedge Fund Operational Due Diligence: Understanding the Risks* (John Wiley & Sons, 2008). Mr. Scharfman has participated in operational due diligence reviews of over 200 private equity and real estate funds of multiple strategies across the globe, including REITs, clean-tech funds, direct property holdings, multi-year vintage funds, Asian infrastructure funds, Eastern European utility and infrastructure funds, commodity funds (timber, oil, gold, etc.), and private equity funds of funds.

Before founding Corgentum, he oversaw the operational due diligence function for Graystone Research at Morgan Stanley and was a senior member of a team that oversaw all of Morgan Stanley's operational due diligence efforts for hedge funds, private equity, real estate funds, and funds of hedge funds. Prior to joining Morgan Stanley, he held positions that focused primarily on due diligence and risk management within the alternative investment sector at Lazard Asset Management, SPARX Investments and Research, and Thomson Financial.

Mr. Scharfman received a BS in Finance with an additional major in Japanese from Carnegie Mellon University, an MBA in Finance from Baruch College's Zicklin School of Business, and a JD from St. John's School of Law. He holds the Certified Fraud Examiner (CFE) and Certified in Risk and Information Systems Control (CRISC) credentials and has consulted with the U.S. House Judiciary Committee on the subject of hedge fund and private equity regulation. Additionally, he has provided training to financial regulators on the subject of hedge fund and private equity due diligence. Mr. Scharfman has served as a consultant and expert in hedge fund and private equity litigation, and has lectured on the subject of alternative investment operations and operational risk as an adjunct professor at New York University. He has written extensively on the subject of operational due diligence and travels and speaks worldwide on hedge fund operational risks.

About the Website

This book includes a companion website, which can be found at www.wiley.com/go/privateequityduediligence.

This website features a number of useful spreadsheets and templates which investors can utilize to assist them in performing operational due diligence reviews of private equity funds. This website also includes links to laws and regulations that are cited in the book. The password to enter this site is: Scharfman.

Index

A

AA Capital fraud, 318–321
Accessory liability, 212–213
Actual fraud. *See* Fraud
Administrator, 143–145, 341–345
ADV. *See* Form ADV
Advisory board, 301–313
Agape World, 18
Allianz SE, 325–326
Alternative Investment Fund
    Managers Directive
    ("AIFMD"), 21, 58, 355
Alternative investments, 4–16, 56,
    58, 74, 146, 159, 210
Amazon.com, 20
American Research and
    Development Corporation
    (ARDC), 19
Assembly Bill 1743, 161
Asset allocation, 275–300
Assets under management (AUM),
    57, 100, 129, 193, 220
Audit materiality, 238–240
Audited financial statements. *See*
    Financial statements
Auditor, 143

B

Background investigation, 177–179
Bad faith, 221–226
Baden v. Societe Generale, 213
Balance sheet. *See* Financial
    statements
Barings Bank, 22

Barlow Clowes International Ltd
    (In Liquidation) v. Eurotrust
    International Limited, 213
Basel Committee on Banking
    Supervision, 21
Benchmarking. *See* Operational
    Benchmarking
Berman, Todd, 321–323
Blackstone Group, 20
Board of directors, 26, 205, 302,
    322
Boesky, Ivan, 19
British Venture Capital Association
    (BVCA), 58, 183
Broker-dealer, 162
Bullmore v. Ernst & Young
    Cayman Islands, 217
Business continuity and disaster
    recovery planning (BCP/DR),
    26, 114, 132, 165–168
Business risk. *See* Operational risk

C

Cadbury Commission, 21
California Public Employees'
    Retirement System (CalPERS),
    161
California State Teachers'
    Retirement System (CalSTRS),
    161
Carlyle, 9
Carnegie Steel Company, 18
Carnegie, Andrew, 18
Carried interest, 140, 227, 270

Cash oversight, management and transfer controls, 23, 162–165

Cayman Islands, 34, 91, 145, 218

Channel Islands, 34, 215

Chartwell Investments, 321–323

Chief Compliance Officer, 92, 178

Chief Financial Officer, 92, 178

Chief Operating Officer, 178

Chief Technology Officer, 92

Cliff vesting. *See* Compensation structures

Committee of Sponsoring Organizations (COSO), 21

Committee of Wise Men, 57

Compensation structures, 138–139

Compliance
  Infrastructure, 23, 26, 52, 136
  Manual, 113–115, 153, 347, 357

Compton, Carl, 19

Confidentiality agreement, 106–113

Conflicts of interest, 266–267, 334–335

Continental Airlines, 20

Cooke, Jay, 18

Core operational due diligence process. *See* Operational due diligence

Core operational due diligence process. *See* Operational due diligence

Corgentum Consulting
  Benefits of operational due diligence case studies, 17
  Increased use of operational due diligence consultants, 350–352
  Operational due diligence process documentation, 53
  Operational benchmarking, 54
  Operational due diligence frameworks analysis, 91–95
  Trends in indemnification and exculpation clauses, 217–227

Cosmo, Nicholas, 18

Counterparty oversight, 131

Counterparty risk. *See* Counterparty oversight

Country specific risks, 33–35

Credit Mobilier, 18

Crossover funds, 8

Custodian, 146

Custody 23, 104, 136–137, 146–147, 170, 293–294, 344, 356

Custody Rule, 146

Customer relationship management (CRM) systems, 147, 174

D

Dedicated framework, 91–95

Department of Justice, 162, 320

Deutsche Bank, 9

Digital Equipment Company, 19

Director liability, 213

Directors' and officers' liability coverage (D&O), 173

Discovery, 81–82

Dishonesty, 212–213

Distressed debt investing funds, 8, 223

Dixon, Roy, Jr., 324–325

Dodd-Frank Wall Street Reform and Consumer Protection Act, 21, 57, 355–357

Dom, Telonge, 160

Domino's Pizza, 20

Doriot, Georges, General, 19

Draper Gaither and Andersen, 19

Dreier, Marc, 18

Drexel Burnham Lambert, 19

Due diligence equation, 39

Due diligence file, 81

Due diligence questionnaire (DDQ), 87, 121–123

E

EBITDA, 139, 187
Effectively connected income (ECI), 176
Enron, 20
Equity ownership model, 178
Errors and omissions (E&O) insurance, 173
EU passport, 58
European Association for Investors in Non-listed Real Estate Vehicles (INREV), 237
Exculpation and Indemnity
  Exception to, 211–220
  History of, 207–208
  Uses in private equity offering memoranda, 208–211
Exculpation. *See* Exculpation and Indemnity
Exogenous risks, 60, 65, 165–166, 220
Expanded operational due diligence process. *See* Operational due diligence
Expert research networks, 345–348

F

FAA System Safety Handbook, 2
Fair value. *See* Valuation
FAS 157, 189–191, 251–253
FASB ASC 820, 190
Fat-tail risk
  Defined, 1
  Relation to fraud detection, 5
Financial Accounting Standards Board (FASB), 189, 235
Financial Highlights, 248
Financial Institutions Reform, Recovery and Enforcement Act of 1989, 19

Financial statements
  Audit standards, 233–237
  Due diligence on, 233–255
  Review of in core process, 23
  Sections, 245–248
Firm and employee reputation, 130–131, 177–179
Foreign Corrupt Practices Act, 162, 325
Form ADV, 59
Form PF, 59
Fraud
  Applicable to exculpation and indemnity, 211–212
  Benefits of case studies in, 17
  Case studies in, 315–326
  Detection of, 5–7
  Investor recovery from, 5
  Levels of, 6
  Private equity fund failure considerations due to, 68
Fraud in fact. *See* Fraud
Fund Administrator. *See* Administrator
Fund advisory board. *See* Advisory board
Fund reporting, 3, 23, 131, 136, 183, 277, 356

G

Galleon Group, 345
Geithner, Timothy, 57
General Counsel, 92
General Partner (GP)
  Defined, 10
  Distinction in valuation approaches, 181–182, 197
  Relation to advisory boards, 302–303
  Information flow with Limited Partners, 306–307

Generally Accepted Accounting
  Principles (GAAP)
  Convergence with IFRS,
    236–237
  U.S. GAAP, 176, 235–236, 248
  U.K. GAAP, 235–236
Generally Accepted Auditing
  Standards (GAAS), 234
Global Investment Performance
  Standards (GIPS). *See*
  Valuation
Goldman Sachs, 9
Goldstein, Philip, 56
*Graham v. Allis-Chalmers Mfg.
  Co.*, 215
Greenbury Committee, 21
Gross negligence, 213–214
Guernsey, 34, 218, 224, 328
Guidelines for Disclosure and
  Transparency in Private
  Equity. *See* Walker Guidelines

H
Hampel report, 21
Harvard, 19
Health care fund, 12, 333
Hedge Clauses, 209–111
Hedge fund operational due
  diligence
  Differences with private equity
    operational due diligence,
    44–49
  Similarities with private equity
    operational due diligence,
    40–44
Hedge fund Registration Rule, 56
Hedge Fund Transparency Act,
  56–57
High Voltage Engineering
  Corporation, 19
Human capital, 23, 26, 136, 280
Hybrid framework, 91–95

I
ILPA. *See* Institutional LPs
  Association (ILPA)
  Guidelines
In pari delicto, 216–217
Indemnity. *See* Exculpation and
  Indemnity
India private equity funds, 34–35,
  61
Industry specific risks, 35–39
Information barrier, 72–76
Information security, 26, 132
Information silo, 200
Information technology (IT). *See*
  Technology and systems
Information technology
  consultants, 147
Informed operational opinion
  formation, 25
Institutional LPs Association (ILPA)
  Guidelines, 354–355
Insurance coverage, 26, 130,
  173–174
International Auditing Standards
  (ISA), 234
International Business Machines
  (IBM), 18
International Financial Reporting
  Standards (IFRS), 176,
  236
International Private Equity and
  Venture Capital Valuation
  (IPEV) Guidelines
  Discount cash flows or earnings
    (of underlying business)
    approach, 188
  Discounted cash flows (from the
    investment), 188
  Industry valuation benchmarks
    approach, 188–189
  Multiple valuation methodology,
    186–187

Net assets approach, 187
Price of recent investment
   approach, 185–186
International Standard of Assurance
   Engagements (ISAE) 3402, 349
Interval funds, 8
Investment Adviser, 10
Investment Advisers Act of 1940,
   56, 146, 161, 210
Investment decision making
   authority model, 178
Investment due diligence
   Comparison to operational due
      diligence, 99, 275, 351
   Defined, 51
   In shared due diligence
      framework, 91
   Integration with operational due
      diligence, 39
   Process timing, 36–37, 65, 98–99
   Relation to fraud detection, 6
   Resource allocation versus
      operational due diligence,
      27–30
   Role in private equity
      decision-making process, 11
   Stages of analysis, 13
ISDA, 26
Isle of Man, 34, 218, 224–225

J
Jersey, 34, 215, 218, 224–225
Jurisdictional risks, 35
J.P. Morgan, 18
Junk bonds, 19

K
K1 Group, 18
Key person clause, 227, 291, 312
Key person insurance, 174
Keynes, John Maynard. *See*
   Keynesian economics

Keynesian economics, 22, 62
Kiener, Helmut, 18
KKR, 9
Klomp, Danny, 321

L
Lamfalussy procedure, 57
Lascaux Cave, 2
Legal and compliance risks, 130,
   171–173
Legal counsel, 145–146
Legal documentation review. *See*
   Legal due diligence
Legal due diligence, 23, 198–228
Lesson, Nick, 22
Leveraged buyout (LBO)
   LBO funds, 8, 19
   RJR Nabisco takeover, 19
Levine, Dennis, 19
Liability releases, 214–2146
Liechtenstein, 34
Limited liability company, 10
Limited Partner
   Defined, 10
   Distinction in valuation
      approaches, 181–182, 197
   Serving on Advisory boards,
      302–303
   Information flow with General
      Partner, 306–307
   Fund of funds due diligence
      considerations, 307–308
Litigation support, 80–82
Lockup, 65–68, 79–80
Luxembourg, 34

M
Madoff Effect, 17
Madoff, Bernard, 6–7, 16–18, 59,
   146, 250, 294, 315
Malfeasance, 214, 221–225
Malta, 34–35, 60–61

Manager. *See* Investment adviser
Markets in Financial Instruments
    Directive ("MiFID"), 21, 57
Material nonpublic information,
    345–348
Mezzanine financing funds, 8, 222
Minimum operational risk regime
    (MORR), 280–285
MIT, 19
Modular framework, 91–95
Moral fraud. *See* Fraud
Mortgage fraud, 269–270
Müntefering, Franz, 9

N
Nadel, Arthur, 18
National Commission on
    Fraudulent Financial
    Reporting, 21
Negative operational due diligence.
    See On-site visits
Netscape, 20
No-fault divorce provision, 311
Nondisclosure agreement (NDA),
    106–113
Noninvestment risk. *See*
    Operational risk

O
Offering memorandum (OM). *See*
    Private placement
    memorandum
Offshore block corporation, 177
Offshore jurisdictions
    Onshore versus offshore
        considerations in legal
        document analysis, 205
    Private equity fund managers
        choice of, 61
    Service providers location in, 145
    Tax policy, 34
Ongoing monitoring, 292–296

On-site visits
    Documentation for litigation
        support, 81–82
    Interview techniques and
        question design, 150–154
    Negative operational due
        diligence, 148–150
    Private equity fund manager
        considerations, 125–128
    Underlying private equity
        portfolio companies, 156
Onyx Capital Advisors, 324–325
Operational Benchmarking,
    353–354
Operational Drag, 286–290
Operational due diligence
    Arguments in favor of performing
        on private equity, 75
    Below-core process, 27
    Compared to operational risk, 4
    Contrasted with an insurance
        policy, 68
    Core process, 8, 23, 85–133
    Defined, 4–5
    Distinguished from operational
        management, 9–10
    Document collection, 113–133
    Expanded process, 26
    Filtering stages, 12
    Five-stage process, 101–103
    Frameworks, 91–95
    Lack of universal definition, 4
    Private equity program design,
        87–100
    Process goals, 52–55
    Process timing, 10–13, 97–99
    Resource allocation, 90–91
    Time versus resource allocation,
        72
    Trends in, 341–358
    Understanding time allocation to,
        27–29

Universal definition, 7
Versus operational risk, 3–4
Operational due diligence
  consulting firm. *See* Corgentum
  Consulting
Operational fringe, 87–90
Operational Lift, 286–290
Operational Lift-to-Drag ratio,
  286–290
Operational risk
  Common private equity
    operational risk categories, 3
  Compared to operational due
    diligence, 3–4
  Defined, 1–3
  Operational risk plane, 68–71
  Risk commonalities between
    private equity and real estate,
    30–31
  Risk differences between private
    equity and real estate, 32–33
Operational risk consulting firm.
  See Corgentum Consulting
Operational risk management
  (ORM). *See* Operational risk
Operations risk. *See* Operational
  risk
Opinion letter. *See* Financial
  statements
Ops dd. *See* Operational due
  diligence
Orecchio, John, 318–321
Organizational risk. *See*
  Operational risk

P
Palminvest, 321
Pang, Danny, 316–318
Paper Trail. *See* Litigation support
Pari Passu, 116, 157–158, 218.
  226, 242
Pay-for-play. *See* Pay-to-play

Pay-to-play, 160
PEMGroup Fraud, 316–318
Performance vesting. *See*
  Compensation structures
Personnel and employee turnover,
  129
Petco, 20
Petters Group Worldwide, 18
Petters, Tom, 18
Philips Pension fund fraud,
  323–324
Picasso, Pablo, 2
Piñata problem, 118
PIPE transactions, 8, 20, 345
Ponzi scheme, 5–6, 16–18, 56,
  146–318
Ponzimonium, 18
Portfolio companies, 9–10
Positive fraud. *See* Fraud
Private Equity
Private equity fund of funds,
Private placement memorandum
  (PPM), 201–206
Process homogeneity, 95–97
Public Company Accounting
  Reform and Investor
  Protection Act of 2002. *See*
  Sarbanes-Oxley Act

Q
Quaker Oats, 20

R
R. Allen Stanford, 18
Rajaratnam, Raj, 345
Real estate
  Distinguished from private
    equity, 257–278
  Feasibility study, 258
  Fund fees, 270–271
  Property management, 260–261,
    267–269

Real estate (*Continued*)
  Risk commonalities with private
    equity, 30–31
  Risk differences with private
    equity, 32–33
  Sample process, 258–262
  Technical due diligence, 259
  Third-party developers, 260
  Valuation, 262–266
Rebate. *See* Sales charge
Regional risk. *See* Industry specific
    risks
Regulatory risks, 26, 171–173
Reputational risk. *See* Firm and
    employee reputation
Resource dilution, 95–97
RICS Valuation Standards, 264,
    266
Risk control model, 178
Rogue trader events, 21
*Royal Brunei Airlines Sdn. Bhd. v.
    Tan*, 212–213
Royal Institution of Chartered
    Surveyors, 266
Rule 206(4)-2. *See* Custody Rule

S
Sales charge, 159
San Diego v. Amaranth, 213
Sarbanes-Oxley Act (SOX), 20–21,
    234
Savings and loans (S&Ls), 19
Schedule of investments. *See*
    Financial statements
Scoop Management, 18
Securities and Exchange
    Commission (SEC), 56, 91,
    146, 210, 321
Service level agreement (SLA), 137
Service providers, 23, 132, 141–147
SFAS 157. *See* FAS 157

Shared framework, 91–95
Side letters, 290–292
Signaling effect, 104
Silicon Valley, 19
Snapple Beverages, 20
Snowball Effect, 330–332
Standard Chartered, 317
Stanford Financial Group, 18, 146
Statement of Assets and Liabilities.
    See Financial statements
Statement of Cash Flows. *See*
    Financial statements
Statement of Changes. *See* Financial
    statements
Statement of Financial Accounting
    Standards 157. *See* FAS 157
Statement of Operations. *See*
    Financial statements
Statement on Auditing Standards
    (SAS) No. 70, 348–350
Straw-man borrower, 269–270

T
Tax haven, 327–328
Tax practices, 26, 175–177
Technology and systems, 26, 131
Third-party marketer, 159–162
Timber investment management
    organization (TIMO), 36, 238
Time vesting. *See* Compensation
    structures
Trade flow analysis, 23, 26,
    168–171, 257–258
Trade life cycle. *See* Trade flow
    analysis
Transcontinental Railroad in the
    United States, 18
Transparency and fund reporting,
    131
Treadway Commission, 21
Tyco International, 20

U

U.S. GAAP. *See* GAAP
U.S. Generally Accepted Auditing
    Standards (GAAS). *See*
    Generally Accepted Auditing
    Standards (GAAS)
Ultra vires, 215
Uninterruptible power source
    (UPS), 167
Unrelated business taxable income
    (UBTI), 176

V

Vaisey, Harry Sir, 107
Valuation
    Considerations for newly formed
        funds, 182
    Consultants, 264–265
    Distinction between fund and
        portfolio company level,
        181–182
    Fair value, 183, 185–195
    GIPS Statement of Private on
        Private Equity
    Real estate, 262–266
    Review of in core process, 23
    Third-party consultants, 191–196

Venture capital funds, 8, 19–20, 40,
    45, 57
Vesting. *See* Compensation
    structures
Villalobos, Alfred, 161
Vintage fund
    Financial statement due diligence
        on, 241–244
    Valuation considerations,
        182
    Side letter negotiation concerns,
        291
*Viscount of the Royal Court of
    Jersey v. Shelton*, 215
Voortman, Remco, 321

W

Wagoner Doctrine, 216–217
Walker Guidelines, 21, 58
Weather-related risks, 24, 165
Willful default, 211–212
Willful fraud. *See* Fraud
Worldcom, 20

Y

Yahoo!, 20

Printed and bound by CPI Group (UK) Ltd, Croydon, CR0 4YY

23/04/2025

14661009-0005